Restoring Women's History through Historic Preservation

CENTER BOOKS ON CONTEMPORARY LANDSCAPE DESIGN

Frederick R. Steiner
CONSULTING EDITOR

George F. Thompson
SERIES FOUNDER AND DIRECTOR

Published in cooperation with the Center for American Places
Santa Fe, New Mexico, and Harrisonburg, Virginia

Restoring Women's History through Historic Preservation

EDITED BY GAIL LEE DUBROW
& JENNIFER B. GOODMAN

The Johns Hopkins University Press
BALTIMORE AND LONDON

© 2003 The Johns Hopkins University Press
All rights reserved. Published 2003
Printed in the United States of America on acid-free paper
2 4 6 8 9 7 5 3 1

The Johns Hopkins University Press
2715 North Charles Street
Baltimore, Maryland 21218-4363
www.press.jhu.edu

Library of Congress Cataloging-in-Publication Data

Restoring women's history through historic preservation / Gail Lee
Dubrow and Jennifer B. Goodman, editors.
p. cm. — (Center books on contemporary landscape design)
This essay collection draws upon work presented at three national conferences
on women and historic preservation: the first held at Bryn Mawr College in
1994, the second held at Arizona State University in 1997, and the third held at
Mount Vernon College in Washington, D.C. in 2000.
Includes bibliographical references (p.   ) and index.
ISBN 0-8018-7052-6 (alk. paper)
1. Women—United States—History. 2. Historic preservation—United States.
3. Historic sites—United States. 4. Landscape architecture—Conservation and
restoration—United States. 5. Women historians—United States. 6. Women
conservationists—United States. 7. Women museum curators—United States.
I. Dubrow, Gail Lee. II. Goodman, Jennifer, 1964–   III. Series.

HQ1410 .R47 2002
305.4'0973—dc21

2001007988

A catalog record for this book is available from the British Library.

Contents

Acknowledgments   ix

CHAPTER 1

Restoring Women's History through Historic Preservation: Recent
Developments in Scholarship and Public Historical Practice
Gail Lee Dubrow   1

PART I

Documenting the History of Women in Preservation

CHAPTER 2

Women in the Nineteenth-Century Preservation Movement
Barbara J. Howe   17

CHAPTER 3

Special Places Saved: The Role of Women in Preserving
the American Landscape
Shaun Eyring   37

CHAPTER 4

Four African American Women on the National Landscape
Fath Davis Ruffins   58

PART II

Revisiting Women's Lives at Historic Houses and Museums

CHAPTER 5

Uncovering and Interpreting Women's History at Historic House Museums
Patricia West   83

CONTENTS

CHAPTER 6
Domestic Work Portrayed: Philadelphia's Restored
Bishop William White House—A Case Study
Karie Diethorn with John Bacon 96

CHAPTER 7
Putting Women in Their Place: Methods and Sources for Including
Women's History in Museums and Historic Sites
Edith Mayo 111

PART III
Claiming New Space for Women in the Built
Environment and Cultural Landscape

CHAPTER 8
Rooms of Their Own: The Nurses' Residences
at Montreal's Royal Victoria Hospital
Annmarie Adams 131

CHAPTER 9
On the Inside: Preserving Women's History in American Libraries
Abigail A. Van Slyck 145

CHAPTER 10
Women in the Southern West Virginia Coalfields
Susan M. Pierce 161

CHAPTER 11
"A Night with Venus, a Moon with Mercury": The Archaeology of
Prostitution in Historic Los Angeles
Julia G. Costello 177

PART IV
Exemplary Projects

CHAPTER 12
The Power of Place Project: Claiming Women's History
in the Urban Landscape
Dolores Hayden 199

CONTENTS

CHAPTER 13

Best Practices for Saving Women's Heritage Sites:
Nonprofit Case Studies
Jennifer B. Goodman   214

CHAPTER 14

"It's a Wide Community Indeed": Alliances and Issues in Creating
Women's Rights National Historical Park, Seneca Falls, New York
Judith Wellman   230

CHAPTER 15

"Raising Our Sites": A Pilot Project for Integrating Women's
History into Museums
Kim Moon   248

CHAPTER 16

Finding Her Place: Integrating Women's History
into Historic Preservation in Georgia
Leslie N. Sharp   263

CHAPTER 17

Blazing Trails with Pink Triangles and Rainbow Flags: Improving the
Preservation and Interpretation of Gay and Lesbian Heritage
Gail Lee Dubrow   281

PART V

Toward an Inclusive Agenda for Preservation
Policy and Practice

CHAPTER 18

Searching for Women in the National Register of Historic Places
Carol D. Shull   303

CHAPTER 19

Reflections on Federal Policy and Its Impact on Understanding
Women's Past at Historic Sites
Page Putnam Miller   318

CONTENTS

CHAPTER 20

Parks Canada and Women's History
Alan B. McCullough 337

AFTERWORD

Proceeding from Here
Heather A. Huyck 355

Appendix A: Participants in the Pilot of
"Raising Our Sites: Women's History in Pennsylvania" 365

Appendix B: Women, Women's Organizations, and Buildings Related
to Women Which Have Been Commemorated by the
Canadian Minister Responsible for National Historic Sites 367

Notes 371

List of Contributors 429

Index 435

Acknowledgments

This book grew out of papers presented at the first National Conference on Women and Historic Preservation, which began in 1994 with the leadership of Philadelphia-area preservationists Deborah Filipi, Ellen Freedman Schultz, Gail Greenberg, Jennifer Goodman, Dorothy Guzzo, Donna Ann Harris, Audrey Johnson-Thornton, Deborah Kelly, Howard Kittell, Cindy Little, Gayle Samuels, and many others. Their vision of bringing together scholars, practitioners, and activists to discuss better approaches to identifying, interpreting, and saving women's heritage sites seeded not just this publication but also new collaborations and strategies and what has now become a traditional gathering. The original conference committee, chaired by Barbara Irvine of the Alice Paul Centennial Foundation, generously invested proceeds from the conference in this book project, for which we are indebted, and enlisted us as coeditors, which has been a gratifying experience.

Page Putnam Miller's expert counsel and her leadership of the National Women's History Landmark Project has helped to make the Women and Historic Preservation conferences into a showplace for the best new work in the field. Heather Huyck provided both intellectual and political leadership in securing resources to bring attention to this issue within the National Park Service. Marie Rust, Director of the Northeast Regional Office of the National Park Service, stands out as an early and steadfast supporter of the National Conference. Her willingness to make a long-term commitment to this issue has ensured continuity for nearly a decade.

Mary Logan Rothschild, Jannelle Warren-Findley, Vivien Rose, and Gail Dubrow carried the spirit of the National Conference forward while steering it westward as the organizers of the 1997 meeting in Tempe, Arizona. Gail Dubrow and Edith Mayo hosted the 2000 meeting in Washington, D.C., with support from Vivien Rose, Neile Graham, Connie Walker, Richard Longstreth, and many colleagues. The conference benefited from the participation of additional partners, such as George Washington University, the Smithsonian Institution, and the National Trust for Historic Preservation. The conference program drew out some of the best work in progress on the subject of women and historic preservation. The editors wish to express their appreciation to the authors with whom we worked and to acknowledge the existence of many more experts whose work we were unable to include on account of space limitations.

Because published work on the subject of women and historic preservation is dispersed over a relatively wide range of fields—from archaeology, art history, women's history, and cultural resources management to travel guides and interpretive programs—our hope was that bringing the best work together under one cover would make it more widely accessible. The editors wish to convey their gratitude to the crew at the Center for American Places for seeing the value of bringing this collection into print and express appreciation to Norman Johnston and Jane Hastings for establishing a Publication Support Fund at the College of Architecture and Urban Planning at the University of Washington, which ensured that the book was amply illustrated.

Coll-Peter Thrush provided significant research assistance, for which we are grateful. Lisa Raflo coordinated revisions to the manuscript and whipped it into shape for submittal to the Johns Hopkins University Press. She brought to the project considerable expertise in historic preservation as well as enormous reserves of tact and patience. Elizabeth Gratch's editorial suggestions vastly improved the manuscript.

We dedicate this book to our young daughters, Rachel and Kathryn, in the hope that their generation will be able to take for granted accurate depictions of both men's and women's lives at the places they eventually come to think of as historically significant.

Restoring Women's History
through Historic Preservation

Restoring Women's History through Historic Preservation
Recent Developments in Scholarship and Public Historical Practice

Gail Lee Dubrow

On the eve of the American bicentennial the cartographic company Rand McNally published a guide to the nation's landmarks titled *Discover Historic America*. Overlaying the company's popular highway maps with nearly three thousand places of historic interest, the guidebook furnished travelers and armchair tourists alike with a road map to the nation's tangible past in the form of historic houses, canals, iron furnaces, and logging museums. As the nation approached its two hundredth birthday, there was a growing appreciation of what the guidebook termed "the rich mixture of ethnic groups that makes up our heritage"; hence, Spanish forts, French trading posts, Indian pueblos, Scandinavian farms, and Russian churches were among the many landmarks it featured.[1] Core sites associated with military and political history, particularly battlefields and the homes of presidents, were joined by a handful of places devoted to slavery and its abolition and the homes of woman's rights activists, reflecting the growing influence of the civil rights and feminist movements in contemporary politics as well as the cultural sphere.

But this version of Rand McNally's guidebook was not yet available during the late 1960s and early 1970s when my family took most of our trips to historic sites on the eastern seaboard, so we relied on its immediate and more conservative predecessor. Crossing out of New York City in our faux wood–paneled station wagon, my parents, younger brother, and I headed north to Hancock Shaker Village in Pittsfield, Massachusetts, and the recreated country town of Old Sturbridge Village; west to Gettysburg, Pennsylvania; and south to Mount Vernon and Colonial

Williamsburg, Virginia, on trips intended to animate the history lessons contained in our schoolbooks.

Having been a history major in college, my mother genuinely enjoyed these trips. Never one to relish touring, my father perked up only at the battlefields, our tour of FBI headquarters, or the occasional military museum, which resonated with his branch of historical knowledge and his experience of military service. As for my brother and I, we were rather poor students of public history in those days. Mostly, we fought over elbow room in the car, debated who would get the blue or gray cap at Gettysburg, and stood united on the question of stopping for ice cream. If the truth be told, I found our family visits to historic sites significantly less exciting than my grandfather's ideal outing, which consisted of a visit to the bizarre and fascinating collection of objects in Ripley's Believe It or Not Museum and other forbidden pleasures such as Bette Davis's most grotesque movie, *What Ever Happened to Baby Jane?* Clearly, his taste for the sensational and the macabre engaged my preteen sensibilities at a more visceral level than the average historical exhibit of the period did.

If Gettysburg at the time was an exclusively white male military landscape neatly divided into shades of blue and gray, at least places such as Sturbridge and Williamsburg included women in their historical reenactments. Although I thought spinning yarn and dipping candles were mildly interesting demonstrations, they left me with a hazy picture of women's part in history. Some landmarks of women's history were accessible to the public even during our station wagon years, the homes of Emily Dickinson, Susan B. Anthony, and Harriet Beecher Stowe prominent among them. But we never visited them. The historic places we toured so closely fit our shared belief that men were the agents of historical change that the absence of women's history totally escaped notice.

By the time of the bicentennial I was off to college and learning with others of my generation that women and other overlooked groups had a considerably more complex and interesting history than grade school texts and visits to historic sites had led us to believe. I had the good fortune of attending college at a time when many scholars had begun to make the case for recovering the history of women (echoing historian Mary Ritter Beard, who had begun the project a generation earlier). Since then, untold numbers of women's historians have worked to make sense of female experience in particular times and places while theorizing about broader patterns in the social relations of the sexes. This body of work has provided a base for those dedicated to increasing public awareness of women's history through museum exhibitions, films, oral history projects, archival collections, and historic sites and buildings. The collection of essays in this volume represents the fruits of more than two decades of individual and collective efforts to restore women's history through historic preservation.

Visited by millions of people each year, historic sites and buildings play a major role in educating the public about the nation's past. Yet, taken together, these places present an incomplete picture of women's contributions to American history. Relatively few properties significant in women's history are listed on the National Register of Historic Places, or its state and local equivalents, and women's history has yet to be represented in an accurate and complete way at the vast majority of designated landmarks.

The critiques of women's status at historic sites and buildings, along with ambitious new initiatives to identify, interpret, and protect places significant in the history of women, have arisen wherever women are present in the field of preservation: as interpreters at historic house museums, preservation activists in nonprofit organizations, staff within state historic preservation offices and the National Park Service, as well as from within the academy. Together, in recent years, the individuals involved in these historic preservation efforts have developed a body of work which is potentially useful for those interested in improving the coverage of women's history at historic places, including several model projects, books, and articles scattered in the periodical literature. This volume draws upon work presented at three national conferences on women and historic preservation: the first held at Bryn Mawr College in 1994, the second at Arizona State University in 1997, and the third at Mount Vernon College in Washington, D.C., in 2000.[2] These gatherings were landmarks in themselves, because they provided opportunities for those dedicated to improving the status of women within historic preservation to meet one another. The relationships forged at these conferences have cross-fertilized and nurtured many of the projects discussed in this collection.

As the organization of the book suggests, work on women and historic preservation is divided among several themes, including efforts to: (1) rewrite the history of the preservation movement to account fully for women's participation; (2) improve the interpretation of women's history at historic houses as well as in museum settings, the places where the public is most likely to encounter presentations and displays that address female historical experience; (3) widen the variety of building types and landscapes associated with women's history which are listed on landmark registers and open to the public; (4) develop strategies for improving the identification, interpretation, and protection of women's landmarks; and (5) remove barriers to the protection of women's history landmarks in existing preservation policies and practices. My hope is that this overview and assessment will entice readers to take on projects in areas that beg for attention, which will expand the base of knowledge and raise the level of discussion and debate in this field.

Part 1 reassesses women's contributions to the historic preservation movement. Although standard histories, such as Charles Hosmer's *Presence of the Past,*[3] superficially acknowledge women's contributions to the rise of the preservation movement, it is only in recent years that scholars have begun a detailed exploration of the gender dimensions of the subject. In chapter 2, Barbara J. Howe traces women in historic preservation into the middle of the nineteenth century, when female activists, shaped by the "cult of domesticity," began taking leadership roles in commemorating the past at historic places. Working through the Mount Vernon Ladies' Association of the Union, the Daughters of the American Republic, and other patriotic and genealogical organizations, women led the campaigns to save some of the nation's most treasured landmarks. Howe describes the values that defined these middle-class white organizations then contrasts them with African American women's preservation efforts and the work of women in the Southwest to preserve sites associated with Native Americans.

An appreciation of women's contributions finally has entered broader histories of the preservation movement, most notably James Lindgren's *Preserving the Old Dominion* and *Preserving Historic New England.*[4] The challenge ahead is continuing to move the literature in this field beyond the "contributions" model of women's history to address more complex questions such as, what motivated women to engage in preservation, and to what ends did they use history? Given the rather elite and reflexively patriotic origins of the historic preservation movement, what sources, roots, and traditions might sustain preservationists whose work is guided by a more democratic and inclusive vision?

Shaun Eyring (chap. 3) augments this story by chronicling women's contributions to the preservation of historic landscapes from the mid-nineteenth century onward. She reexamines Mount Vernon as an early example of a unified approach to preserving both the built environment and historic landscape. It served as a model for later groups dedicated to saving historic houses, gardens, and the grounds in which they were set and protecting the scenic views associated with them. Eyring locates women's organizations such as the Garden Club of America in the broader context of women's contributions to the historic preservation movement. She credits women's clubs with playing an instrumental role in the rise of federal and state parklands preservation initiatives. Finally, she documents women's leading role in fighting visual blight in the form of outdoor advertising. Eyring's contribution marks the beginning of a broader history of women's contributions to landscape preservation.

In the final contribution to this section (chap. 4), Fath Davis Ruffins looks at historic sites associated with Mary McLeod Bethune, Harriet Tubman, Madam C. J. Walker, and Maggie Lena Walker. Ruffins examines the churches, homes, and other places associated with these four notable African American women to explore the conditions that have allowed some notable black women to be remembered at historic places, while others have been the focus of more ephemeral forms of commemoration. This chapter, taken together with Ruffins' other published work on African American public history and memory,[5] provide a welcome corrective to the elite white focus of past histories of the preservation movement.

Outside of Fath Ruffins' efforts, little work published to date fully mines the subjects of race, class, and ethnicity in the history of preservation. Yet these social relations are central to the project of explaining why particular groups of women organized to save particular remnants of the past. And they are key to understanding the process by which the cultural heritage of a few (and versions of others' history appropriated by an elite) became equated with the nation's history. More inclusive histories of women and preservation are needed. Doing so requires preservation to be reframed in broader ways, particularly to include women's historic role in maintaining and transforming cultural traditions, only some of which include historic landscapes and buildings. In the process it is essential to address the subject of real property and to account for sharp differences in various groups of women's relationship to it historically. Only then will it become possible for us to write histories of women and preservation which have broader explanatory power than for a propertied class of white women.

In part 2 the authors take a closer look at the place of women's history at existing landmarks, particularly historic houses and museums. One of the founding mothers of the field, Heather A. Huyck, first brought attention to the problem of interpreting women's history in national parks in her 1988 essay "Beyond John Wayne."[6] The recognition that historic houses have been the predominant type of site where women's history is presented to the public has prompted debate over how interpretive programs can be improved in these settings as well as a movement to diversify the property types that mark women's accomplishments and activities. Patricia West's early work on the Martin Van Buren National Historic Site, in Kinderhook, New York, showed that the historical experiences of female domestic servants can be woven into the interpretive programs at the homes of "wealthy, white, male, political figure[s]," even American presidents.[7] In chapter 5 she identifies the rules of interpretation which effectively marginalize women's history in the public programs of historic house museums.[8] She has pointed to the directive that fosters the development of a primary interpretive theme at historic house museums, which tends to push women's interests to the periphery. West shows how combined attention to the history of women and domestic labor has reinvigorated historical interpretation at Lindenwald. Including Irish domestic servants in the interpretive plan there has enriched the public's understanding of Van Buren's political career, the social context of mid-nineteenth-century America, and the spatial arrangements of Lindenwald. West suggests that it is not necessary to "turn our backs on the patriarchs" to tell the history of women; instead, the two can complement each other.

Thanks to the persistence, ingenuity, and creativity of the staff at some historic houses, we have begun to realize the untapped potential for interpreting women's lives through a detailed reexamination of domestic space. The National Trust for Historic Preservation's 1994 conference, "The View from the Kitchen: Interpreting the Lives of Domestic Workers," is a promising sign that some of the fundamental tenets of a feminist historical perspective on the subjects of work, family, and household have gained ground in the mainstream of historic preservation.[9] Since that time new interpretive initiatives have brought together the staff at sites owned by the National Trust for Historic Preservation to take a fresh look at how the difficult subject of slavery is presented to visitors. Karie Diethorn and John Bacon's careful study of the Philadelphia home of Bishop William White, chaplain to the Continental Congress (chap. 6), provides another demonstration of how the story of domestic labor can enhance the interpretive program of a house museum. Diethorn and Bacon link the seemingly peripheral spaces of the Bishop White house—the kitchens, cellars, and garrets—with the previously ignored lives of the free black servants who worked there, the majority of whom were women. The authors show how incorporating the "servants' sphere" into interpretation sheds new light on early American technology, systems of class deference, notions of privacy, and structures of group identity. Turning to museums more generally, Edith Mayo (chap. 7) reviews recent exhibitions to illustrate the ways in which everyday objects, categories of historical experience, and the structure of museum exhibits can be given new meaning through the integration of women's history.

Despite these improvements in the presentation of women's history at historic houses, there is cause for concern about the continuing focus on interpreting women's history in these settings. The ubiquitous presence of historic houses as locations for the public interpretation of women's history inadvertently may buttress the myth of women's confinement in the domestic sphere while missing vital opportunities for marking women's history in the more public arenas of the paid labor force and the community. The continued dominance of grand houses presents a distorted view of the modest and varied conditions under which most women have lived and continues a long-outmoded tradition of viewing women through the narrow lens of their subordinate relationships to notable men. Our enormous collective investment in preserving historic houses justifies the effort to reinterpret women's lives in these settings. But the need remains for new initiatives in the arenas of preservation and interpretation which will provide the public with a more democratic and inclusive view of how Americans have lived. The boardinghouses preserved in Lowell National Historical Park and the Lower East Side Tenement House Museum in New York City provide rare glimpses into shared and ordinary aspects of the American historical experience. An expanded view of historic houses, beyond the mansions of the elite to include a wider variety of types—such as YWCA residences for working women built in nearly every American city,[10] 1920s bungalows, public housing projects, and Levittown's mass-produced suburban housing—might form the beginnings of a broader public curriculum about American living patterns and women's work in the domestic sphere.[11]

Beyond the ubiquitous historic houses and formal museum settings, the third group of essays in this collection examines women's history in a wider array of cultural landscapes throughout North America. The work of a new generation of architectural historians and historical archaeologists committed to exploring social relations of gender provides a model for conducting detailed analyses of these sorts of places. Annmarie Adams (chap. 8) looks at nurses' residences at Montreal's Royal Victoria Hospital, where "a room of one's own" for women in medicine involved both new degrees of freedom and continued surveillance by male administrators. Her work is an outstanding example of how the built environment can be used as a primary source for understanding the lives of women. Turning to another institutional setting, the United States' historic libraries, Abigail A. Van Slyck (chap. 9) critiques preservation programs that have saved library exteriors while stripping their interiors of significant historic features. Van Slyck calls for a reappraisal of standard preservation practices, arguing that library interiors are rich sources for understanding the role of architecture in defining and reinforcing gender-appropriate behavior, reflecting both women's aspirations to professional and personal autonomy and men's attempts to control them.

Changing the scenery, Susan M. Pierce (chap. 10) takes us to the coalfields of southern West Virginia, a space traditionally defined as male but which remains an untapped vein of women's history. Drawing on the practices of social and labor history, Pierce mines local sources for patterns of work, segregation, sexuality, and political reform, emphasizing that industrial landscapes and other spaces customarily associated with the lives of men need to be reinterpreted to include women's stories. Finally, Julia G. Costello's account of an archaeological dig in downtown Los Angeles (chap. 11) brings new attention to the experiences of prostitutes. The material remains of prostitution recovered from two old privies—fine china and elegant perfume bottles, opium paraphernalia and patent medicines—offer new understandings of the everyday lives of women who worked in elegant parlor houses and ramshackle cribs. Costello's approach as a historical archaeologist suggests the combined power of written documents and archaeological investigations to shed light on poorly understood and stigmatized aspects of female historical experience. All of these essays, however, suggest that the challenge ahead is to forge fruitful connections between academic historians and their counterparts at relevant historic properties, to ensure that scholars incorporate the material culture of women's lives in the process of writing history and visitors have access to the latest interpretive advances in the scholarly literature.

The limited information on women's landmarks contained in most guides to historic sites prompted the development of two national guidebooks, *Women Remembered* by Marion Tinling and *Susan B. Anthony Slept Here* by Lynn Sherr and Jurate Kazickas,[12] as well as guides to women's history in various cities. To some extent the authors' focus on places associated with notable individuals, as opposed to women's collective accomplishments and experiences, reflects the limits of their vision. Yet it also mirrors the reality of what was saved by a previous generation of women who worked to preserve a now outmoded version of women's history which revolved around "the woman behind the man"—that is, George Washington's mother and sister, the spectacular homes and gardens of the elite, as well as shrines to woman's rights leaders such as Susan B. Anthony and Frances Willard.[13] Some of the self-published guides to women's landmarks in various cities reflect richer and more sophisticated conceptions of women's history; most have suffered from limited distribution, however, and have quickly gone out of print.[14] Perhaps more important, these projects generally have not been linked to practical efforts to gain official landmark designation and ensure the protection of these cultural resources for future generations.

Guidebooks to women's landmarks have sometimes failed to distinguish between the presence of historic resources and subsequent construction on sites of significance in women's history, making an actual visit to the site a somewhat disappointing experience for visitors. For that reason, a study published in 1987 by historical archaeologist Suzanne Spencer-Wood is particularly important, since she identified the tangible remains of the domestic reform movement in Boston and Cambridge, Massachusetts, providing accurate information on the status of the artifacts themselves.[15] My 1988 study identified two hundred sites significant in Boston women's history, of which approximately fifty were still standing, and more than a dozen were clustered in the downtown in such a way as to readily constitute a coherent itinerary for a walking tour illuminating several centuries of women's history in Boston.[16] Many of the historic properties identified in these studies eventually were folded into a walking tour developed by teachers in the Boston Public Schools.[17]

If there is a substantial base of knowledge about places significant in American women's history, thus far it has fed one major national preservation planning initiative, focused on increasing the number of National Historic Landmarks associated with women's history. This four-year congressionally funded study, now complete, added nearly forty nationally significant properties to the roster of National Historic Landmarks, including:

- Maria Mitchell's observatory at Vassar College
- the Brown Building in New York City, site of the horrific Triangle Shirtwaist fire
- the Washington, D.C. headquarters of the General Federation of Women's Clubs
- Ellen Swallow Richards's home in Jamaica Plain, Massachusetts, which served as the Center for Right Living, her station for experiments in the field of home economics
- the New England Hospital for Women and Children, the oldest existing example of the institutions designed for the training of women physicians
- the Fort Pierce, Florida, home of black folklorist and anthropologist Zora Neale Hurston

This project also generated the major published work in this field, Page Putnam Miller's edited collection *Reclaiming the Past*, whose essays provide a critical context for assessing the significance of properties associated with such themes as women and architecture, the arts, community, education, politics, religion, and work.[18]

Part 4 of this volume highlights exemplary projects that have improved the identification and protection of places significant in women's history, as well as public awareness of their significance, through a wide range of preservation activities. To extend work begun by Page Miller at the national level, parallel studies are needed at the state and local levels, yet the limited funding available for preservation planning has made it difficult for women's history to compete for attention in the work plans of state historic preservation offices. Wisconsin was the earliest state to have "conceptualized a framework for surveying structures" related to women's history.[19] Georgia's Historic Preservation Division was the first state agency to address directly gender issues related to the identification, documentation, and evaluation of historic properties through its Women's History Initiative. In chapter 16 Leslie N. Sharp explains the potential of the Georgia initiative to change public perceptions of women's contributions to the state's history.[20] No doubt the conceptual frameworks, methods, and strategies developed in the context of Georgia will be useful to those interested in launching similar projects in other states such as New Jersey, which in September 1999 appropriated seventy thousand dollars for a comprehensive survey of historic resources that are significant in women's history.[21] Beyond the work included in this volume, a valuable model for future work at the local level can be found in Shanna Stevenson's study of women's history in the city of Olympia, Washington, which provides a context for nominating individual properties to the National Register of Historic Places.[22]

Kim Moon (chap. 15) focuses on an initiative of the Pennsylvania Humanities Council begun in 1992 to raise the visibility of women's history in the state's historic sites and museums. Recognizing the limited capacity of resource-poor historical organizations to undertake the research and planning needed to improve the presentation of women's history, "Raising Our Sites" developed a program of scholarly assistance and mutual support that resulted in improved coverage of women's history at more than a dozen historic Pennsylvania historic sites open to the public. This project provides a blueprint for other states and regions seeking to bring women's history into view at sites already designated.

Preservation advocate and activist Jennifer B. Goodman (chap. 13), the coeditor of this volume, looks at the practices of three nonprofit preservation organizations that focus on the history of women or ethnic communities of color. While sharing similar values and structures, each organization employed dramatically different strategies to save its site. Through her examination of the restoration, reuse, and interpretation of the homes of Charlotte Perkins Gilman and Alice Paul and the free black community of Weeksville, Goodman proposes a series of "best practices" for community-based preservation programs. Judith Wellman (chap. 14) provides another analysis of the practices of preservation advocacy groups in her case study of the establishment of Women's Rights National Historical Park in Seneca Falls, New York. She shows how alliances between local and national supporters, private citizens and government, and scholars and the general public proved crucial to the successful opening of the park in 1982. The park has become the premiere place for interpreting women's history within the National Park System. In her essay on The Power of Place project, Dolores Hayden (chap. 12) discusses her work with local communities to uncover, commemorate, and interpret sites of women's, ethnic, and labor history in the urban landscape of Los Angeles. From the homestead of Biddy Mason, midwife and former slave, to the Embassy Theater, a venue for women's labor organizing, and the remains of Little Tokyo, Hayden shows the possibilities for collaboration between artists, community activists, design professionals, and scholars.

There are some frontiers of women's history still considered too controversial to address in public. This applies, to some extent, to the history of radical social movements at historic sites and buildings. Despite its obvious historical significance, it was impossible to secure National Historic Landmark designation for anarchist and free-love advocate Emma Goldman's New York City apartment. Page Miller writes about the political difficulties of getting Margaret Sanger's New York City birth control clinic listed as a National Historic Landmark, yet she eventually succeeded. Managers of historic sites generally have avoided dealing with the difficult topics of sexuality and sexual orientation, deeming them inappropriate for a family audience. Prior to 1999, none of the more than seventy thousand properties on the National Register of Historic Places had been listed on the basis of its significance in gay and lesbian history, nor did any nomination mention this subject. The June 1999 National Register listing of the Stonewall Inn, site of the uprising that sparked the contemporary gay and lesbian movement, and the inn's subsequent designation as a National Historic Landmark, have paved the way for future listings.[23] Some designated landmarks are perhaps the most obvious places to begin remedying long-standing omissions and silences, including Walt Whitman's Mickle Street row house in Camden, New Jersey, and Willa Cather's childhood home in Red Cloud, Nebraska.[24] In outlining the controversies inherent in reinterpreting much-loved sites (and the myths associated with them), my essay on gay and lesbian historic sites (chap. 17) offers a reminder that preservation and politics are intimate bedfellows.

The collection ends with three perspectives on preservation policy and practice. Carol D. Shull, keeper of the National Register of Historic Places, analyzes the capacity of the National Register Information Service, a searchable Internet database, to help researchers find places associated with women's history. Shull finds that a wide range of women's sites already exists on the register, many of them awaiting scholarly attention. Page Miller's reflections on federal preservation policy and practice (chap. 19) focus on two initiatives, the Women's History Landmark Project and the Women's History Education Initiative. As collaborations between the National Park Service and the Organization of American Historians, these projects have made significant progress in increasing the number of National Historic Landmarks significant in the history of American women and improving the interpretation of women's history at existing units of the national park system. Together, these initiatives point toward a new commitment to women's history on the part of the federal government.

Yet roadblocks remain. Debates over what constitutes "national significance," conflicts over the inclusion of sites associated with controversial topics, concerns about the physical integrity of surviving resources, and methodological differences between academic scholars and preservation professionals will provide challenges to designating women's landmarks in years to come. Although the collection focuses on preservation in a U.S. context, the final chapter provides readers with an understanding of how Parks Canada has incorporated new concern for women's history into its preservation programs. Recognizing that change will be slow, Alan B. McCullough (chap. 20) shows how women's history has forced the federal agency to rethink its processes and practices of commemoration. Finally, Heather A. Huyck's afterword offers her reflections on more than twenty years of action intended to improve the preservation and interpretation of women's history and concludes with a call for new initiatives that will allow the story of all American people to be told at historic sites and buildings.

At this early stage in the development of a body of work that guides preservation policy and practice, there is a pressing need for women working in the preservation movement to reflect on their personal experience and to begin to tell their stories publicly: from front-line interpreters, historians, and educational specialists to curators and supervisory personnel. Historians working in public settings enjoy far less freedom of speech and job security than their counterparts in the academy, resulting in few published accounts of a sharply critical nature. Yet we need to hear their stories to develop a clearer understanding of the forces of sexism, racism, and homophobia within the preservation establishment as they affect women workers in this field and as they shape daily decisions that are made about the presentation of history to the public.

All the more reason that it is imperative for women and their male allies in preservation to create spaces for sharing their experiences and perspectives. The new tradition of holding national conferences on women and preservation provides a needed forum for sharing new work. New vehicles of communication are needed to foster an exchange of information in the interim. This network of scholars, professionals, and activists is likely to provide a more lasting basis for institutional change than any single project or initiative. Despite the disciplinary and professional differences among the contributors to this book, the collection as a whole suggests a common sense of purpose and significant progress in advancing the goal of restoring women's history through historic preservation.

PART I

Documenting the History of Women in Preservation

CHAPTER 2

Women in the Nineteenth-Century Preservation Movement

Barbara J. Howe

Ann Pamela Cunningham (1816–75), a contemporary of Lucretia Mott, Susan B. Anthony, and Elizabeth Cady Stanton, rarely appears in the texts that unfailingly include those other heroines of the nineteenth-century women's movement. Nor do the Mount Vernon Ladies' Association of the Union (MVLA), the Association for the Preservation of Virginia Antiquities (APVA), or the Confederate Memorial Literary Society (CMLS) merit mention in texts that include the General Federation of Women's Clubs (GFWC) or the Daughters of the American Revolution (DAR). This neglect illustrates the gulf between academic historians and historic preservationists, for whom all of these names should be familiar.

Our preservation foremothers had common ground with the better-known, nineteenth-century, white, native-born, middle- and upper-middle-class club women. Imbued with the cult of domesticity which appointed them guardians of society's culture and morals, they took their responsibilities as seriously as modern preservation professionals do when upholding the governmental programs undergirding their work. The cult's virtues of piety, purity, domesticity, and submissiveness helped define a separate sphere for women, at least those in the middle and upper classes, and women exercised these virtues through voluntary association to improve the communities they considered to be extensions of their Christian homes.[1]

Nineteenth-century women saw preservation as an avocation and as an amateur, in the best sense of that word, pursuit. As did temperance or suffrage supporters, they networked through membership in multiple groups, such as the DAR and United Daughters of the Confederacy (UDC).[2] These volunteers led the preservation movement, for government efforts to save the nation's shrines were secondary to private endeavors. Like women who rescued prostitutes or alcoholics, they rarely acted solely in an all-women's world. Men spoke on their behalf, "brother" and "sister" organizations such as the Sons of the American Revolution and the DAR preserved the same buildings, and women negotiated with men as property owners.

Women generated publicity, raised money, and bought and restored properties to save some of the nation's most treasured landmarks, sites that reflected the dominant perspective on the country's history. These were, overwhelmingly, sites and structures related to the founding fathers of the new nation, so that visitors would be infused with patriotism when visiting these secular shrines. If the early preservationists saved a slave cabin, it was because it was on the grounds of Mount Vernon, not because they consciously preserved and interpreted a site related to African American history.

There certainly were nineteenth-century efforts to preserve the history of African Americans. The African Americans who led these efforts focused, however, on markers, libraries, and archives, topics outside the scope of this chapter.[3] The sole African American woman identified to date who actively worked to save a site was a former slave, Selina Gray, who guarded her master's family home, Arlington House, during and after the Civil War. And it was two white women, Helen Pitts Douglass and Kate Fields, who initiated the efforts to preserve the first sites specifically designated to commemorate African American history: the home of Helen's husband, Frederick Douglass, and John Brown's Fort at Harpers Ferry, West Virginia.

One of the first examples of women's preservation efforts came in 1830, when Sarah Josepha Hale led a women's committee to raise funds to complete Boston's Bunker Hill Memorial. In the middle of a recession Hale organized New England women to raise money through their "industry, economy or self-denial." Hale later aided the campaign to save Mount Vernon.[4]

The first history of American architecture was Louisa Tuthill's 1848 *History of Architecture from the Earliest Times; its Present Condition in Europe and the United States; With a Biography of Eminent Architects and a Glossary of Architectural Terms by Mrs. L. C. Tuthill, with Numerous Illustrations.* Tuthill dedicated her work "to the Ladies of the United States of America, the acknowledged arbiters of taste," so they would promote an American architecture that fit the American landscape.[5]

Some twenty years after Hale began her crusade, African Americans in Boston started their own campaign to erect a statue to honor Crispus Attucks, who was killed during the Boston Massacre of March 5, 1770. The only individuals identified from this group, however, were men. After decades of work the City of Boston dedicated the statue in 1888.[6]

Women were less organized in the South than in the Northeast, but sustained organizing efforts for historic preservation began in the South. The movement to save Mount Vernon is the best-known example of women's leadership in historic preservation, for it is unlikely that Mount Vernon would have survived without the MVLA, which still owns and operates the home (fig. 2.1). "A company of Northern and Southern capitalists" reportedly had purchased Mount Vernon by mid-1853, "with a reservation to allow the Government the privilege of repurchase."[7] Popular orator Edward Everett was one of a group of men that summer who suggested a "voluntary subscription among the people" to generate $350,000 to buy and endow the building; a board of trustees would manage the property for the public.[8]

Ann Pamela Cunningham, a South Carolinian, first heard about the dilapidated condition of the estate from her mother, who saw it from a boat on the Potomac River and wrote to her daughter: "Why was it that the women of this country did not try to keep it in repair, if the men could not do it? It does seem such a blot on our country!"[9] On December 2, 1853, driven "by patriotism, and a sense of national and, above all, Southern honor," Cunningham published a letter in the *Charleston Mercury* appealing to southern women to save Mount Vernon from possible development as a hotel. She initially hoped that these women would rise up to save Mount Vernon and that she could stay behind the scenes. Instead, at age thirty-seven and as an invalid, she initiated a crusade that lasted until her death. The first meeting took place in February 1854.[10]

Cunningham's planning took place amid continued public discussion of the fate of Mount Vernon. The *Wheeling (Va.) Intelligencer* thought the Commonwealth of Virginia should purchase the building.[11] The New

Fig. 2.1. Mount Vernon, Va. Mount Vernon. The crusade to save Mount Vernon united women around the country and served as a model for future preservation organizations. Photo by the author.

York legislature urged Congress to buy it.[12] The *New York Express* soon urged that the "movement among the ladies of the South" be a national one, reminding readers in July 1854 that the "Bunker Hill Monument was finished by our countrywomen, without regard to section or feeling, and every true American woman has almost as much interest in that monument as the male descendants of those who fought there more than seventy-nine years ago. We hope then, to see our Northern and Southern women joining hand in hand, and with hearty good will, in this patriotic duty of making Mount Vernon the property of the nation."[13]

Northern women asked to join what Cunningham had envisioned as a southern movement, making the MVLA the first successful national preservation effort, the first national women's organization, and one of the nation's first successful women's organizations.[14] Cunningham soon saw the MVLA and Mount Vernon as a way to join all Americans "hand in hand" in a patriotic cause while sectional strife otherwise threatened to destroy the Union.[15]

In 1855 Virginia's governor, Joseph Johnson, announced that a group of ladies from throughout the South had collected money to purchase Mount Vernon. The legislature chartered the MVLA on March 17, 1856, allowing the Commonwealth of Virginia to own the property after the MVLA had purchased it. In June 1856 John A. Washington, who had inherited the property in 1849, agreed to sell Mount Vernon to the association instead of directly to the commonwealth, as he had preferred. That year the commonwealth amended the MVLA charter to allow the association to hold title to the property, leaving "the work of saving Mount Vernon in the laps of the women of the nation."[16] Cunningham and Washington signed a contract to confirm the MVLA's purchase in April 1858.[17] His high price and neglect of the property subjected him to scathing criticism, however, for his "heathenish grasp" on the "'holy sepulchre'" of his ancestor.[18]

MVLA members raised money relentlessly. In 1858 Cunningham appealed to Americans living in the Sandwich Islands (now Hawaii) and Cuba. Everett raised over fifty thousand dollars through 139 fund-raising speeches.[19] In January 1859 "the country [was] being dunned from one end to another for dollars and half dollars wherewith to purchase the tomb and tombstead of the 'Father of his country' . . . the delicate office of canvassing for alms has been delegated to the ladies it being supposed, and very properly, too, that Mount Vernon, through a temporary identification with their smiles and charms, would not be half so likely to be turned away empty from the doors of 'the sons of the sires,' as it would be under the aegis of sterner patriots."[20]

In May 1859, for example, "young girls of Martinsburg," Virginia, held a fair for the MVLA. The girls netted $110.80 and had already raised $30; the Society of Masons intended to contribute $100. The newspaper editor proudly reported that the grand sum was "as much as can reasonably be expected from Martinsburg" and concluded, "We were much pleased to notice the general and gratifying interest evinced on the part of the citizens of the town and country in this laudable and praiseworthy effort of the girls to raise a fund for the purchase and repairing of the home and grave of Washington."[21]

Almost all the money needed to buy Mount Vernon was on hand by December 1859. Cunningham then asked the clerk of the Fairfax County

Court to circulate a letter nationwide to confirm that the MVLA had legal title to the property, while she set out to raise more funds to repair and maintain the estate.[22] Maintaining the estate grounds gave MVLA members the distinction of being among the earliest women landscape preservationists.[23] The MVLA took possession of the property in the summer of 1860. During the Civil War a superintendent and MVLA secretary Sarah C. Tracey, who lived on the estate, guarded Mount Vernon.[24]

Also during the war, Selina Gray protected George Washington's family treasures at Arlington House, just across the Potomac River from Washington, D.C. Gray's family were slaves of George Washington Parke Custis, George Washington's adopted son and Martha Washington's grandson. He built Arlington House in the early nineteenth century as his family's home but also as a shrine to the nation's first president. Slaves from Mount Vernon moved to Arlington House with Custis and cared for the Washington possessions there. In 1831 Custis's only child, Mary Anna Randolph Custis Lee, married Robert E. Lee. Gray lived at Arlington House from 1833 on and eventually became Mary Lee's personal maid. When the Civil War broke out and Union troops prepared to occupy Arlington House, Mary Lee packed up some of the Washington items, including portraits and papers, and shipped them out of harm's way. She then packed up the Washington china, artwork, knife boxes, and tea table and locked them away in Arlington House's cellar, garret, and closets. As Lee was ready to leave in May 1861, she gave Gray the keys to the house and designated her as the head of the household. By the end of the month Union troops occupied the house and grounds.[25]

Gray guarded the Washington artifacts until December 1861, when she discovered that troops had broken into the secured areas and stolen some of the items and notified Brig. Gen. Irwin McDowell, who was in command of the troops there. McDowell transferred the items out of the house to the Patent Office in Washington, D.C., where they stayed until 1901. Gray received her freedom in 1862 and lived at Arlington House for many years thereafter, continuing to care for the house throughout the war, while Q.M. Gen. Montgomery Meigs transformed the estate into a national cemetery and freed slaves later converted the grounds into a "Freedmen's Village." A prize of war, Arlington House eventually became a unit of the National Park Service.[26]

Ann Pamela Cunningham became a national leader among women after the war as she continued her efforts to save Mount Vernon. In 1869 she succeeded in getting federal dollars to compensate for the loss of revenue from the MVLA's tourist boat that Union troops had confiscated. Before retiring from the MVLA in 1874, she collected the group's records, making this one of the few early preservation groups with adequate records.[27]

Meanwhile, the MVLA became a truly national organization with vice-regents raising money throughout the country. Kansas women raised a thousand dollars to reconstruct the former slave quarters. Alice Longfellow, daughter of poet Henry Wadsworth Longfellow, paid an architect to restore the library, and Phoebe Hearst, mother of journalist William Randolph Hearst, gave six thousand dollars to drain and fill the swamp near the mansion.[28]

The MVLA persevered in spite of criticism. Some felt there should be no admission charge to see Mount Vernon, but defenders argued that this group simply wanted control of a political patronage position as guardian of Washington's home. The MVLA thus augmented the definition of *domesticity* to include Mount Vernon and the concept of "family" to include the father of our country while giving members valuable experience in "making speeches and passing resolutions like men!"—a rarity in the mid-nineteenth century.[29]

Almost every early preservation group had ties to the MVLA. William Murtagh noted that "most preservation efforts throughout the end of the nineteenth century were characterized by the kind of pietism and private support typical of the Mount Vernon effort."[30] The Valley Forge Association, organized in 1878, used the MVLA's charter and bylaws as a guide, and Mrs. William H. Holstein, an organizer, asked the MVLA for names of its regents and vice-regents to tap for money for Valley Forge. Unfortunately for Holstein, saving George Washington's campgrounds lacked the appeal of saving his home. Col. Andrew Jackson's grandson (by adoption) and his wife looked to the MVLA for leadership in organizing to save Jackson's home, the Hermitage (fig. 2.2). The Ladies' Hermitage Association never gained the national stature of the MVLA, in part because Jackson did not have the same appeal as Washington, yet the group did manage to keep the Hermitage from being converted into a home for Confederate veterans when, in 1889, the governor of Tennessee turned it over to the association.[31]

Fig. 2.2. Nashville, Tenn. The Hermitage. The Ladies Hermitage Association modeled itself on the Mount Vernon Ladies' Association of the Union in its efforts to save Andrew Jackson's home. Photo by the author.

The cult of domesticity could not account for all women's historic preservation activities after the Civil War, for, by the 1880s, the nation faced enormous stress and turmoil from increased immigration, financial fluctuations from the depression of the 1870s, Jim Crow racism, and trade unionism. Patriotism and preservation were inexorably linked on the agendas for organization such as the APVA and the DAR.[32] It was a patriotism that was based, however, on a nativist and xenophobic view of the nation's past which too often excluded the contributions of those who came to the United States after the American Revolution and, of course, the contributions of Native Americans.

The Association for the Preservation of Virginia Antiquities, the first large, state-focused private preservation group to appear in the South, was informally founded in 1888 by Mary Jeffery Galt and formally organized the following year by Cynthia Beverley Tucker Coleman. The group first acted "as an appendage" to the Virginia Historical Society, as the historical society saved manuscripts while the APVA saved buildings. Most members, the incorporators, officers, and board members, were all women. Advisory board members, who spoke publicly for the organization until the 1910s, were men. At least one early advisor, James Alston Cabell, admitted that the group was successful because the women members did "most of the work."[33]

James Lindgren argued that these women saw themselves as "the representative women of Virginia," but the Virginia they represented was that of the state's First Families. The founders solicited membership by appealing to Virginians who "still feel themselves a part of that great family, leaning on Virginia as children resting on the bosom of a mother." In fact, Lindgren almost described the APVA members as similar to those in the Daughters of the American Revolution, the United Daughters of the Confederacy, or the National Society of the Colonial Dames, all of which date from about the same time period. "In a remarkable way," noted Lindgren, "the APVA became a defining element in the life of proper Virginia ladies," as the group helped ensure "the cultural cohesion of the dominant class."[34]

APVA women, like MVLA members, felt that it was their responsibility to preserve history. Episcopal bishop A. M. Randolph, who was an advisor to the APVA, told the members, "As a general rule, society develops [sic] these ideas [respect for tradition and history] in the realm of religion and ethics, through the impulse originating in the mind of woman." Women could best protect the sites that perpetuated a sense of duty to the present and future. Thus, some southern white men idolized Gilded Age women such as those in the APVA, setting them up on pedestals as their antebellum ancestors had done and giving them moral authority to save the nation's historic sites.[35]

Still, Lindgren correctly questioned the role of the male advisor in "an organization committed to traditionalism." In the areas of acquisitions, interpretations, and daily policy, men "wielded significant influence," and "a complex relationship existed in the distribution of power." Women took the lead to acquire such prominent sites as the Williamsburg Powder Magazine (then called the Powder Horn, 1889), the Mary Washington House (1890 [fig. 2.3]), and, after 1893, the Jamestown church ruin. While negotiating to buy the land for the Powder Magazine, Annie Galt's "nerves became frayed. Only her nervous tonic kept her going" (fig. 2.4).[36]

Fig. 2.3. (top) Fredericksburg, Va. Mary Washington House. Association for the Preservation of Virginia Antiquities women identified the Mary Washington House as a shrine, "The Home of Mary, Mother of Washington." Photo by the author.

Fig. 2.4. (bottom) Williamsburg, Va. Powder Magazine. Association for the Preservation of Virginia Antiquities women led the effort to preserve historic buildings in Williamsburg by purchasing the Powder Magazine in 1889. Photo by the author.

Incongruously, APVA women used the powder magazine, a masculine military space, for activities consistent with female gender roles, such as afternoon teas and soirees. These informal social events and formal balls helped unite Richmond's elite in a common cause, recruit new members to the APVA, and, in a common goal with all preservationists, raise money.[37]

APVA men and women differed in their interpretation of the historic sites. Men saw the Capitol in Williamsburg and Richmond's John Marshall House as traditional bastions of Virginia power and economics against challenges from Populists and radicals. Women focused on "acceptable codes of individual behavior," emphasizing family and church at the Mary Washington House and various Anglican churches and even interpreting the Jamestown church ruins as "a Garden of Eden where America's first Adam could make an Anglo-Saxon home for his Eve."[38]

Women set daily policy when they presided over all-female meetings held when men were at work. When a man attended, he presided under the "rhetorical argument that [men] were more capable of ensuring efficiency, order, and professional discipline." Both men and women, apparently, thought it would be "un-Virginian" to act otherwise. Female leaders also allowed men to speak for the APVA at the local level and before the legislature.[39]

Nineteenth-century preservationists also protected cemeteries and marked graves, again linking the cult of domesticity and the patriotic fervor that drove women's preservation efforts. The romantic concept of death prevailed in American culture, and people strolled among the graves of the dead as they did along the paths of gardens. Caring for the resting places of one's ancestors was, therefore, an extension of women's responsibilities in the domestic sphere, like caring for part of one's home and family. Richmond women joined the Hollywood Memorial Association (HMA) in 1866 to honor Confederate dead in that cemetery.[40] Cynthia Beverley Tucker Coleman, later active in the APVA, formed the Catharine Memorial Society in 1884, in part, to help repair Williamsburg's Bruton Parish Church and its surrounding graveyard.[41]

APVA members followed Coleman's lead in preserving graveyards, particularly those associated with colonial and Revolutionary War leaders. APVA work in this area "revealed distinct elements in historic preser-

vation: the South's preoccupation with cemeteries, the filiopiety of preservationists, their links with organized Protestantism, and their advocacy
of the civil religion." Coleman argued that preserving colonial graves was
"all calculated to stir the blood of those who can trace their ancestry to
these Colonial grandees. Their old homes in many instances are gone or
else crumbling into decay, but their dust remains a sacred legacy, and the
epitaphs on their tombs, broken and falling away, record their abounding
virtue."[42]

In 1890 APVA member and HMA president Isobel Lamont Stewart
Bryan formed the Confederate Memorial Literary Society to save the
White House of the Confederacy and, with her husband, Joseph, led the
effort in 1894 to persuade the City of Richmond to give the building to
the society. The CMLS "endeavored to represent all Southern women,"
with UDC support and regents in fourteen former Confederate and border states who "attracted contributions of money and relics." The society
opened the White House as a Confederate Museum on February 22,
1896, making it "a kind of monument . . . to vindicate what Southerners
called the 'Lost Cause.'" The CMLS thereby "rescued one of the most
significant structures associated with the Confederacy and saved thousands of 'relics' of the war from the ravages of time and neglect" to exhibit
them in its "Treasure House." Wealthy and well-connected Richmond
women, relatives of Confederate veterans, provided the primary support
and served as vice-regents for the state-based exhibits, with assistance
from their men's advisory board.[43]

Patriotism and preservation also were inexorably linked on the agendas
for other organizations, most notably the Daughters of the American Revolution. Organized in 1890, several months after the Sons of the American
Revolution officially excluded any female descendants of Revolutionary War
soldiers from auxiliary or unofficial membership, the DAR worked through
local chapters and state societies. Its objectives included "the acquisition and
protection of historical spots, and the erection of monuments," making the
DAR the first national organization to protect historic sites around the country. Floride Cunningham of South Carolina, one of the eighteen original
signers of the DAR, was a relative of Ann Pamela Cunningham.[44]

The DAR initially focused on Philadelphia sites. In 1892 chapters organized to save the city's Betsy Ross House (fig. 2.5). The Philadelphia

Fig. 2.5. Philadelphia, Pa. Betsy Ross House. Daughters of the American Revolution efforts to save the Betsy Ross House illustrate the group's focus on Revolutionary War sites. Photo by the author.

Chapter received sole custody of Independence Hall from the City of Philadelphia in 1896 and opened the "restored" second floor in 1898. During the summer of 1899 the city permitted the DAR to move the chapter's museum in Independence Hall to the wings of the building, so that the east wing contained Revolutionary War relics and the west wing colonial relics. In 1900 the 324-member chapter had its own permanent rooms but held its annual meeting and other important meetings in Independence Hall. The Pennsylvania Society of the Colonial Dames of America started to join the effort to restore Independence Hall but decided to restore the Senate Chamber in Congress Hall, next door, instead of tackling the larger building.[45]

In 1899 the DAR Continental Congress encouraged its members to contribute to save the Greenbush Manor House on the east bank of the Hudson River across from the City of Albany. The house was better known as Fort Crailo, the Vlie House, or the "Yankee Doodle house," for it was there that the well-known song was "said to have been composed." Albany founder Kilaen Van Rensselaer ordered the house built as a fort in 1642, and the city's mayor had erected a plaque in 1886, proclaiming this was "supposed to be the oldest building in the United States." The DAR was most interested in the "Yankee Doodle" connection. When members failed to respond as expected, reportedly due to the fact that the DAR was raising money for its own headquarters at that time, Mrs. S. deL. Van Rensselaer Strong, a DAR member, purchased the property and "repaired the building sufficiently to keep it from decay" until it could be restored and made into the planned "museum of relics."[46]

Like other patriotic organizations of the day, DAR members ignored African American and Native American history, other than to acknowledge that their ancestors had owned slaves or had fought Native Americans.[47] Chapters worked alone, with others in their state, or as part of the national organization. Philadelphia's Quaker City Chapter sent circulars to every Pennsylvania chapter, seeking help in getting the legislature to pass a law to preserve Valley Forge. The chapter became one of the first members of the Valley Forge National Park Association and used its DAR ties to solicit each regent in the country for help in having Congress designate Valley Forge as a national military park and provide funding to acquire and maintain the site. The bill was before Congress in 1900, but

Valley Forge did not become a national park until July 4, 1976.[48] Meanwhile, the Valley Forge DAR chapter raised $103.45 through "an entertainment" to furnish the old headquarters at Valley Forge.[49] DAR chapters also honored women and commemorated women's history by naming chapters after Revolutionary War–era women such as Deborah Sampson (Brockton, Mass., organized and chartered in 1897).

DAR chapters installed plaques as early as 1896, when the Norwalk, Connecticut, chapter, engraved a boulder with "This rock marks the site of a battle [Flax Hill] between the Americans and British, July 12, 1779. This cannon ball [embedded in the rock] was found on the battle field a hundred years later."[50] These plaques and monuments, although intended as commemorative, are now themselves historic resources, documenting the history of the historic preservation movement.

The DAR also located and marked graves of Revolutionary War–era citizens, including French allies and "Real Daughters," the biological daughters of Revolutionary War veterans. The Abigail Adams Chapter of Boston marked the DAR's first grave, that of its namesake in Quincy. This was a particularly important project for chapters in East Coast and southern communities, but, since veterans moved west after the war, even the Caroline Scott Harrison Chapter of Indianapolis, named for the DAR's first president general, marked graves in that city.[51]

Melusina Fay Peirce used her DAR ties when she became one of the first women members of the "Trustees of Scenic and Historic Places and Objects" in January 1900. Organizing in New York in 1895 after the model of the British National Trust, the "substantial, respected and well-known" trustees incorporated to "make recommendations to any municipality in the State of New York, or its proper offices, respecting movements in the scenic or material conditions thereof, to acquire by purchase, gift, grant, devise, or bequest, or in any other lawful manner, historic objects or memorable or picturesque places in the State or elsewhere in the United States."[52]

On April 28, 1900, sixty-three women gathered in New York City to form a "Women's Auxiliary" to cooperate with the trustees. Peirce was already well known as an authority on cooperative housekeeping, and, under her leadership, auxiliary members ran their own organization, paying dues to the trustees. Peirce's goal was to save the Fraunces Tavern,

Fig. 2.6. San Antonio, Tex. The Alamo. The Daughters of the Republic of Texas preserved sites such as the Alamo which were related to the early European-American settlement of Texas. Photo by the author.

where George Washington bade farewell to his officers on December 4, 1783, and some early auxiliary members also belonged to the Fraunces Tavern Committee of the Mary Washington Colonial Chapter of the DAR and other DAR chapters. Peirce also had organized the Poe Cottage Association in 1895 to save the poet's home. Members worked with the trustees to save the tavern, the Jumel Mansion (Washington's Headquarters), and the cottage.[53]

In a final example of patriotic preservation, Adina De Zavala organized the De Zavala Chapter of the Daughters of the Republic of Texas in 1893 to preserve the state's missions and landmarks. In 1899 she met Clara Driscoll, the daughter of a wealthy Texas rancher, and drafted her into the cause, using Driscoll's money to buy the siege and massacre site next to the Alamo in San Antonio in 1903 for the Daughters to operate as a historic shrine (fig. 2.6). [54]

Preservation was not a primary focus of members of the General Federation of Women's Clubs (GFWC), as it was for the DAR. Yet club women took seriously their mission to improve their communities by promoting art, libraries, public health, playgrounds, and suffrage. The preservation efforts of clubs such as the Woman's Club of Denver, founded in 1894 and active in the effort to save Mesa Verde, are less well known.

Virginia Donaghe McClurg (1857-1931) was the first woman prominent in the campaign to protect Mesa Verde. She arrived in Durango, Colorado, in 1882 as a correspondent for the *New York Graphic* to "investigate lost cities of the prehistoric Indians of the Southwest," but a Ute Indian uprising thwarted her goal. She returned in 1885, explored a few ruins, and organized her own expedition to the site the next year. McClurg's expedition is credited with the discovery of Three Tiered House and Echo Cliff House. Her companion, Cassius Viets, discovered Brownstone Front, now known as Balcony House, which she explored on that trip.[55] McClurg began her crusade to save Mesa Verde in 1887, as she wrote poems published in prominent magazines and lectured around the country and in Europe, "decrying the wanton destruction of ancient walls by treasure-seekers who were carrying off artifacts to sell." She began to work with members of Congress in 1894 to pass bills protecting Mesa Verde. She also negotiated with Weminuche Ute Chief Ignacio to protect the lands while the Utes retained grazing rights.[56]

McClurg's interest in saving Mesa Verde reflected widespread romantic interest in Native Americans and shifting federal policy toward land ownership for Native Americans in the 1880s and 1890s. The United States' official policy was "one of assimilation (as opposed to extermination or isolation on reservations), which meant the eradication of Indian cultural forms" during these years. As part of this policy, the 1887 Dawes General Allotment Act ended the collective ownership of lands for most tribes, with the exception of the Pueblos. At the same time, Leah Dilworth has called the 1880s and 1890s a "boom time for American ethnology, and the Southwest was a major area of interest." The Bureau of American Ethnology, established in 1879 in the Smithsonian Institution, led many of the expeditions.[57] Anthropology departments in universities and museums also documented a vanishing past.[58] Ethnographers in the Southwest were particularly interested in the Zunis, Hopis, and other Pueblo groups "because they appeared less influenced by European cultures" than other Native Americans.[59] Worried that these groups would soon lose their distinct cultures, ethnographers carefully documented an "'ethnographic present'" of rituals and practices, such as the Snake Dance, which were perceived as still supposedly "culturally intact," that is, unchanged by "civilization."[60]

As ethnographers hurriedly documented a fading past, images of Native Americans permeated American culture. "Dime novels, museums and expositions, Wild West shows, paintings, illustrations, lithography, photography and sculpture, and advertising, as well as sheet music" helped shape perceptions of Indians.[61] Sometimes Native Americans became "artifacts" on display. During the 1893 World's Fair in Chicago, for instance, Navajos lived on the fairgrounds next to the Anthropological Building, and Pueblos inhabited a plaster pueblo on the Midway Plaisance.[62]

Railroads played a key role in shaping perceptions of Native Americans in the late nineteenth century, for railroads brought tourists to the Southwest to see Native American sites and settlers and businesspeople to "colonize" the land. The Atchison, Topeka and Santa Fe Railroad, for instance, began promoting tourism in 1895 and hired ethnographers to publicize the Southwest's attractions.[63]

Given the country's interest in Native American sites and artifacts, McClurg was wise to try to protect Mesa Verde from potential destruction from overdevelopment as a tourist site or looting of artifacts. Fortunately, she could draw on the growing interest of western women's organizations to protect the environment and their organizational skills to help her crusade.

Enlisting the support of the General Federation of Women's Clubs, McClurg had 250,000 women behind her.[64] The GFWC was better known for its work in the conservation of natural resources as the women's club members "identified environmental conservation with a panoply of cherished white, middle-class ideals: motherhood, family, community, religion, and patriotism" as they sought to preserve "God's natural resources and American abundance" for their children. She eventually persuaded the Woman's Club of Denver to organize the Colorado Cliff Dwellings Association and led the group from 1895 to 1930. The association was influential in the eventual establishment in June 1906 of Mesa Verde National Park, "the greatest collection of archaeological ruins in the Southwest," as the first national park founded to preserve cultural resources.[65] Even this story may be incomplete, for there is no evidence to date that Native American women participated in the nineteenth century in the early efforts to save Mesa Verde or other sites related to Native American history. Nor do we know enough about how Native American women preserved memories of these places, in light of the profound dislocations that occurred as they were forced to move from their homelands and live on reservations that, by design, tried to destroy their traditions and heritage.

Two final preservation efforts deserve note here, the simultaneous efforts during the mid-1890s of Helen Pitts Douglass and Kate Fields, both white women, to save sites significant to African American history. Frederick Douglass died in 1895, and Helen, his second wife, devoted the remaining years of her life to saving Cedar Hill, their home, as a memorial to the work of the most prominent African American of the nineteenth century. This was the first home preserved specifically because of its relationship to African American history and became the "first Black historic house." Helen Pitts Douglass died in 1903, and the Frederick Douglass Memorial and Historical Association took over the house.[66] Also in 1895 Mary Katherine Keemle began her crusade to save John Brown's Fort, which the John Brown Fort Company had moved from Harpers Ferry, West Virginia, to Chicago for the 1893 World's Columbian Exposition and then abandoned when only ten people paid the fifty-cent admission charge to see the building. Fields leased five acres of land from Alexander Murphy and his wife and arranged to move the dismantled fort back to Harpers Ferry. Unfortunately, Fields died in 1896, without leaving an estate large enough to reimburse Murphy for his expenses, as she had promised to do. In July 1896 Mary Church Terrell led a delegation of women attending the first national convention of the National League of Colored Women, meeting in Washington, D.C., to the John Brown Fort in "the first known event of African Americans explicitly embracing the fort as a symbol of their struggle for freedom and equality."[67]

By 1900, then, women across the country led the effort to save historic sites. Acting alone, with male advisors, or as auxiliaries to men's organizations, women established a pattern of working through private organizations, sometimes pressuring government agencies, to save historic buildings. By today's perspectives most had a narrow view of the past, ignoring the history of African Americans, Native Americans, and the immigrants who arrived after their own ancestors. They did, however, identify nationally significant sites, raise money, organize cadres of women throughout the country, and interpret their version of the nation's history by placing plaques on buildings, engraving boulders, and saving relics. Although they did not have the vote to pass legislation to save historic sites themselves, they put political pressure on their husbands, sons, and friends to provide that protection when possible. Most important, they used the formal and informal networks that dominated women's lives in the nineteenth century to provide today's preservationists with outstanding examples of the effectiveness of the "old-girl network" and of the patience and perseverance that is so necessary for successful preservation projects. Their actions set precedents that continued to be critical.

Today federal regulations, legislation, and dollars provide many more tools for preservationists, but women still organize in voluntary associations and network through professional organizations to save historic sites. Equally important, they use the most sophisticated current scholarship to enrich their work, including discussions of issues such as slavery which their foremothers had never envisioned when they organized to protect Mount Vernon. Unfortunately, however, we still know far too little about the work of women of color in this crusade. This volume may encourage future preservationists to explore the history of historic preservation in their own communities to uncover the still-hidden stories of these women's efforts.

CHAPTER 3

Special Places Saved
The Role of Women in Preserving the American Landscape

Shaun Eyring

Women have figured prominently in preserving significant American landscapes from the mid-nineteenth century onward. Their contributions range from restoring small historic gardens and protecting large natural systems to preserving diverse urban neighborhoods. The extensive work of women in preserving historic, scenic, and vernacular landscapes, however, is not well documented. Landscape preservation traditionally has been associated with restoring gardens and grounds belonging to historic estates; male professionals are usually credited with these restorations from the early to mid-twentieth century. Preserving scenic and later vernacular landscapes was a strong American focus from the early twentieth century, but, again, the role of women has been overlooked by those who have studied this subject.

A closer look reveals that women have long been involved in preserving landscapes of many scales and types, but they were more likely to contribute through organized groups such as women's clubs. As clubwomen united throughout the late nineteenth and early twentieth centuries, they undertook civic improvement projects that ranged from establishing libraries and improving schools to preserving national treasures and protecting the environment. The club network allowed like-minded women to extend their mission to the local, state, and even national level.[1] Working in groups, women often were the major force behind preservation projects, raising public awareness, fund raising, and lobbying legislatures. Women's groups also offered continuous support for preservation projects, from their launch to meeting ongoing maintenance needs. By profiling the contributions of leading women's organizations within the context of the historic landscape and the scenic and vernacular landscape preservation movements, this chapter begins to illuminate the critical role of women in preserving the American landscape.

Women Preserving Historic Landscapes

According to Charles Hosmer in *Presence of the Past,* the primary focus of the historic preservation movement through the mid-twentieth century was on structures, not on the associated landscapes and settings. But preserving the landscape was clearly a concern even in early preservation projects, in which women played a major role. Women's groups that preserved historic landscapes appear to have been motivated by a sense of patriotic duty; a desire to preserve a local, regional, or even national identity; and a commitment to educating others about the country's landscape heritage.

By today's professional standards, these groups' approach to physical preservation may be dismissed as selective, romantic, or inaccurate. Their approach was significant, however, because it looked beyond the footprint of the building to include the associated landscape. They also recognized that saving a place required a long-term commitment to preservation, restoration, and maintenance. Finally, they brought to their work in landscape preservation a host of management skills honed in the domestic sphere and an ability to network with groups that would support their interests. This overview of women's record in the field of historic landscape preservation focuses on three groups: the Mount Vernon Ladies' Association of the Union (MVLA), the Garden Club of Virginia (GCV), and the Garden Club of America (GCA).

THE MOUNT VERNON LADIES' ASSOCIATION OF THE UNION

Preservation at Mount Vernon was one of the most important early examples of a unified approach to a historic landscape. The effort was spearheaded by the all-woman Mount Vernon Ladies' Association of the Union, whose purchase and protection of George Washington's home on the Potomac River became the first nationwide effort at historic preservation.[2]

Gardens and Grounds. Soon after the MVLA acquired Mount Vernon in 1853, efforts at managing the landscape were under way. Planned projects from as early as 1879 included planting the farm in field crops, restoring George Washington's deer park, reconstructing the ha-ha wall following the original foundation lines, carefully maintaining the lawn, and restoring the Old Avenue used by Washington. The Mount Vernon Ladies' Association set a precedent for using colonial-style materials and construction details that were compatible with the eighteenth-century surroundings for new construction. This approach foreshadowed the colonial revival that later became prevalent in landscape architecture and landscape preservation.[3]

After 1900 the MVLA typically sought professional input on preservation projects. Charles Sprague Sargent, renowned horticulturist and director of the Arnold Arboretum, was one of the first landscape professionals to consult with the Mount Vernon Ladies' Association. Sargent enthusiastically embraced the goal of authentic restoration. He convinced the MVLA to approach the biotic elements of the landscape with the same concern for accuracy which was applied to the structures.[4]

Following Sargent's death in 1927, two noted landscape architects served as directors of research and restoration at Mount Vernon in the 1930s. Harold Abbott, a landscape architectural graduate from Harvard, served from 1932 to 1936; Morley Williams, also a Harvard graduate, consulted for a brief time from 1936. Several noted garden restorations were accomplished during this period. The projects always included intensive research and sometimes archaeological investigation. Although the detailed layout of the gardens and species selection of the period may not meet today's stringent preservation standards, the MVLA has always shown a willingness to challenge past decisions as new information becomes available. In 1935 the association approved the redesign of the Lower Garden based on new information uncovered by Morley Williams and Harold Abbott. In recent years new evidence led to the redesign of the Upper Garden. Advanced technologies in archaeology now play a major role in providing information about the Mount Vernon that George Washington knew. The MVLA also continues to consult with top landscape architecture and preservation planning professionals.[5]

The Larger Landscape Setting. Preserving the larger landscape setting has also been a leading concern of the MVLA from early in its history. Between 1889 and 1915 vistas were cleared to expose views to George Washington's Old River Farm and to the West Lodge Gate. In

Fig. 3.1. The Mount Vernon Ladies' Association of the Union has worked since the mid-nineteenth century to preserve its setting, including this view across the Potomac River. Photo by Robert Page.

addition, the prospect up and down the river was cleared of trees and vegetation to restore views known to Washington.[6]

Protecting the plantation from modern intrusions was an ongoing challenge for the MVLA, and between 1886 and 1926 the group acquired large tracts of land within the property's view shed. This effort ensured the integrity of the landscape setting by eliminating such potential visual intrusions as a hospital, prison, public picnic grove, or hotel complex. By 1950 the surrounding landscape within view of Mount Vernon was securely within its control, and the only possible visual intrusion came from across the Potomac River (fig. 3.1).

Protection of the view shed across the Potomac River was accomplished, at least in part, in 1955 when the vice-regent of Ohio purchased a 485-acre tank farm site across the river. After receiving much broadly based political support, this land and some additional acreage became designated as Piscataway National Park. The development boom of the 1980s prompted the association to hire landscape architectural consultants to prepare an assessment of the view shed and a computer model that would assist in preparing a view shed protection plan. The MVLA soon after joined forces with Congress. On George Washington's birthday of 1994, Senator Paul Sarbanes of Maryland introduced Bill 1703, the Piscataway National Park Expansion Act. This legislation, signed into law in October 1994, may provide the complete view shed protection the association has been striving for years to secure.[7]

Mount Vernon emerges as an early leader in landscape preservation and has served as a model for other preservation groups. The Wakefield Memorial Association, led by Josephine Rust (1923), secured the land related to George Washington's Birthplace and built a memorial house and landscape in honor of George Washington. The Ladies' Hermitage Association was formed in 1889 to administer the Hermitage, Andrew Jackson's home in Nashville, and the Robert E. Lee Memorial Foundation, founded by May Lanier, acquired and preserved the house and grounds of Robert E. Lee's Stratford Hall. A women's group in Colorado also looked to the MVLA for its structure when it organized to preserve the cliff dwellings of Mesa Verde in 1898.[8]

THE GARDEN CLUB OF VIRGINIA

Professionalism in preservation became a standard for completing projects during the 1920s. Colonial Williamsburg in many ways set the precedent for the concept of professional collaboration,[9] as attention to research and accurate details characterized the restoration process. The Garden Club of Virginia extended the professionals' traditional focus on historic structures to include historic gardens. The organization's best-known works include Kenmore (1929), Stratford Hall (1932), Monticello (1938), the University of Virginia's pavilion gardens (1952), and the kitchen garden at Bacon's Castle (1988).

The Virginia garden clearly stirred a strong cultural, if not romantic, connection for the women of The Garden Club of Virginia, who have been among the leading advocates for its perpetuation. These women foresaw that without organized protection the Virginia garden, a hallmark of genteel culture, would be destroyed. Beginning with Kenmore in Fredericksburg, The GCV made it a primary mission to save Virginia's most historically significant gardens.[10] The GCV from its earliest work has

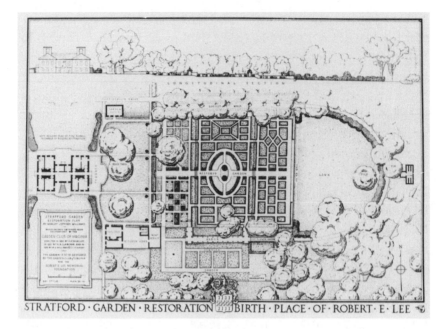

STRATFORD · GARDEN · RESTORATION BIRTH · PLACE · OF · ROBERT · E · LEE

Fig. 3.2. Stratford Hall restoration plan of 1932 completed by landscape architect Morley Williams for the Garden Club of Virginia. Courtesy of the Garden Club of Virginia.

promoted professionalism in planning projects and common sense in their execution. Garden restorations were selected by application. A long and thoughtful study of each proposal by the Restoration Committee of The GCV was part of the process. Two basic principles still apply today to gardens selected as GCV restoration projects: first, each garden must be opened to the public on a regular basis; and, second, the property's governing body must both approve the project and agree to maintain it.[11]

The Garden Club of Virginia's approach to garden preservation was innovative yet sensible. Each project was seen as an act of restoration, preservation, or interpretation. Which approach was selected depended on the level of available documentation and what was found in the existing conditions. The club made every effort to document and restore original landscapes, although this was not possible for every project. At Stratford Hall, for example, the early walls and terraces were archaeologically documented and followed in the restoration plan of 1930. At the

University of Virginia, however, no individually detailed plans for the Pavilion gardens were ever located. The GCV, through Alden Hopkins, completed a conjectural restoration of each garden to suit the style, period, and needs of the property (fig. 3.2).[12]

The Garden Club of Virginia has always worked with landscape professionals. Leading restoration landscape architects such as Morley Williams, Charles Gillette, Arthur Shurcliff, Alden Hopkins, and Ralph Griswold provided research, designs, and working drawings for the restorations. The GCV enjoyed a close working relationship with the project landscape architect throughout the design process, and an annual inspection of each property ensured that the plan was maintained as the two had envisioned.[13] Since the 1970s The GCV has hired accomplished landscape architects to serve as the club's lead professional, thus guaranteeing continuing commitment to a high standard of professionalism in its projects.[14]

The Garden Club of Virginia always understood that maintenance was the key to true preservation success; without proper funding, beautiful and expensive garden restorations would not succeed in the long term. The GCV sought ways of funding projects that would ensure not only the initial restoration work but also the long-term care. A mammoth flower fair at Monticello in 1927 raised the tremendous sum of seven thousand dollars to put toward historic tree maintenance on that site. In 1929 The GCV initiated a statewide tour of homes and gardens opened to the public during the height of blooming season. The proceeds from the tour went to funding current and future garden restorations. Historic Garden Week, today a leading tourist attraction in Virginia, grosses over a half-million dollars annually for historic garden projects.[15]

The Garden Club of Virginia has been a model for how organizations can take the initiative to protect and manage important historic gardens in their region. The club had the vision to hire talented landscape architects to execute the design of their projects and then ensure that they would be maintained in the long term. This combination has allowed the work of The Garden Club of Virginia to perpetuate the Virginia garden, a tradition that long ago would have been lost without such help. In fact, some of the gardens from the 1920s and 1930s are gaining historic significance in their own right as examples of colonial revival landscape architecture in the United States.

The Garden Club of Virginia set a precedent for professionalism in regional garden preservation and practicality in preservation maintenance. Other women's groups also adopted similar approaches with landscape preservation projects. These include the Garden Club of Natchez, Mississippi, which organized a house and garden pilgrimage to raise funds for the deteriorating Greek- and Federal-style mansions in their town, and the Maryland Federation of Garden Clubs, which advanced the automobile tour idea in May 1930 to benefit the restoration of Stratford Hall.[16]

THE GARDEN CLUB OF AMERICA

Besides preserving the physical fabric of a structure or landscape, documenting historic sites through drawings and photographs gained popularity between the late nineteenth century and the mid-twentieth century. Books documenting historic landscapes, largely written by women, began to appear around the turn of the century. Alice Morse Earle wrote *Old Time Gardens* in 1901 and Louise Shelton completed *Beautiful Gardens in America* in 1915.[17] In 1922 the Garden Club of America began making significant contributions to this growing body of work by carefully documenting both historic and contemporary landscapes (fig. 3.3).

The Garden Club of America's Committee on Historic Gardens began collecting material for its now seminal two-volume work *Gardens of Colony and State*, by Alice G. B. Lockwood, in 1922. The first volume was published nine years later, the second in 1934.[18] Organized geographically, Lockwood and other contributors documented through plans and photographs, and with great accuracy for the time, extant gardens and landscapes in the United States whose origins could be traced to the midnineteenth century or earlier. Many of the gardens disappeared not long after the book's publication due to the gardeners' shift to wartime activities and the broader effects of postwar suburbanization.[19]

The GCA's second major project began in the early 1920s with the commissioning of a nationwide set of glass lantern slides to record the gardens of their members. Recently, The GCA, along with Mac Griswold and Eleanor Weller, provided support for amassing the scattered slide collection in one spot. The GCA worked jointly with the Office of Horticulture at the Smithsonian Institution to create Archive of American Gardens, which now houses the nearly fifteen hundred lantern slides as

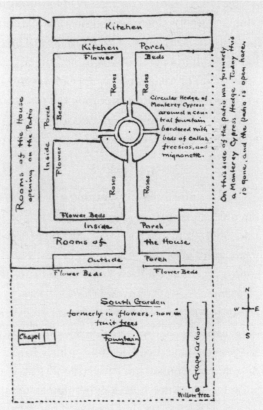

Fig. 3.3. Photograph (*top*) and garden sketch (*bottom*). Camulos Ranch, Calif. From *Gardens of Colony and State*. Courtesy of the Garden Club of America.

well as other garden documentation, both historic and modern. According to Griswold and Weller, the archive preserves the record of women's history in the garden. Since many of the gardens no longer exist or are in serious decline, the photographs may also provide remaining clues to the styles and garden techniques in practice in the early twentieth century. These slides were the focus of Griswold and Weller's 1992 publication, *The Golden Age of American Gardens.*

Local clubs affiliated with the Garden Club of America also documented historic gardens by publishing photographic essays about exemplary properties. Documentations include *Historic Gardens of Virginia,* compiled and published by the James River Garden Club in 1920.[20] In 1923 the Garden Club of Philadelphia published a book documenting the beautiful Wissahickon Valley, and in 1929 Louise and James Bush Brown wrote *Portraits of Philadelphia Gardens.* Other published books by women and women's groups documenting historic gardens include the *Descriptive Guide Book of Virginia's Old Gardens* (1929), assembled by the Garden Club of Virginia as a handbook for its annual garden tour. The Peach Tree Garden Club of Atlanta published *Garden History of Georgia, 1733-1933,* and Winifred Starr Dobyns completed *California Gardens.*[21] In 1996 the Garden Club of Virginia created a fellowship to document privately owned historic gardens in the state.

SUMMARY

Women have played a critical role in securing a place for the American landscape within the historic preservation movement. Further research is needed to illuminate the contributions of other women's groups that have influenced historic landscape preservation. The Society of the Colonial Dames of America, the Daughters of the American Revolution, the Valley Forge Centennial Association, and the Association for the Preservation of Virginia Antiquities, for example, promoted American battlefield preservation as early as the mid-nineteenth century.[22] More recently, minority women have been leading efforts to preserve historic landscapes. For example, woman-run African American Heritage Preservation Foundation has identified and documented landscapes associated with African American history, including the Stanton Family Cemetery and the Historic Aberdeen Gardens, both in Virginia.[23]

Women Preserving Scenic and Vernacular Landscapes

Although landscape preservation traditionally has been perceived as restoring the gardens and grounds of historic sites, since the nineteenth century there have been efforts to address and protect scenic and vernacular landscapes. Throughout the nineteenth century Americans began to identify scenic landscapes that were distinctly American and therefore worth protecting.[24] By the twentieth century preserving scenic and natural American landscapes became a popular issue on the agendas of civic organizations. The movement to address vernacular landscapes began slowly in the early twentieth century and gained momentum in the 1950s. When postwar suburbanization and urban renewal brought enormous physical destruction to once-familiar neighborhoods, towns, and countryside, preservation-minded groups organized to stave off mass destruction of the physical landscape and its associated cultural traditions. Within this spirit of preserving scenic and vernacular landscapes, three women's organizations emerge as leaders: the General Federation of Women's Clubs, the National Roadside Council, and the San Antonio Conservation Society.

GENERAL FEDERATION OF WOMEN'S CLUBS

The General Federation of Women's Clubs (GFWC), founded in 1890, encouraged women to participate in public affairs and provided the vehicle for them to take their concerns from the local to the national level.[25] Women who were members of the GFWC had the opportunity, with the support of its large membership, to push for change. The group had a profound influence on identifying and protecting large landscape systems and ensuring their protection as national and state parks

Support for a National Park Service. Led by Mary Belle King Sherman of the General Federation of Women's Clubs, the collective interests of thousands of clubwomen brought major support to the bill establishing the National Park Service in 1916. So dedicated to the cause was Mary Sherman that she became known as the "National Park Lady," even changing the emphasis of the GFWC's Conservation Department from conserving natural resources to protecting scenic landscapes. Sherman led the GFWC on a crusade to establish national parks, even implementing a national scenic area survey in which member clubs from every state were asked to identify parks in their state that should be protected. The GFWC passed a resolution in 1916 supporting a national park service and, in addition to lobbying congressmen, produced a mailing list of 275,000 names for the Department of the Interior, which was undertaking a publicity campaign to garner support for the bill.[26]

Wide Support for State Park Preservation. Most noted among the efforts to preserve land at the state level was the work of the Florida Federation of Women's Clubs at Paradise Key. In the early 1900s Mary Barr Munroe, a vocal activist, learned of the south Florida location, then owned by a local land developer, where palms grew wild and vegetation was so lush that it was aptly named Paradise Key. Mary Munroe was convinced that Paradise Key was a national treasure and determined that it should be donated to the Florida Federation of Women's Clubs to preserve as parkland. The club was able to secure land donations from the developer and the state with the influential assistance of the club's president, Mae Mann Jennings. This resulted in the establishment of the 4,000-acre Royal Palm State Park under the ownership of the federation. Funds for its management were scarce, but the clubwomen persisted by lobbying the Florida state legislature for an appropriation. In 1947, after managing the park for nearly thirty years, the federation donated the land to the Department of the Interior to be included in the Everglades National Park.[27]

The New Jersey Federation of Women's Clubs led a persistent crusade to preserve the Palisades of New Jersey. In 1896 the towering, rocky cliffs bordering the Hudson River were in danger of destruction from commercial enterprise. The club women decided to "Save the Palisades for Posterity," after listening to many papers on preserving state forests and taking a convincing boat trip up the Hudson to view the damage. As a joint scenic asset between New York and New Jersey, legislatures of both states formed commissions. The New Jersey State Federation of Women's Clubs had representation on the New Jersey commission (fig. 3.4).[28]

Many plans were reviewed by the commissions, but only one eventually was considered acceptable to the New Jersey Federation of Women's Clubs: the establishment of a permanent interstate park. In 1899 the club formed the Palisades League to raise funds for the project outside its own commission activities. Despite those who deemed it a hopeless task, the

Fig. 3.4. A 1998 image of the Palisades, a successful preservation effort led by New Jersey clubwomen. Photo by Richard Newton.

group raised sufficient money to halt the destruction. Their persistence evidently paid off, for on April 4, 1900, the Palisades Bill was passed by the legislature, an action acclaimed by conservationists nationwide. The New Jersey Federation of Women's Clubs has continued to monitor the Palisades, ensuring its long-term preservation. In 1964 the federation supported Bluff Point, another site in the Palisades; in 1993 a resolution asked that the Palisades be placed in the New Jersey Register of Natural Areas.[29]

Other women's groups also addressed large landscape preservation issues. Beginning in the 1920s, a devoted member of the Save the Redwoods League, Mrs. Philip Lansdale, led the longtime crusade to purchase individual Redwood Groves to keep them from being destroyed. In the 1940s the Garden Club of America promoted national park preservation.[30]

THE NATIONAL ROADSIDE COUNCIL

Believing that a "bad physical environment meant a bad moral environment," many women's groups waged campaigns to beautify their cities by promoting or regulating clean, tree-lined streets free of trash and unsightly billboards. The effort to control roadside billboards in the name of preserving scenic beauty began in the early decades of the twentieth century.[31] By the 1920s women's groups such as the Garden Club of America and the General Federation of Women's Clubs gained recognition as significant voices in the quest for roadside beauty. The National Roadside Council was born to help win the war against the billboard industry.

Creation of the National Roadside Council. Elizabeth Lawton created the National Roadside Council in the 1920s (founded as the National Coalition for Roadside Beauty) as a vehicle to speak out against the impending blight upon the landscape caused by outdoor advertising. Lawton's opposition to billboards virtually became her life's work. Her basic philosophy was that "beauty and the billboard cannot exist on the same landscape." By the mid-1930s fifteen state and regional roadside councils, with predominantly women as members, had been established under the National Roadside Council.[32] This created a unified voice for opponents of roadside advertising against the powerful male-dominated Outdoor Advertising Association of America (fig. 3.5).

In the 1930s Mrs. Lawton, her husband, and the National Roadside Council performed many highly acclaimed roadside inventories for states across the country—including North Carolina, Georgia, Illinois, Oregon, and Washington as well as the District of Columbia—to emphasize the extensive visual damage caused by outdoor advertising. The explicit re-

Fig. 3.5. From "Highway Entrances to the Federal City," the 1930 survey completed by Elizabeth Lawton and her husband for the American Civic Association.

sults of these photographic inventories were published in the American Civic Association's annual reports and in *Nature* magazine. They were also used to support the cause of scenic beauty and the need for legislation to control billboard proliferation. The National Roadside Council would survive past Lawton's death in 1954 and would play a key role in the next generation of advocacy for roadside beauty in the United States.

A New Interstate Road System. Renewed efforts to protect the country's scenic beauty along highways emerged in the 1950s when legislation came before Congress to create a new interstate highway system. Representatives from the state roadside councils, such as Hilda Fox of the Pennsylvania Roadside Council and Helen Reynolds of the California Roadside Council, campaigned for the protection of natural scenery along the growing U.S. highway system. Fox used several public tactics to highlight "blot of the month" billboards in her state.[33] She also created the famous "litterbug" in 1951 to promote roadside beauty. This character eventually was adopted by the "Keep America Beautiful" antilittering campaign and soon became a nationally recognized symbol along the nation's highways.[34]

When national billboard legislation was introduced in the late 1950s, women from local civic clubs, garden clubs, and roadside councils were present to prevent the new interstate from becoming a "billboard canyon." Perhaps the most significant addition to the highway beauty coalition during this era was Lady Bird Johnson, the wife of President Lyndon B. Johnson. Her efforts led to the passage of the contentious and highly controversial Highway Beautification Act of 1965. Although flawed in its execution and widely criticized by proponents of roadside beauty, the act forced a continuing public debate that kept the issue of national roadside beauty at the forefront.[35]

The efforts of women who addressed beauty along American highways have left a profound legacy that can be seen today in the work of such groups as Scenic America and in programs such as the Federal Highways Administration's Scenic Byways. Some state roadside councils continue to exist, while others, like Fox's Pennsylvania Roadside Council, formed new groups that have expanded their mission to deal with a range of environmental and scenic issues. Many women's organizations, including the Garden Club of America, continue to place scenic beauty and conservation issues at the top of their national agendas.

When driving long stretches of many interstate highways and state turnpikes which embrace the surrounding landscape and are noticeably devoid of outdoor advertising, one must look to a past that sought to secure a beautiful landscape in the face of a growing highway system. Although the role of women in this movement has often been trivialized, they deserve widespread credit as catalysts in making roadside beauty and billboard control enduring aspects of the effort to protect the nation's scenic landscape.

THE SAN ANTONIO CONSERVATION SOCIETY

Although the preservation community in the nineteenth and twentieth centuries focused on the physical fabric of structures and landscapes, there was a small movement afoot in the early twentieth century which looked to preserve the everyday character of places, including cultural traditions and land uses. This trend grew as post–World War II development began to destroy much of the country's common landscape, including farms, small country towns, and decaying urban communities. The San Antonio Conservation Society, founded by a group of women artists in 1924, was one of the earliest groups in the United States to seek an integrated preservation of the built, cultural, and natural environments.[36]

The San Antonio Conservation Society formed when artist Emily Edwards and civic activist Rena Maverick Green sought to prevent the loss of the Old Market House to a street-widening project in San Antonio's booming downtown. This focus was an early indication of the emphasis this group would place upon the vernacular qualities of the city, since at this time there were few examples of preserving common places that had no links to famous individuals or formative events in American history. To protect fully the heritage of this uniquely multicultural city, the women reached out to different parts of the city to give their group a community focus. As a result, the society gained a rich and varied membership. The goal of the group became saving not only landmarks but traditions and ambience as well.[37]

In the 1920s and 1930s the society worked persistently for the preservation of San Antonio's Spanish Missions. In the 1930s and 1940s the group campaigned for the proper preservation and treatment of the San Antonio River and the buildings and communities along its path. The river, whose curvilinear thirteen-mile route wound through the heart of the city, was threatened by a flood control project designed to straighten its characteristically meandering route. Through the support of the society and its convincing arguments that the simple, natural beauty of the river was San Antonio's greatest asset, the basic character of the river was conserved, and some of the communities adjacent to it were restored.[38] In the 1940s and 1950s, like other American cities, San Antonio felt the impact of the automobile. The San Antonio Conservation Society took a firm stand on conserving the local public parks and open spaces that were threatened with demolition or drastic reduction to accommodate this increased traffic, parking spaces and expressways.[39]

Like other women's groups of the period, the society realized the importance of fund raising to support its cause effectively. Its approach was to celebrate the local color and traditions of San Antonio. The group's first fund-raising activity was the Indian Harvest Festival in 1936, which recalled the harvest festival customarily observed by Indians of the area prior to the establishment of the missions.[40] This early festival evolved into the society's annual fall river festival, later named "A Night in Old San Antonio." The event continues to represent the multicultural character of the city.

CONSERVING INNER-CITY NEIGHBORHOODS

After World War II more groups emerged which supported conservation of the everyday landscape. During this period neighborhood-based groups of both women and men became increasingly vocal and politicized as large-scale urban planning projects affected their communities.[41] Federal legislation, specifically the National Housing Act of 1949 and the Federal-Aid Highway Act of 1956, was a significant catalyst in fueling the nationwide trend to revitalize decaying city centers. Renewal often meant demolishing deteriorating historic business and neighborhood districts and building modern developments and expressways. But thousands of proposed projects never moved forward or were substantially altered when middle- and lower-income urban neighborhoods formed strong alliances to challenge unwanted new construction. Women-led neighborhood organizations in 1960s Baltimore, Philadelphia, and New York, for example, blocked expressways from bisecting their neighborhoods. In Pittsburgh, with the support of the private Pittsburgh History and Landmark Foundation, men and women in the lower-income African American neighborhoods of Manchester and the Central Northside formed citizens' groups targeted at rehabilitating their decaying housing stock. The primary motive was to resist plans for urban renewal by preserving the physical and social fabric of the neighborhoods. Out of each of these efforts, new historic preservation precedents were set. In Manchester, for example, the first preservation program that served the needs of low-income and minority families was established.[42] Similar preservation-minded, low-income and ethnically diverse groups organized in Detroit, Boston, New York, Washington, D.C., and Cincinnati. In Philadelphia groups worked successfully to beautify their neighborhoods to change perceptions of urban blight (fig. 3.6).

In 1953 Louise Bush-Brown, director of the Pennsylvania School of Horticulture, initiated the Philadelphia Neighborhood Gardens Associa-

Fig. 3.6. Planting a garden block in Philadelphia, Pa., 1953. Reprinted with the permission of Scribner, a Division of Simon and Schuster, from *Garden Blocks for Urban America,* by Louise Bush-Brown. Copyright 1969 by Louise Bush-Brown.

tion (PNGA). The focus of this group was to combine conservation of community with neighborhood beautification. A diverse group of mostly women spearheaded the effort. Their goal was to create garden oases in some of Philadelphia's most blighted neighborhoods, including African American, Latino, and Lithuanian communities. Using William Penn's original concept for Philadelphia of the "Greene Countrie Towne," this organization planted over five hundred garden blocks with thousands of window boxes and containers throughout the city between 1953 and 1968.

The group's hallmark was the active involvement of neighbors, local community leaders, and suburban garden club chapters. Neighbors from each participating block took direct responsibility for planting and taking care of the gardens and often constructed the window boxes and containers; the suburban garden clubs donated plants and supplies and sometimes gave technical assistance. The PNGA became a national model for garden block programs created in other cities such as Pittsburgh, Boston, and New York.[43] Moreover, this urban block beautification played an important role in changing both the residents' and the public's perceptions of the physical environment and was instrumental in promoting neighborhood conservation. The work of the PNGA has been perpetuated in the Pennsylvania Horticultural Society's "Philadelphia Green" program.

SUMMARY

Clubwomen and community groups such as the General Federation of Women's Clubs, the National Roadside Council, and the San Antonio Conservation Society have played a leading role in protecting vast scenic landscapes and corridors and preserving the country's ethnically diverse heritage.

As women began to enter the field of historic preservation as professionals in the 1970s, they continued to speak out for an integrated approach to landscape preservation. For example, the Alliance for Historic Landscape Preservation, which was founded by both men and women in the late 1970s, advocated rural landscape preservation and supported a revised approach to evaluating these landscapes for the National Register of Historic Places. These efforts foreshadowed the most recent historic preservation trends, which include an emphasis on diverse landscape types and the relationship between the environment and its cultural traditions.

Conclusion

Women have played a significant historical role in preserving American landscapes from small historic sites to the large scenic areas to diverse urban neighborhoods. Ensuring that these contributions are well recorded remains a challenge for the future. Overall, the breadth and influence of women in landscape preservation has not been widely documented. Moreover, modern preservationists may dismiss their early efforts as amateurish or irrelevant.

There are four areas that current preservation must address to expand the scholarship on women who have preserved the American landscape. First, more emphasis must be placed on documenting groups of women who labored collectively and often anonymously to preserve, restore, protect, or design landscapes, rather than on notable individuals. The women discussed here and the groups to which they belong may not appear in a history of landscape architecture or landscape preservation. Their efforts have been extremely influential, however, in shaping the future of specific landscapes and clearly had an impact on subsequent preservation efforts. Second, the full range of contributions that women have made to landscape preservation, not just physical results, must be fully considered, including the process of initiating, developing, implementing, and maintaining a project. Women's groups have been exceptional leaders in mobilizing support, raising money, making and implementing decisions, and planning for the long term. Third, the growing role of minority women in preserving landscapes must be studied in detail; this may include revisiting past contributions. The substantial role that many minority women played, for example, in safeguarding their neighborhoods from destructive postwar urban renewal projects was not viewed at the time as historic preservation. But, because of their efforts, numerous historic neighborhoods were saved from complete demolition. Finally, the evolving role of women's groups in more recent preservation efforts must be documented and placed in context, especially as women have pursued landscape preservation as individual professionals. As more women have entered the field, for example, they have become significant voices in national landscape preservation organizations and in that capacity shaped future preservation trends.

In summary, expanding the view of historic landscape preservation is fundamental to understanding the wide and diverse historic role of women in this field. The result will be a more comprehensive history of women who have preserved the American landscape.

CHAPTER 4

Four African American Women
on the National Landscape

Fath Davis Ruffins

Four African American women officially appear on the national landscape of historic preservation. Their names are Harriet Tubman, Mary
McLeod Bethune, Madam C. J. Walker, and Maggie Lena Walker (no relation). Apart from Harriet Tubman, these women's names are probably
rather obscure, yet Mary McLeod Bethune's memory is preserved in two
different sections of Washington, D.C. This chapter is an initial investigation of how these sites came to be preserved and why these four women
continue to be remembered formally in buildings, whereas some others
who are more famous today do not. I distinguish between memorial
plaques and buildings named in memory of someone to focus on those
places with direct historical connections to the individuals named.

In 1998 First Lady Hillary Rodham Clinton made the preservation of
sites related to particular African American women part of her mandate
for the Millennium Project,[1] which focused on the preservation of ten
physical pieces of the national heritage, including the Harriet Tubman
Brick House. This project was announced at the Smithsonian's National
Museum of American History, home of the Star Spangled Banner, which
is the first priority. Designer Ralph Lauren gave thirteen million dollars
for preservation and educational programming related to the flag.

Also in 1998, the National Park Service (NPS) developed a website on
"Places Where Women Made History" and a National Register travel
itinerary series, "Discover Our Shared Heritage."[2] These efforts were to
celebrate the 150th anniversary of the Seneca Falls, New York, conference in which leading American women formulated the *Declaration of*

Sentiments, announcing the formal beginning of the struggle for women's rights. This website has four locations devoted to African American women.

These places truly need illumination because they are little known to the general public and are rare examples in which the memory of Black women is present on "the ground," that is, on the national landscape of historic preservation. To be sure, there are an uncounted number of plaques, named school buildings, and other forms of local remembrance devoted to Afro-American women, mainly in New England and the Middle Atlantic States, where genealogical and historical interests run high.[3] For example, because of generations of active work by a historically conscious Afro-American community, Philadelphia has numerous markers, street names, plaques, and other memorials.[4] In Sag Harbor, New York, there is also a memorial to Maude Terry, the founder of Azurest, an Afro-American resort community that has operated since the 1930s.

In roughly chronological order, the six sites of national significance which are dedicated to four Afro-American women are:

1. Harriet Tubman's Home for the Aged (1908) and estate, including her residence, the Brick House (1869–72), and her grave site (1913), in Auburn, New York
2. Mary McLeod Bethune's Council House in Washington, D.C. (1874), the Retreat (1915), and grave site (1955) on the campus of Bethune-Cookman College in Daytona Beach, Florida
3. Madam C. J. Walker's Villa Lewaro in Irvington-on-Hudson, New York (1917), and the Madame Walker Theater Center in Indianapolis, Indiana (1927)
4. Maggie Lena Walker's residence in Richmond, Virginia (1883)

Of these four women, Harriet Tubman (1820 [1821?]–1913) is by far the best known today because the history of the Underground Railroad and the struggle against slavery are taught in most elementary and secondary schools. Tubman's role as a major "conductor" on that freedom train and her service during the Civil War as a nurse, spy, and unrewarded brevet commander are familiar to most Americans, if only lightly. Madame Walker and Bethune were nationally, even internationally, known in their own times, but today they are primarily known to scholars, advanced students of history, and attendees at Black History Month exhibits and festivities. Maggie Lena Walker was once known through-out the South but now is obscure to those outside of her hometown of Richmond.

These sites are in different states and reflect distinct historical eras and aesthetic sensibilities. Only some were designed by Afro-American archi-tects. Yet these four women share important characteristics that explain why they remain physically on the landscape whereas other equally sig-nificant Black women do not.

The Harriet Tubman Home for the Aged, originally named the Home for the Aged and Indigent Colored People, is a National Historic Land-mark in Auburn, New York, owned and managed by the African Methodist Episcopal (A.M.E.) Zion Church. It is regularly open to the public. Founded by Tubman herself in 1908, she spent the last two years of her life in the home and died there in 1913 at the age of ninety-three. Today there are a number of buildings on the property: the Home for the Aged, which includes an exhibition on Tubman's life; the "Brick House," where Tubman lived for most of her life in Auburn (after about 1869); and a multipurpose building.[5] The Brick House is included in the Millennium Project, and the A.M.E. Zion Church is currently seeking the status of National Historic Landmark for it.

Along with Sojourner Truth and Frederick Douglass, Tubman forms a well-known Afro-American trinity of individuals who struggled and ulti-mately won against the slavocracy. Tubman, whose incredible life can only be summarized here,[6] was born into slavery in Dorchester County near Cambridge, Maryland (fig. 4.1). In 1849 she escaped to Pennsylvania alone and unaided after her 1844 marriage to John Tubman, a freeman. By 1857 she had made fifteen trips back to Maryland and freed her whole family, including her aged parents and three hundred other souls. Because of the threat of recapture, especially after the passage of the Fugitive Slave Law (1850) during the next decade, she moved her family to St. Catharines in western Canada.

As civil war loomed, Tubman moved to Auburn, New York, after about 1857. Located off U.S. Highway 90 in western New York state, Auburn was a small community nestled within a hotbed of Quakerism, abolitionism, suffragism, and other millennial causes. Auburn was close to Seneca Falls and Rochester, the homes of important suffragists and abolitionists such as

Fig. 4.1. Auburn, N.Y. Harriet Tubman. Photo courtesy of the Tubman Home, A.M.E. Zion Church, Auburn, N.Y.

Elizabeth Cady Stanton, Susan B. Anthony, and Mary McClintock—key conveners of the first women's convention in 1848. It was patterned after the Negro Convention movement begun in the 1830s and reflecting the religious links between abolitionism and women's rights. Further, Auburn was the home of William H. Seward, a staunch antislavery activist, former governor of New York, and secretary of state under President Abraham Lincoln. Today Auburn is probably the most rural of the four NPS sites.

Tubman's relocation to Auburn (from Canada) also reflected a crucial organizational choice. The presence of the local African Methodist Episcopal church, Zion Church (now known as Thompson Memorial), was almost certainly as important to Tubman as the relative safety of this location among a nest of white abolitionists. The A.M.E. Zion Church became a separate denomination in 1820 when it formally withdrew from the older Methodist Episcopal Church. A.M.E. Zion congregations sprang up in various places, especially in New York State. Sojourner Truth joined the Zion Church in New York City, as part of her larger journey through millennial religious communities. In New Bedford, Massachusetts, Frederick Douglass became a local minister of the Zion Church.[7] Clearly, the A.M.E. Zion Church deeply appealed to a number of Afro-American abolitionists, who believed that their life's work was to bring about the end of slavery in their own time.

Of this abolitionist trinity, only two of the three are preserved on the ground: Douglass and Tubman. Douglass's last home in Washington, D.C., is now a part of the National Park Service after a long history of private preservation beginning in 1896.[8]

Sojourner Truth is not present in tangible form on the historic landscape. While there are numerous schools and other buildings named after her, materials related to her life primarily live in archival collections.[9] Yet Truth lived an extraordinary life. Born about 1797, Isabella von Wagener (whose first language was Dutch) was freed in the last of New York State's gradual manumission laws by 1820. Soon she began to call herself "Sojourner," meaning a brief visitor to this earthly vale of tears who would speak the "truth" about slavery and women's rights while still on this earth. Sojourner Truth was a member of numerous religious, radical, indeed millennial sects. Some renounced all forms of wealth, including private property. At times she was involved in protracted legal battles related to the dissolution of one or another of these communities.

Truth was a key combatant against the slavocracy, but she neither allied herself with nor founded any continuing organizations. Twenty-five years older than either Tubman or Douglass, Truth did not live into the era in which (some) people wished to memorialize the fight against slavery. For all of these reasons, Truth is not present on the ground.

It is critical to recognize the difference between memorial plaques and buildings named in memory of someone and the preservation of places with direct historical connection to a person.[10] In addition to their homes, however, Tubman and Douglass have other forms of direct commemoration. There are plaques to Tubman near City Hall and in a downtown Freedom Park in Auburn, New York. Further, her grave site in a local private cemetery is also a pilgrimage site. At his request Douglass was buried in Rochester, New York, alongside his first wife and a child whom they lost. There is also a statue of him in a Rochester park which was erected in 1896 and is believed to be the first statue dedicated to an Afro-American. Douglass is also remembered in Washington, D.C., with a plaque in a row house on Capitol Hill which he once owned, which became the original home of the Smithsonian Museum of African Art.

The story of the preservation of the Douglass homes and the Tubman buildings and estate reflects a fundamental truth about African American cultural history. Although some, such as Bethune and Maggie Walker's homes, are now part of the National Park Service as National Historic Sites, all of these buildings were preserved for most of their history by an extraordinarily small number of Afro-American organizations, principally by women's groups. In Tubman's case she bequeathed the Home and the estate (minus the Brick House) to the A.M.E. Zion Church,[11] whose cultural preservation work cries out for an exhaustive historical investigation. Tubman formally joined in 1857, although she might have known about the Zion Church's work in New York City anytime after her 1849 escape. She was a stalwart of the church during her lifetime. Her life's work during and after the Reconstruction era involved trying to help Afro-American orphans and indigent elderly. Her daring rescue of her aged parents from slavery bespoke a tremendous devotion to older people who had lived enslaved for a longer period of their lives; Tubman was in her late twenties when she escaped. She brought her parents to Auburn and cared for them until their deaths. In 1896, as a delegate to the first conference of the National Federation of Afro-American Women, Tubman gave a talk entitled "More Homes for Our Aged." She later founded the Home to carry on her work and willed it to the A.M.E. Zion Church.

How Tubman came by the money to purchase the twenty-five acres and have the buildings erected is another story that needs greater investigation in the antislavery, missionary board, and church archives of New

England. Present sources agree that she raised this money through unsolicited donations. Illustrious people such as Thomas Wentworth Higginson asked for monetary donations at his local church and at various speeches and lectures he gave after the Civil War. Moreover, Tubman was offered the land at very reasonable prices by former Governor Seward.

Such private compensation for her heroic deeds was truly necessary because, when Tubman applied a pension for her work during the Civil War, the U.S. Congress denied her any payment because she did not fall into any recognized legal category, such as military veteran (all male), trained nurse, or spy (all white). She did collect a small widow's pension because her second husband was a Union veteran. In 1897, thirty-two years after the end of the Civil War, Congress did enact a private bill authorizing a small pension for the rest of her life.

While support by white philanthropists was essential for her to purchase her own ground, her alliance with the A.M.E. Zion Church allowed her to found an institution (the Home) which has preserved her memory. After her death, the church ran it as a facility for the aged, but over time the church's concern shifted to highlighting the Tubman legacy within the church and across the nation. The A.M.E. Zion Church has supported the Tubman estate for eighty-five years without any government support and has developed a complex strategy for ensuring the integrity of the estate, managing its care, and financing its preservation work. In recent years the church installed a resident minister as director of the property, and the Home is open regularly to the public (fig. 4.2). Busloads of schoolchildren, families, and people passing through the region come to visit.

Perhaps the most interesting of the A.M.E. Zion traditions is the Decoration Day, or Memorial Day, Pilgrimage to the Tubman Home which occurs every May. People come from all over for a banquet, grave site visit, and festival that focuses on the interests of young people. A king and queen of the festival are named based on the number of contributions they have raised over the year for the support of the Tubman Home. Clearly, Tubman made a prescient choice when she left the primary part of her estate not to individuals who might have been unable to keep it but, rather, to the A.M.E. Zion Church, which has preserved the Home for future generations despite the fact that the church has had to respond to many other pressing needs.

Fig. 4.2. Auburn, N.Y. Harriet Tubman Home for the Aged. Photo courtesy of the Tubman Home, A.M.E. Zion Church, Auburn, N.Y.

During the 1920s and after, the estate did languish somewhat. The bed in which Tubman died is in the Home today, although many other objects of historic significance were lost, sold, or destroyed through use over the years. Professional curation was not present for some decades. At times the Brick House neared derelict status as the economic and social justice needs of Afro-American communities threatened to overwhelm the resources of Negro churches in the Depression.

Fortunately, however, during these years Afro-American women's clubs aided in the preservation of the estate. In particular, the National Council of Negro Women (NCNW) worked to support the Home. They purchased the Brick House from its private owners and returned that parcel to the larger Tubman Home estate around 1930. During World War II, NCNW, along with other Afro-American organizations, helped sponsor a Liberty Ship named for Harriet Tubman. In 1978 NCNW was instrumental in having Harriet Tubman named as the first in a series of Black Heritage stamps.

The recognition by the First Lady Hillary Clinton's Millennium Project garnered a $10,000 contribution to the Brick House by the Washington, D.C.–based Folger Foundation. It is important to realize, however, that this donation represents the first financial support from outside the world of black churches and women's clubs since those unsolicited donations by Tubman's white comrades a century ago.

The link between the Tubman home and the NCNW is especially intriguing because Mary McLeod Bethune (1875-1955) founded the National Council for Negro Women in 1935. Today Bethune is the Black woman most commemorated through historic preservation (fig. 4.3). She is marked at four sites in three locations. The NCNW headquarters is known today as the Council House. In 1982 it was declared a National Historic Site and was acquired by the National Park Service in 1994. It is located at 1318 Vermont Avenue in the Logan Circle neighborhood of Washington, D.C. (fig. 4.4).

Bethune's amazing life is too complex to give more than a summary here. While Tubman was born into slavery and was emblematic of the last generation of enslaved Americans, Bethune was a member of the first postslavery generation. Born in 1875 in Mayesville (Sumter County), South Carolina, Mary McLeod was the fifteenth of seventeen children; both of her parents had been born enslaved. She studied at the local Presbyterian church schools and wanted to become a missionary. She applied to the Presbyterian Board in about 1895 but found that they took no Negroes. Although temporarily stymied, by 1904, Bethune had founded the Daytona Educational and Industrial Institute for Colored Girls, supported by the wealthy and white Ladies Advisory Group. Two significant patrons were Thomas H. White of the White Sewing Machine Company and James Gamble of Procter and Gamble, who both left relatively large trust funds to continue the expansion of the school.

By 1922 the institute had grown to three hundred girls and twenty-five staff members. Bethune and her female staff all voted in elections after 1920, despite the Ku Klux Klan's threats of violence.[12] In 1923 Bethune's school joined with the Cookman Institute for Boys, creating a coeducational school, and in 1941 Bethune-Cookman became a four-year liberal arts college.[13]

Fig. 4.3. Washington, D.C. Mary McLeod Bethune. Photo courtesy of the Council House, National Park Service.

Bethune became deeply involved in the Progressive women's clubs movements of the 1890s and beyond. In 1920 she became head of the Southeastern Association of Colored Women (SACW). As chair of the association for five years, she participated in the Southeastern Interracial Committee, which became the Colored Contingent at the Women's General Committee of the Atlanta-based Commission on Interracial Cooperation. From 1924 to 1928 she served as the president of the National Association of Colored Women (NACW). She sought to transform this

Fig. 4.4. Washington, D.C. Council House. Photo courtesy of the Council House, National Park Service.

amorphous association of local groups into a united organization at regional, state, and city club levels. In 1928 she secured a national headquarters for NACW in Washington, D.C., because she felt that the organization needed a permanent, fixed national home. Ultimately, Bethune felt frustrated with her efforts to transform the NACW into a truly effective advocacy group. Many of the traditionalists within the NACW focused on more local concerns rather than national interracial politics. After a complex power struggle within the NACW, Bethune left the group. In

December 1935 she founded the National Council of Negro Women (NCNW) and served as its president until 1949 (fig. 4.5).

Bethune knew Eleanor Roosevelt through clubwomen's groups working on social tolerance, community uplift, and other educational programs. After Franklin Roosevelt's election in 1932, Bethune used her Roosevelt connections to help organize the Federal Council on Negro Affairs (known unofficially as the "Black Cabinet") and sponsored, along with others, national labor conferences from 1937 through 1939. In 1939 she was named director of Negro Affairs for the National Youth Administration. At least some of the NCNW's success had to do with Bethune's insider status in the long-lived Roosevelt Administrations.[14] Bethune began to suffer health problems in the 1950s and died of a heart attack in 1955. She was buried in Daytona Beach, Florida, on the campus of Bethune-Cookman College (fig. 4.6).[15] Bethune's professional life re-

Fig. 4.5. Washington, D.C. President Harry S. Truman with Mary McLeod Bethune. Photo courtesy of the Council House, National Park Service.

Fig. 4.6. Daytona Beach, Fla. The Retreat, Bethune home. Photo courtesy of Bethune-Cookman College, Office of Public Relations.

flected not only her membership in the "up from slavery" generation but also her effectiveness in linking religious, institutional, and financial arrangements for the purpose of racial uplift, equal justice, and social tolerance.[16]

Today Bethune would be described as an "activist," yet she also had a profound interest in cultural preservation. She was involved in nearly every important effort to preserve individual Afro-American historic sites, chairing committees and organizations devoted to preservation. She established an archive on Afro-American women's history. Through the NCNW Bethune provided financial support to the Tubman and Douglass homes and to key organizers and founders of Afro-American libraries and museums, especially Dorothy Porter, librarian of the Moorland-Spingarn Research Center at Howard University and Sue Bailey Thurman, later the founder of the Museum of Afro-American History in Boston. Thurman was also the founding editor of NCNW's *AfraAmerican Journal* and essentially the co-founder of the Black Women's Research Archives, housed then and today in the carriage house of the Council House in Washington, D.C.[17]

In explaining her extensive representation on the landscape, one critical factor is that she was the founder of two ongoing organizations that sustain her memory as a part of their basic work.[18] While not well known to the general public today, Bethune has four important sites, both public and private, in Washington, D.C., Florida, and South Carolina. Recently, an annual arts festival began in Mayesville, South Carolina, where Bethune's birthplace is located, which is now listed on the South Carolina register of historic buildings.

The presence of these buildings reflects the deep taproots of Bethune-Cookman College and the NCNW in an era of self-organized Colored uplift and Progressive-era white philanthropy. Yet their continuance in the present involves the growth of funding mechanisms such as the private, nonprofit United Negro College Fund, legislative mandates to support "historically Black colleges and universities," preservation initiatives focused on the tangible resources associated with them, and state and federal grants to plan social service programs that have been awarded to NCNW in increasing amounts since Bethune's death. Bethune was clearly prescient in understanding how important the role of the federal government was to the future of Afro-Americans.

Madam C. J. Walker of Indianapolis and New York and Maggie Lena Walker of Richmond were both members of the same postslavery generation as Bethune. Their lives, however, reflect a different spirit within that generation. Although both Walkers joined a large number of religious, civic, and benevolent societies, their primary impetus for "uplift" was through business, that is, through the accumulation of wealth. While Madam C. J. Walker ultimately became wealthier than any other Afro-American of her era, both Walkers were quite successful, prominent enough to leave private homes that have entered the national preservation landscape. Madam Walker left a thirty-five-room mansion and estate in Irvington-on-Hudson, Villa Lewaro (1917). In addition, she is remembered through the Madame Walker Theater Center in Indianapolis. This vibrant performing arts space and arts education facility is located in the second factory building of the Walker company, which was built in 1927 on the land of the original plant (1913). What's more, in January 1998 the

National Postal Service released a Black Heritage stamp commemorating Madam C. J. Walker, twenty years after the release of the first such stamp which honored Harriet Tubman. Maggie Lena Walker left her residence and twenty-four thousand related objects in Richmond, Virginia, which is now open to the public as a National Historic Site owned by the National Park Service. These two women are quite well represented on the ground.

Both of these women's homes and memories are preserved today, though in different ways. Madam C. J. Walker's Harlem brownstone has long since been demolished, though many of the organizations she supported survive today. Villa Lewaro is privately owned by an African American investment banker, Harold Doley, and his family.[19] It is not open to the public, but it is listed as a National Historic Landmark. Villa Lewaro is unusual because it was designed by an Afro-American architect, Vertner Tandy, who has few buildings still extant.

Maggie Lena Walker bought her 1883 house in 1904 and lived in this mansion with her children and grandchildren until her death in 1934. She expanded it dramatically in 1922 to accommodate her sons' families. Her family owned it until 1979, when it was purchased by the NPS. In 1996 the residence opened to the public as a National Historic Site. Through the accumulation of private wealth and the foresight to buy and build impressive homes, the two Walkers have been preserved on the landscape in a far more traditional way: as the architecturally significant homes of wealthy Americans judged by later generations to be deserving of historical designation.

Born Sarah Breedlove on a Louisiana plantation in 1867, Madam C. J. Walker became quite wealthy before her sudden death in 1919. Madam Walker wrote: "I am a woman who came from the cotton fields of the South. From there I was promoted to the washtub. From there I was promoted to the cook kitchen. And from there I promoted myself to the business of manufacturing hair goods and preparations. . . . I have built my own factory on my own ground." She spoke these words in 1912 to a convention of the National Negro Business League. These words also appear at the beginning of a website devoted to her memory maintained by her great-great-granddaughter and biographer, A'Lelia P. Bundles.[20]

Being the first person in her family to be born free, Sarah Breedlove led an improbable and astonishing life. Orphaned during a yellow fever epidemic in 1874, she and some surviving family members moved to Vicksburg, Mississippi. As was not uncommon in the rural South in these years, at fourteen she married Moses McWilliams, a laborer. She became a laundress, which was backbreaking work. She gave birth to a daughter in 1885 whom she and her husband named Lelia. In 1887, however, Moses McWilliams was killed in a construction accident. Left a widow and single mother and seeing greener pastures elsewhere, she left for St. Louis, Missouri, in 1888. There she married again and became part of a much larger Afro-American community. She listened to the Colored leaders who came and lectured during the 1904 St. Louis World's Fair. She met women in the NACW who sponsored an address by Margaret Murray Washington, wife of Booker T. Washington, the founder of Tuskegee Institute.

She was impressed by the good grooming, bearing, and style of these leaders and their wives. In St. Louis she also came into contact with the locally based Poro Company, which was the first large-scale Colored hair care company. Colored women in this era had enormous difficulty with their hair. Many of the fashionable styles of the late nineteenth century required huge bunches of hair. White women could supplement their natural hair with wigs and falls designed to create the effect of volume, but Colored women did not have much access to appropriate hairpieces. A number of products were on the market, but McWilliams had used them with little success. Her biographer, A'Lelia Bundles, wrote: "In early 1905, McWilliams informed friends that, with divine help, she had learned how to make the mixture she wanted. God, she later told a reporter, 'answered my prayer, for one night I had a dream, and in that dream a big black man appeared to me and told me what to mix up for my hair. Some of the remedy was grown in Africa, but I sent for it, mixed it, and put it on my scalp, and in a few weeks my hair was coming in faster than it had ever fallen out. I tried it on my friends; it helped them. I made up my mind I would begin to sell it.'"[21] Perhaps in order to find a more fertile selling territory, Mrs. McWilliams decided to leave St. Louis. She divorced her second husband and married Charles Joseph Walker, a sales agent for the local Afro-American newspaper. Together they headed for Denver, Colorado.

In 1905 Afro-Americans in Colorado numbered no more than ten thousand, and the whole state had just a few more people than the city of

St. Louis. Mrs. Walker, however, turned out to be a natural marketer: she pictured herself on the box of her products, assuming that Colored people would be more likely to buy something if the person on the box looked like them. She began using the term *Madam* to refer to herself, both as a reflection of her married station and because this invoked an association with French sophistication and elegance. By 1906 she was out on the road doing direct sales, which developed into a mail-order catalog business.[22] Due to segregation, she was housed in the railway car closest to the coal and had to use church connections to make arrangements to stay in the homes of local people rather than hotels.

In 1908 she moved to Pittsburgh and established Lelia College, where she trained scores of hair culturists. By 1910 she was scouting new locations for the construction of a permanent national headquarters, settling on Indianapolis, the "Crossroads of America," at the center of a major transportation network, which was a great asset for a mail-order business. The city also had a thriving Negro business community, including a well-known newspaper, the *Freeman*. Her business grew by leaps and bounds. By about 1913 her factory was completed. Meanwhile, her daughter, A'Lelia Walker Robinson, developed their territory in New York City. Madam Walker decided that they needed a New York base of operations. In 1913 she acquired a house on 136th Street near Lenox Avenue in Harlem, which became a beauty salon and their home.

Since joining St. Paul's A.M.E. Church in St. Louis, Madam Walker had been an active "race woman," working assiduously in benevolent associations, church organizations, women's clubs, and education programs and helping to endow the Colored YMCA in Indianapolis in 1913. Not satisfied with founding Lelia College, she decided to create a national organization. In 1917 more than two hundred delegates met at Philadelphia's Union Baptist Church for the first national meeting of the Madam C. J. Walker Hair Culturists Union of America.[23] While increasing her business and becoming involved on a national political level advocating equal rights for Afro-Americans, Walker was also able to begin building her dream home.

In 1916 Walker purchased an estate in Irvington-on-Hudson, about nineteen miles from Manhattan with panoramic views of the river and the New Jersey Palisades. After an initial local furor created by white fears, she and her family moved in June 1918. Soon after, they entertained the era's most celebrated opera tenor, Enrico Caruso. Her home reminded him of great estates in Italy, and he suggested that they call it a villa and use the first two letters of A'Lelia Walker Robinson's name: hence, Villa Lewaro. Madam Walker was proud of the villa "that only Negro money had bought."[24] Both her New York City townhouse and Villa Lewaro were designed by Negro architect Vertner W. Tandy.[25] The Walkers began to entertain a wide set of American and European literati and diplomats from Liberia and began to host events for the boards of organizations such as the National Association for the Advancement of Colored People (NAACP).

Walker was also directly involved in historic preservation. For example, she gave five hundred dollars to the fund for the preservation of the Frederick Douglass Home, the single largest contribution. She spoke at annual conferences and was involved in numerous projects with Carter G. Woodson's Association for the Study of Negro Life and History (ASNLH). A magnificent and wealthy woman, who pushed herself until her body gave out, Walker died in 1919 at the age of fifty-one. She left bequests to dozens of organizations and individuals, including an orphan home in St. Louis, an old-age home in Pittsburgh, the NAACP, and the Tuskegee Institute in Alabama.

After Madam's death, A'Lelia went on to become an important patron and figure within the Harlem Renaissance. Her Harlem townhouse became a salon for an integrated group of American and European intellectuals, artists, musicians, writers, and social activists. Unfortunately, A'Lelia also suffered from the high blood pressure that ran in the family, and a stroke led to her premature death in 1931 at the age of forty-six. Although Madam was an arts supporter, it was A'Lelia who became an arts patron. The only Negro in the Harlem Renaissance to be able to purchase and own artworks, her memory is most clearly visible in the Walker Theater Center in her mother's former company headquarters.[26] Indeed, the preservation of both Villa Lewaro and the spirit of the Walker Theater in Indianapolis celebrate the lives, tastes, and priorities of both Madam C. J. and A'Lelia Walker.

Maggie Lena Walker's life bears important similarities to that of Madam C. J. Walker (no relation). As the first American woman to found a bank, Maggie Lena Walker entered into finance through her work in a beneficial burial society, the Independent Order of St. Luke. The burial and benevolent society was a traditional form of mutual self-support in Afro-American (and other working and poor) communities which went back to the eighteenth century in the American colonies.

Born in 1867 in Richmond, Virginia, the former capital of the Confederacy, Maggie Lena Mitchell was the child of Elizabeth Draper, a young former slave and assistant cook in the home of Elizabeth Van Lew, a Civil War spy. Maggie's father was a white northern newspaperman, but Draper married William Mitchell, a former butler who became a waiter. He was found dead in 1876, probably murdered, and Elizabeth Mitchell was left "a penniless widow with two small children."[27] Mrs. Mitchell also became a laundress. Maggie Lena's job was laundry pickup and delivery, yet she managed to graduate from high school, a remarkable accomplishment for the child of a former slave. As with Bethune, Maggie Lena saw her education as the key to her future. Her first job was teaching first grade in 1883. She taught for three years then married Armstead Walker Jr. in 1886.

Long before her marriage, she had joined the local Richmond council of the Independent Order of St. Luke. This fraternal burial society had been founded in Baltimore in 1867, pointing to the continuing linkage of Afro-American communities in the Chesapeake region which had been divided by the Civil War. Walker served in greater ways in the society until she was named the right worthy grand secretary in 1899 and kept the position until her death in 1934. Walker wrote: "Through sound fiscal policies, a genius for public relations and enormous energy, she took a dying organization, gave it life, and helped it thrive."[28] St. Luke's eventually opened both an insurance agency and a clothing store for its members. By 1927 St. Luke had more than one hundred thousand members in several states and a staff of two hundred in its Richmond headquarters.

In 1902 Maggie Lena Walker founded a newspaper, the *St. Luke Herald,* to communicate better with the membership. Two years later, in 1903, she founded the St. Luke Penny Savings Bank. Perhaps Walker's most famous statement was: "Let us put our money together. . . . The interest paid to depositors would 'turn nickels into dollars.'" She became the first woman bank president in the United States. When children came to the bank, she gave them cardboard play banks to be filled with pennies. When filled, they were returned to the bank for safe depositing. When the bank later merged with two others to become the Consolidated Bank and Trust Company, she became chairman of the board. Lasting through the entire Depression, this bank exists today and remains the oldest continually operating African American bank in the country. In a similar fashion to Madam Walker, Maggie Walker established a successful business that exists today and a prominent family whose members were wealthy enough decades later to aid in the creation of the Maggie Lena Walker National Historic Site.

Mary McLeod Bethune, Madam C. J. Walker, and Maggie Lena Walker were "firsts." Being extraordinary individuals, they were acknowledged in their lifetimes as leaders: the first Negro woman to found a college; the first in a government post; for many years Walker was believed to be the first self-made millionaire; the first woman to found a bank. After World War II formal acknowledgment of Afro-American firsts became an important trope in Black newspapers and magazines.[29] In the era of desegregation it became especially important to acknowledge and celebrate the individual achievements of particular Black Americans. Many felt that these individuals' lives demonstrated that Black people were equal to other Americans and therefore should have equal citizenship rights. Within the larger context of the history of preservation, their concerns were expressed by the saving of buildings associated with singular individuals. The four women discussed here met that criterion. Not only were they high achievers; they had led morally exemplary lives. Legally married (although not always happily), mothers all, religious women devoted to their churches and their race, these four women were the sort of woman deemed worthy of individual celebration.

Other people, especially women, who had led much more irregular lives were not seen as exemplary. For example, blues queens such as Ma Rainey were associated with many lovers and a rural backwater background. A writer and folklorist such as Zora Neale Hurston had descended into poverty and problematic political opinions in later life. These sorts of women had not accumulated wealth, did not leave architecturally significant buildings, and had not allied themselves with organizations devoted to preserving their memory. It was not until the feminist, or "womanist," awakening of the 1970s that such women's stories became more widely known. Novelist Alice Walker, for example, was crucial in the rediscovery of Zora Neale Hurston's life.[30]

In the 1990s more preservation emphasis has come to be put on saving community settings and whole districts. In Kansas City, Kansas, for example, the "18th and Vine" section of town associated with Black businesses and the development of jazz has been named a historic district in which numerous buildings are being preserved and a newly erected Black museum has been built. In Atlanta, Georgia, and in Birmingham, Alabama, similar historic districts have been set aside for preservation. Anchored by newly constructed museums, these historic districts represent an effort to preserve and memorialize a way of life, not just a single individual. But the preservation efforts associated with the four women discussed here are very much part of that earlier era of preservation activity in which unusual individual achievement was highlighted.

Of these four women, Tubman's life is quite different from the other three. Her struggles and triumphs aided the sacred cause of freedom in its most critical hour. But, once the slavocracy was dead, new and complex issues arose for the children of the first postslavery generation. Bethune and the two Walkers were members of that generation. Like Tubman before them, these three were sui generis, they imagined a future for themselves and their people quite different from the enslaved past of their parents' time and before. They invented themselves and in so doing helped bring about that future they had once imagined. All this they share. What is different among these three women is how they decided to go about creating that new future.

Bethune chose to concentrate on religious training and formal education as a strategy for community uplift. She aligned herself with the high moral fervor and energy that at its best characterized the Progressive Era in American politics. She mobilized traditional sources of white philanthropy in the service of educational goals by establishing Bethune-Cookman College. She tirelessly organized women's clubs to tackle not only the problem of educating children but also the formal preservation of Afro-American history in buildings and in collections. She successfully used the platform of the New Deal to garner government support for the work of the NCNW, which continues to exist today.

Although they were religious, churchgoing women, Madam Walker and Maggie Walker did not view the church as the primary site of their work toward individual and community uplift. Both women were supportive of formal preservation efforts and contributed to various Negro history lectures and events, yet they saw their work as being in the arena of business. These two women saw the crucial role of accumulating capital as a source of upward mobility for their families, as a vehicle for community improvement, and as a way of exerting greater control over the future. Both women were justifiably proud of the wealth built by "Negro money."

Within the context of business both women appear to have been concerned with wide community interests. Madam Walker wanted to encourage her route of self-reliance and hard work, and thus she sponsored the first national organization of Afro-American hairdressers. She contributed heavily to the NAACP and early on put her wealth behind the legal struggle against discrimination. Although she had been born in the South, Madam Walker's business was largely in the North. She is undoubtedly the wealthiest of all the Negro rural-to-urban migrants of that era. Maggie Walker's business success took place in Richmond, a city that bore all the scars of the northern victory. Perhaps that explains why she saw the older organizational model of the benevolent society as a way of building wealth in her community. Perhaps she simply never had a specific product-oriented dream such as the one that inspired Madam Walker. Much more biographical work needs to be done on Maggie Walker before we can understand exactly why she took the route that she did. We know, however, that she used the Order of St. Luke to establish a bank. This kind of financial work has most frequently been described by historians in European ethnic communities in New York, Chicago, and throughout the country's major urban areas of the late nineteenth and early twentieth centuries, but not for African Americans. For complex reasons both Madam and Maggie Walker saw the road to uplift as one paved by financial success. Both left enough wealth and prominence on the ground so that their buildings were available for later generations to preserve.

The history of the private and public preservation of the two Walker homes is far more similar to the preservation histories of homes and buildings left by wealthy non-Black Americans than the stories of Bethune's and Tubman's preservation. In that sense the two Walkers may well have anticipated the economic surge of the Black middle class, which has grown dramatically since the early 1970s.[31] In sum, the histories of all four women point toward two distinct roads to historic preservation. Tubman and Bethune chose the levers of religion and community organization. The two Walkers chose the strategy of business success. Their lives provide a lesson for our present. These two roads remain the most viable tactics for individuals who want be stewards of their own history: either they can found an organization with sufficient resources, or they can create enough personal wealth to own the ground themselves.

PART II

Revisiting Women's Lives
at Historic Houses and Museums

CHAPTER 5

Uncovering and Interpreting Women's History at Historic House Museums

Patricia West

It is paradoxical that the historic house museum, largely initiated by women's voluntary associations and embodying the domestic life of the past, should need active revision in order to represent women's history. Yet widespread revision is necessary, for these museums have a long history of memorializing the economic and political activity of wealthy white men. The task of revision requires nothing less than shifting the institution's field of vision in order to identify and dissolve existing barriers to meaningful interpretation of women's history in house museums.

The first such barrier is the perception that the call for revision is merely a manifestation of "political correctness," an attempt to politicize an institution that has previously been neutral or apolitical. In fact, the political agenda of house museums has merely been submerged because traditional interpretations focusing on the public achievements of patriarchs have become so familiar as to seem politically neutral.[1] Presenting the "main," usually male, historical occupant of a house as having been disconnected from a wider social world—from women, servants, or slaves; from the poor side of town—is a highly political yet utterly familiar approach.[2] The shift in focus necessary to incorporate women's history recognizes that historic houses existed in a diverse social context and that portraying such past diversity enriches the site's potential for interpreting history in general.

Another barrier to the interpretation of women at historic sites can arise from the interpretive planning process itself, which frequently generates narrowly defined interpretive "themes." In the past half-century the need to advance the state of house museum interpretation generally has produced how-to books and interpretive primers such as Alderson and Low's *Interpretation of Historic Sites*, originally published by the American Association for State and Local History (AASLH) in the mid-1970s, during the boom years of academic women's history. While the emphasis on the "clearly defined interpretive objective" may have had a salubrious effect overall, the problem for women's history is revealed by Alderson and Low's stern warning that "secondary themes" are "legitimate only as fringe benefits." Unfortunately, this prescription can easily be used to bolster arguments against substantive interpretation of female historical occupants as diversions from the "primary objective."[3]

The conservative history and orientation of house museums, together with overzealous attempts to eliminate secondary themes, have combined to eradicate much of women's history, in particular the history of the domestic servant, from the typical house museum. House museum visitors are generally treated as guests, brought in through front halls to view formal areas. This presentation is often reinforced by the architecture itself, which conspires to keep workspaces and maintenance functions from visitors' eyes.[4] The narrow back halls and impassable stairways and the fascinating servants' rooms where museum staff so often find their offices or storage spaces located were the heart of the working house. When these spaces are unavailable to the public, it becomes difficult to interpret the house as anything but a static entity, and the opportunity is missed to represent it as the context for domestic life, a dynamic, functioning space that could reveal the daily lives of past women, particularly as they engaged in myriad forms of household labor. If these areas are inaccessible because of fire codes or file cabinets, then the museum can draw visitors' attention to its replication of the way the "primary" historic occupants wished their home to be viewed by guests. This approach can provide insight, for example, into the symbolic function of the house in the historic period. In the case of Victorian houses, we can note that, as American class structure solidified across the nineteenth century, upper- and middle-class homes increasingly reflected a kind of material code of propriety, the desire to display taste in consumer items on a scale previously unimaginable. An accent on the display function of the Victorian house highlights such areas of women's history as the role of social class in the ideology of the "cult of domesticity." While "ladies" were encouraged to cultivate a public and private "delicacy," ethnic and African American women were assigned the backbreaking labor of maintaining stylish parlors and wardrobes, the props upon which the iconography of the refined home (and the house museum) were constructed.[5]

In part the house museum's disposition toward the interpretation of parlor furniture over parlor maids arose from the connoisseurship tradition of collecting. Exceptionally well-crafted, rare, old, or beautiful objects were quite appropriately analyzed and collected, but common, unaesthetic, or utilitarian objects, if they didn't wear out and get discarded, were far less frequently collected and even less frequently displayed.[6] Historically, house museums were often conceived of as repositories and exhibit venues for high-style or quaint objects, limiting the extent to which a broad social network could be evoked by period rooms arranged deploying such collections. When women's history is interpreted in the house museum's beautifully appointed period rooms, it is often romanticized, and the enormous amount of housework necessary to maintain elite lifestyles is downplayed or misrepresented. The ubiquitous gingerbread-baking program conjures up a beguiling though inaccurate image of women's past domestic labor. Likewise, spinning demonstrations, which, if underinterpreted, convert a dull and backbreaking chore to an entertaining experience. A nostalgic vision of past forms of domesticity serves not only to undermine the historical value of such attempts at women's history; it also fosters the elimination or distortion of servant labor.

Similarly, another traditional interpretation of women's history in museums features elite women as tranquil and charming wives to the "great man" of the house in a kind of historic "feminine mystique." Particularly if the historic couple is detached by omission from the wider community of servants, slaves, and workers, elite homes converted into house museums often appear to be the equivalent of single-family suburban homes. Again, this phenomenon can be traced to an effort to maintain an interpretive focus on that part of the past which is considered more historically significant, that is, on "the great white male," to paraphrase Melville. The pull to diminish these women to a sort of 1950s wifely stereotype can be counteracted by thoughtful critiques catalyzed into vigilance and a heightened commitment to research.

Fig. 5.1. Kinderhook, N.Y. Lindenwald, Martin Van Buren National Historic Site. Photo by Michael Fredericks. Courtesy of National Park Service, Martin Van Buren National Historic Site.

Considering the range and long history of the barriers to recognizing and interpreting evidence of women's lives—in particular, the fact that house museum history has not generally drawn upon the innovations of social history, the notion that women's history is somehow a "secondary theme," the limitations of the museum collection as a source of evidence, and the tendency to suppress the history of housework and to romanticize the domestic life of the past—it may be tempting to some administrations to postpone the interpretation of women at historic houses indefinitely. Yet, as the following case study of the domestic service at Martin Van Buren National Historic Site in Kinderhook, New York, demonstrates, these barriers are not as formidable as they appear (fig. 5.1).[7]

Domestic service—in terms of the history of class, ethnicity, race, and gender—is an excellent subject for inclusion in the interpretive programs of high-style, nineteenth-century houses, although the received notion is that it is a difficult topic about which there is too little evidence to be a viable interpretive focus. It is true that domestic service has been a problem for historians, not only because of the lack of a broadly representative body of material culture but also because the preponderance of documentary evidence about servants was written from the perspective of Anglo-American employers. Yet this very problem signals the topic's richness in understanding the complexities of the domestic and public world of the nineteenth century.

Domestic service was an uncomfortable subject to nineteenth-century Anglo-Americans. Political ideology celebrated republican equality and independence; "servitude" and "slavery" were metaphors for the worst political perils. And domestic ideology glorified the home as an insular "haven in a heartless world," safe from the discord of public life.[8] Yet these ideals clashed with their wish for household servants, which introduced large numbers of Irish Catholic immigrant women into northern homes, blurring the supposedly separate public and private "spheres" and causing that bane of nineteenth-century "true womanhood," the "servant problem." As Faye Dudden explains, domestic service introduced into the private sphere the ethnic and class conflict that had rocked the political world. The transition from the traditional employment of "help," the familiar neighbor girls of essentially the same cultural background as their employers, to the hiring of Irish Catholic "domestics" was the equivalent of the change in the public male workplace. Dudden points out that "the home" of Victorian prescriptive literature was in reality highly permeable to the infusion of such values as "time discipline" from the public world of men.[9] Nevertheless, as both the trades of men and the textile production of women gradually left the home to be taken over by factories, the home took on greater symbolic power as the culture's moral center, locus of women's special responsibility to offset the turmoil of the morally corrosive, highly competitive male world of business and politics. Middle-class women, now ensconced in "woman's sphere," were less engaged in productive labor and more engaged in the symbolic labor of elaborate calling and dining rituals that are so deeply associated with Victorian life. Dudden suggests that the paid labor of poor women freed middle-class employers from the drudgery of housework to pursue education and participation in reform as well as making the "cult of domesticity" so well represented by house museums possible.[10]

Of course, because men could vote and women could not, the modernization of the male workplace translated into the unmuffled political excitement of the Jacksonian Era. It was this climate of political experimentation which nurtured the rise of the brilliant and opportunistic Martin Van Buren (1782–1862), dubbed by detractors and boosters alike the "Little Magician" and the "Red Fox of Kinderhook." Historians have linked the decline in republican values in the workplace to the political ferment that spawned the second American party system, that is, to the rise of the Whigs in opposition to the Democrats, the latter the vehicle of Van Buren's ascent to power and the former the agent of his downfall.[11] The contours of the Jacksonian period have been the subject of a legion of books and articles and the source of rich debate. In summary the era was characterized by increasing urbanization, growth in business and banking, westward expansion, technological advances (in particular in paper production and printing), and the "transportation revolution." Mass immigration and the expansion of the electorate provided the immediate catalyst for the development of the second two-party system, the amplification of egalitarian political rhetoric, and the dubious invention of the mass media political campaign.[12] Van Buren's rise from obscurity to lead the New York political machine and to initiate the establishment of a two-party system that he hoped would reorder politics and transcend the looming North-South split was a classic example of the possibilities and limitations of the Jacksonian moment.[13]

The problem of domestic service, of the so-called stranger in the gates, resonated with conflicts that matched the mercurial nature of antebellum politics. Thus, Martin Van Buren's political career was inextricably linked to the social changes well symbolized by his Irish domestic servants. The mass immigration of the Irish, beginning in the 1820s and 1830s and reaching colossal proportions by the 1840s, was both a major source of political innovation and at the root of the domestic transformation described by Dudden. In general, the Irish came to the United States because of limited economic opportunity in Ireland. By the famine years, from 1845 to 1849, they were pushed from their homeland by sheer unmitigated poverty.[14]

Meanwhile, in the world of American politics, Martin Van Buren's career had waxed and waned. Having steadily advanced from New York politics to the Senate, the vice presidency, and finally the presidency in

1837, Van Buren was resoundingly defeated in his bid for a second term in 1840. His avoidance of controversial issues (such as the extension of slavery) in hopes of maintaining the Union, his Jeffersonian minimalism in response to both the economic Panic of 1837, and the boisterous campaign tactics of the Whigs cost him reelection.[15] As his stormy presidency ended, Van Buren came to terms with his move from the White House to Kinderhook, wearily vowing: "I will mature my plan for that life of quiet contentment for which I have so long looked in vain and the opportunity to enjoy that which has been so suddenly, and I cannot think but fortunately, thrust upon me."[16]

Some years before, President Van Buren had purchased a plain but commodious Federal-style, brick house he renamed "Lindenwald." Urged on by his fashion-conscious son, Smith Thompson Van Buren, the former president hired sought-after architect Richard Upjohn to renovate the house in 1849. An amazing metamorphosis resulted: the formerly stolid house now sported a rather imposing Italianate tower, copious Gothic Revival details, and a puzzle of a floor plan featuring numerous additional rooms and halls. This was the workplace the Lindenwald house servants knew, a federal house in eclectic Victorian garb. It was the perfect analogy to the aging Van Buren, the Jeffersonian cum Jacksonian whose political career had risen and fallen in accordance with the vast cultural changes that swept the first half of the nation's nineteenth century.

At Lindenwald, Van Buren entered a new phase of life as elder statesman and gentleman farmer. The home of the gregarious Van Buren, a widower with four sons, was regularly filled with visiting family and friends. Yet documents describing his formal parlors and lavish dinners also imply the other side of the coin of Victorian life: that of the domestic servant. The museum's recognition of the lives of house servants has the potential to historicize the romantic image of antebellum culture and politics to which house museums have so often subscribed.

The mission of Martin Van Buren National Historic Site, founded in 1974, emphasizes two major historical themes set forth by its early interpretive planners: first, Martin Van Buren's political career; and, second, his life at Lindenwald.[17] Given these established interpretive themes, the initial task was to find a way to make women's history central to the museum's interpretive orientation, in this case to demonstrate exactly why the house servants were germane to both of the primary objectives that had been identified.

Consider the "main" interpretive theme, "Martin Van Buren, president and statesman."[18] A useful definition of Van Buren's political life links politics with social change, making it easy, if not essential, to find an interpretive niche for the Irish domestic servants. Examining how house servants lived is an ideal way of demonstrating some of the important changes in American political culture across Van Buren's lifetime, most significantly mass immigration, a feature of American history which has shaped its politics as well as its social structure in fundamental ways. Lindenwald's floor plan and layout of decorative detail suggests a social stratification within the household which reflects that occurring in society at large (figs. 5.2 and 5.3). Van Buren's activity as leader of an early political machine, his support of the ten-hour day, and his role in the elimination of imprisonment for debt take on richer meaning when there are real people to work with in reflecting on these issues. Comparing the use of waged servants in Van Buren's home and the use of slaves in southern homes—both kinds of labor crucial to the support of extravagant lifestyles such as the ones we often see in museums—provides a dramatic perspective from which to understand the regional differences that plagued Van Buren's goal of forming a national political party.

The second major interpretive theme, "Martin Van Buren's life at Lindenwald," lends itself even more easily to the interpretation of house servants, because this lifestyle was utterly dependent on the availability of inexpensive domestic servants. For example, Lindenwald's formal "Best Bedroom," with its upholstered furniture and ingrain carpet, bespeaks a way of life supported by an enormous amount of housework (fig. 5.4). This period room simply could not have existed in that form without the availability of inexpensive servants. If we look closely at the details of Van Buren's public and private life, we see that the hallmark is not isolation from other social groups but, rather, interdependence.

Material culture proved to be a critical source of evidence as objects were reexamined for clues about the work lives of the servants. For example, when the curatorial staff discovered an object previously cataloged as a "pen holder," it was obvious that something was amiss because this was a singularly ugly pen holder and Van Buren liked elegant things.

Fig. 5.2. Kinderhook, N.Y. Martin Van Buren's armoire. Photo by Michael Fredericks. Courtesy of National Park Service, Martin Van Buren National Historic Site.

A study of period household guidebooks identified it as, in fact, a ruffle iron, a long, slender upright shaft into which a heated cylinder was placed so that a ruffle could be drawn across it (fig. 5.5). With the perspective that not all the museum's objects were display oriented and used by the great man, interpreters now could call upon an artifact through which to discuss the idea that Van Buren's notoriety as a dandy (which played a role in campaign rhetoric, contributing to his loss of a second term) depended completely upon the labor of servants. A narrow view of the associational meaning of artifacts can disguise the rich social context in which historic objects existed.

Because much of the household labor performed by women was hid-

Fig. 5.3. (top) Kinderhook, N.Y. Pegs where Van Buren's servants stored their clothing. Photo by Michael Fredericks. Courtesy of National Park Service, Martin Van Buren National Historic Site.

Fig. 5.4. (bottom) Kinderhook, N.Y. "Best Bedroom," Lindenwald. Whether visitors view a period room such as this one as a showplace or a workplace depends on the museum's interpretive strategy. Photo by Michael Fredericks. Courtesy of National Park Service, Martin Van Buren National Historic Site.

Fig. 5.5. Kinderhook, N.Y. Ruffle iron. Photo by Michael Fredericks. Courtesy of National Park Service, Martin Van Buren National Historic Site.

den from "guests" and therefore museum visitors, it was crucial to design period rooms in the basement areas of the house, even though furnishings for the spaces were lacking. The misleading physical impression presented by the working spaces, however, undermines the accuracy of existing interpretation. Clean and pleasant, Lindenwald's kitchen exhibit is the coolest place in the house in summer, quite the contrast to what it would have been like for the Lindenwald servants (fig. 5.6). Some of the methods used to offset this powerful information include directly discussing the misrepresentation on tours and employing storytelling techniques in order to communicate the reality of the historic kitchen, defined by heat, dirt, and heavy work.

Fig. 5.6. Kinderhook, N.Y. Kitchen, Lindenwald. The tidiness and charm of Lindenwald's kitchen remain an interpretive problem. Photo by Michael Fredericks. Courtesy of National Park Service, Martin Van Buren National Historic Site.

Other dimensions of the servants' work lives have been uncovered through a reconstruction of the labors necessary to maintain the lifestyle the formal period rooms represent. Elaborate meals described in Van Buren correspondence suggested the problems of cooking and serving meals. The parlors pointed to an enormous amount of housework (rug care, dusting, tending the lamps). Those lovely evenings of feasting and withdrawing into the parlor, so often the fond subject of house museum tours, take on a new meaning when interpreted from the perspective of the household worker. Studying the lives of the Lindenwald domestics highlighted the fact that the prevailing popular image of a precious and charming Victorian past has a harsh underside, since it is built upon the repression of laboring women. In this sense we have based our collective memory on the nineteenth-century rhetorical constructs of egalitarian politics and the "cult of domesticity" rather than on historical reality, merely reflecting rather than interpreting the ideological dilemma of affluent Victorians.

The case of the Lindenwald domestics reveals the impossibility of sifting politics from "the home," the private from the public, men's history from women's history. Uncritical readings of biased material culture and documentary evidence has led to serious underestimations of the historical significance of the lives of domestics. We need to uncover these stories and demystify the ideology of the home, our inheritance from the nineteenth century and beyond. There are important reasons why conventional house museum interpretation ought to be expanded to include more kinds of people, not the least of which is simple accuracy. Although in many cases the houses have been preserved as the sole reminder of another time and survive without much context, the historical reality is that they were once enmeshed in complex social networks. Historians have a responsibility to reconstruct the contexts that give rich meaning to historic places, if not literally through preservation, then through the vehicle of interpretation. This critical interpretation challenges the old-fashioned, antiquarian approach that implies that women, the poor, slaves, and Irish domestics were invisible or in some way peripheral to the history of the house or, for that matter, to the history of the United States. Because there are so few historic sites dedicated explicitly to women, it is imperative that we find a permanent, broadly based territory for women's history in house museum interpretations. And, reassuringly to those attached to conventional house museum interpretation, it is not necessary to turn our backs on the ever-popular American patriarchs. It is at the house museum that an established public audience could come to grasp one of the truisms of women's history: that men's lives, public and private, cannot be fully understood without reference to women, be they mothers, wives, sisters, daughters, servants, or slaves.

CHAPTER 6

Domestic Work Portrayed
Philadelphia's Restored
Bishop William White House—A Case Study

Karie Diethorn with John Bacon

Traditionally, America's historic house museums have celebrated the great personalities and mammoth events of the past in a view character-ized by traditional definitions of political, economic, and social achieve-ment. The individuals recognized for these achievements are predomi-nantly white adult males of British or Western European heritage. Other populations—women, children, and racial and ethnic minorities—have been included in the drama as supporting cast members, but usually they play their parts offstage, incidental to the main action.[1]

This characterization of history's less visible denizens is reflected in the restoration and interpretation of house museums, which rely upon sur-viving documentary and material evidence associated with the time and place in question. Traditional sources such as tax and census records, newspapers, decorative and fine arts, diaries, and letters generally reflect the lives of those propertied and literate groups who dominated the his-toric scene. Other people appear occasionally in these sources, usually when they take some action in defiance of societal norms. Generally, and especially for those eras that predate the Industrial Revolution, evidence for the lives of society's rank and file has been particularly difficult to ob-tain and thus to interpret.

During the last two decades, however, the study of America's past has broadened to include a greater range of peoples, places, and cultures. Reinterpreting traditional forms of evidence through new means of study and recognizing new information sources have fostered an expanded view of history and its occupants. This development has touched the historic house museum community, occasionally resulting in new programming and in the preservation of previously overlooked sites. This evolutionary process brings with it new challenges in terms of integrating expectations of familiar and unfamiliar pasts.[2]

At Independence National Historical Park in Philadelphia, Pennsylvania, the familiar past is one populated by universally recognized figures (George Washington, Thomas Jefferson, Benjamin Franklin) and events (the signing of the Declaration of Independence, the drafting and implementation of the United States Constitution) which unfolded in hallowed spaces (Independence Hall, Congress Hall). These restored sites are both public and private, the latter being a group of residential structures restored to reflect the lives of those occupying them during the last two decades of the eighteenth and the beginning decades of the nineteenth centuries.

The house museum sites at Independence National Historical Park provide a complex resource for exploring the lives of past Philadelphians. The house at 309 Walnut Street was finished in 1787 for the family of William White, Pennsylvania's first Episcopal bishop, the rector of Christ Church, and a chaplain to the Continental Congress and United States Senate. For forty-nine years, until his death in 1836, Bishop White occupied the house with his wife, children, grandchildren, houseguests, and staff (fig. 6.1).

In the late 1950s the National Park Service included this residence in its restoration program because of the high degree to which the building's historic fabric had survived and because of the range of William White's involvement in the important events of the post–Revolutionary War era. Park Service historians also considered White's home to be a good representation of patrician Federal Philadelphia and proceeded to research and refurnish the house accordingly in the 1960s. The original interpretive program at the house focused on a guided tour of the building's first- and second-floor rooms showing how the White family entertained and where the bishop conducted his ecclesiastical affairs. Before Mrs. White's death late in 1797, she and her husband had eight children. Later, three of these children would return with their own children to live with the bishop in a large, extended family household.[3]

Beginning in the mid-1980s, a reassessment of the interpretive program manifest in the Bishop White House's furnished rooms began. At

Fig. 6.1. Philadelphia, Pa. The Bishop William White House. Courtesy of Independence National Historical Park.

the heart of the reassessment was the expansion of the interpretation in the house to areas previously undeveloped in the site's educational programming. In the course of this study a range of new topics was explored, among them the theme of domestic service and a study of the potential for interpreting the spaces in which servants worked. The purpose of this research was to identify, explain, and reintegrate into the interpretive program the previously unacknowledged occupants of the building and their essential role in sustaining it.[4]

Few details exist, however, regarding the identities of the Whites' servants. Only two members of this staff, Mrs. Boggs (a cook-housekeeper whom the federal censuses list as a "white woman") and John (an African American coachman) are known by name through family letters. The remaining staff is discernible only in the public record. This evidence consists of federal censuses in which investigators noted the race, sex, and age (but not the name) of each occupant in the White household at the beginning of each decade from 1790 onward. Removing from these records the entries clearly associated with the bishop's immediate family identifies those remaining as servants. In this way the structure of the Whites' domestic staff becomes clearer. Over four decades the servant population in the house remained constant: at any one time the family (ranging from four to fourteen members) employed two or three women and one man.

Detailed analysis of the nonfamily entries on the censuses reveals a hierarchy of age among the servants which corresponds to the level of responsibility assigned to each. The oldest woman, regardless of race, probably served as cook. Younger women, usually teens, acted as kitchen help and maids. Some of the girls were probably indentured, a common practice in eighteenth-century Philadelphia, especially among free African Americans.[5] The Whites' sole male servant was a coachman–stable hand, who occasionally may have served as a waiter.

The census also reveals that black servants consistently outnumbered whites in the bishop's household. These blacks were free people, members of a substantial African American community that had been growing in Philadelphia since the end of the Revolution. Like most white eighteenth-century Philadelphians, the bishop owned no slaves. Although very little survives to document his personal opinion of slavery (e.g., he was not a member of the Pennsylvania Abolition Society), we know that he provided economic support to free blacks in the city by hiring them as domestics (fig. 6.2).[6]

The previous discussion reveals the limits of written evidence pertaining to servants employed by the bishop and his family. In one respect this blurry picture imparts an eighteenth-century reality: employers indeed wished that their servants were not too closely seen or heard, yet this ideal seldom existed. The unintentional perpetuation of it in the restored Bishop White House therefore misrepresents the nature of late-eighteenth- and early-nineteenth-century domestic life. In order to represent accurately those who served the bishop's household, a reconstruction of the physical realities of their service is necessary. By observing and experiencing the spaces used by servants from their point of view, visitors

Fig. 6.2. Philadelphia, Pa. *Life in Philadelphia, Sketches of Character: At Home, by H. Harrison* (Soho: W. H. Isaacs, 1830s). After scraping off the dinner plates, servants soaked them in hot water. In the eighteenth and early nineteenth centuries soap played no part in the dish-washing process. Pots were rubbed with sand, not soap, to remove food and grease. Courtesy of The Library Company of Philadelphia.

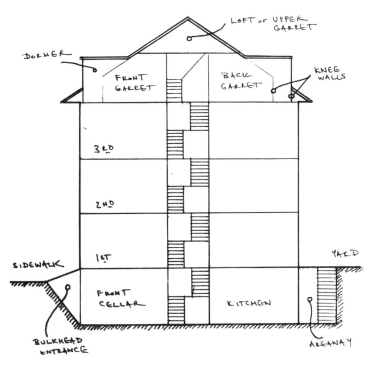

Fig. 6.3. Philadelphia, Pa. Cross-section of a room in a typical early-nine-teenth-century row house. Drawing by John Bacon, courtesy of Independence National Historical Park.

to the Bishop White House can achieve a deeper understanding of how one household functioned and how its occupants interacted with one another on a daily basis.

Cellars and garrets, among the least visited areas in a historic home today, were in constant use during a typical eighteenth-century day. The cellar is the enclosed space within the foundation walls below the level of the ground floor; the garret is the uppermost usable room or floor, often partly or entirely under the roof (fig. 6.3). In Philadelphia's temperate climate, cellars naturally maintain a relatively low and stable temperature throughout the year but are frequently damp. Garrets in the same buildings are dry by comparison but with widely fluctuating temperatures. These basic conditions suggest that the spaces were suited to distinct and different functions. Cellars received and housed bulk provisions that were not overly sensitive to cold or damp. Garrets served as auxiliary sleeping and dry storage areas, although they were certainly less convenient and more cramped than rooms on the main floors of a house.

The Bishop White House cellar was divided into four distinct spaces: the open cellar and storeroom under the main house, the piazza cellar, and the kitchen cellar (fig. 6.4). Bulkhead doors provided direct access from the street or yard to the open cellar; access to the interior of the house took the form of a flight of steps behind a closed door under the main stairway. Goods and people entering and exiting the cellar, notably those from outside the household, never entered the primary living spaces. The open cellar was thus a permeable, but controllable, space subsidiary to the primary living spaces.

Open cellars had three major uses: fuel storage, food storage and processing, and laundering. Until well into the nineteenth century, wood (chiefly hickory and oak) was the only significant fuel used in Philadelphia; coal became common only after the 1820s. Both types of fuel were delivered directly from the street or yard via a cellar bulkhead door. Philadelphia author Eliza Leslie described a similar scene in her 1840 *House Book:* "Besides the coal and wood are kept the charcoal barrels; the cinder-sieve; the coal scuttle, when not in immediate use; the fire-pan for carrying live coals that are wanted for kindling; the saw, and the wood axe."[7]

Along with wood and coal storage, the cellar housed food. Preserved foodstuffs and other bulk provisions were readily available in Philadelphia, and cellar inventories of the period often mention barrels of salt fish and pickled meat, grains and flour, and root vegetables. Philadelphia's renowned markets supplied fresh food too, which consumers stored in covered dishes in the coolest part of the cellar, often

---

Fig. 6.4. (opposite) Philadelphia, Pa. Floor plan and furnishing recommendations for the Bishop White House cellar. This cellar has a full complement of architectural spaces and finishes; furnishing these spaces can suggest a similarly broad range of usages , including food storage and processing, fuel storage and processing, and clothes washing. Because these and other service activities were concentrated in the cellar, back building, and yard, they should be interpreted together. Drawing by Denise Rabzak, annotated by John Bacon, courtesy of Independence National Historical Park.

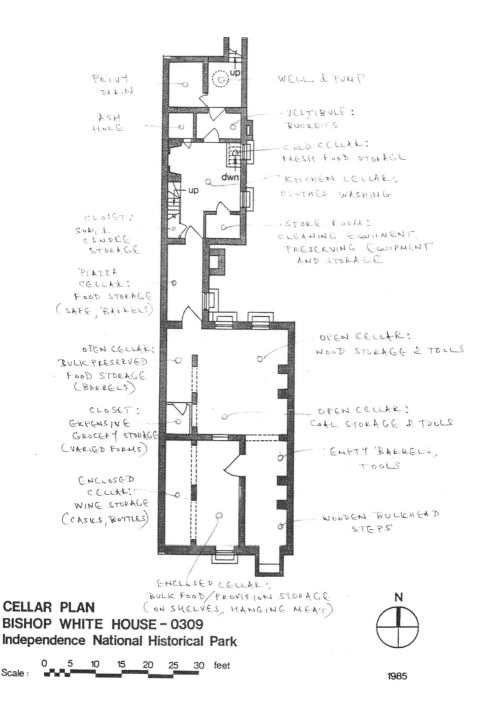

PRIVY DRAIN

WELL & PUMP

ASH HOLE

VESTIBULE: BUCKETS

COLD CELLAR: FRESH FOOD STORAGE

KITCHEN CELLAR: CLOTHES WASHING

up

dwn

up

STORE ROOM: CLEANING EQUIPMENT, PRESERVING EQUIPMENT AND STORAGE

CLOSET: SOAP & CANDLE STORAGE

PIAZZA CELLAR: FOOD STORAGE (SAFE, BARRELS)

OPEN CELLAR: WOOD STORAGE & TOOLS

OPEN CELLAR: BULK PRESERVED FOOD STORAGE (BARRELS)

CLOSET: EXPENSIVE GROCERY STORAGE (VARIED FORMS)

OPEN CELLAR: COAL STORAGE & TOOLS

EMPTY BARRELS, TOOLS

ENCLOSED CELLAR: WINE STORAGE (CASKS, BOTTLES)

WOODEN BULKHEAD STEPS

ENCLOSED CELLAR: BULK FOOD/PROVISION STORAGE (ON SHELVES, HANGING MEAT)

CELLAR PLAN
BISHOP WHITE HOUSE – 0309
Independence National Historical Park

Scale: 0 5 10 15 20 25 30 feet

N

1985

directly on the floor. Under the kitchen cellar, the Bishop White House also has a brick vault with a circular ice pit for use in preserving fresh meat and dairy products during the summer.

Food processing and preservation, done in large powdering or pickling tubs, was not always successful in the pre-refrigeration era. Philadelphia diarist Elizabeth Drinker reported in August 1803, "Some time ago [my husband] bought 8 Barrels of salt fish, we discovered soon after that the pickle was tainted, empty'd ye two worst in our dung heap . . . [in] such hot weather it wd. not do to keep such things in ye Cellar."[8] Dry or liquored foodstuffs, on the other hand, usually were safe from spoilage. Generally, such items were stored in a locked stand or safe. The Bishop White House cellar has a sizable room with a heavy, locking door and is traditionally regarded as a storage area for wines in casks, demijohns, and bottles. It probably also contained costly bulk groceries such as sugar, coffee, and tea as well as dried meat, which hung from the ceiling.

Laundry was the third major activity that took place in urban domestic cellars. In the Bishop White House the cellar kitchen area has a brick floor, large fireplace, and direct access to the yard with its cistern and pump. Laundry equipment included wash kettles, buckets, soap tubs, clothes baskets, and stools. There is also a brick ash hole where ashes from the fireplaces in the house were stored safely until needed to make lye, soap's principal ingredient. The lye also served to clean the house's privy drain, which was accessible below grade just outside the cellar's back door. The Whites' privy drain, subcellar vault, well, and cistern are all located within ten feet of one another at cellar level. This proximity was common in eighteenth- and nineteenth-century Philadelphia, with noxious and sometimes dangerous results: "This afternoon a Laboring Man lost his Life," reported Elizabeth Drinker in 1784, "who was diging a Seller up Town—by ye bursting out of an nesesary against which he stood."[9]

Like cellars, garrets were utilitarian in design and multipurpose in use. What was being stored there varied with the seasons. During spring cleaning, carpets and rugs were rolled and placed in the garret along with coal grates and fireplace tools. Heavyweight bed and window draperies were replaced with lighter materials or simple mosquito netting. In the fall the stored items returned to their regular use. The garret also served as a storage place for stylistically or functionally outmoded furniture. The trove of things found in a garret could make for a measure of a household's evolution, as "Anthony Afterwit" (aka Benjamin Franklin) noted when a new looking glass served as the catalyst for a wholesale removal of parlor furnishings to the garret: "In a Week's time, I was made sensible by little and little, that the Table was by no Means suitable to such a Glass. And a more proper Table being procur'd, my Spouse, who was an excellent Contriver, inform'd me where we might have very handsome Chairs in the way; And thus, by Degrees, I found all my old Furniture stow'd up into the Garret, and every thing below alter'd for the better."[10]

Whether in the cellar, garret, or kitchen, domestic labor cast its practitioners as distinctly different members of the household. Servants' work was necessary, but it had no status compared to that of the master. And, although he depended upon his servants, the master submerged this dependence beneath the prevalent eighteenth-century perceptions of servants as naive or willful incompetents in need of strict guidance. For these reasons servants (perceived as social inferiors engaged in menial activities) held positions of unrecognized intimacy; the ideal servant was ubiquitous but invisible. To deny servants' existence in this way while depending upon their labor created a dichotomy in the household. Master and servant were cohabitants of a single house but residents of different spheres.

The definition of these spheres went beyond the nature of their inhabitants' social origin or occupational activity. Being identified with the part of the house in which they spent most of their time, a family and its servants came to be known as the "parlor" and the "kitchen," respectively.[11] The parlor(s) and bed chambers belonged to the family; the kitchen, wash house, cellar, and garret were assigned to the servants. Although the two groups entered each other's appointed areas frequently during the day, their activities there were limited and their presence temporary.

Keeping servants in the work areas of the house not only controlled the negative aspects of their presence such as dirt, noise, and intrusion; it also ensured that masters would find their servants at a moment's notice. Although servants worked intermittently throughout the day at a variety of tasks, time between jobs was always subject to their employers' demands.

For this reason servants ate their meals in the kitchen and slept in rooms nearby.[12] These secondary spaces, used for dining and sleeping, combined the social characterization of servants as inferiors with the menial, perpetual nature of their work. Together, they reinforced the notion that the servants' sphere was separate from that of their employers.

This designation of rooms for servants' use accompanied developments in domestic architecture which emphasized the existence of distinct areas in the home. During the eighteenth century service spaces increasingly became formalized as such. Houses contained servants in interconnecting hallways, piazzas, and back buildings and isolated the family from servants' work with backstairs and doors between rooms.[13] These additions engendered further architectural developments by hindering interhousehold communication and thus prompting the creation of bell systems.[14] A series of brass bells mounted in the kitchen connected the servant and family areas of the house by means of a wire and pulley mechanism. The bell for each room responded with a distinct tone to the pull from a lever. Hence, the servant, if unable to see which bell was ringing, could discern from where the summons came. Intended as a connecting device, the bell system actually reinforced the social distance between employer and servant. The system's mechanical nature depersonalized contact and audibly represented the servants' subordinate status: a bell's jarring sound frequently interrupted the privacy of the servants' meal.[15] Clearly, the location of work areas in the house, as well as their structural and mechanical conduits, established an architectural identity for servants similar to that given to them socially as a separate, "kitchen" sphere.

Despite their clear identification with the kitchen and cellar, servants slept elsewhere in the house. These quarters, however, contributed no distinct quality to servants' identity other than that defined as work. The character of most servants' quarters was fairly anonymous. Garrets and above-the-kitchen chambers were less refined than those rooms used by the family. Often these rooms were unpainted, with little or no applied woodwork, low ceilings, and small windows (if any).[16] These were not chambers to which people retired for conversation, study, or private reflection. Rather, the nature of this environment suggests that people spent as little time as possible there.

Accordingly, the contents of servant rooms also reflected their occupants' ephemeral presence. A study of forty-three Philadelphia probate inventories (dated 1780 to 1835 and labeled by their evaluators as having some form of a garret) reveals that 73 percent of the rooms were used as sleeping quarters.[17] Of these, a large majority contained some sort of bedstead, indicating that the occupants had slept off of the floor. In general, however, this allotment of bedsteads characterizes the sole attempt to make these garrets into living spaces. Only 18 percent of the garrets with bedsteads contained other furniture, which suggests the rooms were for private, personal use. Tables or stands, chairs, chests of drawers or bureaus, looking glasses, or any combination of these items were rare. Garrets mostly contained odd, broken, or old pieces of furniture, scraps of metal, bundled Venetian blinds, rolled carpets, chests, and trunks. The majority of these garrets, then, primarily were used as storage spaces. Only secondarily could they be considered areas of habitation, having the servant's bedstead and possibly a chest containing personal possessions.[18]

The multipurpose character of servants' quarters complemented the defined status of their work areas; in fact, the two were often the same. The dual sleeping-storage nature of garrets reflected an older tradition of building in which all the rooms in a house served several functions simultaneously, and the personal status of the people in them was not necessarily reflected in the architecture.[19] This undifferentiated quality of garrets represented servants' intended anonymity in the house as a whole, as did their specific containment in the cellar, kitchen, and stable. The interchangeability of work and rest activities in these areas reiterated servants' subordinate status. The constant state of readiness required by employers placed servants everywhere at all times. By contrast, the work-oriented and impersonal nature of their environment put servants nowhere at any time.

In order for servants and their work to assume a more central role in the interpretation of the Bishop White House, visitors must see the servants at work and rest in various areas of the house through the presentation of artifacts in meaningful arrangements and contexts. In many restored residences, evidence of servant activities is concentrated in the kitchen with the display of culinary implements. Additional means of conveying domestic work and workers in a household, however, are available.

In the Bishop White House the physical structure of the entire house informs visitors about servants. During a tour visitors progress through the first floor of the house (as the servants did) from the front hall to the parlors and into the piazza. There a single door, when closed, conceals the kitchen (and its occupants) from the rest of the house. Leaving this door closed between tours provides the new visitor with a physical barrier that sets the tone for further discussion of the servants' presence in the house. Once in the kitchen, a view of the small winding stairs leads to the servants' quarters above. No doorway connects the above-the-kitchen chamber with the second- and third-floor rooms in the main house. This simple, but striking, fact succinctly illustrates the dichotomy of servitude: one of necessity combined with anonymity.

In the servants' quarters above the kitchen or the cellar below, visitors may encounter the duality of the occupants' lives. While climbing the back building's steep stairs, visitors experience the inconvenience that must have occurred for servants when they ran up or down (often with a heavy load) to their rooms or work. In the cook's chamber there is a walk-in closet with many shelves used for storing the family's Chinese export porcelain, which was brought down whenever the occasion required and then carried upstairs again after washing.[20] Other aspects of the cook's quarters relate to her domestic duties, such as the small anteroom, which offers an ideal place to iron clothes (fig. 6.5).

Above the cook's chamber was the kitchen garret, where the maid probably slept. The appearance of this room reflects the subordinate status of its occupant compared to that of the cook. The garret's low ceiling, limited light, and lack of heat illustrate the room's relative unattractiveness as a private apartment. In addition, off-season or discarded furnishings probably shared this space with the maid's bed. Overall, the cluttered and cramped maid's quarters provide a vivid contrast to the bed chambers inhabited by the bishop's daughters and granddaughters and contributes to visitors' understanding of the diversity of female experience, by class, in this period.

Upon reflection, the reassessment of the Bishop White House's servants and their work supports the National Park Service's original goal to present this Federal-era urban residence as a microcosm of its contemporary context. This goal, however, has been significantly expanded to include more of the complex society that was late-eighteenth-century

Fig. 6.5. Pennsylvania. "Woman Ironing by a Window," John Lewis Krimmel Sketchbook 5, plate 8. In a Pennsylvania farmhouse a woman irons sheets on a table. Her cold, sad iron sits on the table to her left and its trivet on the right. The wooden trough on the floor behind her holds the clean, unpressed laundry. Courtesy of The Winterthur Library, Joseph Downs Collection of Manuscripts and Printed Ephemera.

Philadelphia. Now the house presents visitors with a window into the lives of those Philadelphians who provided the comforts that sustained the city's leading public figures. Among the issues raised by the presence of these men and women include those of class deference in a democratic society, group and individual identity defined by work, personal privacy, and the impact of technology on daily life.

As the work spaces of the Bishop White House are refurnished and opened to visitors, the nature of the interpretive tour there has begun to change. No longer are today's visitors to the house simply echoes of their privileged predecessors who visited the Bishop two centuries ago. Now those who tour the building also represent elements of Philadelphia's citizenry who came to 309 Walnut Street as trades people, job seekers, charity cases, and extended family members.

The interpretation of domestic servants within the Bishop White

House opens the tour up for a deeper understanding of the dynamic that resulted from the intersection of individual lives in a single place. Opportunities to reflect upon the personal relationships and the circumstances that defined them—marriages, illnesses, births, deaths—within one house create paths between the past and the present. These are the events that mark a human life; they provide the context for deeds of lasting import. They and all of their participants are the true stuff of history.

CHAPTER 7

Putting Women in Their Place
Methods and Sources for Including Women's History in Museums and Historic Sites

Edith Mayo

Gender is one of many factors that structures society, shapes points of view about life and, of course, informs exhibitions. Until relatively recently, history was written by men and considered in male-defined terms. Exhibits that incorporate only male experiences and points of view skew the historical reality of over half our population. Filtered through the prism of gender, history becomes inclusive, correcting past distortions and incorporating both halves of human experience. Done well, women's history can profoundly reshape our perceptions of the past and foster an irrevocably altered perspective on the present and the future.

How can museum professionals ask questions of the past which are appropriate to women's experiences and create exhibitions that accurately reflect women's past experiences and their viewpoints about those experiences? How can the creators of exhibitions be more attentive to women's experiences—and sensitive to the ways in which exhibits are understood by museum visitors? Historians and curators must incorporate and present the historical realities of women in order to create a balanced historical perspective and to legitimize women's experiences as valid, rather than as "deviant" or "exceptional."

Increasing concern in the museum and historic preservation community about including gender in exhibitions and historic sites prompted a series of conferences to examine the topic. During Women's History Month in 1986 the Smithsonian Institution sponsored a conference, "Women's Changing Roles in Museums," which dealt with women's career paths, promotion, and leadership potential; and women as colleagues and supervisors in the workplace. A later Smithsonian conference, "Gender Perspectives: The Impact of Women on Museums," held in 1990, focused on a more critical examination of the impact of feminist scholarship on research, collections, exhibitions, and publications.[1]

Other initiatives to incorporate women's history into existing historic sites not specifically related to women included "Raising Our Sites," a pilot project by the Pennsylvania Humanities Council launched in 1992, funded by the National Endowment for the Humanities. This three-year project fostered collaboration between historians and museum professionals to design comprehensive plans for the inclusion of women's history at fourteen sites in Pennsylvania. Project sites created special exhibits centered on women's experiences, developed interpretive strategies, and integrated women's history into existing exhibits, with the hope that the initiative will impact collection policies as well as future interpretation.[2]

In a joint effort between the Organization of American Historians and the National Park Service, two workshops were conducted, one at Lowell, Massachusetts, in 1995, and the other in Chapel Hill, North Carolina, in 1996. These workshops brought together scholars and museum professionals to design plans to include women's history at National Park Service sites throughout the country.[3]

Two major conferences brought together academic historians, curators, and historians from the National Park Service and other museums and preservationists of women's historic sites across the country. The first conference, "Reclaiming Women's History through Historic Preservation," held at Bryn Mawr College in 1994, and the second, "Women in Historic Preservation," at Arizona State University in 1997, sought to build permanent working dialogue, cooperative exchange, and networks among those attending. The ultimate goal is "how to interpret and reinterpret historic sites as documents of women's history and to recognize the significance of women's leadership role in the American historic preservation movement."[4]

Despite growing interest in women's past by the public and the history community, comparatively little published material exists on the actual practice of how to include women in exhibitions and how to conceptualize exhibits that incorporate a feminist framework from the outset. My article

"Women's History and Public History: The Museum Connection," which appeared in the *Public Historian* in 1983, was an early attempt at suggesting how objects could be used to interpret women's history. Three years later two volumes appeared, written by academic historians who had become interested in or taught in the field of public history: Barbara Howe and Emory Kemp's collection, *Public History: An Introduction*, and Susan Porter Benson, Stephen Brier, and Roy Rosenzweig's *Presenting the Past: Essays on History and the Public.* These were essentially critiques of how history was done in museums and historic sites, some of which included women. But the omission of articles by museum professionals who had actually conceptualized and curated exhibitions about women, using historical artifacts, was both glaring and telling.[5] A work edited by Rosenzweig and Warren Leon, *History Museums in the United States: A Critical Assessment* (1989), is a more sophisticated approach that includes articles by practicing curators.[6] A growing literature on the use and interpretation of material culture, much of it produced for the expanding market in museum studies, museum education, and cultural resource management courses in colleges and universities, is heavy on the theory of material culture but lighter on its application and practice.[7]

Despite this growing professional literature, most public visitors to museums and historic sites do not understand what constitutes "history." Contrary to what the public thinks, history is not a series of agreed-upon, immutable facts; rather, it is a "construct"—a deliberate selection, interpretation, and presentation of the facts from a particular point of view. The construction of the historical past is usually done by the dominant group in society, which looks to the past to understand, give meaning to, or justify the present.[8] Museum professionals must examine who is selecting and interpreting the historical record. Who is constructing what the public "sees" as history? It is crucial to examine whose point of view and, therefore, whose value system is being enshrined and legitimized in constructing the historical record.

In the past quarter-century new scholarship in women's history has vastly increased historical information concerning women's experiences and contributions in the past. As a result, museums have sought to include women in exhibits, but many have simply incorporated them into traditional history, that is, the preexisting historical categories developed by and about men. This approach adds women to the historical list of "achievers" but does not change the historical categories, the standards of achievement by which one's accomplishments are judged. History remains fundamentally unaltered; the viewpoint remains male.

Exhibits That Include Women in Male-Defined Categories

Viewpoint can be expressed in every element of an exhibition from the conceptualization, design, and wording of labels to the museum collections and historical research on which the exhibition is based. Some examples from Smithsonian exhibitions illustrate questionable uses of women in displays that blatantly represent them only as sex objects. This does not constitute "inclusion" of women in the historical record.

In *Engines of Change*, a permanent exhibit on the Industrial Revolution in the National Museum of American History (NMAH), a full-scale replica of sculptor Hiram Powers's *Greek Slave* (a nude figure of a woman bound in chains) is used to draw visitors' attention to the exhibit. In the introductory section, curators intended to depict American objects shown at the Crystal Palace Exhibition in London in 1851. The curators felt that the naked sculpture of *The Greek Slave* would suggest to visitors the cultural impact of industrialization. On the body of the sculpture, upon close visual inspection, are fine metal points that allowed the statue to be reproduced exactly with a pointing machine; that is to say, the use of the statue was intended as a demonstration of industrial ingenuity. While a lengthy label explains this nuance of the curators' presentation, the predominant visual image is that of a large statue of a naked woman. Only when the label is read in great detail does one notice the visually minute points, or "get the point" about technological advances that made it possible to easily reproduce works of art. Most visitors to the exhibit "see" the statue as a sexual come-on and wonder aloud what the "naked lady" has to do with the Industrial Revolution! This less-than-auspicious introduction undermines the excellent presentation, later in the exhibition, of ways in which the Industrial Revolution dramatically altered women's lives (fig. 7.1).

Perhaps not coincidentally, located directly across from *Engines of Change* is the *Hall of American Maritime Enterprise*, where museum goers are again greeted by semi-naked ladies, represented as figureheads on ships. While this lusty representation of the maritime experience of

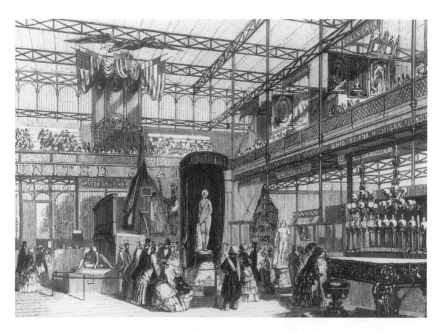

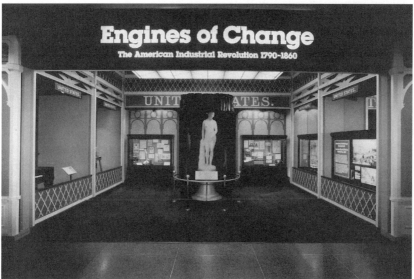

Fig. 7.1. Washington, D.C. The figure of Hiram Powers' *Greek Slave*, in *Engines of Change,* National Museum of American History, visually fails to "make the point" about technological advancement (*top*). Try to locate the points for the pointing machine on the "naked lady" (*bottom*). Courtesy of the National Museum of American History.

men is grounded in historical reality, one might suggest that representing the work of women and their contributions to the economy in maritime communities would balance this somewhat sexist presentation. We must begin to ask ourselves, "Are both male and female historical experiences represented in this kind of exhibitry?"

Another example where the view presented is more subtly, but decidedly, from the male historical experience is *Legend, Memory, and the Great War in the Air* at the National Air and Space Museum. This exhibition about the military use and nostalgia surrounding the role of the airplane in World War I clearly reflects a masculine construct. In "The Enthusiast's Room" section the male cap on the bedroom door and the knickers on the bed clearly indicate these were legends and memories of boys and men. A woman working in a war factory and another serving as a courier in the British Royal Air Force introduce women into the scenes, but their supportive roles remain unexamined. The exhibit presents women who participated in a masculine-defined enterprise. The conceptual "construct" is male (fig. 7.2).

Fig. 7.2. Washington, D.C. "The Enthusiast's Bedroom," in *Legend, Memory, and the Great War in the Air,* presents male-defined memories of World War I. Courtesy of the National Air and Space Museum.

Fig. 7.3. Washington, D.C. This scene of men and women hoeing indicates the shared experiences of men and women in *From Field to Factory.* Courtesy of National Museum of American History.

Exhibits That Transcend Categories of Gender

Some topics are presented in ways that transcend gender differences. In the Museum of American History's *Field to Factory* exhibit, the curator examined an experience shared by both African American men and women: twentieth-century migration from the South to the North. From conceptualization the curator and designer incorporated experiences of both sexes, displaying historical concepts and experiences that both sexes shared (fig. 7.3). In presenting scenes of work, the curator clearly depicted the gendered division of labor (fig. 7.4). Another scene shows work implements used by men and those used by women.

In concentrating on experiences shared by men and women, *Field to Factory* reinforces a sense of cohesiveness and bonding in the African American community. Often themes of race and ethnicity tend to obscure issues of gender difference. Centuries of suffering discrimination at the hands of the dominant white society makes it even more difficult to examine divergent experiences of class, gender, and color within the

Fig. 7.4. Washington, D.C. A woman washing clothes presents gender differentiated experiences in *From Field to Factory.* Courtesy of National Museum of American History.

shared experience. While the very human tendency is to emphasize experiences that bond the group together, it might also be useful to examine where the male and female experience diverged.

Similarly, *A More Perfect Union,* about the Japanese and Japanese American internment in the United States during World War II, which is a permanent exhibit at the National Museum of American History, depicts the shared experiences of men and women as well as gender-defined experiences. A scene of a family grocery store illustrates common aspects of social life, while the depictions of a woman with her child and men in battle point to gender-specific historical experiences.

When Is It Women's History?

Although women may curate exhibitions and both men and women may do their best to insert women into exhibitions at appropriate junctures, in many exhibitions the fundamental conceptualization of the topic, the "construct" of the history, the "viewpoint" of the subject matter, remains male defined. Categories in the historical record and questions being framed about the past are shaped or defined only by the experiences of men. When the male experience is presented as the "norm," women's experiences will always be "deviant" or "less than."

At present exhibitions by and about women abound in museums, but that is quite different from incorporating women's history scholarship into the exhibit framework.[9] Some years ago an exhibit at the Museum of the City of New York entitled *Beyond the Golden Door* focused on the Settlement House Movement and its work with immigrants and the poor. Although it was a wonderful and informative exhibit, I looked in vain for the historical impact of women—who largely structured and ran the settlements—or for an explanation of why they were called "settlement houses." It was no accidental term; the women who founded them "settled" in the neighborhoods they served and deliberately employed a woman-defined, woman-controlled, politicized domestic space, a space that intentionally brought the domestic ethic into public life. *Beyond the Golden Door* offered a unique opportunity to define and conceptualize an exhibition structured from a gender-defined view of women's work in the public sphere which created the profession of social work and profoundly influenced twentieth-century American social policy. Although this exhibition was curated by women about work that was primarily women defined, it was not a women's history exhibit, in my view.

To constitute women's history an exhibit must: (1) place women's point of view as the central frame of reference about experiences in the past; (2) define which group of women's experiences one is presenting in terms of race, class, or geographic locale; (3) emphasize female-defined historical experiences such as housework, childbirth, women-defined work/labor/economic experiences, or women's impact on male-defined arenas and ask what further historical questions are raised by such an approach, and (4) recognize that questions about what is meaningful in the past are often quite different for women than for men. Placing women's experiences and women's questions at the vital core of the historical record defines a new angle of vision on the past, one that has the power to redefine the basic narrative of American history.[10]

Barbara Clark Smith, a curator at the National Museum of American History, wrote about her experience in conceptualizing *Men and Women: A History of Costume, Gender, and Power:* "In the midst of working on 'Men and Women,' I realized that I was only addressing women as my audience . . . [and] came to the conviction that my best work, my strongest thinking and writing, came when I constructed my audience in this way."[11] Smith's powerfully persuasive argument for conceptualizing exhibits for a female audience is one way to ensure that women's questions about the past are central to the framework of the presentation. It ensures a women's history exhibit. "Surely women who work in museums and those who attend museum programs and exhibitions need to be responsible for placing ourselves, our questions, and our experiences at the center."[12] Using this women-centered paradigm, Smith found that her "costume" exhibition was really about power relationships between men and women and how clothing was infused with that cultural meaning.

Using Objects to Communicate Women's Past

In conceptualizing *From Parlor to Politics: Women and Reform in America, 1890–1925,* which I curated at the National Museum of American History, I deliberately focused on women's questions about the past and informed the exhibit with a women's history framework. I, too, made women my target audience. I strove to overcome the fact that past museum collecting had largely omitted women, particularly in political and reform movements. There were few artifacts in our own collections, or in those of other museums and libraries, which adequately conveyed the concepts I wanted to present. With the help of a talented and imaginative designer, Constantine Raitzsky, we overcame this deficiency by creating "evocative settings" to convey ideas that could not be illustrated with actual objects. With his assistance I structured the exhibit around three domestic spaces: the parlor, which evoked the concept of middle-class women's power and place within the home in the nineteenth and early twentieth centuries (fig. 7.5); the tenement, which represented the experiences of European immigrant life in the nation's urban centers as well as the lives of laboring class and poor Americans (fig. 7.6); and Hull House, the famous Chicago settlement, which symbolized both the settlement movement in the United States and the coming together of various classes of women to negotiate reform and social policy in a woman-defined space. Through the spatial metaphors of physical settings, I literally wanted to take museum visitors on women's journey "from parlor to politics."

Fig. 7.5. Washington, D.C. This parlor setting, indicating experiences of middle-class women in *From Parlor to Politics: Women and Reform in America, 1890–1925,* visually conveys how women used domestic concerns as a rationale and mandate to enter reform and politics. Courtesy of National Museum of American History.

Using common artifacts in a reinterpreted women's context can be a crucial step in changing both the curator's and the audience's historical perceptions. Redefining the meanings of objects, placing them within a framework of women's history, can lead to a redefinition of historical meaning itself. To overcome a dearth of political objects representing women, we used our collection's personal "association pieces" from notable women and located them in a new interpretive context to convey that, for women, "the personal becomes political." The tea sets given as ceremonial gifts to Susan B. Anthony on her seventieth birthday and to African American woman's club leader Josephine St. Pierre Ruffin at the first convention of Colored Women's Clubs, transcended mere personal "association items," or a testimony to the middle-class gentility of the recipients. The inscriptions engraved on the tea sets carried a decidedly political message recognizing both women in their capacity as political

Fig. 7.6. Washington, D.C. The domestic objects used for this tenement scene juxtapose the experiences of immigrant, working-class, and poor women with the fashionable furniture of the parlor to indicate class difference in *From Parlor to Politics: Women and Reform in America, 1890–1925.* Courtesy of National Museum of American History.

leaders. These tea sets also attest to the deliberate intention of women to infuse domestic artifacts with political meaning and to the use of the "tea party" as a powerful ritual of women's political culture, much as the "smoker" served as a bonding ritual in men's political culture.

Banners, strike posters, and union cards from our labor history collection—previously viewed as male objects—assumed new meaning in the reinterpreted context of the women's movement. These artifacts, juxtaposed with graphics from the women's labor movement, became powerful testimony to women's struggle for better wages, working conditions, and unionization.

Barbara Clark Smith explained that, when she worked on an exhibition about life in the late eighteenth century and noted the lack of attention to women's history, she was informed "that there were no artifacts available pertaining to women. This exhibition, however, included period rooms and furnishings, pots, pans, toys, spinning wheels, costume and jewelry, artisan tools, and ceramic wares! This incident reflects not an idiosyncratic blindness, but a common one shared among many museum professionals and among many visitors who . . . are a product of an invidiously gendered society that has been blind to women and their lives."[13]

In sections of *Parlor to Politics* for which artifacts and settings were unavailable, we used period photographs in photographic "essays" to convey historical concepts. Placing photographs of the women leaders of Hull House together with labels about their pioneering reform work, thus evoking a page in the "women's section" of an early-twentieth-century magazine or newspaper, proved quite effective in conveying that these women were central actors in the creation of innovative twentieth-century social policies.

Placing women's questions at the center of historical inquiry constructs a new context for the interpretation of everyday objects. Common artifacts, found in most museum collections, can be used to tell women's history. These include costumes, textiles, decorative arts materials, and household artifacts. In *Parlor to Politics* household artifacts, diagrams of the spatial layouts of period kitchens, period advertising, and home economics tracts were used to create a "model kitchen" of 1915. This enabled us to contextualize the home economics movement to demonstrate its critical impact on women's education and professions, illustrate women-defined changes in domestic spatial arrangements, and convey the impact of home economics on twentieth-century politics and reform.

Costumes, a collections category common to almost every museum and historic site, were the starting point for the politicized reinterpretation of that most traditional of women's exhibitions, the First Ladies Collection. Begun in 1912 by Mrs. Cassie Myers James, a leading figure in Washington, D.C. society, and Mrs. Rose Gouveneur Hoes, a descendant of President James Monroe, the collection was part of a widespread movement in the early twentieth century to preserve the nation's cultural heritage. It fit neatly into the Smithsonian's approach to history at that time, which presented the lives of notable people (virtually all distinguished white men) as examples of civic virtue. One of the oldest themes in American commemorative activity is the idea that, if the public were given worthy role models, they would become good citizens.

Into this framework Mrs. James introduced the idea of a collection of American historical costumes (then the primary object category relating to women) "illustrative of the fashions of the women of the United States from colonial times . . . and the articles of their particular sphere in home life. . . . The costumes assembled do not include those of the lowly, but belong entirely to at least the well to do, and mainly to the wealthy and distinguished." When Mrs. Hoes, with her presidential connections, was asked to contribute to the costume collection, the idea was born for a display of dresses worn by first ladies.

Although it presented only upper-middle-class and upper-class women, the new First Ladies Collection at the Smithsonian was itself a radical step in its day, for it introduced women as important in the pantheon of "worthies" at the Smithsonian and established "women's sphere in home life" as an important category in its own right. Virtually all other collection and display categories were entirely male. The collection gave American women visibility in the nation's museum and paved the way for future collections on women's history.

In reconceptualizing the collection and exhibition, First Ladies' clothing was used to illustrate the social and ceremonial role of the president's spouse, placing these women within the political context of their husband's presidential administration. Using portraits of First Ladies Louisa Catherine Adams and Lucy Webb Hayes enabled me to present Mrs. Adams's astute use of her entertaining skills to further her husband's political agenda and career and to talk about Lucy Hayes's White House endorsement of the Temperance movement. In fact, the portrait of Hayes had been commissioned by the Woman's Christian Temperance Union to honor the First Lady as a model for temperance advocates.

The Division of Political History's large political campaign collection, universally recognized and used as male cultural artifacts, enabled me to reinterpret First Ladies as political partners and political campaigners. A photographic scrapbook of Warren Harding's famous "front porch" campaign of 1920 documented the central role of Florence Harding in creating her husband's campaign image. As a partner with Warren on his Ohio newspaper, Mrs. Harding was acutely aware of the importance of the candidate's image. She became, in effect, the master of what we call today the "photo opportunity," astutely orchestrating the visits of such key constituency groups as African Americans, women (who cast their first vote in the 1920 election), ethnic community representatives, and Hollywood and radio stars to the Hardings' "front porch." Making sure that they were photographed prominently with the candidate, she saw that these photos were widely distributed through her connections with Republican newspapers nationwide. Here we begin to see all the trappings of the modern media campaign.

Using a large woman suffrage postcard collection in the *Parlor to Politics* exhibit permitted us to explore the use and manipulation of political images of women, both pro- and anti-suffrage, to create a distinct female political culture in the early twentieth century. Further examination revealed that this distinct female political culture has had a dual legacy: while women in the early part of the century employed the political imagery of the home and family as a rationale and mandate to enter American political life, the continuing power of these images has served to inhibit women's political progress in the latter part of this century as they seek to transcend and move beyond political concerns that deal solely with home and family.

Period prints, common to collections in most museums and historic sites, usually from *Harper's* or *Leslie's Illustrated Newspapers,* prove helpful in including women's history. This particular print from *Harper's* helped to chronicle women's direct political action in protests for the Temperance movement, which pioneered virtually every aspect of the women's reform agenda from the 1870s into the 1920s. Other period graphics such as cartoons, political drawings, and book and magazine illustrations offer a variety of visual representations of women's experiences.

In addition, a variety of artifacts that could easily be collected to tell women's history include costume accessories such as hair products and adornments, makeup, shoes and jewelry; textile materials; furniture, home artifacts, and domestic appliances; children's furniture, toys, and clothing; table settings, china, and glassware; portraiture; posters, period books and magazines; etiquette books, cookbooks, and recipes; medical instruments; dancing manuals; fashion plates; work costumes and tools related to women-defined occupations; period imagery and advertising about women; and decorative arts objects. These artifacts can be used to explore women's roles in the home and family—as producer, consumer, wife, mother, healer, and nurturer—which most women played. The period and subject matter of the site you wish to interpret will dictate other materials that are possible to acquire. Keep in mind that objects associated with women have great power to explain gender relations; nontraditional objects in women's hands (large power machinery, guns, military uniforms) have enormous power to convey the gendered meanings and value judgments society attaches to these objects. Photographic essays can inexpensively include women's history in exhibits or sites without changing the existing text or installation. Photographs can present how women were, or were not, involved in the experiences your site or museum exhibits or suggest parallel or alternative activities in which women were engaged.

If one is interested, and inventive, ways can be found to reinterpret existing sites to include women's history which are informative and powerful as well as fascinating to the public. The paramount point is how an existing collection, exhibit, or site, or reasonably priced additions to it, can be used to illuminate the new angle of vision on the past which women's history provides.

Challenges to Including Women's History in Public Sites

Many challenges face museum professionals committed to exhibiting issues of gender in the public sector: questions of legitimacy, the creation of a community of women scholars, and the perception of women's history as "subversive." My own experience has indicated that, in many instances, questions about the legitimacy of women's history still linger, within one's own administrative structure as well as with the public. For many, women's history is still not considered "real" history. Women, themselves, robbed of knowledge of their past, often ask me, "What could you possibly exhibit?"

Curators are often faced with administrative disinterest or collaborators' trivialization of women's history. When collaborating with design teams or public relations and fund-raising colleagues, this can spell potential disaster. It is critical for the curator or historian to establish clearly, within his or her own mind and within the museum administration, the importance of the women's story to be presented. Remember, women's history is not minority history nor the history of a "special interest group." It represents the experiences of over half our population. Although the legitimacy of "minority" history (African American, American Indian, Hispanic, or other ethnic or racial groups) is now seldom questioned and is often viewed as a healthy expression of American "diversity," the legitimacy of women's claim is still disputed. Have the necessary historical and ideological ammunition ready. The claim to legitimacy must be clear, persuasive, and forceful.

Creating a community of women scholars can be a powerful tool for supporting women's history in the public sector. Fortunately, the dichotomy between academic history and public history is breaking down as women scholars in both sectors find a commonality of interests. Since most members of the American public obtain their view of history through public, not academic, sources, collaborative ventures between academic and public historians broaden the base on which women's history rests. Such cooperation greatly aids public historians in their quest for legitimacy within their own communities as well as with funding sources. Academic scholars should view public history venues as conduits to the public for their historical scholarship, garnering a wide public audience for their research. Academic women might also play a powerful and effective role in encouraging museum and historic site administrators to support women's scholarship by making available research time, publication possibilities, adequate monetary support, and defense of possibly controversial issues.

Finally, women academics and museum professionals must address the perception of women's history as subversive. Let us understand clearly that, for those imbued with a male vision of the past, women's history will remain controversial—not only in its presentation of women's past contributions but also in its implications for women's continuing empowerment. Throughout this chapter I have spoken about the power to alter historical understanding and meaning by applying women's angle of vision. As Barbara Clark Smith suggests, "The ideology of masculinism [is] a point of view that privileges men's experiences, aspirations, and perspectives, not only imagining these to be most important but also believing them to be most representative of all. . . . We should not underestimate or fear to acknowledge to one another the difficulty and radicalism of our objectives."[14]

Reshaping enshrined value systems within a society is a radical political statement, viewed by many as possessing the power to subvert the dominant male order. Yet not until women as well as men define the theories and methodologies by which we research and present history, not until historical periodization reflects the patterns of women's lives and consciousness, not until the questions historians and curators ask about the past are those of women as well as men, will meaningful women's history appear. Not until these conditions are met will the impact of the new scholarship on women emerge in museums and public history sites. Not until women themselves demand to see their own history and claim their past will women's history have real power. We can commit ourselves to no less.

PART III

Claiming New Space for Women in the Built Environment and Cultural Landscape

CHAPTER 8

Rooms of Their Own
The Nurses' Residences at Montreal's
Royal Victoria Hospital

Annmarie Adams

The Historic Sites and Monuments Board of Canada reaffirmed its commitment to women's history in 1998 by commemorating several sites associated with the history of nursing. Among them was the Hersey Pavilion at the Royal Victoria Hospital (RVH) in Montreal (fig. 8.1), a nurses' residence designed in 1905 by Edward and William Sutherland Maxwell, with major additions by Hutchison and Wood (1917) and Lawson and Little (1931–32).[1] While the board had considered other types of sites for possible designation as heritage buildings, it was decided that the purpose-built nurses' residence in a hospital setting best illustrated the dual themes of professionalization and nurses' work culture.[2]

Little remained of the original design at the time of the building's designation. Like other Canadian nurses' residences, the Hersey Pavilion and its additions had been converted to other hospital functions following the closure of hospital-based training schools in the 1960s and 1970s. It fell to the building's exterior and two restored interior spaces to illustrate what the board determined to be the three major functions of a nurses' home: residential, recreational, and educational.

Nonetheless, from the perspective of architectural history, much could still be culled from what evidence remained. When supplemented with information gleaned from original drawings, architectural intentions, and photographs of the lost interiors, the Hersey Pavilion reveals the truly paradoxical relationship of domestic and institutional women's architecture in the early twentieth century. This chapter explores how a real

Fig. 8.1. Montreal, Quebec. Maxwell watercolor perspective of the nurses' residence. Photo Brian Merrett. Courtesy of the Maxwell Archive, Canadian Architecture Collection, McGill University.

"room of one's own," at least for nurses at the Royal Victoria Hospital, simultaneously offered women autonomy and restraint.

The educational program for nurses based at the Royal Victoria Hospital did not begin with the realization of the Maxwells' new residence. Since the founding of the Training School in October 1894, nursing students at the RVH had lived amid the large, open wards, exposed to the fetid air, contagious diseases, and never-ending duties of turn-of-the-century nursing.[3] In earlier plans of the Royal Victoria Hospital, the women who worked day and night, trained countless others, and cared for the city's "sick and injured persons of all races and creeds, without distinction," had few rooms of their own.[4]

Unsigned plans of the hospital dated 1905 (which were in the possession of the Maxwells) seem to show some of these spaces in the original hospital intended for nurses but never built: a large dining room in the western section of the administration block (on level F) and a single space intended for the head nurse in the east tower (level E).[5] The original drawings for the hospital, however, which also do not necessarily reflect what was constructed, show a series of small rooms and a waiting room for nurses in the central administration building, in addition to a tiny space "with inspecting windows, which command the entire wards."[6] There was also a special office on the principal floor in this early scheme assigned to the head nurse, or lady superintendent.[7] Yet there is little evidence at this point to ascertain where the first nurses at the RVH may have slept.[8]

The main building of the RVH was designed by British architect Henry Saxon Snell in 1889–93, who was well-known in England and Scotland as the designer of workhouses and hospitals and as the author of two significant books, *Charitable and Parochial Establishments* (1881) and *Hospital Construction and Management* (1883). A central administration block and two long and narrow open wards form a U-shaped ensemble facing south, toward McGill University, with which the hospital is affiliated (fig. 8.2). Influenced by the ideas of Florence Nightingale, Snell's building was a "pavilion hospital," in which the separation and isolation of both patients and diseases were thought to discourage the spread

Fig. 8.2. Montreal, Quebec. Photograph by William Notman and Son of the Royal Victoria Hospital, designed by Henry Saxon Snell in 1889–93. This view shows Pine Avenue, its intersection with University Street, and the wooded slopes of Mount Royal. Photo courtesy of Royal Victoria Hospital.

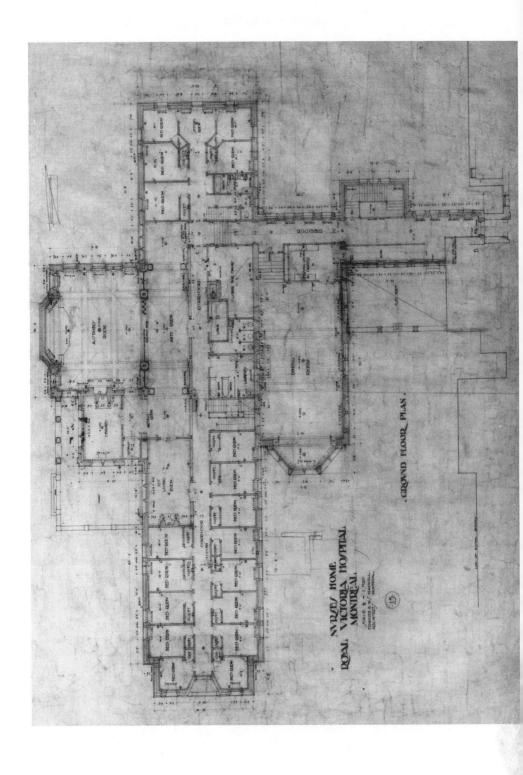

NVRSES/ HOME.
ROYAL VICTORIA HOSPITAL.
MONTREAL.

SCALE ⅛" = 1 FOOT
EDWARD S. W.
ARCHITECT
MONTREAL.

· GROUND FLOOR PLAN ·

of infection.[9] Constructed of Montreal limestone, the hospital was also distinguished by romantic turrets framing generous sun porches at the corners of its imposing medical and surgical wards. Snell modeled the Montreal hospital on Edinburgh's Royal Infirmary, constructed by David Bryce in 1870. This "Scottish baronial style" pleased the hospital's upper-class patrons, whose families had emigrated from Scotland.[10]

The construction of the new residence was intended to improve the daily lives of the nurses at the busy urban hospital. Separate quarters were considered particularly imperative after a fire in 1905 damaged many of the nurses' bedrooms on the fourth floor of the Snell building, forcing them to sleep in the surgical wing for several months.[11] Adjoining the ventilation tower of Snell's west or surgical wing on the slopes of Mount Royal, the Maxwells' five-story, fireproof residence gave the nurses private space within their sphere of work as well as status and visibility in the community (fig. 8.3). In its heavy masonry construction, stepped gables, and details intended to evoke a particularly Scottish medical tradition, the new building mimicked, to some extent, its older neighbor, to which it was directly connected through a passageway above the east entrance.

The RVH nurses' home also drew heavily on middle-class domestic architecture, offering its aspiring residents 114 bedrooms, 10 sitting rooms in which to socialize in small groups, a grand dining room, and a sequence of elegant spaces on its west side, including a library, living room, anteroom, and a large assembly hall with a stage. These spaces were deliberately homelike, intended to reflect the residential function of the new building, and were given special emphasis in the massing and elevations of the building. The nurses' home as a building type, at this early stage of its development, knew nothing of the more institutional classrooms and demonstration labs characteristic of later nurses' homes.[12] The education of nurses at this time was largely conducted in the hospital itself.[13]

Fig. 8.3. (opposite) Montreal, Quebec. Ground-floor plan of the nurses' residence by Edward and W. S. Maxwell. The connection to the original hospital by Henry Saxon Snell is at the bottom of the drawing. Photo courtesy the Maxwell Archive, Canadian Architecture Collection, McGill University.

Fig. 8.4. Montreal, Quebec. Aerial photograph of the Royal Victoria Hospital Montreal, early 1940s. Photo courtesy of Royal Victoria Hospital.

Even the siting of the building was romantic (fig. 8.4). Nestled among the trees and poised on the steep ground west of the Snell building, the original nurses' residence was only partially visible from Pine Avenue, the busy thoroughfare in front of the RVH. The winding pathways and angled gateways of the growing hospital complex ensured that the residence was mostly seen in oblique views.

The agitated silhouette of the home's stepped gables, presumably inspired by Snell's extensive use of the Scottish feature on the hospital wards, ventilation towers, and administration block of the earlier building, added to the romantic perception of the building. So did the fact that the Maxwells' nurses' residence was the first major extension to the hospital to break the apparent symmetry of Snell's monumental courtyard.[14] This gesture expressed the newer building's noninstitutional nature, which was further differentiated by the proliferation of dormers and stone railings on the Maxwell building. Indeed, the Maxwells' perspective view (see fig. 8.1) emphasizes their building's isolation from the Snell hospital, whose west tower and ward loom behind the new building in the drawing. The vantage point selected for the drawing and for many photographs of the building completely obscured the residence's connection to the hospital, making it appear, instead, as a freestanding, isolated (and therefore smaller, domestic) structure (fig. 8.5).

This idea of having a separate, seemingly domestic structure situated in a romantic landscape was essential to the experience of the first nurses' residence. In addition to the winding flagstone path, which, as one resident of 1933 described it, "entices us to follow whither it doth lead; we yield and follow it to the door of the Home,"[15] the location of the nurses' residence to the west of the hospital ensured that it was seen against the backdrop of Mount Royal's wooded slopes. The area above the original hospital was vacant at this time; Percy Nobbs's Pathological Institute was

Fig. 8.5. Montreal, Quebec. This photograph shows the Maxwells' reception room in the foreground and the Lawson and Little gymnasium in the background. Photo courtesy of Royal Victoria Hospital.

constructed to the east in 1924, across University Street from the Snell building. As was the case with many late-nineteenth-century institutions for women, particularly colleges, it is likely that the western site was considered more appropriate for the nurses' residence because of its more natural, "untouched" character.

This association of women and wilderness was central to the process of suburbanization in the nineteenth century as well as in the location of the first colleges for women at universities, which were typically relegated to the periphery of the campuses or even cities. It stemmed from long-established conceptions of nature, understood in the late nineteenth century as healthier, safer, and more beautiful than the unpredictable, industrialized city.[16] In the cases of both suburbs and early colleges this widespread belief that women required protection from the dangers of urban life meant that they were removed or separated from the masculine centers of power, which tended to be located in more urban (less natural) locations.[17]

The eastern section of the large RVH site has been perceived for a century as a more masculine, technology-oriented (urban) area.[18] In addition to several prestigious medical buildings, it housed the powerhouse and laundry building (1900) and ambulance garages (1911), while the western and northern edge of the roughly triangular site—the steep, rocky, wooded mountainside—was reserved for women (and wealthier patients).[19] Today the edge is still marked by the Allan Memorial (a renovated mansion), the former nurses' residence, the Ross Memorial Pavilion (1915-16), and the Women's Pavilion Hospital (1925–26). Just beyond lie the heavily wooded, rocky slopes of Mount Royal.

Despite the separateness of the building as expressed in the drawing and photos, the actual connection of the nurses' residence to the hospital building proper was a blatant statement of the institution's expectation of total commitment on the part of its student nurses. The narrow passage, carefully detailed by the architects, expressed—maybe even ensured—the fact that the nurses' six and a half–day workweek left little time for any life outside the hospital.[20] The actual intersection of the hospital and nurses' residence was given elaborate architectural attention; the Maxwells designed a special door for the juncture.[21] Its decorative ironwork must have warned unwelcome visitors of the more private, domestic quarters beyond.

This close connection between hospital and nurses' residence was uncharacteristic of buildings constructed later in the century. Indeed, the influential *Survey of Nursing Education in Canada,* conducted by George Weir in 1932, recommended that the nurses' residence be separated from hospitals, allowing "adequate opportunity for privacy, rest, quiet retirement for study and for cultural recreation."[22] By then the modernization of both the hospital and the professionalization of nursing meant that nurses could demand a certain degree of autonomy from the hospital. This autonomy was expressed in spatial terms by the physical distance separating their places of residence and work. Edward Stevens, an expert on hospital architecture and designer of two major buildings at the RVH, described the separation of residence and hospital in the 1920s as beneficial to the patients, taking the nurses' need for recreation for granted: "Any hospital of considerable size should have its nurses' residence. This should be a separate building, not too remote from the hospital, but far enough away so that the noises of an entertainment, a dancing party or a romp will not disturb the patients."[23] Stevens also emphasized the need for nurses to "go out of the environment of the sick room, out of the sound of suffering, out of hospital smells, and in fact out of the hospital atmosphere."[24] In this earlier period of development, however, the need for nurses to escape their workplace was unacknowledged in spatial terms.

The building's interiors, too, were quite domestic in terms of their physical form as well as their intended use. The new reference library, for example, replaced the earlier library by the Maxwells, which was subsumed in the new wing's entrance, while a new gymnasium extended from the Maxwells' original reception room (fig. 8.6).[25] These rooms were furnished with comfortable chairs and tables, typical of middle-class houses at the time. The furniture was arranged casually, loosely grouped around fireplaces and pianos, probably intended to simulate intimate, homelike gatherings. The yearbook praises the domestic character of the new residence, remarking on the foyer's "soft lights," which, the author suggested, "invite us to linger." The reception room on the first floor, "tastefully and comfortably furnished," was the setting for bridge parties and teas. The library also illustrated in the yearbook, was "luxuriously furnished with piano, chesterfields and occasional chairs."[26]

Fig. 8.6. Montreal, Quebec. This photograph shows student nurses in the classroom, part of Lawson and Little's addition made during the 1930s. Photo courtesy of Royal Victoria Hospital.

Martha Vicinus has pointed out how many early buildings for women—colleges, schools, settlement houses—looked like large houses. This domestic imagery was probably intended to smooth the transition for middle-class women to the world of paid work while at the same time offering the promise of gentle protection in that realm. "The surroundings," says Vicinus of the first colleges for women in England, "bespoke permanence, seriousness of purpose, and the same solidity that marked the middle-class families from which the bulk of them came."[27] The house-like appearance of the RVH nurses' residence probably reassured anxious parents that their daughters would be looked after, protected, and separated from the hospital, the street, and the city beyond.

The class-conscious profession of nursing may have presumed that the association of the residence with upper-middle-class houses would attract young women from wealthier families. Just as the nurses' uniforms made young graduates feel "dignified and poised," the new building may have been intended to impose middle-class values on working-class women, whose backgrounds were increasingly unacceptable to the profession in the decades following Florence Nightingale's sweeping reforms.[28] Edward Stevens pointed to the domestic character of the architecture, expressing concerns over both class and performance: "The more attractive and homelike this building can be made and the more alluring it can be made to the young woman who is taking up nursing, the better will be the class of women who will come to it and, in the end, the better will be the care that the patient will receive."[29]

In spite of the traditional, domestic attributes of the nurses' residence, the building type became a trademark feature of the "modern" hospital throughout urban North America. An implicit assumption in the development of the type was that the more efficient the nurses' residence, the more efficient the hospital in general. This led to the gradual inclusion of educational spaces within the program of the nurses' home, a mark of both decreasing reliance on the hospital as the primary site of nursing education and of increased specialization within the nursing profession.

Modern nurses' residences built after the 1920s included social spaces that tended to be multifunctional, accommodating complex changes in use, relative to the earlier near-replicas of traditional domestic spaces. This is particularly evident in the transformation of the Maxwells' assembly room of 1905 into the expanded assembly room/gymnasium space of Lawson and Little in the 1930s. "It is a convertible room appearing now as a ballroom, now a gymnasium and again as a lecture theatre, seating comfortably two hundred and fifty persons," boasted the 1933 yearbook. Despite this modern, multifunctional conception, social rooms in nurses' residences typically were furnished in an extremely conservative manner. The rooms at the RVH, for example, featured Oriental rugs, upholstered armchairs and couches, Windsor chairs, and heavy draperies with sheers.

Lawson and Little's new wing to the west of the original nurses' home provided 132 rooms and a reference library, in addition to the multipurpose room. In the basement were classrooms and labs, reflecting the full integration of educational spaces into nurses' residences by this time.[30] Although this "teaching unit" occupied an entire floor, these rooms received no special treatment in the massing or elevations of the extension.

In terms of planning, however, the educational rooms were considered extremely up-to-date, planned as they were on "scientific" principles. The classroom, for example, had a sloping floor, allowing each student to view the blackboard in the front of the room (see fig. 8.6); the demonstration room included beds, model trays, and mannequins, simulating the real hospital environment next door.[31]

At the same time as the building saw the introduction of these supposedly modern features, the nurses' residence remained an arena in which the private lives of nursing professionals could be closely supervised and controlled by the hospital administration. Student nurses could not marry, they kept strict curfews, and their friendships were carefully monitored.[32] In the 1920s nurses were required to wear hats when leaving the building and to return home by 10:00 P.M. Smoking, dating the so-called housemen (residents), or mentioning the issue of salary were strictly prohibited.[33]

Lawson and Little's monumental extension to the Maxwells' building in the early 1930s gave physical form to many of the restrictions imposed on nurses' lives. The new building continued the general massing of the earlier residence by extending the west end of the Maxwell project with a new entry sequence (through the former Maxwell library). This hallway led to the generous gymnasium behind the former stage of the Maxwell assembly room. A Medieval Revival tower housed the elevator, another modern feature.

The tower also marked the crossing of this long hallway and the double-loaded corridor that commanded the more residential section of the new extension. Like the educational rooms in the basement, bedrooms in the new wing were considered extremely up-to-date, "artistically furnished in a green, rose or tangerine color scheme."[34] Special bedroom furniture, like the multifunctional social spaces in the new wing, served several purposes at once. A single piece, for example, served as dresser, desk, and bookcase.[35] The section of the building running from the elevator lobby in the tower, southward, toward Pine Avenue, was known as "Peacock Alley" because of its bright colors and highly decorated appearance.[36]

The expansion of the residence so soon after its completion may have sprung from the hospital's desire to segregate nurses to an even greater degree than the original home prescribed. Of great concern to the hospital administration, after all, was the fact that, even after the construction of the original residence, student nurses continued to have close contact with the male staff. In the early 1920s, for example, when the Maxwell building no longer accommodated the number of nurses working at the RVH, students whose names began with the letters A through J had been housed in part of the former Ward K, which had been converted into a temporary residence. The other half of the former ward was occupied by the housemen (residents), separated from the student nurses by only a particle board partition. "In no time a direct communication system had been established," recounted Eileen Flanagan fifty years later, "by means of a clothesline stretched across the alleyway between the two wings. Many a note and batches of homemade candy were passed across."[37]

The confinement and surveillance of student nurses in early-twentieth-century hospitals was primarily the responsibility of the lady superintendent. Lawson and Little's plans of the early 1930s reflect the important place occupied by Miss Mabel Hersey, who served as superintendent from 1908 to 1938 and figured centrally in the development of nursing education and the profession in Quebec.[38] While the inclusion of the classrooms, library, and gymnasium must have appeared as fairly progressive at the time, contributing as they did to the institution's maintenance of the students' minds and bodies, the subtle renovations made to the Maxwell building by the later architects are extremely telling. Four bedrooms in the south end of the original building were transformed at the time of the new addition into a relatively luxurious four-room apartment for Hersey. Critical to its function in the growing complex, of course, was the new suite's strategic position overlooking the entrance area and stairs. Inside the building, Miss Hersey could easily survey the long corridor of the residence's main floor.

This form of direct surveillance was unknown in other residential sections of the hospital complex and may not have even occurred in the earlier nurses' residence of 1905, as the Medical Board had suggested that the lady superintendent's quarters should remain in the Administration Building, even after the construction of a separate Nurses' Home.[39] The (male) superintendent of the entire hospital, for example, did not even live at the hospital, underlining again the gendered dimensions of the question of which employees were permitted to live apart from their place of work.

Historian Judi Coburn has noted how nursing has been shaped by two powerful ideological forces: the "bourgeois ideology of femininity," which attempted to "contain women's work outside the home within the duties of homemaking," and the allure of professional status.[40] The architecture of the RVH nurses' residence reflects this duality of forces which shaped the profession. While the building's homelike character was intended to attract middle-class women to join the ranks of the growing profession, the same architectural features also served to limit women's participation in the world of health care.

Yet the buildings also served very positive roles in shaping the Canadian nursing profession. Residences gave nurses real space in which to live and work, in contrast to their prior "invisible" contribution to hospital life; the residences' clear connection to the hospital—in terms of both a real physical link and stylistic congruity—acknowledged the students' grueling schedules and total commitment to nursing. Most significantly, the architecture of nurses' residences offered single women a place to live in the city, outside the traditional middle-class (or working-class) home.

In addition, the history of this much-neglected building type should remind architectural historians of the pitfalls of isolated typological studies. The dynamic interplay between the architectures of the hospital and the homes of the surrounding neighborhood is material evidence of the murky distinctions between domestic and institutional architecture at this time. The study of architecture designed for women underlines this danger, as it nearly always represents a carefully negotiated compromise of private and public space.

CHAPTER 9

On the Inside
Preserving Women's History
in American Libraries

Abigail A. Van Slyck

Turn-of-the-century public libraries were among the most popular American preservation projects in the 1990s (fig. 9.1). As such, they offer a useful means for assessing the current state of historic preservation practice in the United States. In the post–World War II period these modest classically detailed buildings were easy targets for demolition. Hopelessly dowdy to Modernist eyes, they frequently were pulled down to make room for larger library facilities with sleek, metallic interiors flooded with cool fluorescent light. Today these same modest buildings have benefited from an approach to preservation which values the cultural importance of historic sites as much as their aesthetic qualities, while a postmodern sensibility has prompted a renewed appreciation of their architectural charms. From Pittsburgh, Pennsylvania, to Pittsburg, Kansas, proponents of historic preservation can point with pride to the sensitive renovation of many such buildings, some of which continue to serve as libraries and others that have been adapted for reuse (often as local history museums or art centers).[1]

Yet these preservation efforts tend to be skin-deep. To step inside a "preserved" library is often to step into an interior space that has been stripped of its original fittings. Even if the preservation architect is dedicated to maintaining the historic character of the interior, this often means retaining or (in the case of a new addition) matching the material, profile, and finish of permanent woodwork while removing the charging desk, card catalog, and other "impermanent" furnishings that were once integral components of library interiors. This practice is perfectly in keeping with

Fig. 9.1. Stillwater, Minn. Stillwater Public Library. The renovation of this Carnegie library in the 1980s maintained the historical character of the building's architectural shell but moved the charging desk from the top-lit oval foyer, stripping the building's focal point of its original symbolic and functional role. Photo by Abigail Van Slyck.

the secretary of the interior's Standards for Rehabilitation, which emphasize the integrity of the architectural shell and its exterior context by calling for "minimal change to the defining characteristics of the building and its site and environment."[2] Likewise, when such interior changes facilitate putting an old building to new use, preservation professionals argue (with good reason) that they also "extend the building's life since occupied structures are less likely to be demolished than vacant ones."[3] In short, the sacrifice of the historic interior has been readily accepted as the best way to ensure the preservation of a building's street-front appearance. Indeed, it is difficult to imagine a viable approach to historic preservation which allows no changes in historic interiors whatsoever.

However common, this tendency to sacrifice historic interiors has gender implications worth acknowledging. An emphasis on preserving the building's exterior appearance tends to highlight the activities of men: the design activities of male architects; the construction activities of male carpenters, masons, and members of other building trades; and the civic improvement activities of male boosters who raised the funds for municipal and commercial buildings. Conversely, the destruction of historic interiors disproportionately obscures the activities of women—housewives, schoolteachers, shop assistants, waitresses, librarians, and others—who often accepted responsibility for arranging the interiors of architectural shells designed, built, and paid for by men. To destroy these interior arrangements is to erase important primary evidence of women's lives. Particularly in nondomestic buildings, the destruction of historic interiors eradicates evidence of women's work lives outside the home, reinforcing historical inaccuracies that suggest that women were once exclusively domestic creatures.[4]

This is certainly true of early-twentieth-century libraries, which served as workplaces for the first generation of American women to enter professional librarianship. To the extent that architecture defines and reinforces deeply held assumptions about appropriate gender behavior, these library interiors have untapped potential to illuminate the daily realities of women's lives. Interpreted in the social context of early-twentieth-century librarianship, the interiors demonstrate how male librarians attempted to use library design to constrain the professional activities of their female colleagues, while women used these same buildings in creative ways to subvert male control.

Interpreting the Library Interior

In the last years of the nineteenth century American librarianship was a male-dominated profession in crisis. Despite having campaigned for professional status since the organization of the American Library Association (ALA) in 1876, librarians commanded neither the prestige nor the salaries enjoyed by their contemporaries in law and medicine. The economic depression of the 1890s brought the crisis to a head and triggered a flurry of activity aimed at bolstering librarians' claims to professional status. Professional schools were established to give institutional recognition of specialized knowledge. A new focus on public service reinforced the librarian's social usefulness. And a new emphasis on masculinity in the language of librarianship was intended to dispel a stereotype of the male librarian as bookish and meek.

The last point is critical to understanding the gender politics of American librarianship. The old-style librarian was variously described as an "older custodian" or "a crabbed and unsympathetic old fossil." In each case the mental image is of someone of advanced age, inactive, physically diminished, all but emasculated.[5] In contrast, the new librarianship was associated with vigor and action. According to leaders in the profession, the new librarian needed a knowledge of the world of affairs, a head for business, a willingness to experiment, and the ability to exercise authority over others. This list of traits parallels almost exactly the qualifications that the nineteenth century had required for successful businessmen and suggests that librarians sought to take book work out of the feminine sphere of culture and to associate it with the masculine realm of commerce. In the process they undoubtedly hoped to push their field closer to the "true" professions of law and medicine.[6]

Ironically, these were the same years in which women were entering the profession in increasing numbers. By 1910, 78.5 percent of American library workers were women, many of whom were educated at women's colleges that had opened in the last quarter of the nineteenth century. With few other outlets for their skills, these women were often drawn to librarianship by what they understood as their natural aptitude for disseminating culture.[7]

Few male library leaders were happy about accepting women into their ranks, sensing that the women's presence threatened their campaign for professional recognition.[8] Yet other factors came into play. Not only were college-educated men choosing other careers, but, as one librarian so bluntly put it in 1904, women "do not cost as much as men." Indeed, the salary for a woman working in a small library in 1904 was two-thirds the pay that her male counterpart received for the same work.[9] For libraries with tight budgets, hiring a woman was an increasingly attractive option.

Faced with this reality, male librarians began to support a highly gendered professional hierarchy. In this official version of librarianship men would continue to dominate key executive and management roles, while women were encouraged to fill less prestigious and lower-paid positions. Even proponents of women in library work espoused this view. In 1911 John Cotton Dana of the Newark Library spelled out with unselfconscious clarity that women could aspire to be "assistants" and "subordinates" but rarely more. He also identified technical work such as cataloging, classifying, and index making as particularly well suited to female skills. In each case intellectual ability was not a job requirement. He suggested cataloging, for instance, for women who "write clearly, . . . are painstaking and accurate and can . . . follow exactly rules set for [their] guidance," while work at the lending desk was suited to those who "have an agreeable presence and [who] tend to be obliging rather than the opposite." Even Dana's description of reference work was stripped of its intellectual content when applied to women; although it is arguably the most intellectually rigorous area of library work, Dana felt that women could take it on if they were able to "feel almost instinctively what a book . . . can tell you."[10]

Dana's presentation of library work for women was based upon conventional stereotypes of the ideal woman as attractive, pleasant, malleable, detail oriented, naturally intuitive, but not too smart. By suggesting that women were innately suited for library tasks, Dana welcomed them into the field but also helped to rationalize their lower pay. After all, if women's work was innate, it was also largely unskilled. At the same time, by denying women the chance to exercise professional authority in the workplace, this definition of women's aptitudes would ensure that most women would remain subordinate within the hierarchy of the library staff. Indeed, Dana did nothing to challenge the accepted notion that management of others was a male aptitude and that the supervision of female workers a male prerogative. For library leadership, which remained predominantly male, it was an ideal means of tapping a pool of low-paid but highly skilled workers while reserving positions of authority for themselves.

This influx of women coincided with a library building boom, financed in large part by Andrew Carnegie, who provided funds for the construction of over sixteen hundred public library buildings in more than fourteen hundred American communities in the years before World War I. Fortunately for male librarians, Carnegie took the unprecedented step of following the design advice of professional librarians, maintaining a close working relationship with William Howard Brett of the Cleveland Public Library. Thus, the profession's officially approved principles of library design were outlined in *Notes on the Erection of Library Bildings* [*sic*], a brief pamphlet issued by the Carnegie Corporation in several editions from 1911 to 1917. It is worth noting that the *Notes* focused exclusively on the form of the small public library, in which the librarian was likely to be a woman, suggesting that Carnegie and his professional advisors were anxious to define the scope of activity for the female librarians who had appropriated the supervisory roles understood to belong more naturally to men.[11]

At first glance the *Notes* themselves present a remarkably simple setting, with only two spaces within the library designated for the librarian's use (fig. 9.2). Of primary importance was the charging desk, around which the rest of the library was planned. Here the librarian was expected to pass the greater part of the workday, overseeing the entire library from its central position. Of secondary importance was the multipurpose staff room, located in the basement, serving the staff as a resting room and providing a venue for the messier aspects of the librarian's job.

This seemingly straightforward arrangement represents a dramatic change in the way in which librarians worked. In the closed stack public library of the late nineteenth century, librarians and readers conducted much of their business at a long, straight counter designed primarily as a physical barrier, keeping the public from the library's treasures and marking the boundary between public space and staff areas (fig. 9.3). Here readers handed in request slips, approaching again a few minutes later to receive their books.

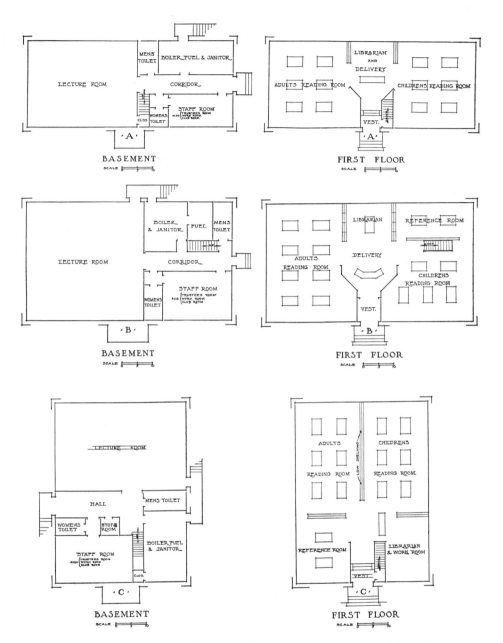

Fig. 9.2. James Bertram, "Notes on the Erection of Library Bildings [*sic*]," c. 1917, schematic plans A, B, and C. The low partitions subdividing the first floor plans allowed the librarian seated at the charging desk to supervise the book-lined reading rooms and reference areas. Photo courtesy of Carnegie Corporation Archives, Rare Book and Manuscript Library, Columbia University.

Fig. 9.3. Pittsburgh, Pa. Smithmeyer and Pelz, Carnegie Library and Music Hall, Allegheny City (now Pittsburgh), 1886–90. Delivery room, c. 1891. Although financed by Andrew Carnegie, this library predated the architectural reforms associated with Carnegie libraries erected in the twentieth century. Photo courtesy of Carnegie Library of Pittsburgh.

In the twentieth-century library represented in the *Notes,* the delivery counter was replaced by the charging desk. This was still the place where readers charged out books for home use, but it no longer served as a barrier between the reader and the books nor as a boundary between public and staff areas; indeed, in the open stack library of the twentieth century readers helped themselves to books directly from the shelf and (reversing nineteenth-century practice) presented the books to the librarian at the desk.

This change in library practice had an impact on the form of the charging desk. In the *Notes* all of the plans show the librarian's post as a small, compact desk, which did nothing to prevent readers from reaching the bookshelves. In plan B the ends of the charging desk are canted back toward the interior of the library, actually encouraging and speeding up the encounter between readers and books.

The charging desks in the *Notes* are little more than schematic representations, but their size, location, and shape are consistent with the charging desks sold by the Library Bureau, a commercial purveyor of library supplies organized by Melvil Dewey, inventor of the Dewey Decimal System. Custom fit to each library, the desks varied dramatically in size and shape, from the tiny U-shaped desk at the Solvay (N.Y.) Public Library (to be used by a single librarian) to the large square enclosures installed in Manhattan's branch libraries, with desks that were the size of small rooms and could accommodate five library workers (fig. 9.4).

Whatever their size, charging desks were meant to maximize book-handling efficiency, something that is particularly evident in their small-scale design (fig. 9.5). The interior of each Library Bureau charging desk

Fig. 9.4. Illustration from a Library Bureau catalog, showing the charging desk, or pen, in a branch library in Manhattan. "Library Bureau, Charging Desks: A Description of Representative Types . . . ," Boston, n.d., 7. Positioned to force library patrons to exit the library in a single file, this desk enhanced the librarian's ability to scrutinize each departing reader.

Fig. 9.5. Library Bureau charging desk, c. 1902. Library Catalog: A Descriptive List with Prices, (Boston), 1902, 50. The sales literature for this desk highlighted its "patent adjustable blocks" and other new technologies that allowed the librarian to achieve externally determined standards of "proper" library practice "with the minimum of effort."

contained drawers and cupboards, specially shaped to accommodate a full battery of library devices (also marketed by the Library Bureau). Date stamp, rubber bands, and paper clips all had their place at the charging desk, arranged within easy reach of the staff member seated there. Hinged and roller covers warded off dust, hid the clutter of cards, and gave the desk an unencumbered surface that signaled efficiency to turn-of-the-century eyes. In short, the centrally placed charging desk was the control center of the early-twentieth-century library: without it, the library was incomplete; with it, the library was transformed into an efficient machine for book distribution.

Such industrial analogies were favorites in turn-of-the-century library literature, which allowed male librarians to compare themselves to great business magnates. Yet the actual physical environment of the library suggested something less prestigious. Unlike the factory manager who supervised his workers from an elevated position, the librarian sat among her charges; if she could supervise their activities, they could subject her to comparable scrutiny. In their writings female librarians often described their sense of exposure at the desk. At the Hudson Park Branch of the New York Public Library a librarian equated the experience of the after-school rush with both natural and man-made disasters. At three o'clock, she explained, "the storm broke. There was what might be called a 'preliminary warning.' It was the sound of many feet pressing swiftly on from every direction and growing each instant nearer, then the big double doors swung open and an army of children marched in." In reality the charging desk was hardly a command post where the librarian reigned with calm composure. Instead, it was more a defensive fortress protecting the librarian in a losing battle against hostile attack. At the Hudson Park Branch the staff were unable to maintain authority from the desk and eventually stationed a police officer at the door who "only admitted one [child] when we sent one out."[12]

In practice the librarian in a small Carnegie library was less like a manager than she was like other pink-collar workers, and the charging desk was remarkably like the workstations of other jobs increasingly assigned to female workers at the turn of the century. Whether she was a librarian or a typewriter or telephone operator, the middle-class working woman found herself working in a seated position at a workstation shaped to minimize unnecessary movement (fig. 9.6). She was surrounded by technologically advanced tools that defined and structured her work into a series of repetitive tasks that she was unable to complete without specialized tools. Women's work was also measured quantitatively, in the number of cards filed, the number of letters typed, and the number of calls put through.

Although such feminized tasks often were described with elevated titles such as file executive, their physical settings were substantially different from the work spaces of male professionals. By the end of the nineteenth century professional men used control over their work space as one of the symbols of authority, carefully orchestrated to intimidate laymen and make them more receptive to expert advice. Having made an appointment to see a doctor or a lawyer, even the most prompt of clients was shown into an outer office. Left there to wait, the client had time to peruse the impressive framed certificates hanging on the walls and to peer at the spines of the leather-bound textbooks. In addition to these

Fig. 9.6. Buffalo, N.Y. Typewriter Operators' Department in Frank Lloyd Wright's Larkin Building, 1904. By requiring typists to reach and leave their desks in unison, Wright introduced a degree of synchronized movement to the workplace which enhanced the visual and symbolic elision between the female worker and the technological apparatuses that defined her work. Photo courtesy of William Clarkson.

signs of erudition, the practitioner also maintained control over the timing of the consultation, either by entering the room himself or by having a receptionist usher the client into his room.[13]

In contrast, women in predominantly female occupations had no such control over their work spaces. Whether seated in tight rows in the Typewriter Operators' Department of the Larkin Company Building or at a long bank of switchboards at the local telephone exchange, their work environment was completely controlled by others, with their work equipment bolted in place and themselves under the scrutiny of a male supervisor. Instead of having offices of their own, women in female occupations often had jobs that centered on reinforcing the spatial barriers that underlined and enhanced the professional prestige of men, who actually wielded authority and enjoyed professional status.[14]

Women's work environments were particularly insidious in encouraging women to enact a specific set of gender roles and thus in involving women in reinforcing the gender assumptions that oppressed them. Consider Lillian Gunter's description of a typical afternoon at work at the Carnegie library in Gainesville, Texas, in 1923: "The monthly report must be handed in to the new commissioner's court and it is not yet finished. The assistant librarian is at home, ill with the flu. I have a reference to look up, 'Find a copy of a mock marriage.' . . . Ten children want to use the same number of the 'Reader's Guide.' Ten more want to find a recitation or declamation. Six or seven are hovering around the loan desk to have their books charged or discharged. A branch librarian is selecting books to take back with her. Two teachers from the country want help with their work." After recounting a number of telephone interruptions, Gunter finished the passage with the editorial comment, "Ye Gods!"[15]

In fact, Lillian Gunter was a leader in her profession, a founding member of the Southwest Library Association, an early advocate of the county library idea, and the author of Texas county library legislation. Yet her work environment reinforced a very different public perception of her. In this setting her own work seemed unimportant, interruptible. Because she was always on call, she was bombarded with a large number of simultaneous requests that made it difficult for her to complete the easiest task. Constant interruptions required mental agility, stamina, and patience, but, if any of those qualities slipped even for a moment, she risked seeming scattered, even scatterbrained.

Gunter was not a helpless pawn in this situation; like others of the first generation of female librarians, she used a variety of means to break her connection with the charging desk. Gunter found refuge in the mobility of county library work, spending much of her time driving country roads to deliver books to outlying ranches. Other women found work with children, which took them into specially designed children's rooms and story hour niches. Although built upon conventional definitions of the female sphere, these new professional specialties actually helped combat the loss of professional prestige which threatened women in librarianship. The children's librarian, for instance, had to be well versed in emerging theories of child psychology, claiming a theoretical knowledge base that al-

lowed her to claim greater autonomy than others within the library hierarchy, if not actually higher pay.[16]

Preserving the Library Interior

In order to use historic buildings more effectively to interpret women's
lives, preservation advocates and design professionals who share their
concerns need to give more serious consideration to saving their interiors. Yet the issue of preserving early-twentieth-century library interiors is
complicated by the subsequent actions of the women whose lives we seek
to interpret. Female librarians were in fact early advocates of the liberal-
ization of library policies. As they became less concerned with monitor-
ing readers' movements, they became more willing to relocate the centrally placed charging desk. At the same time, a professional ethos that
placed a high priority on collection development put added pressure on
librarians to rearrange library interiors in order to eke out more book
storage space from the building's finite architectural shell. As directors of
small libraries, female librarians often played key roles in dismantling the
material traces of their own professional past.

What is more, the process of remaking the library interior has acceler-
ated in recent years, thanks in large part to computer technology. Libraries
that can afford the cost of retrospective conversion (typically university libraries and public libraries in large cities such as New York, Seattle, and
Cincinnati) have destroyed their card catalogs, burning the cards and selling off the golden oak Library Bureau cabinets that once protected them.
As an exact contemporary of the charging desk and the feminization of librarianship, the card catalog is seen by some observers as the victim of
contemporary gender politics. In an in-depth consideration of the value
of the card catalog, Nicholson Baker has suggested that "the impulse to
burn [catalog cards] is there . . . because library administrators (more
often male than female) want so keenly to distance themselves from the
quasi-clerical associations that surround traditional librarianship" and
from "the lowly, meek-and-mild [female] public librarian as she exists in
the popular mind." For Baker the functionalist argument that a library is
"out of space" simply masks a more complex network of highly gendered
value judgments about the past, present, and future of library work.[17]

In such a context attempts to preserve historic library interiors are sure to face both practical and ideological obstacles. Nonetheless, there have already been calls to make historic library interiors more visible. Confronted with the fact that Seattle's 1906 central library building was torn down in 1957, that city's Public Art Commission engaged Judy Anderson, Gail Lee Dubrow, and John Koval to produce *The Library Book,* a limited-edition publication that combined historical narrative, oral history, and period photographs to evoke the richness of the library experience. Although the library interiors are long gone, the book reminds readers of the old library's "subtle system of spatial controls" and its role as a work space for female librarians.[18]

Within the library profession the focus has been on extant buildings. George Bobinski, dean of the School of Information and Library Studies at the State University of New York at Buffalo, has instigated a campaign to identify one well-preserved Carnegie library building in which to establish a museum commemorating the Carnegie library program and the history of early American public libraries more generally. His goal is to fit out the building with turn-of-the-century library furniture and equipment in order to "show what a public library was like" for users and for librarians.[19]

Yet such efforts on their own can do little to challenge the underlying value system that sees library interiors as expendable. In part the issue is bound up with the larger question of preservation's very purpose. If the goal of preservation is merely to save appealing architectural elements from the past, then it may continue to seem more prudent to sacrifice interior elements that may impede adaptive reuse. But, if preservation aspires to do more—to enhance public awareness of urban history, to illuminate the gendered division of labor—then it is time to recognize interior furnishings and fittings as integral components of a building's historic character. Instead of beginning the preservation process by discarding old library fittings, we need to begin with the assumption that the charging desk and other library furnishings are indispensable features of the historic library, as much defining characteristics of the building as the rusticated basement and classical columns on the street facade.

How, then, might the charging desk coexist with newer library arrangements? Even if it no longer serves its original function, it might well stand as a relatively compact three-dimensional exhibition of an important aspect of library history. Provided with a chair of the right height, it can allow readers to get a librarian's-eye view of the original library rooms. Outfitted with the appropriate library tools and facsimile library cards, it can encourage the curious to discover for themselves just what each specially shaped drawer was designed to hold. Stocked with a well-prepared information sheet, it can direct library users to other sources that have been compiled to suggest the character of life in the early-twentieth-century library, which might include period photographs of the library in use as well as oral histories collected from longtime members of the library staff and from adults who checked books out from the other side of the desk as children.

In short, historic interiors play a key role in preserving women's history. If we continue to sacrifice interior spaces in order to maintain the historical integrity of the streetscape, we risk perpetuating the gender inequalities of our history. If we venerate architectural containers that were the products of male building skill, we also need to value the material evidence of women's activities outside the domestic sphere. The built environment can tell us much about the interaction between men and women in the public arena, but we have the responsibility to rethink the practices of historic preservation in order to allow that environment to speak.

CHAPTER 10

Women in the Southern West Virginia Coalfields

Susan M. Pierce

The story of the southern West Virginia coalfields traditionally has belonged to men. It is an industrial story, characterized by its masculine personification: King Coal. The lead characters are the mines and the men who work in them and run them. In the late nineteenth and early twentieth centuries, when roles were strictly divided above or below ground, women played supporting roles within the company, community, and family unit. The daily lives of women in the coalfields have not been the primary focus of scholarship or of interpretative exhibits at museums or historic sites and buildings associated with the industry.[1]

Careful study of social and labor history, as well as recent historic preservation initiatives, reveals the variety of roles played by women in the coal camps and communities (fig. 10.1). Women were wage earners as well as family and community leaders. For the miner's wife or mother, her life centered upon the mine. She prepared meals for the miners and was up as early or late as the assigned shift schedule required. She walked past the coal-loading tipple on her way to the company store. From the door of her house she could view coke ovens burning as she washed coal dust from curtains and clothing. She tended the garden and raised pigs, chickens, and cows.

According to Janet Greene: "Women earned cash by taking in boarders and laundry, selling butter and eggs, and serving as bootleggers and prostitutes. They scavenged coal for fuel and sold company scrip for cash. Women worked as clerks in company stores and as nannies and maids in the homes of company officials, while others cooked and made beds in

Fig. 10.1. Unknown location. Coal camp women sewing and ironing on the porch, n.d. Photo courtesy of the Eastern Regional Coal Archives.

company owned boardinghouses."[2] Greene's essay looked primarily at the women of the coal camps. However, there are examples from each class of society. Using photographs, oral histories, and diaries, personal accounts can be drawn to reveal details of both men and women's lives. These stories bring to life the history of the West Virginian coalfields. Unfortunately, the sites and buildings that are remnants of this history are rapidly vanishing. Actual mining structures have been broken apart, reused, or scrapped. Whole towns have disappeared after the associated mine has closed.

In response to the continued destruction of this built environment, the West Virginia State Historic Preservation Office completed a five-county Coal Heritage Survey in 1991. Funded by the National Park Service, this survey documented the Pocahontas and Flat Top Coal Fields, which are located roughly within Boone, Logan, McDowell, Mingo, and Wyoming Counties. The historic inventory documented approximately thirty-seven hundred extant resources, including workers' housing, company stores, community buildings, hospitals, churches, hotels, coal tipples, mine portals, coke ovens, and other associated structures and equipment.

Ironically, the coalfields remain largely represented by residential building types of the extant company towns. Of the total number of inventory forms completed, only 156 were directly associated with mining activity; 752 community buildings, including commercial, governmental, educational, and religious resources, were surveyed. The remaining 2,774 photos record the coalfield housing. These buildings are readily identified with the domestic life associated with the history of this extractive industry.[3] Using documentary sources that reveal the experiences of individual women, one can interpret the remaining buildings to understand women's daily lives in the coalfields.

Pocahontas, Virginia, and Bramwell, West Virginia: Towns Segregated by Social Class

Company towns in the Pocahontas Coal Fields were segregated by job position. The established hierarchy of company employees was evident in the location and style of housing for the officials and the miners. The housing set aside for the superintendents was usually larger and more architecturally distinguished, reflecting popular styles of the period. In contrast, the rows of workers' housing for the miners relied upon a set of repetitive patterns drawn by company engineers.[4] A woman's home and its location identified her status within this hierarchy. Two neighboring towns, Pocahontas, Virginia, and Bramwell, West Virginia, reflect the social divisions set up by corporate management.

Pocahontas, Virginia, was laid out in the early 1880s by the Southwest Virginia Improvement Company to serve as a residential community for miners. The primary commercial area of the town consists of late-Victorian, two-story, brick, commercial buildings with cast-metal storefronts and cornices. The majority of the town's residential buildings are modest frame dwellings for the miners, supervisors, and engineers associated with Pocahontas No. 1 Mine, located about one mile from town. Laid out in a block plan of fifty-foot lots, many of the town's original buildings have survived, including the company doctor's office, the millinery shop, the opera house, and several saloons.[5]

From 1881 to 1885 Pocahontas was the home of Harriet Lathrop, wife of

Fig. 10.2. Pocahontas, Va. Portrait of Harriet Lathrop, wife of Pocahontas Coal Company superintendent. Photo courtesy of the Eastern Regional Coal Archives.

the company mining engineer, who was also the mine superintendent (fig. 10.2). Her memoirs document her early married life in this company town. Originally from Pennsylvania, she described her life in letters home to her mother. Her house was the first finished in the new town, a "double house much like the miners' houses."[6] Each side of the two-story, board-and-batten duplex contained five rooms and a cellar. Although she first lived in a duplex provided by the management, this lodging was considered inappropriate to the couple's position in the community. They were moved to a single-unit home considered more in keeping with their company status.

Lathrop's memoirs record the development of the town. "By July 1883 we had a company store, a milkman who came every day with printed milk tickets and who rang a bell, a ten pin alley, a butcher who knew how to cut meat properly, a dress making and millinery establishment. . . . What more could one ask for?"[7] She also described events that affected her outlook on life. She described the first mining accident, on March 13, 1884, which killed 150 men,[8] and she described her fear during a miners' strike. But what was perhaps the most personal event reveals the harshness of their lives:

> As a girl I had always avoided . . . seeing my friends who were ill, or attending funerals, so that at the time of my marriage I had visited only a few who were ill and had attended only one funeral. My first experience came after we had moved in to . . . Pocahontas when the young telegraph operator sent for me to come. His wife was ill and the newborn baby had died. . . . When, with a lump in my throat so large I could hardly swallow, I arrived at the house, the young husband put his head on my shoulder and sobbed. They were so young, and were crushed by the loss of their baby . . . when they asked me to make a dress for the baby, and lay it in its casket, again, there was nothing for me to do but say "yes."
>
> There was no way of getting a small casket in time, so I took a small box (the baby was very tiny) lined it with silk, and covered it with white broadcloth, made a little dress for the baby, and did the best I could with what there was to be had.[9]

Lathrop created personal relationships despite her status as the superintendent's wife. She seems not to have minded that she lived in a duplex nor that she assisted grieving parents. Her husband held a key role as liaison in the coal camp, representing the company and its management to the miners. Their housing was likewise distinguished. Despite these restrictions, perhaps the flatter topography of Pocahontas encouraged mingling despite their social status. If Pocahontas' layout contributed to social flexibility, the topography of nearby Bramwell contributed to its social inflexibility.

Established in 1885, Bramwell was founded in order to provide a socially appropriate community for investors and operators of the coalfields. The primary commercial avenue of shops, Town Hall, the Bank of Bramwell, and several churches are located within the tight meander of the river. Several homes are located here and along the hillside above. Their architectural style reflected the owners' prosperity and sheltered them from the mining activities around them. A concerted effort was made to "overcompensate for the lack of 'society' in southern West Virginia [in the early twentieth century] by building large homes."[10]

Bramwell was the home of Phoebe Douty Goodwill (fig. 10.3). Unlike Harriet Lathrop, it appears that she was unaware of her surroundings. In researching the National Register nomination for Bramwell, author Beth Hager learned that Goodwill did not make Bramwell her permanent home. Born in Pennsylvania, Goodwill moved to West Virginia after her wedding in October 1887. Socializing with other former Pennsylvanians in Bramwell, she also returned to Shamokin, Pennsylvania, for a portion of the year. For example, she returned home to Shamokin, Pennsylvania, for the birth of her first child in 1889.[11] Diary entries record parties, dances, afternoon tea, tennis matches, and baseball games. Weddings and parties were decorated with floral arrangements and party goods im-

Fig. 10.3. Bramwell, W.Va. Historic photograph of the Phillip and Phoebe Goodwill Home, c. 1906. Photo courtesy of the Eastern Regional Coal Archives, Craft Memorial Library.

Fig. 10.4. Bramwell, W. Va. Home of Katherine Hewitt, 1994. Photo by the author.

ported by train. Hager describes red carpets stretching from churches to the train station and block-long trellises decorating these affairs.[12] Women of Bramwell generally did not pursue charitable works. Although there was a Red Cross effort during World War I, "not until the Depression of the 1933 do the Goodwill diaries mention relief work through the church for the coal field [poor]."[13]

Unlike the more ephemeral housing provided for workers in most coalfield towns, Bramwell's residential building stock consisted of well constructed buildings that reflected the popular, architectural high styles of the period. Goodwill's three-story home reflects the characteristics of the Victorian and Queen Anne styles. Originally built in 1894 and re-modeled in 1904, the interior woodwork and stained-glass windows are refined and reflect the influences of the Arts and Crafts movement.[14]

At least one building was built for a female client. Katherine Hewitt was the wife of the first mayor of Bramwell and director of the Pocahontas Company. Ten years after her husband's death, Hewitt com-missioned a new home on the property of her first (fig. 10.4). Designed by a Philadelphia firm, the exterior facade is composed of native blue-stone but does not resemble the late-nineteenth-century Victorian styles. The Colonial Revival project included low interior ceilings for the asymmetrical floor plan. Hewitt continued to influence and lead the community through her social status, albeit through decisions of style and construction which were traditionally reserved for men.[15]

Workers' Housing

In early efforts of West Virginia's National Register program, nominations focused on the upper classes of coal community society. The homes of the coal investors, officials, and superintendents were recognized for their association with significant persons contributing to the development of the coal industry. Workers' housing typically was ignored. For example, the original National Register of Historic Places nomination for the Bramwell Historic District included only the commercial district and the homes of the "coal barons." It took twelve years to gain recognition for the subdivisions of workers' housing. In 1995 a boundary increase for the Bramwell district was approved that included workers' residences. The subdivisions noted in this amendment extend along the Bluestone River. They are comprised of the smaller, noncontiguous mining communities that are now incorporated into the Town of Bramwell. The subdivisions, Cooper and Freeman, were named after coal company operators, John Cooper of the Mill Creek Coal and Coke Company and John Freeman of the Caswell Coal and Coke Company.[16]

The delay in gaining recognition for the workers' housing can be attributed to its commonness. Yet its repetitive nature is central to understanding the social and economic relations that dominated coal town life. As the text of the Bramwell Additions nomination states, "Identical design and construction of the individual houses within each cluster [are] indicative of company control."[17] Miners were not viewed as individuals; neither were their homes.

The coal works in McDowell County are another example of standard construction methods instituted by company management. In 1902 J. P. Morgan's U.S. Coal and Coke Company acquired the lease of fifty thousand acres of the Pocahontas Coal Fields from the Flat Top Land Association, a subsidiary of the Norfolk and Western Rail Road. By 1910

U.S. Coal and Coke had built twelve individual company towns linked by hard-surfaced road and rail lines. These were known as the "Gary Works."[18] Remnants of these settlements were identified by the Coal Heritage Survey. At least four were considered eligible for entry in the National Register: Elbert, Filbert, Ream, and Wilcoe. Often these camps were noted by number, such as Elbert No. 7 and Filbert No. 9. The numbering system contributes to the sense of anonymity of the miners.[19]

Existing documentation shows the extensive planning by U.S. Coal and Coke for these towns (fig. 10.5).[20] As plans became reality, framing went up, and company field representatives photographed the new homes.[21] Unfortunately, approximately twelve hundred of them were demolished in the 1950s as U.S. Coal and Coke's successor, U.S. Steel, abandoned its interests in the coalfields (fig. 10.6). Until recently, intact rows of housing remained to demonstrate the impact this construction activity had on the landscape of McDowell County and the domestic sphere.[22] Devastating floods in May and July 2001 damaged several hundred additional buildings. The Federal Emergency Management Agency (FEMA) has begun removal of condemned properties, further impacting the historic character of the federally designated Coal Heritage Area.

Despite the uniform quality of the Gary Works, ethnic characteristics of the community are evident. The Greek Orthodox Church in Gary carries the traditional round dome associated with this denomination.[23] Historic photographs also reveal ethnic and cultural activities in the camps. Christmas, May Day, and other festive activities were celebrated by the community.

Domestic Life in the Coal Camps

The building stock of the company towns and camps is complemented by the depiction of the daily activities within them. The character of the workers' housing illustrates the quality of life in the company camps. Recognition of these buildings by the National Register of Historic Places presents a more complete picture of the coal industry. The use of oral histories in combination with archival collections of photographs, scrapbooks, and boardinghouse ledgers expand our understanding of company town life. Field representatives of the company photographed the everyday life of the coal camps to report the conditions of the camps to absentee officials.

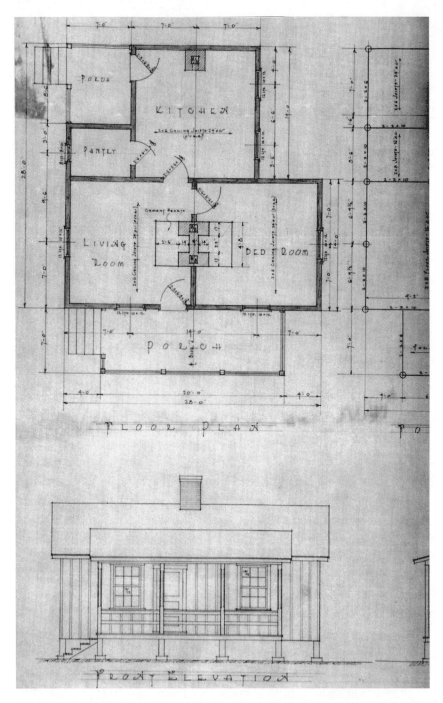

Fig. 10.5. McDowell County, W. Va. Typical floor plan and elevation prepared by the U.S. Coal and Coke Company for construction in the "Gary Works." Plan courtesy of the Eastern Regional Coal Archives.

Fig. 10.6. McDowell County, W. Va. Construction of a row of workers' housing under way in the "Gary Works." Photo courtesy of the Eastern Regional Coal Archives.

Photographs captured women ironing, washing, and tending their gardens. Contests were held to judge the best home gardens. Well-scrubbed children attended elementary school classes, women and families shopped at the company store or worked on household duties on the front porch, and families attended special events such as the arrival of Santa Claus by horse, a wedding procession, and the celebration of May Day.[24]

For women of the working class the company town was their entire world. Unless they left by the railroad to visit friends or family in neighboring camps, they spent most of their lives within the company town. Although teachers and schools were provided, families sent children away to school to live with relatives outside the camp. Monthly deductions to the miner's wages were made for rent, electricity, and running water if available. A running account of purchases at the company store was kept. Company scrip substituted for money.[25]

Many women were responsible only for their personal household, but others worked outside their home as domestics, store clerks, or seamstresses. Sallie B. Robinson, for example, moved to Maybeury, West Virginia, in 1930. She washed, ironed, and cleaned house. From the store she could buy beans, potatoes, coffee, sugar, flour, clothes, animal feed, and cigarettes. She kept a cow and grew a garden, picking berries for canned fruit. Her home did not have indoor plumbing: the company provided water from outside pumps.[26]

Women also supervised the company boardinghouse for single miners. Miss Roddy was manager of the Gary Clubhouse. Her 1903 photograph shows a strong woman.[27] Frances Huffman recalls her mother's responsibilities at the boardinghouse in Bishop, Virginia. Breakfast at 4:30 A.M. included hot biscuits, eggs, sausage, and bacon for some twenty-five to thirty men per day. Sixteen men were housed in the mill house and the same number above the store. Miss Roddy remained on the company payroll until 1957.[28]

Daily activities centered on the company store. A woman would be familiar with its layout: groceries on the left, butcher in the back, and ready-to-wear clothes for women upstairs. Companies also provided health care and education, often importing doctors, nurses, and teachers to the towns.[29]

On the Other Side of the Tracks

While the company's photos can document women's lives in the coal camps, they present a biased point of view. Companies such as the U.S. Coal and Coke Company photographed the camps to share information with their investors, offering a sanitized view of the Gary Works, only showing what the company wanted people to see. Fortunately, other documentation and primary sources also contribute information. Movements for social reform produced another set of sources important for interpreting women's lives in the coal camps. A small temperance tract, *Sodom and Gomorrah of Today or the History of Keystone,* provides a lurid story of prostitution in McDowell County. Written in 1912 by "[a] Virginia Ladd," the author depicts "Cinder Bottom," a neighborhood of brothels. The pamphlet illustrates with several stories the wickedness of this occupation. Miss Mary Miller, a local madam, raises enough money to build her own home but dies before its completion. The pamphlet states that "her guilty, sin-stained soil was called before the bar of God to receive punishment for the deeds done while here on earth."[30] Women suffer from syphilis. Gambling, robbery, and murder are frequent events in Cinder Bottom; dead bodies are discovered along the railroad tracks. One young woman escapes kidnapping, and her abductors are arrested for white slave trafficking.[31] Visiting the town today, it is difficult to imagine Cinder Bottom in this illicit context. Only a few abandoned commercial buildings line the railroad tracks today.

This pamphlet is a unique primary source. Unfortunately, other pamphlets have not yet been found which examine, for example, healthcare or education issues of women living in the coal communities. One must rely, instead, on oral histories, census material, and other surveys.

Reform and Mother Jones

The preceding sections suggest new opportunities for interpreting the lives of women in the coal camps, history most clearly marked by the housing associated with company towns. To date, the recognition of women in the coalfields has been limited to significant or exceptional individuals. Mother Jones has received much attention, for example, for her promotion of unionization among the miners and better living conditions in the camps. Leading parades of women banging "tin pans as if they were cymbals,"[32] "she served as a role model for many [women] in their struggle for freedom from the suffering and oppression of the coal camps."[33] During the 1912-13 coal strikes in the Paint Creek and Cabin Creek areas of Kanawha County, she was arrested and charged with the theft of a machine gun, an attempt to blow up a train with dynamite, and conspiracy to murder. Her imprisonment became the focus of media attention. Press coverage of her illness during her house detention drew national attention to her fight for better living conditions in the coalfields.[34] The National Park Service thematic study of women's history identified her prison site as a National Historic Landmark for its significance in labor history (fig. 10.7). The boardinghouse in Pratt, located outside Charleston, was designated in 1990. The building was in poor condition, however, and was demolished in 1996.[35]

Identifying and Preserving Historic Sites

Only the Mother Jones Prison is directly associated with women's history. Most National Register listings identify company officials and associated

Fig. 10.7. Pratt, W. Va. Mother Jones Prison, c. 1992. Photo courtesy of the State Historic Preservation Office, West Virginia Division of Culture and History.

industrial history. The National Register of Historic Places relies upon the criteria of associated significance with key events and people. Unless the individual is unique or accomplished, the resource is not eligible for listing on the National Register. If, however, an associated broad pattern of history can be developed, listing is possible.

Early survey and nomination efforts do not discuss women's history. The 1991 Coal Heritage Survey focuses on the buildings and structures of the industry. The 1992 National Park Service Special Resource Study for Bramwell identifies significant men associated with the historic resources. The original National Register nomination for Bramwell focuses on the commercial district and the "millionaires' row." The amended nomination now includes the rows of workers' housing. The statement of significance adds new information regarding the workers' housing and their ethnic diversity. It includes two brief references to women as founders of local churches: "Elizabeth Owen Jones provided funds for the Memorial Methodist Church, constructed in 1878"; and "in 1885 Mrs. Cooper provided funds for construction of the Mill Creek Missionary Baptist Church."[36] The nomination also identifies the black poet Anne Spencer as a native of Bramwell.[37] Thus, by finding adequate testimony, women's history can be added to National Register nomination efforts in West Virginia.

Women's history can be revealed through examination of family letters, diaries, and photographs. As stated earlier, the nature of the industry is masculine. In a world in which women played supporting roles, meeting the National Register Criteria will be difficult. Future study may not result in identifying significant individual women and their associated cultural resources, but perhaps research will illuminate the personal relationships within these communities. History will then address not only the role of the miners but also that of the women at home and in the community.

Preservation of the built environment is difficult. The Mother Jones Prison did not have a public constituency organized to protect the deteriorated house. In poor condition and supported by metal rods, it was difficult to repair. Although a plaque on the house identified the building as Mother Jones's prison, the building was privately owned, and its associated significance was simply not enough to save it. Is the building a footnote to this woman's contribution to labor history? Mother Jones on parade through the various coal camps and during speeches at the State Capitol presents more vivid images than those of a sick woman confined to a house in Pratt. Without the building, can history be told as completely?

Future Recognition and Interpretation

As heritage tourism and historic preservation efforts mature and grow, there will be opportunities to conduct additional oral histories and archival research focused on the coal communities. Established by Congress in 1996, the Coal Heritage Area recognizes the national significance of the southern West Virginia coalfields, specifically noting its contributions to the industrialization of the United States, the organization of workers into trade unions, and the unique culture of the Appalachian region.[38] Planning efforts for the area will identify interpretive themes as a framework for developing cultural tourism. The domestic and social history of the coalfields could provide the necessary springboards for interpreting women's lives in the coalfields as mothers, nurses, teachers, and in other roles. These efforts could be made in conjunction with the West Virginia University history programs and the West Virginia Women's Commission.

Current exhibitions focus on mining using company photographs, store scrip, lunch pails, lanterns, and other memorabilia. The Beckley (W. Va.) Exhibition Mine highlights an underground tour of a deep mine. Future exhibitions focusing on social and domestic issues such as nutrition, health care, child rearing, and education in the coal camps could identify significant individuals from among these professions.

King Coal has made a tremendous impact on the lives of all West Virginians in the southern coalfields, but its history remains incomplete. As shown by the examples of Harriet Lathrop, Phoebe Douty Goodwill, and Mother Jones, women chose various roles in the southern coalfields. They provided comfort, entertainment, food, lodging, and support to the miners. Without their anonymous hard work each day, the miner could not have successfully completed his own responsibilities. We will benefit from future studies that recognize the significant contributions of women to the history of the coalfields in southern West Virginia.

CHAPTER 11

"A Night with Venus, a Moon with Mercury"
The Archaeology of Prostitution in Historic Los Angeles

Julia G. Costello

In the spring of 1996 a large archaeological project in downtown Los Angeles uncovered rich deposits related to the city's red-light district circa 1880–1907. A large privy, once located behind a parlor house at 327 Aliso Street, was densely filled with broken household goods including more exotic items such as French porcelain, crystal liqueur tumblers, stemmed water goblets and wine glasses, and a remarkable number of cream jars and medicine bottles. Another artifact-filled privy, associated with a row of "cribs," documented the bleak commerce that had taken place in these small rooms that were rented by the hour. With the buildings long destroyed and documents meager, preservation of this aspect of women's history relies on telling the tale encrypted in the discarded artifacts left behind.

Archaeology, the primary source of information on prehistoric cultures, is also effective for studying more recent times, particularly in illuminating the lives of those who did not dwell in the spotlight of written history. Women, minorities, subjugated peoples, children, and many other populations overlooked (or narrowly depicted) by chroniclers, government documents, and economic accounts are democratically present in the archaeological record. The rubbish of living—what archaeologists study—is edited by universal processes of decay and disruption which are evenly distributed across social, economic, gender, and cultural boundaries. Although little written documentation survives on the Los Angeles prostitutes, their artifacts speak eloquently of their lives in the demimonde.

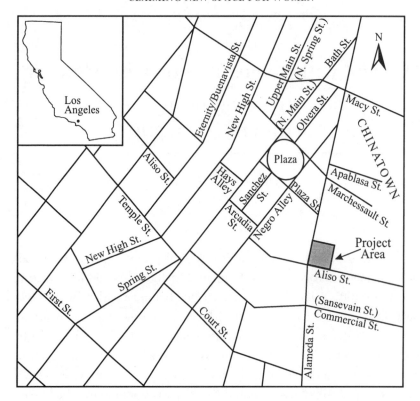

Fig. 11.1. Los Angeles, Calif. The archaeological excavations took place on a site adjacent to Los Angeles' historic Mexican Period Plaza and later Chinatown. Map by Maria Riberio.

I directed the archaeological investigation along with Adrian Praetzellis.[1] The four-acre project area, abutting Union Station on the south, was the building site for the twelve-story Headquarters Facility building of the Metropolitan Water District of Southern California (Metropolitan).[2] As the project area lay near L.A.'s historic Mexican Period Pueblo and later Chinatown, we expected to find important remains (fig. 11.1). California laws require archaeological and historical studies in advance of construction, and Metropolitan provided the funding and support for this research.[3]

Fieldwork was carried out over ten weeks and involved a crew of sixteen archaeologists. During the excavations we were looking particularly for artifact-rich features: historic period pits and depressions that were filled, upon abandonment, with masses of household refuse. These types of features include such once-common facilities as privies, cisterns, wells, and trash pits, all typically located in backyards. As these refuse pits are usually filled in a short period of time (weeks or months), they are unique time capsules of material culture from specific households at specific periods of time.

Heavy machinery was first used to scrape off carefully and remove from five to as much as twenty feet of fill, imported for the Union Station parking lot in the 1930s, and expose the buried nineteenth-century ground surface. This exposure was then cleaned with shovels and trowels to reveal the archaeological features. Historic city maps allowed us to resurvey the old lot boundaries onto the newly exposed surface. We could then tell exactly which lot each archaeological feature belonged to and, through documentary research, who was living on the lot at the time the feature was filled with discarded items.

Our excavations yielded seventeen important artifact deposits: the privy complex behind the parlor house at 327 Aliso Street filled in about 1900; a contemporary privy related to a row of cribs; nine privies relating to middle-class and blue-collar families on Aliso Street from 1875 to 1895; three artifact-rich features documenting the lives of Chinese vegetable sellers in the 1910s; and five deposits of mixed attribution. This chapter focuses on discoveries related to the parlor house and cribs and demonstrates how artifacts have the power to reveal hidden aspects of women's history.

Excavating Women's History

Archaeologists excavate for history, finding stories of the past recorded in the artifacts and landscapes of our predecessors. As anthropologists, we try to use this data to reconstruct past cultures and to view these societies in the context of broad human processes. The rise of feminist perspectives was reflected in the discipline as researchers, particularly women, began to step away from male-centered research questions and interpretations. As models for interpreting historic events become less rigid and stereotyped, artifacts can provide clearer reflections of both men's and women's lives.

In 1991 two important compilations of feminist articles were published, *Engendering Archaeology: Women in Prehistory*, edited by Joan Gero and Margaret Conkey; and *Gender in Historical Archaeology*, edited by Donna Seifert.[4] While Gero and Conkey's work reveals how our unchallenged assumptions about gender in the present guides our interpretations of ancient societies, Seifert's volume examines relationships between site data (archaeological and historical) and gender as a structural principle of culture.

Pioneering research on women's role in history was conducted by Kathleen Deagan on the fifteenth-century Spanish town of St. Augustine, where Native American women, through intermarriage with Spanish males (*mestizaje*), exerted a powerful influence on colonial culture. More recently, archaeologist Diana diZerega Wall has produced a compelling study of how women in New York City in the period from 1790 to 1830 contributed to the developing separation of home and workplace, ironically resulting in a restricted social role that would burden women for over a century. Elizabeth Scott has also produced an illuminating scholarly volume entitled *Those of Little Note: Gender, Race, and Class in Historical Archaeology*. Interpreting women's past has also, thankfully, encouraged not only scientific but empathetic insights, ably represented by Janet D. Spector's feminist fiction about a young Sioux woman in early-nineteenth-century South Dakota, *What This Awl Means*.[5]

A Brief History of Prostitution in Los Angeles

The Spanish town of El Pueblo de Nuestra Señora la Reina de Los Angeles was founded in 1781, relocated several times, and finally settled in 1818 at its present location just above the flood plain of the Porciúncula (Los Angeles) River. Activities centered around the town plaza, and it was adjacent to the plaza, on the block bordered by Alameda and Aliso Streets, that Irish entrepreneur Matthew Keller purchased vineyards and built his winery in the 1850s. Optimistic about the city's future, he developed residential lots along his vineyard's Aliso Street frontage, selling home sites to middle-class professionals.[6]

At this time L.A.'s prostitution trade was in its infancy. The estimated twenty local prostitutes were augmented in 1854 by the arrival of a troop of "lewd women" from San Francisco, an event reportedly inspiring a celebration by established citizens. The profession grew apace with the town, however, and by 1874 was a perceived public nuisance. In an effort to contain sexual pandering, a special district was set up in which prostitution was tacitly legal. By the late 1880s this district was centered on the Alameda–Aliso Street intersection, from which former respectable residents had long fled to more fashionable parts of town (fig. 11.2). A police raid in 1887 included a brothel on Aliso Street which netted madam Hattie Walker and her "boarders" Jane Doe, Ethel Scholer, Georgie French, Gypsy Rivers, and Minnie Palmer.[7] These women may have been residing at 327 Aliso, the site of the excavated privy.

During the 1890s emphasis shifted from brothels to cribs (fig. 11.3). The former were residential establishments run by madams who fed and

Fig. 11.2. Los Angeles, Calif., c. 1899, looking west along Aliso Street to its intersection with Alameda. To the right, in the middle ground, the lines of single-story cribs can be seen. By 1906 seven brothels are on the north side of Aliso in the center of the block. (Cf. map of fig. 11.4.) Photo courtesy of University of Southern California, Regional History Center.

Fig. 11.3. Los Angeles, Calif. A prostitute in the window of a crib, in or near the project area, in 1898. Photo courtesy of Department of Special Collections, Charles E. Young Research Library, University of Southern California.

housed their employees. Madams retained a large percentage of the clients' fees, which ranged from one dollar to five dollars, and all profits from sales of liquor. At the lower end brothels resembled cheap boardinghouses, while more expensive brothels attempted to simulate upperclass Victorian parlors and are sometimes differentiated as "parlor houses."[8] Cribs were the lowest-ranking establishments: complexes of single rooms simply furnished with a bed, washstand, and chair. Crib workers rented these rooms for about seventy-five dollars per shift per month; they lived elsewhere in town. The client was usually charged fifty cents and typically did not even remove his boots.[9]

Once prostitution was established, it became a big industry. Local landlords charged prostitutes higher rentals, and merchants inflated the prices of everything from liquor to lamps. Madams passed the exorbitant prices back to the customer. Such lucrative investment attracted big speculators such as Chris Buckley, crib owner and Democratic Party boss of San Francisco. Closed out of San Francisco in the 1890s by a reform mayor, Buckley teamed up with local developer Bartolo Ballerino, eventually controlling most of the crib district bordering Alameda Street and the Plaza area. Old L.A. families were also involved in red-light real estate. Lines of nearly seventy cribs (10 x 24 ft. each) were erected on Matthew Keller's old vineyard land by his sons-in-law George and Frank Shafer.[10] The once stately Keller home was turned over to location agents Blanche and Jean Rappet, who also managed the Shafers' Horseshoe Saloon, located at the entrance to crib-lined Easy Jeanette Street (the intuitive association of this street name with prostitution could not be confirmed).

The Progressive movement, which gained momentum in the early twentieth century, was to end these halcyon days of L.A.'s prostitution. The first to go were the cribs, targeted not only for their degraded status but also for being controlled by well-known underworld financiers. In December 1903 the citizenry waged war on the district: "Surging up and down and in and out among the alleys and narrow passages of the district of the scarlet women, yesterday afternoon, the hosts of righteousness and the hosts of hell met, and as one of the leading workers in the social-purity crusade expressed it, 'The Battle of Armageddon had begun.'"[11]

Responding to the changing social climate, the Shafers razed their cribs the following month, constructing warehouses and industrial facilities in their place (during this renovation the cribs' privy was filled and paved over). Buckley and Ballerino fought back, however, looking for a loophole. Equipping their cribs with shelves and token merchandise, the prostitutes posed as retailers, displaying new signs proclaiming sales of cigars, tobacco, and chewing gum, or advertised expertise in fancywork, corset work, gents' neckwear, or curling feathers.[12] Yet the tide of social reform could not be denied, and all L.A. cribs were closed within the year.

The brothels and parlor houses were abolished several years later. At the time of the crib campaign, no action was taken against the women who relocated nearby into different types of establishments. By 1906, seven of the eight Aliso Street buildings in the project area contained brothels, four of which were owned by former crib manager Jean Rappet (fig. 11.4). The brothel at 327 Aliso Street appears to have been renovated about 1901. Its discarded domestic furnishings were thrown down the obsolete privy holes, which were replaced by modern toilets hooked up to the Aliso Street sewer line.

L.A.'s crusade against prostitution eventually prevailed, and by the end of 1907 the red-light district was effectively closed. From one end of the neighborhood to the other there were no signs of the "infamous traffic," and property owners were notified that they would be prosecuted if they leased their buildings for immoral purposes ever again. The *Daily Star* reported that the "red lights, curtains, music, and other signs of the Tenderloin were no more."[13] In 1909 the people of Los Angeles reaffirmed their disapproval of vice by electing a reform administration. A much subdued prostitution industry dispersed and went underground.

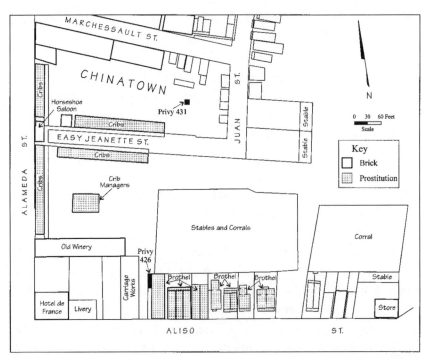

Fig. 11.4. Los Angeles, Calif. The project area in 1903–6, showing the concentrations of brothels and cribs.

Chinatown, long established on the northern edge of the red-light district, filled the void by extending southward over former crib locales. Chinese vegetable sellers built warehouses in which rural produce was sorted and distributed around the city. By 1915 land encompassing the project area and several adjacent blocks was consolidated by speculators into a holding company, awaiting construction of Union Station. This facility was completed in 1937, burying its past under five to twenty feet of fill.

The Archaeology of Prostitution

The rich life of the 1890s parlor house at No. 327 Aliso Street is archaeologically well documented. Over 10,000 artifacts representing 1,845 individual items were recovered (fig. 11.5). Finds related to the rows of cribs, in use between roughly 1895 and 1903, are less distinct. Having few amenities, these latter enterprises had little to leave behind. The contrast between brothel activities and crib life is highlighted by the differences in their archaeological remains.

PARLOR HOUSE ARTIFACTS

It is difficult to discuss the "uniqueness" of something without a baseline of "normalcy." Fortunately, the collection from the brothel privies can be compared to the six collections recovered from blue-collar neighbors on Aliso Street. Being contemporaries in time, location, and ethnic affiliations, these family residences provide a rare archaeological control group. Substantial differences in artifact occurrences between the parlor house and the six dwellings can be attributed to household function: commercial brothel versus domestic residence. Noteworthy contrasts are found in artifacts related to alcohol consumption, disease and its prevention, and beauty maintenance.

Eating Meals. Types of ceramic tableware are often used to distinguish social and economic differences between households: the proportion of porcelain wares (expensive and fragile) is compared to improved white wares (sturdy and affordable "Ironstone" types) and earthenware (inexpensive but fragile). Almost two-thirds of the tableware (plates, saucers, and cups) recovered from the brothel privy were of porcelain, this in comparison with the contemporary neighborhood residences, where porcelain accounted for less than one-third of all tableware. In contrast to the expen-

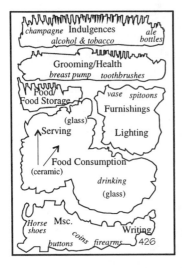

Fig. 11.5. Los Angeles, Calif. Over ten thousand artifacts, representing nearly nineteen hundred individual items, were excavated from the six-seat privy behind the parlor house at 327 Aliso Street. Photo by Alice Olmstead.

sive tableware, serving vessels such as platters and tureens were simple undecorated vessels, and the meats served, which were determined from studying the recovered bones, were the same moderately priced cuts of beef (more than 65 percent) and mutton (nearly 20 percent) typical of their neighbors. Unlike nearby residences, however, there was a variety of fish and shellfish found in the brothel refuse.

The key to understanding this apparent dichotomy between fancy and plain foodways may be found in understanding the distinction between the brothel's private and public spaces. While the working women ate healthy but unremarkable meals themselves, they "entertained" a paying clientele in their parlor,[14] priming them with liquor and delicacies (including seafood) served on porcelain and other expensive dishes. A plethora of pressed, cut, etched, and painted glass containers supports this interpretation. The apparent ambiance of the tableware reflects the staged affluence offered the customers, rather than the dining habits of the women.[15]

Drinking Alcohol. Parlor house preliminaries included some socializing, during which the customer could make his choice of women. Alcohol facilitated these interactions, and its sale added substantially to the house's income. The remarkable consumption of alcohol at 327 Aliso is documented by the large proportion of drinking glasses among the tableware. At the parlor house 65 percent (148 items) of all the glass and ceramic artifacts related to food preparation and consumption were tumblers, goblets, and wine glasses, while the same types of drinking glasses averaged just 28 percent at the neighboring residences. The quality of the glassware at the brothel was also remarkable and included unusual numbers of cut, pressed, etched, hand-blown, and colored items. The activities at 327 Aliso Street not only involved a lot of drinking, but this imbibing was carried out in style.

The percentage of alcohol bottles recovered from the brothel, not surprisingly, is over twice that of the residences. In addition to quantity, what was being drunk is also instructive. Beer, the most popular drink at 327 Aliso Street (at nearly 50 percent), was recovered from only two of the five neighborhood homes (where it averaged 20 percent). The parlor house also apparently went through an unusual abundance of whiskey flasks: barely present in domestic collections, they made up nearly 23 percent of the discards from the parlor house. Interestingly, wine and champagne were equally represented in the brothel and the neighborhood. As much of a madam's money was made in large mark-ups on the resale of alcohol, the smaller quantities provided in beer bottles and pint whiskey flasks were more profitable. How the liquor was served, however, was also important: fancy glassware added to the opulent setting and encouraged imbibing and the abandonment of moral and fiscal inhibitions.

Venereal Disease. Perhaps the most dreaded ailment among prostitutes was venereal disease, with syphilis the most ravaging and gonorrhea and other infections also debilitating. Although specific diagnosis and treatment of these maladies were still elusive in the 1890s, their transmission through sexual intercourse, and particularly by prostitutes, was well known.[16] To combat both disease and conception, "injection brews," introduced as a douche, were very popular in Europe and widely adopted in the United States. Remains of five rubber syringes and injector bulbs attest to their common use at 327 Aliso Street (fig. 11.6). The most popular injection brew at the brothel was Darby's Prophylactic Fluid, imported by J. H. Zeilin and Company, Philadelphia (table 11.1). The cure was purchased in quart-sized bottles, nine of which were found in the brothel refuse.

Although condoms were recognized as being of great use in preventing venereal disease, they were not widely used in brothels. Madame de Stael once described them as "a breast plate against pleasure and a cobweb against danger."[17] The more popular method of guarding against both venereal disease and pregnancies was application of a salve of Vaseline and

Fig. 11.6. Los Angeles, Calif. The rubber syringes and injector bulb were likely used to administer liquid prophylactics, while the glass needle-syringes were used for drugs or medicines. The breast pump indicates a nursing mother. Photo by Alice Olmstead.

Table 11.1. Health Aids and Remedies

Types		Number of Items
Medicine bottles		89
Homeopathic vials		35
Pharmaceutical bottles		27
C. F. Heinzeman Pharmacist, Los Angeles	14	
Fr. Aockerblum Druggist, Los Angeles	4	
Off and Vaughn Pharmacists, Los Angeles	2	
Godfrey and Moore Druggists, Los Angeles	2	
C. A. McDonell Druggist, Los Angeles	1	
Viole and Lopizich, Los Angeles	1	
Shaw's Pharmacy	1	
(Incomplete), Los Angeles	1	
Unknown	1	
Cures		22
Darby's Prophylactic Fluid, Philadelphia	9	
Saxlehner Hunyadi Janos, Hungary	5	
Dr. J. Hostetter's Stomach Bitters	1	
F. Brown's Essence of Jamaica Ginger, Philadelphia	1	
Shiloh's Consumption Cure, New York	1	
Fellow and Co. Chemists, New Brunswick, N.J.	1	
Kola-Cardinette, Yonkers, N.Y.	1	
Ayers Compound Extract Sarsaparilla, Lowell, Mass.	1	
California Fig Syrup, San Francisco	1	
Trask's Magnetic Ointment, Buffalo, N.Y.	1	
Vaseline, Cheseborough, N.Y.		13
Douche syringe and bulb		5
Breast pump		1
Mineral water		5
Syringe (glass)		2
Ointment jars		9
Poison, P. D. and Co., Detroit		1
Total		209

boric acid. A similar concoction was used by Parisian prostitutes, who favored "a bottle of oil to facilitate intercourse and a solution of caustic soda to guard against disease and prevent conception."[18] Thirteen jars of Vaseline were thrown in the privy at 327 Aliso Street. Although this ointment had many other health uses, its unique abundance at the brothel suggests its primary use as a prophylactic.

Mercury was the most relevant antisyphilitic remedy since the sixteenth century. A popular adage of the day, "A night with Venus, a moon with mercury," warning men of the perils of frequenting brothels, was well understood by the populace. Mercury came in several forms, referred to as "life balsams" or "blood purifiers": blue mass (mercury and chalk), calomel (mercurous chloride), and corrosive sublimate (bichloride of mercury).[19] Mercury was injected, eaten, inhaled, smoked, and put on the skin in poultices. The remedy was often worse than the disease.

Sarsaparilla was used in Europe in the sixteenth century to combat syphilis, fell out of favor, and then was revived in the nineteenth century. Ayres Sarsaparilla was the brand chosen at 327 Aliso Street. The only values in its ingredients might be found in the cathartic action of senna and the tonic of iron, the potent potassium iodide, and the soothing qualities of its high alcohol content (26 percent).

Patent Medicines. Illnesses other than venereal diseases plagued the working women at 327 Aliso Street. It was popularly believed that all illness came from related imbalances, and therefore a cure for one symptom was a cure for many. From the late 1800s through the 1920s proprietary (patent) medicines rode a flood tide of popularity: by 1900 there were over a million patents on the market. In addition to liquid tonics, remedies came in the form of pills, pastilles, globules, powders, herbs, and ointments. Succeeding partly because of the infancy of modern medicine, the rage for cures ebbed as the increasingly scientific medical profession publicized their dark by-products: drug addiction, alcoholism, and unnecessary death.[20]

Opium-laden tonics such as laudanum and the stronger derivative morphine were the Victorian woman's "silent friends." Easily obtained from pharmacies and usually initiated by a doctor's prescription, they were taken orally, as a salve, and by hypodermic needle, enema, or suppository. The population of opium and morphine addicts was almost exclusively composed of fashionable middle-class housewives (for whom alcohol was unseemly) and prostitutes.[21]

The Aliso Street prostitutes partook of the lavishly advertised Shiloh's Consumption Cure composed of morphine, alcohol, muriatic acids, extract of henbane, wild cherry and ginger, essence of peppermint, syrup of tar, and water. In addition to unhealthy doses of chloroform and prussic acid, it also contained hydrocyanic acid—a colorless, volatile liquid with a peach blossom odor which was a deadly poison.[22] Chronic opium use produces constipation, and companion laxatives at 327 Aliso Street were California Fig Syrup and the popular Hungarian product Hunyadi Janos.

F. Brown's Essence of Jamaica Ginger, also found in the brothel privies, was advertised as curing cholera, dyspepsia, colic, and cramps. Consisting of over 90 percent alcohol with burnt sugar and ginger flavoring, it was ironically touted as being "especially good for the inebriate to help resist temptation."[23] As it was considerably less expensive than whiskey, it was drunk for a cheap high. Additional payment was extracted, however, in side effects: chronic users would develop "Jake leg," a type of paralysis in one or both extremities. More temperate users drank it as a toddy, reduced with water and sweetened with sugar to relieve cramps and colds.

In addition to specific named cures, many of the 141 medicine bottles and vials recovered from the brothel privies would have had opium, morphine, and alcohol as major ingredients. They were purchased at local pharmacies, and 27 are embossed with the proprietor's name and address. Half of these pharmaceutical bottles were from C. F. Heinzeman's pharmacy at 122 North Main Street, only a few blocks from the Aliso Street brothel. The other druggists were also located nearby.

Pregnancies were usually viewed as personal and professional liabilities. Measures used to prevent conception were generally the same used to prevent venereal disease. In the prostitute's favor, opium addiction and chronic gonorrhea tended to produce sterility. The presence of a breast pump in the Aliso Street privy, however, attests to there having been at least one nursing mother on the premises.

Cosmetics. Like most women of their day, the prostitutes at 327 Aliso indulged in the luxuries of creams and scents (table 11.2; fig. 11.7). The appearance of youth and beauty were tools of the trade, and investments in cosmetics were likely viewed as prudent. Nine percent of the parlor house

Table 11.2. Cosmetics and Grooming Aids

Types		Number of Items
Cream jars and pots		18
Prof. Huberts Malvina Cream, Toledo, Ohio	5	
S and K Italian Cream, London	3	
Wakelee's Camelline, San Francisco	3	
Pond's Extract, New York	1	
Dr. Funk's Cream of Roses, Los Angeles	1	
Creme Simon, Paris	1	
Gouraud's Oriental Cream, New York	1	
Unnamed (cream jars and lids)	3	
Perfume		17
Ed Pinaud, Paris	4	
Lubin, Paris	2	
X. Bazin, Perfumer, Philadelphia	2	
Atkinson, London	1	
Maison Dorin 27, Paris	1	
Ricksecker's Perfumer, New York	1	
Unnamed	5	
Cologne		9
Colgate's Violet Water, New York	6	
E. W. Hoyt's German Cologne, Lowell, Mass.	3	
Florida water		14
Murray and Lanman, New York	14	
Toothbrushes		6
Toothpaste		17
Calder's ALC Dentine, R.I.	11	
Van Buskirk's Sozodont, New York	2	
Hood's Tooth Powder, Lowell, Mass.	2	
Cherry Toothpaste, London	2	
Razor		1
Hairbrushes		3
Combs		8
Soap dish set		1
Pitcher		1
Slop jar		1
Chamber pots		2
Powder-puff handle		1
Unidentified jars and lids		10
Total		109

Fig. 11.7. Los Angeles, Calif. Parlor house residents invested in beauty en-
hancements including toilet waters, perfumes, creams, and hair items. Photo
by Alice Olmstead.

assemblage was related to "grooming" items, compared to an average of 3
percent in the residences. Gouraud's Oriental Cream was promoted for
removing "tan, pimples, moth-patches, rash, skin diseases, and every
blemish on beauty."[24] Wakelee's Camelline was designed "for softening
and beautifying the complexion," while Prof. Huberts Malvina Cream was
a skin cure-all. Also on the brothel dressers were S and K Italian Cream
from London; Dr. Funk's Cream of Roses, locally made in Los Angeles;
and Creme Simon, which cured "in one night . . . chilblains, chaps and all
light curtneous affections."[25] The familiar Pond's Extract, which has out-
lived all the others to the present day, was also used in the L.A. brothels.

Enticing scents were obtained from exotic and expensive perfumes
from Paris—Lubin, Pinaud, and Maison Dorin—as well as domestic perfumes made by Ricksecker in New York. Colognes, less costly, were purchased from domestic manufacturers. The Aliso Street prostitutes also
favored the popular Florida Water, an inexpensive cologne used by both
men and women for over a century.

The quantities of tooth powders present at the brothel were most

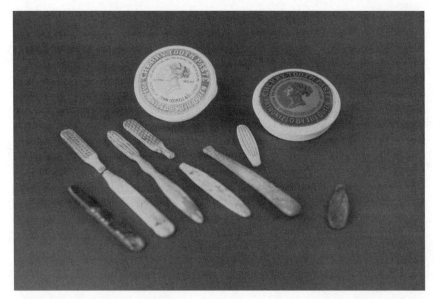

Fig. 11.8. Los Angeles, Calif. Unusual attention to oral hygiene was documented at the parlor house with recovery of numerous toothbrushes and toothpaste jars: the five Vaseline jars represent numerous uses for this product. Photo by Alice Olmstead.

impressive (fig. 11.8), for this was a time when oral hygiene was not well developed. In homes and boardinghouses there was often a common toothbrush in the washroom for anyone who cared to use it. The most popular tooth powder at the parlor house was Calder's Saponaceous Dentine, made in Providence, Rhode Island. Van Buskirk's Fragrant Sozodont for the Teeth and Breath and Hood's Tooth Powder were also present. Cherry Toothpaste from London advertised that it was "patronized by the Queen" and featured a portrait of Queen Victoria on its lid. One wonders if the company knew it was being patronized by a parlor house in Los Angeles.

THE CRIB PRIVY

The crib privy was located behind a line of about twenty cribs that bordered the north side of Easy Jeanette Street from 1895 to 1903 (see fig. 11.4). Although the privy backed onto Chinatown, it is very unlikely that these neighbors would have been permitted to use the facility. Excavations of the feature revealed more details about the outhouse itself than the women it served. A two-holer, it featured an enormous 6 x 6 foot privy pit, which was 6.5-feet-deep and lined with redwood boards. This hole was covered by a two-room frame outhouse fitted with two porcelain toilets. These fixtures, although mimicking modern facilities that were common in better neighborhoods, were not hooked up to the sewer; the privy pit, cut into sandy soils, functioned like a small sump.

When the Shafers closed their cribs in 1903, their rapid renovation of the neighborhood is reflected in the material that was used to fill the gaping privy hole. At the bottom were the privy toilets, pushed in as the outhouse was leveled. On top of the toilets was a layer of large granite boulders, over a dozen of them in excess of two hundred pounds. Above this layer was a palm tree stump that measured two feet in diameter. Soils had been packed into the hole and the new Napier Street laid on top. As the privy hole settled over the years, fill was added to the depression to keep the street level.

The soils of the privy fill contained 500 items (3,667 artifacts), very few of which can be attributed to the cribs. Chinese ceramics dominate the collection, and artifacts such as cooking pots, serving bowls, an opium pipe, and horse tack are clearly related to the adjacent Chinese residences. Many artifacts could have been used by either Chinese residents or prostitutes, as similar examples were found in the other Chinese features and in the 327 Aliso Street brothel collection. The ambiguous items include medicine bottles, liquor bottles, European ceramics, pieces of clothing, and even cologne. Given the spartan setting associated with cribs, it is likely that only a small percentage of items in this collection came from the prostitutes' rooms. The discarded iron bed frame and springs may be one of these items, representing the largest and most important piece of furnishing in each crib. This association is strengthened by discovery of the bed frame near the bottom of the fill, indicating that it was one of the first items thrown in. It is also the only bed found in any of the project area privies.

Conclusion

How can a collection of broken dishes, bottles, and household goods from a brothel transform our understanding of prostitution? The work of historians, sociologists, reformers, and social workers has illuminated many dark corners in the lives of these working women. Archaeologists, however, can supply the vantage of the material record, the very things that were bought, used, and discarded by the prostitutes and their customers. If we can read these collections of artifacts, we can add new stories to those contained in written documents.

Some readings have been attempted in this brief chapter. Parlor house drinking simulated upper-class fashions, and off-duty prostitutes ate meals around the kitchen table similar to neighboring families. Evidence places a nursing mother at the brothel, locates the prostitutes' favorite pharmacy, and identifies these women's preferences in perfumes and colognes. Artifacts also have shown how brothel activities are shaped by market forces. Balancing rapid customer turnover with maximum profits from alcohol sales selected for the pint whiskey flask and bottled beer. The women's concern over maintaining their commercial appeal is expressed in extraordinary expenditures on creams and scents. Procedures are regularly employed to help prevent both conception and venereal disease, while illness and addiction are constant companions.

The collection of fancy items from 327 Aliso Street also adds substance to the justification given by Maimie Pinzer, in her eloquent letters, for returning to her life in the demimonde in 1911: "As I began to see that I was still attractive to men, I began to use what charms I might possess to make it possible to have a few of the luxuries which had become necessities."[26] Also, as historic preservationists know, there is nothing like tangible things from the past to make a personal and emotional connection. Reaching through time to the present, artifacts allow us to see, touch, and feel the actual objects that were used by the working women of Aliso Street and their clients. Although we know prostitutes took medicines and drank whiskey, we now know which patent cures they preferred and can see the decorative floral patterns etched on their glass tumblers. We know the names of their skin creams and that their perfumes came from Paris. Our view into the past is made personal by these pinpoints of reality.

PART IV

Exemplary Projects

CHAPTER 12

The Power of Place Project
Claiming Women's History
in the Urban Landscape

Dolores Hayden

Layered with the traces of previous generations' struggles to make a living, raise children, and participate in community life, the vernacular urban landscape, as John Brinckerhoff Jackson has written, "is the image of our common humanity—hard work, stubborn hope, and mutual forbearance striving to be love,"[1] a definition that carries cultural geography and architecture straight toward urban social history. At the intersection of these fields lies the history of urban space and its public meanings. How do urban landscapes hold public memory? And why should feminists and scholars of women's history struggle to create projects honoring and preserving women's history as part of public culture?[2]

Every American city and town contains traces of historic landscapes intertwined with its current spatial configuration. These parts of older landscapes can be preserved and interpreted to strengthen people's understanding of how a city has developed over time. But often what happens is something else. Cycles of development and redevelopment occur. Care is not taken to preserve the spatial history of ordinary working people and their everyday lives. Instead, funds are often lavished on the preservation of a few architectural monuments along with the celebration of a few men as "city fathers." In New York City, for example, many buildings designed by the architects McKim, Mead and White at the turn of the century are closely identified with an Anglo-Saxon, Protestant, male elite who commissioned the private men's clubs, mansions, banks, and other structures, from which other New Yorkers were often excluded. In contrast, modest urban buildings that represent the social and economic struggles of the majority of ordinary citizens, especially women and members of diverse ethnic communities, have often been overlooked as possible resources for historic preservation. The power of place to nurture social memory—to encompass shared time in the form of shared territory—remains largely untapped for most working people's neighborhoods in most American cities and for most ethnic history and most women's history. If we hear little of city mothers, the sense of civic identity which shared women's history can convey is lost. And even bitter experiences and fights women have lost need to be remembered, so as not to diminish their importance.

To reverse the neglect of physical resources that are important to women's history is not a simple process, especially if preservationists are to frame these issues as part of a broader social history encompassing gender, race, and class. First, it involves claiming the entire urban landscape as an important part of American history, not just its architectural monuments. Second, it means identifying the building types—such as tenement, market, factory, packing shed, union hall—which have housed women's work and everyday lives. Third, it involves finding creative ways to interpret these modest buildings as part of the flow of contemporary city life. This means finding a politically conscious approach to urban preservation, complementary to architectural preservation, which emphasizes public processes to nurture shared memories and meanings. In addition, there may be sites of historic importance where architectural remains are limited—such as the Wesleyan Chapel in Seneca Falls, New York—or nonexistent. Then architects, landscape architects, and artists have important roles to play in interpreting women's history through new construction.

Early in the 1980s, when I was teaching at the Graduate School of Architecture and Urban Planning at the University of California, Los Angeles (UCLA), I founded The Power of Place as a small, experimental nonprofit corporation, to explore ways to present the public history of workers, women, and people of color in Los Angeles. It began as an unpaid effort with a few student as interns—I also had a full-time teaching job. Los Angeles is an ethnically diverse city. It always has been, since the day when a group of colonists of mixed Spanish, African, and Native American heritage arrived to found the pueblo in 1781 next to Yang-Na. It has remained so through the transfer of Los Angeles from Mexican to U.S. rule in the mid-nineteenth century and on into the late twentieth.

Residents—more than one-third Latino, one-eighth African American, one-eighth Asian American, one-half women—could not find their heritage adequately represented by existing cultural historic landmarks. (In 1985, 97.5 percent of all official city landmarks commemorated Anglo history, and only 2.5 percent represented people of color; 96 percent dealt with men and only 4 percent with women, including Anglo women.)

No one has yet written a definitive social history of Los Angeles. By the early 1980s, however, older works by Carey McWilliams and Robert Fogelson were being complemented by new narratives about ghettos, barrios, and ethnic enclaves, as Albert Camarillo, Mario Garcia, Vicki Ruiz, Richard Griswold del Castillo, Ricardo Romo, Rodolfo Acuna, Lonnie Bunch, Don and Nadine Hata, Mike Murase, Noritaka Yagasaki, and many others were creating accounts of Latinos, African Americans, Chinese Americans, and Japanese Americans in L.A.[3] The new work suggested the outline that the urban history of Los Angeles must one day fill. As a feminist scholar concerned with the history of the urban landscape, transplanted from New England to Los Angeles, I was tremendously excited by the new, ethnic urban history and its potential to broaden my teaching in a professional school whose students were concerned with the physical design of the city, in areas such as preservation, physical planning, public art, and urban design. (I was looking for ways to enable students to take something back to their own communities.)

One of the first projects of The Power of Place in 1984–85 was a published, self-guided walking tour of downtown Los Angeles (coauthored with then UCLA graduate students Gail Lee Dubrow and Carolyn Flynn).[4] Organized around the economic development of the city, the itinerary looked at some of the working landscapes various industries had shaped over the previous two centuries (fig. 12.1). It highlighted the city's history of production, defining its core and emphasizing the skill and energy workers have expended to feed, clothe, and house the population. These workers included women, men, and sometimes children of every ethnic group employed in citrus groves, flower fields, flower markets, produce markets, oil fields, and prefabricated housing factories as well as garment workers, midwives, nurses, and firefighters. The State of California's ongoing research on ethnic landmarks, eventually published as *Five Views*, was then available in draft form.[5] The Power of Place ran some public hu-

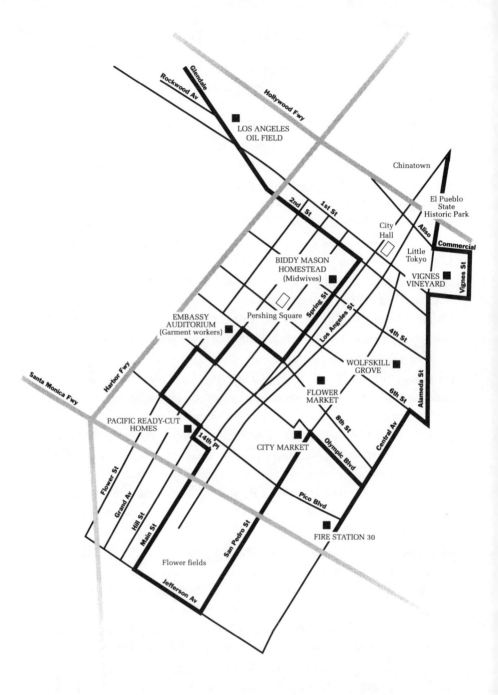

Fig. 12.1. Los Angeles, Calif. The Power of Place, an itinerary of historic places in downtown Los Angeles. Courtesy of The Power of Place.

manities workshops on topics such as Japanese Americans in the flower industry and African American firefighters. The published walking tour pamphlet, distributed through a small press distribution company to local bookstores as well as in teachers' workshops and public history settings, finally identified an itinerary of nine major downtown places (and twenty-seven minor ones): some were buildings eligible for landmark status because of their significant social history, some were buildings with architectural landmark status needing reinterpretation to emphasize their importance to social history, and a few were vacant historic sites where no structures remained but where new public art or open-space designs might be possible to commemorate the site's importance.

In 1986 The Power of Place launched into work of a much more experimental kind, combining public history and public art to commemorate an African American midwife's homestead with no historic structure remaining. The site was one of downtown's endless parking lots. At that time the Los Angeles Community Redevelopment Agency (CRA) was developing a plan for a ten-story commercial and garage building at 333 Spring Street. Because the material in the walking tour had been listed in the agency's computer, the address popped out as Biddy Mason's historic homestead. The Power of Place was invited to propose a component for this new project involving both public history and public art. I served as project director and historian and raised money from arts and humanities foundations. The team included public art curator Donna Graves and artists Susan E. King, Betye Saar, and Sheila Levrant de Bretteville. The first public event was a workshop in 1987 (fig. 12.2), cosponsored by the African-American studies program at UCLA and assisted by the California Afro-American Museum and the First African Methodist Episcopal Church (FAME). The team came together with community members to discuss the importance of the history of the African American community in Los Angeles and women's history within it.

Using Biddy Mason's biography as the basis of the project was the key to finding a broad audience (figs. 12.3 and 12.4). One pioneer's life cannot tell the whole story of building a city. Yet the record of a single citizen's struggle to raise a family, earn a living, and contribute to professional, social, and religious activities can suggest how a city develops over time. This is especially true for Biddy Mason. Her experiences as a citi-

Fig. 12.2. Los Angeles, Calif. Participants at a public history workshop, "The Life and Times of Biddy Mason," run by The Power of Place at UCLA, 1987. Seated at center is Miriam Matthews, a retired librarian who played a key role in preserving documents and photographs on the history of African Americans in Los Angeles. Photo by Drummond Buckley, courtesy of The Power of Place.

zen of Los Angeles were typical—as a family head, homeowner, and church-goer. Yet they were also unusual because gender, race, and legal status as a slave increased her burdens.

Born in 1818, Biddy Mason was the lifelong slave of a master from Mississippi.[6] She had trekked west with his family and other slaves, including her three daughters, herding his livestock behind a Mormon wagon train, first to Deseret (Salt Lake City, Utah) and then to the Mormon outpost of San Bernadino, California. They arrived in southern California in 1851. Biddy Mason brought suit for freedom for herself and thirteen others in court in Los Angeles in 1855. When she won her case and chose to settle in the small town of Los Angeles in 1856 as part of the very small African American community there, her special medical skills, learned as a slave midwife and nurse, provided entry for her into many households. She became the city's most famous midwife, delivering hun-

Fig. 12.3. (top) Los Angeles, Calif. Biddy Mason, undated photograph. Courtesy of The Power of Place.

Fig. 12.4. (bottom) Los Angeles, Calif. Los Angeles in 1857, shortly after Biddy Mason's arrival. Courtesy of The Power of Place.

dreds of babies. She lived and worked in the city until her death in January 1891.

The Biddy Mason project focused on the changing experience of being African American in Los Angeles, the problems of earning a living as a free woman of color in the city, and the nature of home as one woman created it. Although Mason at first lived with another family and then rented on her own, the homestead she built in Los Angeles in the 1880s, a quarter-century after her arrival, was a surprisingly urban place, a brick commercial building with space for her grandsons' business enterprises on the ground floor and for her own quarters upstairs, where the early organizational meetings of the local branch of the First African Methodist Episcopal Church were held.

A working woman of color is the ideal subject for a public history project because in her life all the struggles associated with class, ethnicity, and gender are intertwined. Although she herself was unable to read and write, the history of Biddy Mason was not lost. Through Mormon records of colonization I was able to trace her journey westward. Through the account of her suit for freedom in the local newspaper, I followed the legal proceedings. Some diaries and a photograph from the family her daughter married into provided personal details. Then, using work in the history of medicine concerning other African American midwives and women healers, I constructed an account of what a successful midwife's medical practice was probably like. (A few years later Laurel Ulrich's *A Midwife's Tale*, a marvelous book about a Maine midwife's diary, confirmed the social importance of women's medical work.)[7] Finally, using detailed records of the built environment, I was able to unlock the narrative of how Biddy Mason created her urban homestead. The records of her property happened to be particularly significant because the growth of the Spring Street commercial district in Los Angeles between 1866, when she bought her land, and 1891, when she died, proceeded right down her street and included her property. Thus, her life story spans the wider themes of slavery and freedom, family life in pioneer times, women in the healing professions, and economic development in Los Angeles between the 1850s and 1890s.

The Biddy Mason project eventually included five parts. First, Betye Saar's installation, *Biddy Mason's House of the Open Hand,* was placed in

Fig. 12.5. Los Angeles, Calif., *Biddy Mason: Time and Place*, by Sheila Levrant de Bretteville with The Power of Place. Photo by Jim Simmons/Annette Del Zoppo, courtesy of The Power of Place.

the elevator lobby of the new structure. It includes a photomural and motifs from vernacular architecture of the 1880s as well as an assemblage on Mason's life. Second, Susan King created a large format artist's letterpress book, *HOME/stead,* in an edition of thirty-five.[8] King incorporated rubbings from the Evergreen Cemetery in Boyle Heights, where Mason is buried. These included vines, leaves, and an image of the gate of heaven. The book weaves together the history of Mason's life (drawing on my research and some by Donna Graves) with King's meditations on the homestead becoming a ten-story building. Third, an inexpensive poster, *Grandma Mason's Place: A Midwife's Homestead,* was designed by Sheila de Bretteville. The historical text I wrote for the poster included midwives' architectural rituals for welcoming a newborn, such as painting the shutters of a house blue or turning a door around on its hinges. Fourth, *Biddy Mason: Time and Place,* a black, poured-concrete wall (eighty-one-feet long) with slate, limestone, and granite inset panels, was designed by Sheila de Bretteville to chronicle the story of Biddy Mason and her life as well as the history of urban development in Los Angeles from 1818 to

1891 (fig. 12.5). The wall includes a midwife's bag, scissors, and spools of thread debossed into the concrete. De Bretteville also included a picket fence, agave leaves, and wagon wheels representing Mason's walk to freedom from Mississippi to California. Both the deed to her homestead and her "Freedom Papers" are among the historic documents photographed and bonded to limestone panels. And, fifth, the project included prose in a journal. My article, "Biddy Mason's Los Angeles, 1856–1891," appeared in the fall 1989 *California History.* Eventually, my 1995 book, entitled *The Power of Place: Urban Landscapes as Public History,* documented all the projects.[9]

Everyone who gets involved in a public history or public art project hopes for an audience beyond the classroom or the museum. The poster was widely distributed through workshops for teachers. The wall by Sheila de Bretteville has been especially successful in evoking the community spirit of claiming the place (fig. 12.6). Youngsters run their hands along the wagon wheels. Teenagers trace the shape of Los Angeles on historic maps and decipher the old-fashioned handwriting on the Freedom Papers. One woman, who had tried for years to create a memorial to Mason and failed to get enough support from the city, told me, "Child, you're the answer to my prayers." People of all ages ask their friends to pose for snapshots in front of their favorite parts of the wall. Since the project opened in late 1989, we who worked together on it have had the satisfaction of seeing it become a new public place, one that connects individual women with family history, community history, and the city's urban landscape, developing over time.

The resonance of the Biddy Mason project increased with every additional project undertaken in Los Angeles and around the country: a local museum did an exhibit on contemporary black midwives; a storyteller from North Carolina created a performance about Biddy Mason, the L.A. public library created a special program about photographs of people of color, Chicago historians did a similar walking tour, Philadelphia public art supporters started a program on ethnic history sites. And it continues.

If you lift your eyes above the Biddy Mason wall, you will see a garment factory. The next project that The Power of Place sponsored involved the Embassy Theater as a site of union organizing and community organizing among Latina workers in the 1930s. This project was directed by Donna

Fig. 12.6. Los Angeles, Calif. Visitors at the Biddy Mason wall. The X mark is Biddy Mason's mark from the deed to her homestead. Photo by Drummond Buckley, courtesy of The Power of Place.

Graves, while I remained as president of the organization. It suggests some ways an existing architectural landmark can be reinterpreted in terms of its importance to women's history, labor history, and ethnic history. Designated a Los Angeles Cultural-Historic Landmark (as part of a real estate deal) for its indifferent neoclassical architecture designed by Fitzhugh, Krucker, and Deckbar in 1914, the Embassy Theater is far more important as the historic gathering place for labor unions and community organizations—including Russian Jewish and Latina garment workers, Latina cannery workers, and Russian Molokan walnut shellers. Unions, especially women's unions, met inside and marched outside the Embassy between the 1920s and the 1940s, as did El Congreso (the Spanish Speaking People's Congress), the first national Latino civil rights organization.[10] By the 1990s it had become a residential college for the University of Southern California (USC).

The Embassy in its heyday was frequented by many of that era's most colorful organizers, including Rose Pesotta of the International Ladies' Garment Workers Union (ILGWU), who led the 1933 Dressmakers' strike, Luisa Moreno of the United Cannery, Agricultural, Packing, and Allied Workers Association (UCAPAWA), and Josefina Fierro de Bright of El Congreso. All three reached Los Angeles after epic journeys of the same proportions as Biddy Mason's—from Russia for Pesotta, Guatemala, for Moreno, and Mexico for Fierro de Bright. All three experienced the height of their careers in Los Angeles, recruiting thousands of Spanish-speaking women into their organizations—but it must be added that their work was so controversial and disturbing that Pesotta resigned as ILGWU vice president and Moreno and Fierro left for Mexico during the red-baiting years.

Graves' project highlighted these three organizers. Artist Rupert Garcia created a poster with their portraits to advertise a public humanities workshop, "La Fuerza de Union," held in the historic main auditorium in the spring of 1991. Participants included two artists, Garcia and Celia Alvarez Munoz; a restoration architect, Brenda Levin; and historians George Sanchez and Albert Camarillo (Moreno's biographer) as well as union leaders, students, and retirees. (Historian Vicki Ruiz, whose wonderful book *Cannery Women, Cannery Lives* had first drawn attention to Moreno, also worked on the team briefly.)

Following the workshop, Celia Alvarez Munoz created an artist's book,

If Walls Could Speak, which intertwined public and private story lines in English and Spanish, beginning: "If walls could speak, these walls would tell/in sounds of human voices, music, and machines/of the early tremors of the City of Angels." And on the same three pages she wrote: "As a young child, I learned my mother had two families./One with my grandmother, my aunt, and I./The other at la fabrica, the factory." The end papers were union logos. A typical spread included historic images of Rose Pesotta with her arm around a worker and another worker stitching a banner reading, "Win the war," or Josefina Fierro organizing for El Congreso and workers with linked arms. The small artist's book was distributed free to several thousand people, including union members, retirees, and students.[11]

At the same time, architect Brenda Levin proposed the recreation of two traditional showcases in front of the Embassy Theater to carry history text as well as sculptural representations of the workers' sewing machines, spools, and hammers, while union logos were to be pressed into a new concrete sidewalk. In a storefront adjoining the sidewalk, the faculty hoped to open the "Luisa Moreno Reading Room" for students interested in social history. It was a disappointment to us all that, although the permanent art was fully funded, plans by the owner, USC, to sell the building prevented installation. Then the January 1994 earthquake hit the building so hard it had to be evacuated. Perhaps one day there will be a permanent commemoration on another site.

Today many of us who worked together in L.A. continue activities in other cities, but some subsequent projects in Los Angeles go on too. In Little Tokyo a UCLA student working with me and The Power of Place, Susan Sztaray, proposed a project for a public art sidewalk wrapping the First Street National Register Historic District. Sztaray wanted to tell the history of this community and recall the scale of small, traditional Japanese American businesses flourishing there before the internment. She went to work for the Los Angeles Community Redevelopment Agency and persuaded them to take up her plan and run a public art competition to select an artist to create a work of public art in Little Tokyo. Entering the competition as an independent artist, Sheila de Bretteville, who designed the Biddy Mason wall, won the Little Tokyo commission along with artists Sonya Ishii and Nobuho Nagasawa. Construction was completed in 1996.

Los Angeles now has at least three cultural heritage projects—one African American, one Latina, and one Japanese American—in three very different kinds of settings, ranging from a lost homestead to a reinterpreted theater building to a National Register Historic District. They demonstrate some of the new ways artists and designers can work with preservationists and historians on reclaiming women's history in the public landscape, whether or not architecturally significant buildings survive which can be designated as official landmarks of women's history.

The projects I have discussed are all located in the area of our 1984 walking tour, close to the center of downtown Los Angeles, set near the high-rise buildings of the Bunker Hill redevelopment area. They have challenged the idea that only massive commercial development can provide a downtown with an identity, because The Power of Place presented an alternative account of the process of building a city, emphasizing the importance of both paid labor and work within family life to urban survival. In a city where half the residents are women and more than 60 percent are people of color, these small projects struck a responsive chord.

The projects straddled several worlds: academic urban history and public history, urban planning, public art, preservation, and urban design. Every project had a multiethnic, multidisciplinary team. Teamwork is difficult, especially across disciplines. It was often hard for historians to collaborate with artists, to see them as more than illustrators, just as it was often hard for artists to see historians as more that providers of basic information. Yet over time members of teams began to develop both spatial and historical imaginations and to expand the possibilities of what could be done through collaborative work.

There are rewards for struggling with such difficult interdisciplinary projects. First, public space has a resonance for local history which no other medium can match. Second, locking women's history into the design of the city exploits the permanence of public space as a medium. Over time the exposure can be as great as a film or an exhibit. Third, as projects such as Biddy Mason and Embassy show, when you have one significant public place, there is less pressure to divide history into academic categories (such as women, ethnic, or labor history) which often trivialize and marginalize urban stories. For the university there are also benefits. A fieldwork program such as The Power of Place connected students to urban history and at the same time gave them the chance to work as interns on local projects with diverse organizations as cosponsors.

For the city itself there are also rewards. Putting working people's history into downtown expands the potential audience for all urban preservation and public art. The recognition of important cultural heritage in diverse working people's neighborhoods can support other kinds of community organizing, including neighborhood economic development and planning for affordable housing. Teachers can bring classes to the sites to launch educational projects on women's history. Last, but not least, public space dedicated to women's history and ethnic history, especially to projects focused on working women of color, claims political territory in tangible ways. Women can meet in these historic places and work together on new issues, with the collective knowledge of earlier struggles. And this fosters a public realm in which, at last, we as women are free to be ourselves and to see ourselves as strong and wise people, because we have represented ourselves that way.

Across the country today I see many successful preservation projects focusing on women's history, such as the Seneca Falls Women's Rights National Historical Park. At the same time, promoting ethnic diversity in preservation has become a goal many organizations share, including the National Trust for Historic Preservation, so projects involving African American, Asian American, and Latina/Latino history are receiving higher funding and visibility. Artists, too, are working on many more public projects exploring spatial history. Today there are hundreds of architects, landscape architects, and artists as well as historians and preservationists who enjoy the complex challenges of reclaiming and interpreting women's history in the urban landscape. There are many historic buildings and historic districts where preservationists can save and interpret women's history as well as many opportunities for artists and designers to work on vacant sites to restore the memory of women's lives and work in the public landscape. Finding the stories of diverse working women and inscribing them in public space is one small part of creating a political culture that can carry the American city into the next century.

CHAPTER 13

Best Practices for Saving Women's Heritage Sites
Nonprofit Case Studies

Jennifer B. Goodman

The varied approaches to the preservation and interpretation of places associated with women's history raise the unresolved question of how these sites are best conserved and presented to the public. Grappling with this issue goes to the heart of the preservation movement's ongoing debate about how to treat historic sites whose significance is defined less by their architectural merit and more by their association with events, important historical figures, or broad patterns of cultural life. The issue is particularly relevant for women's heritage sites as preservationists begin more actively to address the growing body of scholarship that is redefining women's role in shaping history.

One of the proving grounds for determining how these theoretical issues are translated into practice continues to be the nonprofit arena.[1] This chapter describes three case studies of preservation nonprofits, illustrating how three different advocacy organizations, all employing similar planning and promotional tools and dedicated to similar preservation ideals, selected dramatically different approaches to the preservation and interpretation of their women's historic sites. Efforts to save homes associated with feminist commentator Charlotte Perkins Gilman, suffragist Alice Paul, and a free black community of women and men strayed from traditional preservation practices with positive and negative results.[2]

In this chapter I argue that, while flexibility is required when pursuing historic preservation goals, certain preservation standards remain necessary to ensure that the preservation of architectural features successfully captures the cultural significance of historic sites. I also propose a series of best practices that nonprofits can employ to build public support and organizational capacity for their community-based campaigns.

Saving a Representation of Charlotte Perkins Gilman

A four-hour journey across seven city blocks capped a three-year effort by Pasadena Heritage to save the California house in which Charlotte Perkins Gilman lived and died (fig. 13.1). Working with city agencies, neighborhood associations, and volunteers, the nonprofit group relocated the building from its original site in 1993, to prevent its demolition and provide housing in a neighborhood characterized by disinvestment and blight. The one-and-a-half-story, wood-frame house built around 1900 features a full-width front porch and Queen Anne detailing.

Perkins is considered a leading figure in feminist circles in the United States and Europe for her charismatic presentation of economic, social, and political arguments for collective domesticity.[3] While she lived less than one year in the house, it holds associations with the flowering of her professional career in Pasadena as well as her social philosophy.

Perkins moved to Pasadena in 1887 at the invitation of her good friend Grace Channing, who hoped that the artistic environment of Pasadena would help her recover from the "rest cure" that limited her reading and prohibited her writing. As Gilman recalled in her autobiography, "With Pasadena begins my professional living . . . [e]verywhere there was beauty, and the nerve-rest of steady windless weather."[4] She wrote thirty-three short articles, twenty-three poems, and ten child verses and published the famous account of her rest cure, *The Yellow Wallpaper*, by 1890.

Subsequently, Perkins left Pasadena and lived several places in the United States and Europe while writing and lecturing. She returned to Pasadena in 1934, after the death of her second husband, to be close to her daughter and two grandchildren. She lived nearby in a studio apartment and then with them, enjoying a modified version of the extended-family social access that was part of her feminist philosophy of domestic culture.[5]

The house was also the site of her suicide. When Gilman learned that she had inoperable breast cancer, in 1932, she bought lethal chloroform, determined not to let herself become incapacitated. In 1935, with her death imminent, she completed her autobiography and then committed suicide.[6]

Fig. 13.1. Pasadena, Calif. Moving the Gilman House. Photo courtesy of Pasadena Heritage.

When Gilman's granddaughter sold the property, in 1993, the new owners applied for a demolition permit, intending to use the property's multifamily zoning status to construct an apartment building. Pasadena Heritage believed that it lacked the legal and political support to preserve the structure on site and felt that moving the house was the best plan.[7] The organization also justified its actions based on an architectural assessment. By the late 1980s, when the house was threatened, roughly 70 percent of the Gilman-era housing stock had been replaced by apartment buildings. Pasadena Heritage sought to recreate its context by choosing a new site surrounded by modest Victorian-era housing.

"We set out to save a house, not just memorialize Charlotte Perkins Gilman," said Pasadena Heritage executive director Susan Mossman.[8] A single mother won the city's housing lottery and purchased the property in 1995 (fig. 13.2). Saving residential properties such as the Gilman house is central to Pasadena Heritage's mission. Founded in 1977, the nonprofit organization's first project was to preserve a historic bungalow slated for demolition. Over the years it has developed a revolving fund for the acquisition and rehabilitation of threatened properties.

On balance the group's preservation strategies were successful; Pasadena Heritage saved the house, and a sensitive renovation of the house by project architect Elizabeth Neaves maintained connections to Gilman. Although the livable space in the house was expanded, the renovation project protected the integrity of the major spaces associated with Gilman's life. A new bedroom and bathroom were added in an unfinished area under the roof; physical assessment and oral history work had indicated that Gilman had no strong association to this area of the house. Gilman-era features such as the kitchen cabinets and bathtub were saved, and a major intrusion, a 1950s-era rear addition, was removed.

Moving the house, a typical "last resort" in traditional preservation practice, severed some obvious physical and interpretative connections to

Fig. 13.2. Pasadena, Calif. Celebrating the rehabilitation of the Gilman House. Photo courtesy of Pasadena Heritage.

Gilman's living patterns in the immediate yard and surrounding community. For example, Gilman spent a great deal of time in the house's back yard, often in a hammock, resting, playing games with her grandchildren, and perhaps revising manuscripts and preparing for speaking engagements, according to her granddaughter. Before moving into her daughter's house, Gilman lived nearby in her own apartment; she dined and visited frequently with the family. The proximity of her rooming house to her daughter's house offered an opportunity to explore Gilman's personal and professional views of her family and domestic social policies. Although the house now stands in a neighborhood in which it fits architecturally, physical connections to significant stories or themes associated with Gilman have unfortunately been lost.

Preserving Paulsdale as a Living Memorial

The nonprofit Alice Paul Centennial Foundation rallied to save Alice Paul's birthplace, Paulsdale, from destruction when its owner of thirty years sold the property in 1987. Real estate professionals had predicted that the property would have been replaced with a subdivision of twelve to fifteen houses if sold on the open market.

Paulsdale stands on a 6.5-acre remnant of a 173-acre farm in Mt. Laurel, New Jersey. Porches wrap around two sides of the three-story farmhouse built in the Greek Revival style (fig. 13.3). A deep lawn with deciduous and evergreen trees buffers the house. Despite acres of mid-twentieth-century suburban development and a major interstate highway near the house, the landscape still evokes an agrarian setting in which one of the most important contributors to the women's rights movement came of age.[9]

Of all the properties associated with Alice Paul's life and political efforts, Paulsdale stands out because it is where she formed the ideals that made her one of the United States' leaders of women's suffrage and equal rights. She was raised in a strong Quaker tradition and was surrounded by family and friends who reinforced the Quaker concept of equality of the sexes.[10] In addition, Paul returned to the house at key junctures in her political career. At Paulsdale she planned the five thousand–person demonstration held during Woodrow Wilson's 1913 inauguration and returned home to recover from hunger strikes and other activities that she introduced in the fight for women's rights.

Fig. 13.3. Mt. Laurel, N.J. Encroaching development at Paulsdale, c. 1955. Photo courtesy of Alice Paul Centennial Foundation, Inc.

The original foundation board members felt a strong connection to Paul and her teachings; the advocates were motivated by a strong interest in promoting equality for women. What began as an effort to educate the public about Paul and the desire to continue her work became a struggle to preserve the house in which she was born, according to Barbara Irvine, president of the organization between 1984 and 1995. None of the original board members were students of women's history or historic preservation, but every member was committed to women's rights.[11]

Fig. 13.4. Mt. Laurel, N.J. Paulsdale, c. 1938. Photo courtesy of Alice Paul Centennial Foundation, Inc.

Although the foundation, which had been formed to celebrate the centennial of Paul's birth, was caught off-guard by the proposed sale of the house, the board's firm belief in saving the entire site, coupled with conservative preservation practices, enhanced its ability to interpret Paul's life and teachings at the site.[12]

The group looked inward, away from the site's suburban surroundings, and embraced a landscape that contained only remnants of the collection of outbuildings and landscape features that had existed on the farm of Paul's era. "We felt that the property's integrity had already been compromised, and to sell off parts of the land would have dramatically diminished its significance," reported Irvine. The board members were motivated by a desire to provide open spaces in a highly congested area and to offer views and outdoor activities that Paul had experienced, according to Lucienne Beard, a longtime volunteer and staff program coordinator since 2000.

The foundation is using the Secretary of the Interior's Standards for Rehabilitation as it restores the house and outbuildings (fig. 13.4). Extant landscape features that the group plans to preserve include a grand copper beech tree, hydrangea plants that marked the front steps, and a highly altered icehouse structure. Further historical research may reveal additional ways for the foundation to revive lost elements that enhance a visitor's understanding of Paul's experience on the farm.

Saving Remnants of Weeksville to Promote Community Assets

The Society for the Preservation of Weeksville has worked diligently for three decades to preserve four mid-nineteenth-century cottages in Brooklyn, New York. Built between 1840 and 1883, the wood-frame houses are the only extant remnants of Weeksville, an early and affluent nineteenth-century free black community. The society's longtime leader, Joan Maynard, believes that saving historic places such as Weeksville gives African Americans, especially children, an essential link to their past. This link to both accomplishments and ordinariness offers a sense of pride and positive outlook, according to Maynard.[13]

Weeksville was named for James Weeks, a free black man who purchased land there in 1838. In the nineteenth century the community offered economic opportunities and drew free blacks from the South as well as African Americans seeking refuge from white mobs following the 1863 riots in Manhattan. Weeksville thrived for nearly a half-century and supported a school, orphanage, old-age home, and two churches. Today vacant land and a 1,100-unit public housing complex stand close to the houses; only two other Weeksville structures, a church and a benevolent institution, survive.

During an era of aggressive urban renewal planning by the city redevelopment authority in the late 1960s, Joseph Haynes, an engineer and pilot, and Jim Hurley, a historian, discovered the small farmhouses that stood along an irregular lane called Hunterfly Road from Haynes's two-seater plane. Their effort to learn more about Weeksville emerged from Hurley's Pratt Neighborhood College workshop on Brooklyn neighborhoods. Following the rediscovery, community leaders in 1968 created the Society for the Preservation of Weeksville and Bedford-Stuyvesant, whose broad mission was to research and disseminate the history of African Americans in central Brooklyn, particularly the nineteenth-century Weeksville community (fig. 13.5).

Over the past thirty years the society has purchased and restored all four cottages, although the effort has not been without setbacks. The first house was opened to the public in 1985. One house was burned in 1973 and had to be rebuilt. Another was nearly destroyed by vandals. A car crashed into another, destroying renovations that had taken two years to finance (fig. 13.6).

In an effort to enhance the visitor experience of Weeksville, Joan Maynard, executive director for twenty-five years, and now Pamela Green have led a complementary campaign to create an institution so that the history of black Brooklynites and New Yorkers as a whole would have a home in Brooklyn. In 1995 the city adopted an urban renewal plan that provides the Weeksville Society with control of land adjacent to the historic houses for erecting a museum.

The type of context that the Gilman House lost in its move is what the Weeksville Society promotes through public programs. The society also plans to recreate the road that the houses stood along in the mid-nineteenth century and other historic features to provide a new sense of place

Fig. 13.5. Brooklyn, N.Y. Joan Maynard viewing one of the Weeksville properties, c. 1968. Photo by William Cary, courtesy of the Society for the Preservation of Weeksville and Bedford-Stuyvestant History.

Fig. 13.6. Brooklyn, N.Y. Weeksville properties, 1998. Photo by Jack Jupp, courtesy of the Society for the Preservation of Weeksville and Bedford-Stuyvestant History.

and connection to the past. "A dream that has evolved for thirty years approaches reality," said Maynard.[14] The new multiyear funding by the city and other sources should strengthen the organization and advance the major preservation and interpretive project.

This chapter highlights the Gilman House, Paulsdale, and Weeksville as case studies because each project illustrates how the mission of the organization, its leaders, and its target audience continue to be decisive factors in how nonprofits decide to preserve and interpret sites. Each nonprofit group's analysis of the historic integrity of its site served as a primary influence as each planned and executed different types of restoration, reuse, and interpretation projects. In its own way each of the three nonprofit organizations has succeeded in preserving an aspect of women's history.

While the case studies show that nonprofit organizations should be prepared to compromise and develop creative solutions, they also show that the organizations should also be guided by standards that ensure that the preservation of architectural features successfully captures the cultural significance of a place. With women's heritage sites, and other sites significant for their cultural heritage, advocates must identify the physical elements that contribute to its significance as a landmark. These elements may be an entire landscape, a whole structure, interior spaces, outbuildings, plantings, open space, and relationships between features. Advocates must fully research and analyze how these architectural elements relate to the site's cultural significance when establishing restoration, reuse, and interpretative plans.[15]

The ability to provide a provocative demonstration of a site's cultural heritage may also relate to use. Folklore offers preservationists a helpful perspective when evaluating how best to preserve a site that is significant for its association with a person, event, or cultural development. Simply stated, significance is tied to patterns of use and the continuity of an activity or tradition.

The Pasadena model offers an example of a simple continuum of activity. The house where Gilman and her descendants lived remains in use as a residence. In a different manner the Alice Paul Centennial Foundation has capitalized on the spirit of the significance of Paulsdale. Because Paul's early years at her family home are seen as influential in the development of her political philosophy and her success, the foundation was drawn to the site as a leadership training center for young women.

The Weeksville model relies heavily on public programs to convey the activities that occurred at the site over one hundred years ago. On another level the society has revived or created a new Weeksville community. Every generation—from children in the Weeksville school to octogenarians—is involved in the preservation and promotion of this historic place. The organization's awareness of its own history is evident in interviews and publications; the deaths of participants are recorded with strong familial tones.

Meeting these preservation objectives requires advocates to raise public awareness and build critical partnerships. In addition to exploring what physical features best related to cultural heritage significance, this chapter offers the nonprofit organizations' "best practices" for generating support for their missions and ideas for building the organizational capacity of local preservation movements.

Building Public Awareness for Threatened Properties

Leaders of preservation projects related to women's history often have difficulty securing supporters. Potential allies, such as members of the general public, preservation professionals, and politicians, are often not cultivated because they do not know the significance of the person or historical theme, they have a misunderstanding of the person or theme, or the issue is controversial. Many of the politicians, preservationists, and educators whom Barbara Irvine approached in the effort to save Paulsdale, for example, first had to be educated about Alice Paul's significance in history. The appearance of cultural heritage sites can also create a challenge for advocates. Potential constituents may need to be convinced that modest places such as the Gilman House or deteriorated properties in highly altered settings such as the Weeksville houses are worth saving.

Advocates stress the need to combine direct public outreach with educational and promotional programs to raise public awareness for threatened properties. The Alice Paul Centennial Foundation secured "VIP" support to add legitimacy to its campaign and boost its national profile. Elected officials, entertainers, and prominent feminists, including Bella Abzug, Marlo Thomas, and Shirley Chisolm, lent their names to the cause. Nominations from the foundation to the U.S. Postal Service helped secure an Alice Paul stamp to commemorate the seventy-fifth anniversary of women's suffrage. Promotional events surrounding the release of the stamp helped increase public awareness of Paul's contribution and the foundation's cause.

The Weeksville Society has engaged children throughout its campaign (fig. 13.7). In the group's publications and presentations it has frequently made point that children from the Weeksville public school, P.S. 243, first had the dream to save the houses and make a black history museum. In 1970 children testified at a New York City Landmarks Commission meeting in support of New York landmark designation for the houses and raised a thousand dollars to start a restoration project. Twenty-five years later students from P.S. 243 spoke at a public hearing in support of funding for a Weeksville museum.

Pasadena Heritage's partnerships with the City of Pasadena and the owners of the Gilman house were essential to its success. Pasadena

Fig. 13.7. Brooklyn, N.Y. A school group at Weeksville. Photo by Jack Jupp, courtesy of the Society for the Preservation of Weeksville and Bedford-Stuyvestant History.

Heritage also secured support of neighborhood groups in the area to which they were moving the house. To draw attention to Gilman and their preservation objectives, the group hosted an on-site celebration the night of the move, produced an exhibit on Gilman and the house's rehabilitation for the city's main library, and celebrated with an open house for neighbors when the project was complete. The Weeksville Society's aggressive programming has generated important data and partnerships with local community groups, area institutions, and a national network of African American scholars and museum professionals. Weeksville projects have included oral history programs, tours, high-profile conferences, and children's activities.

Historic designation can also draw attention to a threatened property. The terms *National Register* and *Landmark* resonate with the general public and the media. Some public sector funding programs and private foundations use National Historic Landmark or National Register status as a criteria for grant funding, and local landmark designation often offers protection from inappropriate alterations or unnecessary demolitions. The Weeksville Society secured New York City Landmark status in 1970. Paulsdale was designated a National Historic Landmark in 1994, and the Gilman House became a City Cultural Heritage Landmark in 1980.

Strong media relations are also essential in broadcasting the message of the preservation cause. Pasadena Heritage produced a video of the Gilman House which ran on local television stations. News coverage and editorial support in New Jersey newspapers as well as several key stories in the *New York Times* helped the Alice Paul Centennial Foundation raise funds for its efforts.

Building the Movement: Preventative Measures for Nonprofits

Although the Gilman and Paulsdale projects were long, arduous, and expensive, their advocates were working with small, single structures, already-identified historic sites, and sites associated with prominent women. There are projects such as Weeksville with greater hurdles to overcome, and over the last decade scholars and preservation practitioners have emphasized the need to look beyond traditional preservation projects such as saving the home of a prominent woman. The identification, preservation, and interpretation of structures and places associated with less prominent women, the contribution of women in groups, and minority communities are essential.

The following principles emphasize expanding the scope of resources that are being saved and building the capacity of the preservation movement at the local level. These activities suggest proactive planning and reduce the need for reactive efforts.

CONDUCT SURVEY OF LOCAL RESOURCES

Advocates need to understand the breadth and significance of historic sites in their cities and towns. Sites that are threatened and documentation of local landmarks which overlooks women's contributions reinforce the need for planning.[16] One of the Weeksville Society's first projects was to gather information on the lost and extant structures from the Weeks-ville community as well as information about the community's history, people, institutions, economics, and work.

UTILIZE THE NATIONAL HISTORIC LANDMARK
STUDY AT THE LOCAL LEVEL

The research and analysis produced for the 1992 Women's History Land-mark Project, which culminated in the publication of *Reclaiming the Past: Landmarks of Women's History* and the designation of forty national his-toric landmarks, provides valuable historic context material for local sites. The publication's essays on politics, architecture, arts, community, edu-cation, politics, religion, and work offer information on the significance of national leaders and historical themes. The essays also serve as models for how to develop a historic context for the assessment of local sites of his-toric districts.

TAP WOMEN'S PHILANTHROPY AND THE RESOURCES
OF WOMEN'S ORGANIZATIONS

Analysis of philanthropic giving shows that women's heritage sites advo-cates have a long tradition of successful fund raising and that they may benefit from new national trends.[17] Women control more wealth than they ever have in the past, and giving to cultural, health, and social ser-vice programs is rising. Work by organizations such as Women in Philan-thropy and the New England Women's Fund to secure more foundation board of directors seats for women should also have a positive effect on donations to women's programs.

Groups such as the Junior League also have a long tradition of preser-vation activity. The Junior League helped to form Pasadena Heritage in the 1970s and maintains a supportive relationship. The Alice Paul Centennial Foundation has secured support from the national and local chapters of the National Organization for Women, Business and Professional Women, the League of Women Voters, and the American Association of University Women. According to president Lucienne, the groups are drawn to the preservation project by the need for equal rights for women and the legacy of Alice Paul. Members of the group give time and money to the

Paulsdale project because of its current mission, leadership training for girls.[18]

ENGAGE NEW CONSTITUENCIES

This long tradition of women saving historic sites should be linked to new goals and new constituent groups. Emerging alliances of African Americans, Latinos, gays and lesbians, and other groups offer opportunities to exchange information about difficult cultural heritage preservation issues as well as to strengthen the preservation movement. The National Association for African American Heritage Preservation wants to increase participation of African Americans in historic preservation and use historic preservation tools to help improve the quality of life for African Americans.

Preservation Pennsylvania, the Pennsylvania Historical and Museum Commission, and local groups launched a city-based model of increasing participation by Latinos in historic preservation in 1997. The sponsors produced a set of workshops to improve communication between preservation leaders and Latino communities in Philadelphia and Lancaster.

SHARE ADVOCACY STRATEGIES AND SUCCESSES

Exchanging information on "wins" and "losses" helps other advocates. Conferences, awards programs, and Internet-based formats continue to offer many possibilities. The ability to organize constituents, apparent in the Weeksville, Paulsdale, and Gilman House examples, remains at the heart of any successful campaign. The three case studies offer models for building public awareness and effective collaborations when faced with demolition, deterioration, or other threats to significant sites. The advocacy projects also provide an opportunity to discuss ways to build the capacity of cultural heritage sites preservation efforts at the local level.

In addition to offering political and planning advice, these examples offer diverse models of preservation priorities for sites that are defined less by their architectural merit and more by association with events, important historical figures, or broad patterns of cultural life. Treatments of their surroundings, interiors, and relationships between features reveal ways to relate architectural features of a place to its cultural significance.

CHAPTER 14

"It's a Wide Community Indeed"

Alliances and Issues in Creating
Women's Rights National Historical Park,
Seneca Falls, New York

Judith Wellman

Women have always been involved in the movement for historic preservation. Usually, they preserve sites related to men. Ann Pamela Cunningham's campaign to save Mount Vernon was only the first of a long tradition. One park, Women's Rights National Historical Park in Seneca Falls, New York, offers a contrast. It commemorates the first U.S. women's rights convention, held in 1848 in Seneca Falls, New York. This is the story of how that park was born.[1]

Located in upstate New York between the major cities of Rochester and Syracuse, Women's Rights National Historical Park (WRNHP) includes a Visitors' Center and three sites related to the first women's rights convention: the Wesleyan Chapel, where the convention actually met (fig. 14.1); the Stanton house, home of Elizabeth Cady Stanton, the convention's main organizer; and the M'Clintock house in nearby Waterloo, New York, where the convention's major document, its Declaration of Sentiments, was written. Complementing National Park Service efforts, the State of New York created an Urban Cultural Park to interpret the broader history of Seneca Falls, and the Village of Seneca Falls defined a historic district to preserve the historic character of village neighborhoods. Two other historical agencies offer visitors additional perspectives. The National Women's Hall of Fame honors famous women of national importance, while the Seneca Falls Historical Society focuses on the history of the local community.

The significance of Women's Rights Park derives from the importance of the Seneca Falls convention. In 1848 Elizabeth Cady Stanton, with the

Fig. 14.1. Seneca Falls, N.Y. Wesleyan Chapel, built in 1843, was the site of the 1848 women's rights convention and is now part of Women's Rights National Historical Park. Photo by Judith Wellman.

assistance of Elizabeth and Mary Ann M'Clintock and several other local people, called this convention to discuss the "social, civil, and religious rights and duties of women." Sixty-eight women and thirty-two men signed the Declaration of Sentiments, patterned after the Declaration of Independence, asserting that "all men and women are created equal" and that women should have equal rights with men in politics, marriage, jobs, education, religion, and the law. As one signer acknowledged, this document was "of the kind called radical." Americans throughout the country responded to its challenge. From 1848 to the present, the ideal that all men and women are created equal continued to challenge American definitions of gender roles.

Given the themes of the Seneca Falls women's rights convention, some would question why the federal government would sponsor WRNHP at all. When the park celebrated its grand opening in 1982, Ronald Reagan was president, James Watt was secretary of the interior, and the American public had defeated the Equal Rights Amendment. This chapter argues that the birth of WRNHP was indeed remarkable, but it was not miraculous. It was made possible by a lively and vocal alliance between government agencies and public advocates, facilitated by key politicians.

Public advocates for a new women's rights park included community boosters, feminists, and scholars. What made this perhaps unlikely alliance work well was the permeability of boundaries between these groups. Community boosters, while sometimes fearful of feminist ideas, recognized the economic value of women's rights. Feminists, motivated primarily by the symbolism of Seneca Falls for contemporary gender issues, recognized the importance of working with real people in a real place. Scholars, whose interest lay in understanding the past on its own terms, were energized by their own commitment to social justice. All three groups remained open to dialogue. What might have become a contest between using the past as "heritage" and understanding the past as "history" (to borrow David Lowenthal's distinction) became instead a collaboration, in which groups with different purposes functioned as a team and infused each other with energy.[2]

In 1858 Ann Pamela Cunningham's work with the Mount Vernon Ladies' Association provided a model. "I was painfully depressed at the ruin and desolation of the home of Washington," she reported, "and the thought passed through my mind: Why was it that the women of his country did not try to keep it in repair, if the men could not do it?" Outraged and inspired, Ann Pamela spoke the words that every preservationist has echoed ever since, "I shall do it!" And, in spite of the seeming impossibility of organizing a national movement when the nation itself was on the road to civil war, she did.[3]

That same year Elizabeth Cady Stanton received a request from the Mount Vernon Ladies' Association to become a "Lady Manager." Stanton replied publicly and scornfully. "Every energy of my body and soul is pledged to a higher and holier work than building monuments," she wrote.

> The constitutions and statute laws of every State in this Republic are in direct antagonism to the immutable truths set forth in our Declaration of Independence, and the ghosts of Washington, Jefferson and Adams should haunt us with "the cry of liberty: 'Go! strike the chains from every

slave! Go! give your mothers their rights to personal liberty, to their children, property, and homes! Go, give to every citizen of this Republic, black and white, male and female, the right of trial by a jury of his peers! Let no citizen be taxed without representation!' . . . What mightier monument can we raise to the memory of Washington than to complete the pure temple of liberty."[4]

In spite of Stanton's opposition, the Mount Vernon ladies had far more success in restoring Washington's home than Stanton did in completing her "pure temple of liberty." In fact, as Charles Hosmer Jr. argued, "Mount Vernon was the first successful nation-wide effort at preservation," and its effect "can hardly be overestimated, for almost every early preservation group had some contact with the Ladies' Association." William J. Murtagh argued that Ann Pamela Cunningham's work at Mount Vernon was so influential that it established "certain presuppositions about historic preservation in America. These assumptions included the idea that private citizens, not government, were the proper advocates for preservation; that only buildings and sites associated with military and political figures were worthy of preservation; that such sites must be treated as shrines or icons; and that women would assume a dominant role in the acquisition and management of such properties."[5]

One hundred and twenty years later preservationists challenged every tenet of this basic model when they organized a new campaign. Ironically, this campaign was to save Stanton's own house. Their intent was not to commemorate a successful revolution but to generate debate about the unfinished challenge of equality for all people. They would treat sites not primarily as shrines but as historical artifacts. And they would involve private citizens as well as government agencies and women as well as men.

Inspired by the resurgence of the women's rights movement in the 1960s, Americans rekindled their interest in Seneca Falls. In 1977 relay runners from Seneca Falls opened the International Women's Year celebration in Houston, Texas. In Seneca Falls President Jimmy Carter's daughter-in-law, Judy Carter, read a new Declaration of Sentiments written by Maya Angelou, proclaiming that "we promise to accept nothing less than justice for every woman." The next morning Millicent Brady Moore, a collateral descendant of Susan Quinn, youngest signer of the 1848 Seneca Falls Declaration, handed the torch to the first runner.

Fifty-one days, fourteen states, and twenty-six hundred miles later, a thousand women accompanied the torch on "its last grand mile." Its entrance into the convention hall was, noted the official report, "one of the most dramatic features of the Conference." Three First Ladies—Lady Bird Johnson, Betty Ford, and Rosalynn Carter—formally accepted the torch.[6]

In 1978 public concern began to coalesce specifically around the preservation of sites related to the Seneca Falls convention. Two organizations, one local and the other national, acted as catalysts to connect contemporary and historic visions of women's rights. Locally, citizens of Seneca Falls organized the Elizabeth Cady Stanton Foundation (ECSF) to save Stanton's own house. Nationally, the National Park Service identified Seneca Falls as a potential new historic park. Existing historical and women's organizations within New York State (including the New York State Studies Group, the Upstate New York Women's History Organization, the Regional Conference of Historical Agencies, the New York State Council on the Arts, and the New York Council for the Humanities) as well as political support from Lieutenant Governor Mary Ann Krupsak helped create a supportive climate. Regional women's groups—including the American Association of University Women, Business and Professional Women, and two Syracuse chapters of the National Organization for Women (NOW)—also embraced the cause.

When private owners proposed to sell the Elizabeth Cady Stanton house, concerned citizens sprang into action. Lucille Povero, Corinne Guntzel, Mary Curry, Marina Brown, Hans Kuttner, and others began a campaign. Meeting in July, almost exactly 130 years since the original convention, representatives from NOW, the Seneca Falls Historical Society, the National Women's Hall of Fame, the Downtown Revitalization Committee, and the Town Young People's Committee developed plans for a Women's Rights Historic District. Mary Curry epitomized this group's emphasis on direct grassroots action when she carried out an informational vigil in front of the Wesleyan Chapel to mark the anniversary of the convention on July 19–20, 1978 (fig. 14.2). By the end of 1978 this group had changed its name to the Elizabeth Cady Stanton Foundation.

From the beginning, the board of the ECSF was motivated by feminist ideals. They intended that Stanton should be interpreted as the rad-

Fig. 14.2. Seneca Falls, N.Y. Mary Curry, Seneca Falls resident, and uniden-
tified passerby at card table display commemorating the 130th anniversary of
the Seneca Falls women's rights convention, July 1978, in front of the Wesleyan
Chapel. Photo courtesy of the Women's Rights National Historical Park.

ical thinker that she was and that her home and the site of the 1848 convention should become vehicles both for understanding the origins of the
women's rights movement and for carrying its spirit into the present.
Preserving the Stanton house and the Wesleyan Chapel, however, quickly
gained support from a much broader spectrum of the community. Although

some citizens were worried about attracting "bra-burners" to the streets of Seneca Falls, everyone recognized the economic potential of tourism. For a community that had lost much of its industrial base, a new national park would be a major economic asset. That potential quickly became more real when two tourists, Ralph Peters and Marjorie Smith, both from Seattle, visited the Stanton house. Shocked to discover its condition, Peters reported the story to the National Organization for Women, and NOW supporters began sending donations to help preserve the house.[7]

Meanwhile, the National Park Service began to survey potential sites relating to women and people of color. As part of this study, two Park Service representatives, Judy Hart and Shary Berg, visited Seneca Falls in December 1978. They were overwhelmed by their enthusiastic reception. Local people "came out of the woodwork," noted Judy Hart, and "just piled onto the car." With interest from the NPS and with support from NOW, what had seemed a few months before to be merely a local concern, with little prospect of success, suddenly assumed larger significance.[8]

In 1979 three developments outside Seneca Falls further energized local support. First, the NPS recommended that Congress create a new national park in Seneca Falls, devoted to the theme of women's rights. Second, Ralph Peters purchased the Stanton house, to hold it until the Stanton Foundation could raise money to buy it (fig. 14.3). And, third, the Regional Conference of Historical Agencies, a network of museums and historic sites in central New York, held a conference in Seneca Falls on women's history. Although they expected only one hundred people, an audience of four hundred attended. There could be no doubt now about public interest in women's history and popular support for Seneca Falls.

Suddenly, the real prospect of acquiring the Stanton house and establishing a new national historical park seemed much more real. Nothing was certain. No one was quite sure where to begin. Everyone, however, recognized that local citizens could make a difference. Under the leadership of the first two presidents—Lucille Povero, a saleswoman at a local car dealership, and Corinne Guntzel, an economics professor at a local college—the ECSF worked creatively and aggressively to generate local, state, and national support for the proposed park.

To generate national support, the Foundation developed an honorary board, made up of well-known feminist politicians, activists, and academics. Among the most influential were actor Alan Alda, *Redbook* publisher Sey Chessler, and special liaison from the lieutenant governor's office, Nancy Dubner. Support from Stanton's great-grandchildren, Rhoda Barney Jenkins and John Barney, and from Rhoda Barney Jenkins's daughter, Colline Jenkins-Sahline, brought extra energy to the cause. One fall day they arrived in Seneca Falls with a load of books and furniture that had once belonged to Stanton. "It's time they came home," declared Jenkins.[9]

Locally and nationally, renewed scholarly interest about Stanton and the early women's rights movement also contributed to the sense that

Fig. 14.3. Seneca Falls, N.Y. In front of the Elizabeth Cady Stanton house about 1979, Lucille Povero, first president of the Elizabeth Cady Stanton Foundation, stands with Ralph Peters of Seattle, Washington, who purchased the Stanton house to save it as a historic site. Photo courtesy of the Women's Rights National Historical Park.

what had happened in Seneca Falls in 1848 had implications far beyond the village itself. Corinne Guntzel, an economist, and Paul Grebinger, an archaeologist, initiated an archaeological dig on the grounds of the Stanton house, funded by the New York State Council on the Humanities, using local volunteers. Pat Holland and Ann Gordon at the University of Massachusetts began to edit the papers of Elizabeth Cady Stanton and Susan B. Anthony. Lois Banner and Elisabeth Griffith published new biographies of Stanton, while Margaret Hope Bacon completed her work on Lucretia Mott.[10]

Inspired by strong constituent support, congressmen and senators formally requested the National Park Service to prepare legislation to create a women's rights park. On February 5, 1980, Representatives Gary Lee (R-N.Y.), Jonathan Bingham (D-N.Y.), and Phillip Burton (D-Calif.) introduced legislation into the House (H.R. 5407) to create a women's rights park. At the same time, Senators Jacob Javits (R-N.Y.) and Daniel Patrick Moynihan (D-N.Y.) introduced identical legislation, S 2263, into the Senate.[11]

The ECSF immediately began to lobby for the new bills. Letters went out to women's organizations. Honorary trustee Nancy Dubner met with the Congressional Women's Caucus. In May ECSF president Lucille Povero testified before Congress.[12]

General public support created a favorable climate for the proposed park. In January *Ms.* magazine helped publicize the cause with an article entitled "Seneca Falls Rises." In March President Jimmy Carter designated the week of March 8 as women's history week. And the ERA continued to plod toward what most people assumed would be its eventual success. On May 20, 1980, supporters of the park rejoiced. The House had voted, 300 to 102, to authorize the new women's rights park.[13]

Meanwhile, the ECSF made considerable progress toward purchasing the Stanton house. In February the Foundation received a matching grant of $16,500 from the Heritage Conservation and Recreation Service, through the New York State Office of Parks and Recreation, to buy the house from Ralph Peters. By July it had raised an additional $3,000 in small local donations.[14]

In late fall public support saved the proposed park from stillbirth. On October 1 Lucille Povero discovered that the Senate was about to adjourn before the park bill had even left the Senate subcommittee. Povero went into action. "Lobbying works," she declared.

> I made phone calls that day to Honorary trustees Sey Chessler, Lynda Johnson Robb and Alan Alda, as well as Senators Javits, Moynihan and Bumpers to see if there was any chance of reviving the bill. But one of the most important calls, it turns out, was to Congressman Phil Burton who promised me he'd see the bill through the lame duck session. I'm just as convinced, looking back, that had I not met the man face-to-face at the House sub-committee hearings in May, he would not have gone out of his way to help us. So I guess the second lesson to be learned is the importance of "in person" contact with legislators.[15]

Burton formally shepherded the Seneca Falls bill through the House as part of a proposal to expand the boundary of Crater Lake National Park. Povero sent Burton a dozen roses in appreciation. "The whole process," reported Povero, "was inspirational. To know that those representing us in Washington can be moved is a real 'high.' And we were successful. It feels good to win one, doesn't it?"[16]

Win they did. On December 28, 1980, President Carter signed into law the bill that established the Women's Rights National Historical Park in Seneca Falls. The ECSF felt properly proud. "Looking back on the brief history of the Foundation (has it only been two and a half years?)," it noted, "the primary goal of preserving and restoring the home of ECS has been realized far beyond the dreams of those who first saw the 'House for Sale' ad in the spring of 1978. The initial idea has grown to encompass all of the sites important to the First Convention for Woman's Rights held in Seneca Falls in 1848."[17]

The park was now a reality, but it existed only on paper. As everyone recognized, the task of park supporters had just begun. Paramount, of course, was the need for money. Just because Congress and the president had declared their intent to establish a women's rights park did not mean they would fund it.

Complicating the situation was a clear change in the national political climate. Jimmy Carter had signed the bill authorizing Women's Rights Park as one of his last official acts. Four days later Ronald Reagan was inaugurated as president of the United States. Reagan appointed James Watt as secretary of the interior, and Watt's goals did not include support for the National Park Service. One of his first acts was to freeze land acquisition monies. Suddenly the future of Women's Rights Park looked doubtful indeed.

Herbert Cables Jr., director of the Northeast Regional Office of the NPS, took immediate action. He appointed Judy Hart as park coordinator, with a budget of ten thousand dollars for summer programming. Hart became a focal point for planning and for channeling information between the Park Service and Seneca Falls. Contacts she developed with members of the ECSF were essential in maintaining local energies and in coordinating local and national efforts.[18]

In 1981 the primary goal of the ECSF was to lobby Congress for park funding. The Foundation's trump card, of course, was the Stanton house. If the ECSF could buy the house and give it outright to the Park Service, Women's Rights Park might have a real future. By the spring of 1981, however, individual contributions totaled only $8,000. At this critical point the Foundation approached honorary trustee Alan Alda. Would he be able to attend a fund-raiser in Seneca Falls? Alda responded with a telephone call to Lucille Povero. He would not be able to attend, he said, but how much money did the foundation need?

"$11,000."

"I'll send you a check," he replied.

In one stunningly generous and completely unexpected contribution, Alda put the campaign over the top. As Povero explained it to the ECSF, "He felt very strongly that this house has to be saved, and that this was the least he could do." By May the foundation had raised $25,450.[19]

The success of this fund-raising campaign reflected success in other areas, too. Local citizens formed the Seneca Falls Historic District Committee and began to lobby the New York State legislature, with support from the ECSF, to form an Urban Cultural Park. By the end of the year the state had created a new Seneca Falls Urban Cultural Park, with $30,000 to implement it.[20]

Most important, the ECSF strengthened its ties with other groups, especially with the scholarly community, by forming a new coalition. The Seneca Falls Consortium included local historical groups (the National Women's Hall of Fame and the Seneca Falls Historical Society), scholarly organizations (the Upstate New York Women's History Organization, the New York State Studies Group, and the Women's Studies Program at Eisenhower College), and Women's Rights National Historical Park itself. To reach beyond local and regional support, this consortium cosponsored with the NPS an exhibit and reception at the Fifth Berkshire Conference on Women's History, held in June 1981 at Vassar College. More than five hundred people attended. Locally, the consortium worked with the Regional Conference of Historical Agencies to develop a series called "Upstate: Dialogues on the Cultural Background," including one on "Community Women's History: Perspectives for Seneca Falls," with a paper by Joan Hoff, the new director of the Organization of American Historians (OAH). The group continued the series in 1982 with presentations on women and the home, fashion, work, government, religion, and history. Support from the New York State Council on the Arts and from the National Endowment for the Humanities, through the New York Council for the Humanities, made these programs possible.[21]

Successes in the spring and summer of 1981 buoyed hopes. So did word of a new proposal from New York State Senator Daniel Patrick Moynihan. To maneuver around the Interior Department's freeze on land acquisition, Moynihan proposed a $150,000 supplement to the 1982 federal budget, not to buy sites but to develop programming for WRNHP. Here, at last, was a concrete proposal that would bring the park into existence as a working entity, and the ECSF began a strong lobbying campaign to support Moynihan's initiative.[22]

Just as park supporters found themselves cheered by possibilities for park funding, one more obstacle appeared, this one from an unexpected place. Ralph Peters suffered a stroke in February 1981 and remained in the hospital until the end of April. By the time that Peters began to recover, he had had an opportunity to observe James Watt's efforts to cut back support for the NPS. As a result, he was concerned that the Park Service would be unable or unwilling to maintain and interpret the Stanton house in an appropriate way. "Reagan and Watt are absolutely the last people in the world that I would want to have anything to do with anything," Peters reported in a telephone interview. "I have absolutely no confidence in the feds. . . . We've seen the Reagan administration chip away at women's issues and the

National Park Service. I've always been a strong believer in public lands and national parks, but now Yellowstone Park will be a slick commercial operation. . . . It's my real wish that the house become some sort of memorial that would do justice to the ideals that Stanton stood for." Wary of the initial agreement he had made to sell the house to the ECSF, he began to explore other options, including the possibility of allowing a private organization to maintain and interpret the house.[23]

By fall park supporters were seriously concerned. The very existence of WRNHP hung in the balance. Appeals from ECSF trustees failed to change Peters' mind. Desiring to protect the Stanton house and impressed with Judy Hart's "exceptional vision," Peters nevertheless refused to relinquish control of the Stanton house. Sey Chassler reminded Peters that "we may lose all we have worked for and you may be left with a historical relic that serves no purpose and has lost its value." Still, Peters refused to budge.[24]

Meanwhile, the house itself deteriorated. A Park Service appraisal in January 1981 concluded that the condition of the house was "very poor" and that the roof and chimney in particular needed immediate repair. Lights, heat, and electricity had been turned off in July. In October the ECSF and Hart returned the keys they held to the Stanton house and absolved themselves of further responsibility for its upkeep.[25]

Threatened with a loss of this magnitude, Emil Bove, attorney for the ECSF, wrote to Steve Lewis, deputy regional director, urging direct contact between Park Service officials and Ralph Peters. The Park Service responded immediately and fully. On December 4, 1981, National Park Service director Russell Dickenson, deputy regional director Steve Lewis, park coordinator Judy Hart, and acting regional director Herb S. Cables Jr. met with Ralph Peters and Marjorie Smith in Seattle. Cables reported the outcome to the ECSF. "During that meeting," he noted, "Director Dickenson assured Ralph Peters that the Park Service is committed to this site, and takes very seriously its obligation to maintain, protect, and interpret properties that it owns. I further assured Mr. Peters of the commitment of the Regional Office to this Park." And then came the best news of all. "Mr. Peters decided in that meeting," Cables reported, "that he would sell the house to the Stanton Foundation." On December 18, two days short of a year since Congress and the president had officially authorized Women's Rights Park, the ECSF, for $43,500, finally acquired the Stanton house.[26]

The Park Service moved quickly. In January, Herb Cables Jr. came to Seneca Falls himself to announce the appointment of Judy Hart as the first superintendent for WRNHP. Just as important, he brought news of a $105,000 appropriation for the park for 1982, enough to hire not only Hart but a secretary, an historian, and two summer park rangers. Finally, Cables announced the allocation of $35,000 to stabilize the Stanton house itself and to begin preservation planning. At last! The park was alive![27]

Alliances between local and national supporters, private citizens and government, scholars and the general public, had created WRNHP, and, as the park came closer to full operation in the spring of 1982, these alliances expanded their functions. Scholars were an integral part of this coalition. When the Organization of American Historians met in Philadelphia in April, Gerda Lerner became the organization's first woman president. She appointed Judith Wellman as chair of the OAH Committee on the Status of Women. The committee made its main theme "Women and Public History" and focused on Seneca Falls as a case study. At the annual meeting Mary Kay Tachau and Carl Degler presented a contrapuntal reading of the Declaration of Independence and the Seneca Falls Declaration of Sentiments, to juxtapose symbolically the ideals of the first American Revolution with those of the women's rights revolution. A panel on "The Seneca Falls Women's Rights Convention: The People and Their World" emphasized the importance of alliances between scholars from different fields, historical agencies, and the public in promoting women's history.

Meanwhile, in Seneca Falls the whole community celebrated. April 21 became "Ralph Peters Day"; Mayor Robert Freeland presented Peters with a key to Seneca Falls; and park supporters held a testimonial dinner. "For the Foundation," reported the ECSF, "the effort to save the House has been like a long journey, filled with peaks and valleys, rough spots, and different forks along the way. With the House now ready for transfer to the National Park Service, it was fitting to celebrate the end of the journey in the company of fellow travelers and honor the trail breaker, Ralph Peters."[28]

Four years of work culminated on July 17, 1982, when the National Park Service officially opened Women's Rights Park to the public (fig.

Fig. 14.4. Seneca Falls, N.Y. The first staff of the Women's Rights National Historical Park, July 1982. *Front row, left to right:* Connie Hasto, ranger; Judith Wellman, historian; Janice Friebaum, ranger. *Rear, left to right:* Stephanie Dyer, administrative assistant; Nancy Hewitt, assistant historian; Debbie Wolfe, ranger; Judy Hart, superintendent; Ann Ritter, ranger; Margaret Bourke, secretary; Mary Beth Thorpe, intern. Photo courtesy of Women's Rights National Historical Park.

14.4). Three special activities made this celebration very different from previous Convention Day celebrations. All of them carried out the goals of building and reaffirming alliances between a local and a national audience, public and private institutions, scholars and the general public. All three focused on how past events related to present concerns. First, in the Presbyterian Church, site of the first call, in 1923, for an Equal Rights Amendment, local residents presented "Seneca Falls 1848: All Men and Women Are Created Equal," a dramatization of events leading to the original convention.[29] Second, the Seneca Falls Consortium and the new WRNHP sponsored a major conference on women and community history, held on the campus of Eisenhower College just east of Seneca Falls.

Fig. 14.5. Seneca Falls, N.Y. Alliances personified: representatives of local and national groups, citizen advocates, and government agencies at the grand opening of the Women's Rights National Historical Park, July 1982. *From left to right:* Robert Freeland, mayor of Seneca Falls; Alan Alda, actor, Equal Rights Amendment (ERA) advocate, and keynote speaker; Mary Lou Grier, assistant director of the National Park Service; Lucille Povero, first president of the Elizabeth Cady Stanton Foundation; Herbert Cables, Northeast regional director of the National Park Service; Corinne Guntzel, second president of the Elizabeth Cady Stanton Foundation. Photo by Kevin S. Colton, courtesy of the Women's Rights National Historical Park.

True to the long-standing goals of park supporters, this conference included not only scholars, historic site interpreters, archivists, and museum professionals but also community activists, representatives of women's groups, government officials, and ordinary people.[30] Finally, the park formally opened on July 17. A crowd of three to five thousand thronged the main street in Seneca Falls to hear a speech by Alan Alda and to witness the formal transfer of the Stanton house from the ECSF to the National

Park Service (fig. 14.5). As Howard Van Kirk, editor of the *Seneca Falls Reveille,* concluded, "What it all adds up to is an enthusiastic community effort, and it's a wide community indeed. Hurray! We've got our National Park!!"[31]

Comparing the development of WRNHP with the classic preservation story of Mount Vernon, it would be easy to emphasize similarities, to see the women's rights movement as an echo of the American Revolution, Elizabeth Cady Stanton as parallel to George Washington, and the ECSF as the modern equivalent of the Mount Vernon Ladies' Association. Such a comparison obscures the real differences between Mount Vernon and Seneca Falls. Seneca Falls produced no one individual with the impact of Ann Pamela Cunningham. Rather, it brought together a variety of local and national leaders. No single person could do it alone. Unlike Mount Vernon, support for Seneca Falls was not organized hierarchically but in a kind of work democracy, in which many people played key roles, often in unpredictable ways. Ultimately, Women's Rights Park was born because its supporters successfully built alliances between local and national

Fig. 14.6. Seneca Falls, N.Y. Statues of participants in the Seneca Falls women's rights convention stand in the main lobby of the Visitors' Center. Photo by Judith Wellman.

audiences, scholars and the general public, and citizens and government institutions.

Underlying support for Women's Rights Park was the women's movement itself. Historic preservation reflects contemporary values, and the new emphasis on sites related to women's rights reflected a profound change in American life, toward a renewed awareness of the importance of women, past and present. WRNHP rode the wave of popular enthusiasm for women's equality which emerged from the Houston convention and the fight for the ERA. Ironically, the country lost the ERA but gained Women's Rights National Historical Park.

While the park's grand opening marked the end of the fight to establish the park, it was only the beginning of the challenge to interpret the women's rights convention in the context both of its own time and ours. Ultimately, history is not only about the past but about the future. It remains for us as citizens to define what these sites meant in the 1840s and what they mean to us today. Preservation of sites relating to the 1848 Seneca Falls convention may, after all, help Americans to define that "pure temple of liberty" to which Elizabeth Cady Stanton devoted her life (fig. 14.6).

CHAPTER 15

"Raising Our Sites"
A Pilot Project for Integrating Women's History into Museums

Kim Moon

When the Pennsylvania Humanities Council (PHC) undertook a project to integrate women into the interpretation of the state's historic sites and museums in 1992, it found that most state sites were unready for the task. That some of the sites participating in the PHC's project offered comments at its conclusion such as "For the first time, staff members are articulating the need to consider women in the exhibitions" and "A major goal has been achieved: there are now women in our exhibit gallery" demonstrates how far many historic sites have to go in conveying half of the public's history to the public at large.

Development of a Project

In the early 1990s the PHC began to develop statewide programs that reflected the growing interest in women's studies topics among the community organizations it served. As one of the more active state councils in the development of its own programming to complement its grant making for local humanities projects, the PHC had achieved nationally recognized success with its innovative initiative on the bicentennials of the Constitution and the Bill of Rights. At the same time, the council was receiving tremendous response from a pilot women's literature discussion program and two statewide conferences it conducted on Pennsylvania women's history. In order to better meet the growing public demand as well as to further relationships with women's studies scholars across the state, the PHC undertook a major statewide programmatic initiative in women's studies beginning in 1991.

The primary audience for the council's various programming efforts was and remains the out-of-school adult. In the broadest context PHC programs are part of a sociocultural infrastructure of lifelong learning that extends to most of the settings in which the majority of PHC programs occur: libraries, historical societies, and community organizations, such as YWCAs and senior centers. The goal of all PHC activity is to bring together humanities scholars with community audiences either through direct association or through programming designed and generated collaboratively between scholars and community members. Central to the PHC's strategic plan of the time was to establish regional and statewide networks drawing on this combination of grassroots and academic resources.

As part of its initial planning for a women's studies initiative, in 1992 the PHC convened a group of advisors to identify specific areas of need across the state and to brainstorm projects that would be responsive to these needs. Among the advisors were several historians and museum professionals who commented on the absence of women's history at the state's historic sites and museums. These advisors reasoned that improvements in the presentation of women's history were essential if the state's historic facilities were to represent truly the full range of American life.

Further consideration of this situation by the PHC revealed more fully the potential for a project that would strengthen the representation of women's lives and experiences at Pennsylvania museums and historic sites. Because of its strategic place in American history, Pennsylvania contains a total of over five hundred historic places that annually serve hundreds of thousands of Americans—schoolchildren, families, and adults—who come to learn about our collective national history. In addition, more than seven hundred archive and manuscript collections are known to exist across the state. No doubt, perusal of these materials would yield significant insights into the lives of Pennsylvania women as far back as the seventeenth century. The large number of colleges and universities across the state provide over one hundred academic history departments that could serve as potential sources of support for scholarship. Yet, even with this plethora of resources, there existed only one known historic site at the time which prominently featured women in its permanent exhibit. As a result, visitors to Pennsylvania museums and historic sites found no exploration of the everyday lives of women of different economic classes, the emergence of women as industrial wage earners, or the contributions of women to intellectual and political life.

Yet the reasons behind these circumstances were critical ones. Despite the extraordinary breadth of scholarship that was being undertaken in women's history, little concentrated on the lives of Pennsylvania women specifically. And, while the scarcity of information had hindered interpretive efforts, the scarcity of financial resources compounded the problem even further. Being chronically underfunded, the small professional staff at the state's sites and museums for the most part worked outside the mainstream of the historical profession. As a result, they had little opportunity to keep abreast of new scholarship. Basically, the everyday demands of site management virtually eliminated the opportunity to conduct meaningful historical research.

The PHC and the Pennsylvania Historical and Museum Commission (PHMC) have had a long-standing relationship; indeed, the PHC receives its state funding through the commission. The PHMC, along with its associate agency, the Pennsylvania Federation of Museums and Historic Organizations, was supportive of the PHC's undertaking of a women's history project at Pennsylvania sites and museums, since such an effort did not directly fit its organizational mission. Other government-funded entities (since disbanded) whose activities dovetailed with the project but were not inherently part of its planning or structure were the Southwest Pennsylvania Heritage Preservation Commission and the Pennsylvania Heritage Affairs Commission. Aside from these organizations, and other interested individual sites, there was no collective activity focused on the history of women in the state or the preservation and interpretation of women's history at historic places.

In 1992 the PHC applied to the National Endowment for the Humanities (NEH) for an exemplary grant (a category then available to state humanities councils attempting to develop model projects) to create "Raising Our Sites: Women's History in Pennsylvania," a multiyear project to incorporate women's history into the interpretation of historic sites throughout the state of Pennsylvania. With initial funding from the NEH in the amount of $25,000, fourteen sites—which had already begun some work in women's history or which expressed a strong interest and had the capacity—developed individual work plans that reviewed collections and resources and outlined in detail their specific objectives for the integration of women's history into various aspects of their site. The work plans included public programming, collections policies, exhibit planning, staff training, and publications. These plans were developed in conjunction with three consultants: one academic and two public historians. The fourteen work plans formed the core of a proposal to the NEH for a three-year exemplary grant, which was awarded to the PHC in February 1993 to implement "Raising Our Sites."

The Essence of the Project: Linking Scholars with Museums

As outlined in the proposal, the goals developed for the project were ambitious and far reaching: to increase the understanding of women's history at the participating historical facilities; to strengthen the exhibitions and programming at each of the sites to include women of all racial, ethnic, and class backgrounds; to broaden the demographic base and increase the overall attendance at the facilities; to build a statewide network among participants to exchange ideas, encourage implementation of the project's goals, and create interest in the project on the part of nonparticipating sites; and to share the results of this project widely with other historical facilities across the state and nation.

At the core of the project was the element of collaboration between academic scholars and museum staff. The project's design provided two distinct opportunities for collaborative activity between scholars and site staff. Each site worked first with a designated "local" scholar, who was based near the site and who had a particular area of expertise that the site staff had established as necessary to achieve their goals. While the role of the local scholar varied from site to site, the activities this person undertook for the most part included assisting the staff in carrying out specific research projects, overseeing research projects by volunteers, and reviewing materials in collections and archives both at the site and at others nearby. The local scholar's activity frequently dictated the direction that the project took at a particular site; often the information and resources uncovered by the local scholar were unexpected and, as a result, forced site staff to reframe their basic assumptions and questions about the way women fit into their larger interpretive story. At the Landis Valley Museum, for example, an examination of account books and diaries revealed that some previous beliefs about the division of labor between men and women were incorrect—a large area of interpretation for a site dedicated to agricultural history. The discovery of photos, artifacts, and scrapbooks in forgotten boxes at Drake Well provided additional information on Laura Drake and other women who had settled the oil fields of northwestern Pennsylvania with their husbands, leading to a more complex analysis of their social and economic roles.

In addition to the local scholar, many of the sites utilized the expertise of the project's advisors, who consisted of academic and public historians affiliated with universities, the Smithsonian Institution, and other museums or research institutions. The advisors worked with individual sites in a consulting capacity, usually reviewing current exhibits and tours, examining collections and other holdings, and then brainstorming with staff about possible sources and direction for exhibits and programs.

Of the two scholarly resources made available to the participating sites, the local scholar was more valued and therefore more utilized. This was mainly due to the scholar's ongoing availability and resulting familiarity with the site. Yet the collaborative relationship was not without its obstacles. Initially, there was prejudice from some academic scholars about the ways in which history is conveyed to the public by museums and sites. Some scholars questioned the authenticity of the history represented, the academic training of the staff, or the need to consider the larger organizational culture. On the other hand, there was a belief among some museum staff that academic scholars did not understand the realities of interpreting history to the public. Some advisors recommended large-scale research plans that engaged multiple staff members for lengthy periods, while others were skeptical of popular interpretive methods such as first-person interpretation and the use of storytellers to recreate historical incidents or characters. The PHC, whose exposure to museum culture was more limited than its familiarity with the academic world, worked carefully with sites to identify and establish contact with scholars and to ameliorate any potential misunderstandings or conflicts that appeared. By the final year of the project many successful collaborations had resulted from the project between sites and their local scholars as well as their individual advisors. Interestingly, as the link between scholars and museum personnel grew, many site staff members were galvanized to pursue their own scholarship, an interest that had brought many of them into the museum field initially but had been subsequently been put aside by the day-to-day demands of museum operations.

In preparation for participating in "Raising Our Sites," staff from each of the sites worked with a project advisor to devise a work plan that detailed specific objectives in integrating women's history into their existing and/or planned interpretive programs and exhibits. These work plans were then reviewed and revised on a yearly basis over the course of the project. Many of the sites saw their goals and direction change as new information on the lives and experiences of women related to their site was uncovered. As a result, the work plans, designed as planning documents, became even more useful as they charted each site's journey, incorporating elements of both discovery and reflection. After submitting its revised work plan, each site then received an annual five hundred dollars in discretionary funds to support project-related activities.

Developing a Network of Historic Sites

The sites selected to participate were a diverse sample of Pennsylvania historic properties in terms of geographic locations, subject matter, and facility structure; they included one National Park Service site, five sites of the Pennsylvania Historical and Museum Commission, six private historical societies and museums, one research library, and one college.

While one of the crucial aspects of the project was the relationships that developed between the site staff and the scholars with whom they worked, the other important element was a series of meetings open to all site staff and volunteers, advisors, and local scholars participating in the project. In the first and final years of the project, two-day conferences were held which featured nationally known speakers and which were structured for maximum interaction among the participants. The conferences were attended by a combination of representatives from every site which included staff, volunteers, and board members. In addition, seven thematic meetings on topics identified by the sites as being of critical importance to their work—such as industrial history and women's lives, inclusionary and innovative exhibiting strategies, and methods for getting

Fig. 15.1. Harrisburg, Pa. Participants in "Raising Our Sites" exchange information and ideas with one another during a roundtable discussion. Photo courtesy of the Pennsylvania Humanities Council.

women's history materials into school settings—were designed and coordinated by various sites over the course of the project.

The meetings were of critical importance to the project's success, since they not only enabled participants to gather new information and renewed inspiration, but they also served as a basis for building a network of historic sites that shared a similar goal (fig. 15.1). Since the staff of many historic sites and museums work in isolation, reaching out only to those resources in their immediate communities or their existing networks, "Raising Our Sites" provided a way for participating sites to reach beyond their established contacts in a structured and ongoing way. Through the project site staff were able to share their successes and challenges with others across the state; take a leadership role in a particular aspect of programming, archival usage, audience development, or educational outreach; and exchange resource information and expertise with other sites that were attempting similar work. While the meetings provided opportunities for informal discussion, in addition to a more structured exchange on topics such as "Audience Development and Community Outreach" and "Building Collaborative Partnerships with Academic Consultants," some site staff contacted one another between meetings and, in a few cases, even traveled to one another's site to continue discussion on a particular theme or idea. The value of cooperation and exchange, which has been a vital component of the way women have carried out their work throughout history, was reinforced by its use in this project.

Another way that the sites were linked was through a project newsletter, *InSites*. Distributed once or twice a year by PHC staff, the newsletter helped to point participants to specific resources in women's history. The network of sites was also extended to include many organizations in the state which were not participating in the project but which shared many of its goals and areas of interest. The staff from these sites were invited to attend the project's thematic meetings and were added to the mailing lists of both *InSites* and the PHC's newsletter, *Pennsylvania Humanities*, which also reported regularly on the project.

A Sample Activity

Participating sites were not simply jumping on a revisionist history bandwagon by involving themselves in "Raising Our Sites." In some cases the work coincided with a site's overall planning effort for the coming years. Both the Historical Society of Western Pennsylvania and the Chester County Historical Society, for example, were in the process of transforming themselves into state-of-the-art history centers and were anxious to make their depiction of their community's history more representative. As a result, the stories of women and girls are prominently featured in the 15,000 square foot permanent exhibit *Points in Time: Building a Life in Western Pennsylvania* at the new Senator John Heinz Pittsburgh Regional History Center in Pittsburgh as well as the museum's Discovery Place for children and its new theater program Stages in History. Meanwhile, a major two-gallery exhibit that opened at the Chester County Historical Society six months after its expansion, *Do Everything: Women and Social Reform in Chester County*, was the recipient of national awards from the American Association of State and Local History and the National Women's History Project (fig. 15.2). Other new components of the Historical Society—including the Introductory Exhibit, the History Lab,

Fig. 15.2. Chester County, Pa. Chester County Historical Society's exhibit *Do Everything: Women and Reform in Chester County* was the recipient of recognition from the Pennsylvania Federation for Museums and Historical Organizations, the American Association for State and Local History, and the National Women's History Project. Photo courtesy of Chester County Historical Society.

and even the gift shop—are "permanent products of our sensitivity to women's history," according to associate director Beverly Sheppard.

The staff at Pennsbury Manor, the reconstructed summer home of William Penn, located north of Philadelphia, used "Raising Our Sites" to expand their focus to include information about specific servants and slaves who lived and worked at the site. The necessary research, which was done by local scholar Jean Soderlund of Lehigh University, involved a detailed search of local probate records, wills, inventories, and court minutes for information on African American men and women who lived in and around Pennsbury during the late seventeenth century. This research led to the development of a new tour that included information about Sue, an enslaved African American woman, her husband, Sam, and their daughter, little Sue, as well as housekeeper, Mary Lofty, and her assistant, Abigail Pemberton (fig. 15.3). An unexpected challenge arose, however, from this expanded interpretation of the site; the staff encountered resistance from many volunteer docents about the de-emphasization of William Penn in order to talk about "other people." In addition, the volunteers found that presenting William Penn as a slave owner was a potential controversy that they would rather avoid. In response, Pennsbury staff enlisted the guidance of project advisor Stephanie Grauman Wolf of the University of Pennsylvania. The site staff then began to conduct group discussions for guides to talk about the new interpretation plan and discuss how to handle uncomfortable issues. As a result, volunteers became more comfortable with the information, and they became eager to take on this new area of interpretation. According to project director Mary Ellyn Kunz: "Facing the affective as well as the cognitive aspects of interpretation was new ground for us . . . this project pointed out that we have to be not just attuned to interpreter emotions, but we also have to be willing to work with them and use them constructively."

Meanwhile, at the Joseph Priestley House, the central Pennsylvania home of the famed eighteenth-century scientist, the staff, in conjunction with local scholar Jane Dupree-Begos and a cadre of dedicated volunteers developed a permanent exhibit and accompanying interpretation for Elizabeth Ryland Priestley's bedroom as part of the regular house tour. This addition provides the public with its first real glimpse into the lives of the women, children, and servants who once lived there through a series of mini-exhibits and discussion by costumed volunteers on women's work, education, legal status, family roles, and childhood during the late eighteenth and early nineteenth centuries. For example, a discussion of the bedroom furnishings—the cradle, work table, tea tray, bed, and writing implements—indicate the multiple uses of the room and its implications for an upper-middle-class woman of the period (fig. 15.4). Issues of class, race, and gender are also discussed in the context of the Priestley family and their servants. The research undertaken by local scholar Begos for the tours led to the eventual completion of an academic work entitled "Priestley's Feminist Legacy."

Fig. 15.3. Morrisville, Bucks County, Pa. Visitors learn about the intersection of spheres among Hannah Penn, her servant Mary, and her slave Sue in the Best Kitchen at Pennsbury Manor. Photo courtesy of Pennsbury Manor.

Fig. 15.4. Northumberland, Pa. Several mini-exhibits at the Joseph Priestley House in Northumberland depict the multiple roles, both public and private, played by Elizabeth Ryland Priestley. Photo courtesy of the Joseph Priestly House and the Pennsylvania Historical and Museum Commission.

The Future

After three years of planning and activity, the pilot phase of "Raising Our Sites" was completed in April 1996. For many of the sites involved, the primary benefit of participating in the project was having the opportunity to pursue and integrate professionally conducted and focused research into the stories they tell. The resulting scholarship in many instances significantly altered previous assumptions by site staff regarding women's lives and contributions. Often, this forced the site to reevaluate its focus—and in one case its entire mission. As Barbara Zolli, site administrator for Drake Well, put it: "[The project] has taken us in directions that would have taken years and years to get to on our own. . . . I believe that it has affected decision-making at every level here."

A follow-up to a few of the participating sites fourteen months later found that activity generated during the pilot "Raising Our Sites" project had continued for the most part. More important, the project had a last-ing impact on staff members' thinking and planning. Beverly Sheppard of the Chester County Historical Society believed that, while the staff had other opportunities to galvanize institutionally around projects, "Raising Our Sites" provided a greater opportunity to involve board members and volunteers. "For the first time, our long-range plan incorporates diversity. While that comes from influence in the field as a whole, I definitely feel that 'Raising Our Sites' has been an important part of our education pro-cess." Cindy Andes, project director for Drake Well, stated that the pro-ject has helped staff and volunteers to expand their vision: "We were thinking so narrowly before. I, for one, wouldn't have made certain links. Now our approach to things is different. I guess this is the 'inclusionary mindset.'"

In a 1989 essay Barbara Melosh suggests that women's history asks not how women fit into history but, rather, how the discipline of history can be reimagined to take account of female experience.[1] This question gets to the heart of the challenge posed to museums and historic sites by an effort such as "Raising Our Sites": how to move beyond token program-ming and predictable exhibits to make the story that is being conveyed to the public fully inclusionary of both men's and women's experiences.

For some sites the project fostered a mere first step toward the larger issues involved in depicting an inclusionary history. The initial activity of developing an archival finding aid that specifically listed images or refer-ences to women or creating a permanent program that placed women's experiences in the larger context of the site's history helped prepare many sites to continue posing larger questions about their general interpreta-tive focus. According to Jeffrey Collins, project director at Hopewell Furnace National Historic Park: "The research that has been done . . . has established a firm foundation for interpretation and for more detailed re-search. . . . 'Raising Our Sites' has planted and nourished a seedling in our park that will continue to grow and flourish."

For those sites that already had laid some groundwork toward expand-ing their interpretive focus to include women's lives and experiences, the project was an opportunity to finally grapple with some of the larger is-sues involved in what Melosh calls the "reimagining" of history. In the words of Mary Ellyn Kunz, assistant director of Pennsbury Manor: "This project was part of a site-wide change that has so radically altered our interpretation that there is no looking back. Women's perspectives are solidly in place in our mainstream interpretation, and we can only grow from here."

In 1997 "Raising Our Sites" expanded its focus to include the examination of other historically underinterpreted groups in addition to women, such as laborers and servants, religious and ethnic groups, and African Americans and Native Americans. Fifteen sites were selected by a panel of advisors, many of whom were veterans of the pilot phase, and PHC staff. Three sites (the Hershey Museum, Pennsbury Manor, and the Joseph Priestley House) had been part of the pilot project, while the other twelve constituted a diverse range in terms of organizational structure and interpretive focus. The sites designed projects that included an exploration of the roles of indentured servants and free blacks at manor houses, the various communities interacting within a military complex, the role of women and domestic help at the nation's oldest botanical garden and nursery, and the lives of Scotch-Irish immigrants in a rural setting. In the five years since the PHC had originally developed "Raising Our Sites," the culture wars over "political correctness" had become part of everyday discourse, and "Take Our Daughters to Work Day" had entered the annual calendar. It is interesting to note, however, that the majority of applicants for the second phase of the project still cited an almost total lack of interpretation of women's history, and social history in general, at their sites.

"Raising Our Sites: Community Histories of Pennsylvania" was conducted by the Pennsylvania Humanities Council from 1998 to 2000, with support from the William Penn Foundation, the Pennsylvania Historical and Museum Commission, and the National Endowment for the Humanities. An important aspect of this project was a concentrated effort to expand the audience at each of the participating sites by broadening the history that each one depicted. The Lancaster County Historical Society, for example, developed new programs that interpreted local African American history which included workshops for educators on the Underground Railroad and an online bibliography of the society's African American historical documents. Families from racially diverse areas of the region were targeted for outreach about a summer camp and other special programs focusing on the region's rich African American history. After her child participated in the summer camp, one woman described a subsequent visit to the society: "We stopped in and [my daughter] eagerly showed us around. We needed more help and the staff happily helped us in our search. [We] actually had fun searching for and learning information we had never known before."

"Raising Our Sites" has provided the Pennsylvania Humanities Council with a creative opportunity to partner with historic sites to advance its goal of bringing humanities scholarship to the out-of-school American public. Once the majority of American adults leave school, a visit to historic sites is often the sole source of formal history instruction that they receive. Therefore, it is crucial that these sites provide as complete and accurate a depiction of history as possible. A project such as "Raising Our Sites" provides a vehicle for historic sites to examine and enhance the stories that they tell and in the process find ways to challenge their visitors to reflect on history as it really was.

Finding Her Place
Integrating Women's History
into Historic Preservation in Georgia

Leslie N. Sharp

In her speech at Tybee Island, Georgia, in 1897, Rebecca Latimer Felton, the first woman to serve in the United States Senate (appointed in 1922), admonished farmers about ignoring their wives' importance in the operations of their farms: "Where would this puffed up farmer be on 'his' farm if he had to hire the labor of a cook, a nurse, a washerwoman and a seamstress to replace the contribution of his wife? I wish I had the power to put them over the cook stove and washpot, until they would be willing to say 'our crop,' 'our farm,' and 'our everything else.'" Her speech underscores how women's roles have historically been regarded as unimportant or even nonexistent.[1] The same thing can be said today about most historic preservationists when naming historic houses, farms, and other places in such a way that the women in the houses are virtually ignored (fig. 16.1). It is also the standard practice in preservation to overlook the females when considering who designed, built, lived in, and died in the house. Overall, the field of historic preservation, made up of historians, architectural historians, planners, archaeologists, and many other scholars and laypersons, lags behind in integrating women's history in their identification, documentation, evaluation, and preservation of historic places.

In 1995 Georgia's State Historic Preservation Office, the Historic Preservation Division (HPD) of the Georgia Department of Natural Resources, recognized that there was a void in its understanding of how women's history should be incorporated into its day-to-day preservation activities. With the leadership of Beth Gibson, former rehabilitation ar-

Fig. 16.1. Coweta County, Ga. Listed in the National Register of Historic Places, the Bob and Sara Alberta Smith House is named for the original owner and his wife, who actually owned and lived in the house longer than her husband. Photo by Jim Lockhart, Historic Preservation Division, Georgia Department of Natural Resources.

chitect with the Historic Preservation Division, and myself, former National Register coordinator, the HPD began a Women's History Initiative to address the topic of women's history as it relates to the process of identifying, documenting, evaluating, and preserving historic places.[2]

The mission of Georgia's Women's History Initiative is to integrate women's history and the preservation of historic places associated with women into the state's existing programs that record, document, interpret, and preserve historic places representing Georgia history. This mission is being accomplished by the following efforts:

1. actively seeking to identify and document historic places associated with women in Georgia—including specific places that are associated with a particular woman or event as well as resources that collectively

reflect broad themes associated with the roles of women in the state's
history;

2. reinterpreting historic places already identified in Georgia based
upon a better understanding of women's history in Georgia; and

3. promoting the awareness, appreciation, and preservation of historic
places associated with women in Georgia through publications, heritage education programs, and guided tours that will increase public
awareness.

Establishing a Need

Although women have always made up half of the population, not much
is known about historic places related to women or about women's associations with commonly studied historic places such as residential, commercial, industrial, and community landmark buildings.

Of the more than sixteen hundred National Register of Historic Places
listings comprising over thirty-eight thousand historic properties in
Georgia, less than 3 percent are listed because of their association with
women. Similarly, of nearly two thousand Georgia historical markers, less
than seventy markers relate to women. Many of them are based on legend or myth or mention a female only because of her husband's historical significance.[3] This is not to say that the other fourteen hundred–plus
listings or nineteen hundred historical markers are unrelated to women
but that the role of women in these places has not been identified, evaluated, or even understood. Historians, architectural historians, preservationists, and planners have been shortchanging history and our historic
environment by not recognizing historical associations with women in
evaluating and interpreting historic places.

Defining a Women-Related Historic Place

Although the need for studying women-related historic places is apparent, the task is daunting. Many issues need to be addressed, such as the
development of a working definition of what makes historic places significant with respect to women's history. Because the National Register of
Historic Places and its criteria for eligibility are the basis for most of the
activities that go on within State Historic Preservation Offices, a women-
related place for the purposes of the Georgia Women's History Initiative

will be defined using the philosophy and terminology of the National Park Service's National Register of Historic Places Criteria for Evaluation found in *National Register Bulletin 15.*

A beginning definition of *women-related historic place* is a historic place significant for its association with a particular woman or the activities of women. Although this definition sounds straightforward, it raises additional questions such as, can a property be significant in women's history even though there is no such "area of significance" in the National Register Information System (NRIS) or in *National Register Bulletin 16 A: How to Complete the National Register Form?* A second question is, how strong an association with women's history is necessary before a historic place can be considered significant in women's history?[4]

Carol D. Shull, keeper of the National Register and chief of the National Historic Landmarks Survey, laments that "women's history" was not included as a data field for significance within the NRIS. Although it was discussed, the area of women's history was decided against for several reasons, the fundamental one being that "the places associated with women were being nominated not because of the gender of the women associated with them, but because these individuals made contributions in [other] areas of significance. There also was concern that to list any property under the "women's history" area of significance just because it was associated with a woman would be patronizing, and the National Register did not want to imply that standards for listing women-related sites were lower than for men. Shull recognizes that research for her essay "Women's History in the National Register and the National Historic Landmarks Survey" would have been much easier had women's history been made an area of significance. More important, its inclusion would make the NRIS a much better women's history research tool. The National Park Service is currently flagging resources related to women in order to make the database more useful to researchers.[5]

In contrast to the National Park Service's argument for not including women's history as a separate area of significance, the National Park Service has included separate areas of significance for various "ethnic" groups. These areas have served to focus research on and attention to historic places associated with specific ethnic groups. In addition to making research on women-related historic place more difficult, by choosing to omit women's history, the National Park Service also missed an opportunity to improve the scholarship behind nominating properties and understanding properties' significance by placing properties in historical context. If, for example, Georgia chose to nominate a property under "women's history," then the state would have to justify why that property is significant in women's history, exactly like the process for any other area of significance. Georgia could not simply state that the Jane Doe House is significant in terms of women's history because Doe was female. Georgia would have to provide a context by which to evaluate the property's significance as it relates to Doe, the time period in which she lived, how the physical characteristics of the property reflect its significance, and how Doe's life and ideas influenced the house and vice versa. This is an elementary example, yet the possibilities for incorporating the wealth of women's history scholarship into the National Register are immeasurable. The Red Bone Community Club in Lamar County, Georgia, listed in 1998, is significant in the category of "Other: Women's History." In justifying Redbone Community Club's significance, the nomination had to address the women's club movement so that the context in which the clubhouse was built could be understood. Through the efforts of the Georgia Women's History Initiative, justifying a property's significance in women's history should be more easily accomplished than in the past.

It must be kept in mind, however, that the National Register of Historic Places Criteria for Evaluation purposefully were kept broad so that they are inclusive rather than exclusive. The basic four criteria (A through D) work well for women's history when a comprehensive approach is taken in documenting a property's history. To underscore this concept, Carroll Van West writes, "To have a more accurate and balanced depiction of all peoples in historic preservation in general, and the National Register in particular, we need not rewrite the process itself; we need only to ask questions that go beyond the facades of our properties."[6]

If women-related historic places can be nominated to the National Register within the existing evaluation criteria, how strong does the connection with women have to be for a property to be considered significant in terms of women's history? Obvious examples of historic places with a direct association to women's history in Georgia are the Rockmart Woman's Club building, the Athens YWCA, designs of architect Lelia Ross Wilburn

Fig. 16.2. Atlanta, Ga. This bungalow, a design of early-twentieth-century architect Lelia Ross Wilburn, is one of many in the Atlanta area attributed to Wilburn, who also published many popular architectural pattern books. Photo by Jim Lockhart, Historic Preservation Division, Georgia Department of Natural Resources.

(fig. 16.2), and the buildings and sites associated with novelist Flannery O'Connor. These types of places are significant in terms of women's history in Georgia. There are other places, however, which have indirect associations whose connections to women tend to be more tenuous and less understood. Some places where there are indirect associations with women are industrial complexes that may have employed women such as the Newnan Cotton Mills, education-related buildings such as schools in which teachers were most commonly women, or houses with spaces commonly associated with women such as kitchens and gardens.

If a clear differentiation can be made between direct and indirect associations, should efforts then be devoted to reinterpreting already-known historic places to include the roles of women, or should efforts focus on identifying places whose significance is more directly associated with women? Furthermore, if an association is indirect, should the property still be considered significant in women's history? These kinds of questions strengthened the Historic Preservation Division's belief that a special initiative was needed to understand women's roles in Georgia's historic environment. Before discussing the Georgia Women's History Initiative, it is worth examining the relationship between women's history and historic preservation in Georgia to understand more fully the need for an initiative focusing on women's history.

Relating Historic Preservation and Women's History

Gerda Lerner identified several stages of development in the scholarship of women's history. Although Lerner's assessment of the women's history field is more than twenty years old, the framework is still useful in evaluating where historic preservation is in terms of women's history. Women's history, as a field of study, has transcended the compensatory and contributory stages to a more complex understanding of history which includes synthesizing women into the historical narrative and viewing gender itself as a shaper of history. In relation to women's history, historic preservation is currently between stage 1 and stage 2. Lerner refers to stage 1 as "compensatory history," meaning scholars identify women who have made great accomplishments and research and write about these women and their achievements.[7] This phase of women's history has produced a bounty of biographical information on important women in a wide range of fields, from science and medicine to social reform and civic leadership.

Historic preservation stage 1 is best exemplified by the recognition of buildings associated with nationally prominent women. The books *Susan B. Anthony Slept Here*, by Lynn Sherr and Jurate Kazickas, and *Women Remembered*, by Marion Tinling, identify historic places associated with well-known women. In Georgia examples of preservation efforts linking women of great achievement to historic places include the National Register of Historic Places–listed Juliette Gordon Low House in Savannah (Low was the founder of the American Girl Scouts [fig. 16.3]); the Crescent Avenue Apartments in Atlanta, which was listed in the National Register for its association with Margaret Mitchell, author of *Gone with the Wind;* and the Gertrude "Ma" Rainey House in Columbus (Ma Rainey is nationally rec-

Fig. 16.3. Savannah, Ga. The Juliette Gordon Low House in Savannah, Georgia, is one of several historic house museums associated with nationally recognized women. The house and adjacent buildings are also the Girl Scout National Center. Photo courtesy of the Girl Scout National Center, n.d.

ognized as the "mother of the blues"). All three historic house museums are open to the public.

As with the field of women's history, the compensatory history stage of historic preservation has produced useful biographical information on many women and has preserved some important historic resources in Georgia. In reference to Caucasian women, however, the historic preservation field in Georgia has followed the same path as traditional history in that most of the recognized historic places associated with women deal with the "great white woman," paralleling traditional history's focus on the "great white man." The focus has been the same with the federal preservation programs, as Page Putnam Miller writes in *Reclaiming the Past:* "While much of the recent women's history and material culture research has been on broad social trends and ordinary people, federal programs, to the limited extent to which they do deal with women, have in most cases emphasized the preservation of sites associated with notable women."[8]

Interesting to note is that, in contrast to the efforts to recognize places associated with white women, Georgia's African American community has done a better job at recognizing historic places associated with locally or regionally significant women in addition to "famous" women. An excellent example is the Beulah Rucker School/House in Gainesville, Georgia, the only surviving historic resource associated with the Gainesville High and Industrial School for the Colored, which was founded by the black educator Beulah Rucker (1890–1963) and later listed in the National Register for its association with Rucker and her role in providing quality secondary education for many blacks in the Gainesville area.

To improve the scholarship and increase the benefit of compensatory history in historic preservation, it is necessary not only to identify the grand and the famous but to continue to study the unknown woman and the modest vernacular buildings in which she lived and worked. In addition, scholarship must follow the African American example by recognizing women who are locally and regionally significant.

The second stage of history, labeled by Lerner as "contributory history," focuses on women's contributions to already accepted aspects of traditional history, such as the abolition movement, industrialization, urbanization, and Progressivism. Historic preservation's progression to stage 2 has not fully developed. Although there has been little conscious effort in Georgia to address women and the built environment specifically, there are several instances in which the field of historic preservation has made progress toward the contributory history phase.

One early example is from 1975, when Darlene Roth, a noted longtime women's historian and preservationist in Georgia, made a presentation to the American Historical Association meeting in Atlanta which identified buildings and places around that city relating to women.[9] Many of these historic places were found significant by Roth due to their association with national movements or organizations. Spelman College (a historic black women's college), two Daughters of the American Revolution buildings, and a Confederate monument at Oakland Cemetery erected by the Ladies' Memorial Association are a few examples identified by

Fig. 16.4. Indian Springs, Ga. Landscaping at Idlewilde. Run by the Bryans sisters, Idlewilde was a boardinghouse that catered to visitors coming to nearby Indian Springs. The landscaping of Idlewilde was designed by Jennie Bryans, the original owner. Photo by Jim Lockhart, Historic Preservation Division, Georgia Department of Natural Resources.

Roth. Unfortunately, the places she identified have not all been further evaluated, recognized, or interpreted as women's history sites.

Other steps toward phase 2 include listing community buildings in the National Register of Historic Places for their significance relating to nationwide activities such as the women's club movement, educational reform, or the development of automobile tourism. Other than the obvious women's club buildings and female education facilities, a boardinghouse run by women is an example of one type of building which falls into the contributory history category. The Bryans sisters played an important role in the economic development of Indian Springs, Georgia, by opening a boardinghouse named Idlewilde which catered to the tourists visiting the nearby springs during the early twentieth century (fig. 16.4). Running a boardinghouse was considered an "acceptable" occupation for females, and it was a typical way for unmarried women to support themselves and their families. This historic property raises broader issues related to tourism, the rising popularity of the automobile, and the limited employment opportunities available to unmarried women prior to the middle of the twentieth century.

With an abundance of contributory history scholarship, the door is wide open for researchers in Georgia to identify and evaluate places associated with already developed historic contexts. The Historic Preservation Division is already trying to do this by asking more questions relating to women and their roles in the function of the historic places in its routine documentation and evaluation of historic properties.

A good example is the work of Gretchen Maclachlan, a political science professor at Clark-Atlanta University, who in her research concerning women and labor practices has identified certain industries and their Atlanta companies that employed a large number of women during the late nineteenth and early twentieth centuries.[10] Candy making, commercial laundries, and textiles businesses have been identified by Maclachlan as large employers of women. Three buildings mentioned by Maclachlan—the Block Candy Company, Trio Laundry, and the Fulton Bag and Cotton Mill—are listed in the National Register of Historic Places, although there is little or no mention of their significance in women's history in the National Register nominations for these properties. In the future, using the available scholarship, properties such as these should have a women's history component in their documentation (fig. 16.5).

Not only can women's history benefit and expand historic preservation, but preservation's use of buildings as material culture and research tools can provide women's history with a different type of resource by which to study women. Two difficulties in researching women's history are that there are not as many written records produced by women as there are by white men and that these records are hard to find. Often, when there is written documentation, the female is referred to as "Mrs. John Doe" or "the daughter of Mr. John Doe" due to social and historical conventions. Frustrating as this is for a researcher, it makes connecting women's history to historic places even more necessary. Buildings, sites, objects, and structures are concrete, physical links to women in the past, and they provide another source for understanding women's many roles in history (fig. 16.6).

Fig. 16.5. (top) Atlanta, Ga. The Block Candy Company is one of several enterprises that employed a number of women. Photo by Jim Lockhart, Historic Preservation Division, Georgia Department of Natural Resources.

Fig. 16.6. (bottom) Thomas County, Ga. Unknown women and child. Although the women in this historic photograph may remain anonymous, the building and landscaping are material culture that tell us something about their lives. Photo courtesy of Thomas County Historical Society, n.d.

Developing a Women's History Initiative

The first major project of the Georgia Women's History Initiative was a regional conference on women's history and historic preservation. Held in March 1996, "Telling Her Story: Expanding the Past of Georgia's Women through Historic Places" brought together twelve scholars and over one hundred people from a wide variety of backgrounds. The three main paper session topics were: case studies of specific women in Georgia and their associated places; the identification of previously undesignated landmarks in women's history; and cross-cultural perspectives of women and historic places.

Feedback from the closing discussion session and the conference evaluation forms revealed a desire among the participants for projects focusing on women and the associated historic places.[11] A majority of the responses centered on the need for greater activity in and awareness of preserving women-related places. One conference participant pointed out that the standard identification tools for historic resources discourage the documentation of places significant for their associations with women's history. For example, women's history is not a historical theme in the Georgia Historic Resources Survey (the state's ongoing survey program of historic buildings and structures), and women's history is not included in the National Register of Historic Places areas of significance, although it can be added in the category of "Other." This again underscores the fact that gender is not routinely considered in the evaluation of historic places either in Georgia or the nation. Another participant wrote in her conference evaluation that "generally, but particularly for women in preservation, we need a unifying interpretive model that will help us ask fruitful questions of the landscape and built environment that lead to enlightening answers about women's experiences."

To help meet the needs identified by conference participants and to further Georgia's understanding of places associated with woman, the Historic Preservation Division began to develop a historic context in which to study historic places associated with women in Georgia. A context study identifies themes, geographical limits, chronological periods, and associated resource types that serve as a framework for identifying and evaluating historic properties and understanding their significance.

After a two-year effort to obtain funding, the Georgia State Legislature, with the leadership of State Representative Doug Teper, appropriated funds for the support of the Georgia Women's History Initiative. In June 1998 a consulting team led by Darlene Roth was hired to develop a women's history context study, to evaluate the Georgia Historic Resources Survey data in key areas of the state in terms of women's history, and to prepare three National Register of Historic Places nominations and two multiple property nominations for women-related historic places.[12] The National Register nominations included the Georgia architect Ellamae Ellis League's House in Macon, Wesleyan College in Macon, and an amendment to expand the significance of the Swan House in Atlanta to include the life of Emily MacDougald Inman. The multiple property nominations included the Historic and Architectural Resources Associated with Women's Clubs and Organizations in the State of Georgia and the Women-Related Historic and Architectural Resources Associated with the Civil War in Georgia.

The context study was completed in the spring 2001 and includes a narrative history of Georgia women, a historiographical review of the literature pertaining to women's history and historic preservation, biographical sketches of notable Georgia women, and special focus studies on Georgia kitchens and landscapes. The report also includes lists of women-related historic places listed in the National Register of Historic Places and recognized by the Georgia Historical Marker program, a discussion of the types of resources associated with Georgia women, and the results of a survey about the interpretation of women's history in Georgia's historical societies and historic house museums. In terms of identifying new resources related to women, the report provides the results from the evaluation of the Georgia Historic Resources Survey data and a discussion of the process and challenges of the National Register program. The report concludes with concrete recommendations for the next phases of the Georgia Women's History Initiative.

Again with the help of State Representative Doug Teper, the Georgia Legislature appropriated funds during its 2000 session to support the third phase of the Georgia Women's History Initiative based on the initial recommendations from the context study report. This phase began in summer 2001 and further fulfills the initiative's mission by promoting the awareness, appreciation, and preservation of historic places associated with Georgia. The main focus will be to produce a two-volume manuscript ready for publication which includes the research from the context study, the papers from the "Telling Her Story" Conference, and other essays relating Georgia women and the built environment. Other goals of this next phase are to complete a multiple-property nomination for the designs of Georgia's three historic women architects, Ellamae Ellis League, Lelia Ross Wilburn, Henrietta Dozier, and a National Historic Landmark nomination for one of Georgia's National Register–listed properties already identified in the context study.

The context study will be an important resource to professionals in historic preservation, women's studies, architecture, landscape architecture, and history for researching women's history. It will also be an invaluable guide for the Historic Preservation Division staff as they evaluate and document historic places. The context study report will be a permanent contribution to the division's capacity for preserving Georgia's heritage. More important, this publication will raise public awareness of, and appreciation for, women's history and its relationship to historic preservation.

The effectiveness of context studies as planning tools can be demonstrated by the activities in African American preservation following the 1984 publication of *Historic Black Resources: A Handbook for the Identification, Documentation, Evaluation of Historic African American Properties in Georgia.*[13] Due to the concerted effort by the Georgia Office of Historic Preservation (now the Historic Preservation Division) to understand African American historic places, African American places were given a higher priority in being nominated to the National Register of Historic Places and in receiving grant funding. The greatest benefit, however, was that the environmental reviewers participating in Section 106 of the National Historic Preservation Act process were able to evaluate and understand historic black places and determine their National Register eligibility.[14] Before the *Historic Black Resources* context was developed, our office was not even able to comment on African American historic places because of a lack of understanding. Whole neighborhoods were being demolished under governmental programs such as the Community Development Block Grants. The context gave our office and others around the state the tools by which to evaluate African American places. Applying this experience to women's history and the current lack of a framework by which to understand women-related historic places, there is no telling how many and what types of significant women-related historic places have been demolished due to ignorance.

Another measurable benefit of the context study is that the historic theme of "African-American History" was added to the Georgia Historic Resources Survey form, which led to the number of African American historic places surveyed increasing from negligible amounts prior to the 1980s to a total of over thirteen hundred properties with an African American theme out of the thirty-eight thousand properties now in the Georgia Historic Resources Survey database. Historic properties listed in the National Register for their significance in "Ethnic Heritage: Black" now constitute approximately 4 percent of the National Register listings in Georgia. Again, due to the *Historic Black Resources* context, these nominations are stronger and better justified. For example, the Morgan Farm in Sumter County was listed in the National Register at the state level of significance because it is an intact African American farmstead that has remained in the same family since the 1880s, which is extremely rare. The *Historic Black Resources* provided the context to understand that in Georgia during the late nineteenth and early twentieth centuries most blacks were either tenant farming, sharecropping, or leaving the rural areas for better economic opportunities in the cities or up north. The Morgan Farm represents the rare ascendancy of a rural Georgia black family from slavery to property ownership.

Two other results of the publication of this context study were formation of a statewide African-American Network in 1989 to guide this initiative and in 1993 publication of *African-American Historic Places and Culture: A Preservation Resources Guide for Georgia* and "Preserving the Legacy: A Tour of African-American Historic Resources in Georgia" by the Historic Preservation Division. Along with the African American context study, the statewide network, resource manual, and tour brochure have furthered the preservation of African American historic places.

Although published in the mid-1980s, the context study still serves as an essential guide for individuals and groups to better determine the significance of historic places. The African American context has also helped make Georgia preservationists more aware of historic places relevant to African American history. Similar results are expected over time from the women's history context study report.

The first steps taken by the Georgia Women's History Initiative may serve as a model for other states as awareness of women's history and its relationship to historic preservation are more appreciated. This awareness and appreciation (and ultimately the preservation) of historic places associated with women may not occur quickly. As Page Putnam Miller so accurately states: "In the field of preservation the progression from preparing a review of the historical context to the actual identification and preservation of structures, and then to the development of an interpretive program is long, difficult, and complex. Yet it is unrealistic to dream of more public historic sites associated with women without being cognizant of the difficult road ahead."[15]

The opportunities and challenges to fulfill the mission of the Georgia Women's History Initiative continue as the initiative moves forward. Already Georgia is integrating what we do know about women's history into National Register documentation, asking more comprehensive questions about historic places, and flagging women-related historic places in the Georgia Historic Resources Survey database. Georgia has also developed a guide to National Register–listed women's history sites in Georgia; planned a women's history tour with brochure for Athens, Georgia, during the fall of 1997 Southeastern State Historic Preservation Offices and Georgia State Preservation Conference; and created a women's history archive. The completed women's history context study, the sampling of survey work, the Multiple Property Nomination Forms, and the National Register nominations will all be used to integrate women's history more fully into the programs of the Historic Preservation Division as well as provide a basis for the next phase of public outreach.

The expected benefits of the Georgia Women's History Initiative are nothing short of revolutionary. Integrating women's history into historic preservation will incorporate the largely overlooked history of half of the state's population into the long-term planning and day-to-day activities of Georgia's historic preservationists. As with the African American history initiative, the Georgia Historic Preservation Division envisions the following results:

1. Preservation professionals and local communities will have the tools necessary to understand historic places significant for their associations with women.

2. The number of women-related historic places surveyed and listed in the National Register for their significance in women's history will increase.
3. Funding for women-related historic places will become a priority.
4. Women-related historic places will be interpreted and preserved.

Finally, and most important, the "whole story" of Georgia's history will be revealed.[16]

CHAPTER 17

Blazing Trails with Pink Triangles and Rainbow Flags

Improving the Preservation and Interpretation of Gay and Lesbian Heritage

Gail Lee Dubrow

In recent years the leading preservation institutions in the United States have made major commitments to diversity. The preservation movement's search for an expanded constituency and growing awareness of the tangible heritage of Native Americans, ethnic communities of color, and women has resulted in a more inclusive approach to managing the nation's cultural resources.[1] Although the issue of preserving gay and lesbian history has arisen from time to time in the context of these initiatives, and at individual historic properties, a movement calling for the protection of sites and buildings associated with gay and lesbian history has lagged behind other cultural diversity initiatives by more than a decade. One can only speculate on the forces that have discouraged gay and lesbian preservationists from organizing to promote the interests of their own communities: a powerful combination of fear, isolation, caution about being pigeonholed, and an alienating ethic of professionalism which shuts its practitioners off from aspects of their own identity, at least during working hours, if not for longer periods.

The nation's "culture wars," played out in the form of conservative attacks on the National Endowment for the Arts' grants to individual artists, National Endowment for the Humanities funding, and the Smithsonian Institution's *Enola Gay* exhibition,[2] among others, give pause for concern about raising the issue of gay and lesbian history within the preservation programs of the National Trust, the National Park Service, and their state and local equivalents. Even the most vocal advocates for gay rights fear damaging the cause of preservation by stating our grievances. No doubt you've seen Gary Larson's *Far Side* cartoon with two deer in the woods, standing and talking. One has a bull's-eye on its chest; the other offers condolences: "Bummer of a birthmark!"[3] But, in spite of the risks, some of us feel a profound need to reconcile our identities as gay people and devoted preservationists. And to be both, in our time, is a troubling experience, since it means rarely (if ever) encountering an acknowledgment of the existence of gays in history, much less a positive depiction of gay identity, at the historic sites and buildings that are our life's work. In the words of Paula Martinac, the author of the first national guide to gay and lesbian historic sites, *The Queerest Places:*

> I can't remember a time when I wasn't attracted to historic places. When I was a child, my parents didn't have to drag me to Civil War battlefields and historic house museums; I went willingly. As an adult, my first professional job was at a restored historic village. I still think a vacation is incomplete unless I've taken in at least one town that time has forgotten. Recently asked about my favorite magazines, I named *Preservation* at the top of the list. But one thing that historic sites and travel guides never taught me was about a most important part of myself—my heritage as a gay person in this country.[4]

Having emerged from a culture of shame to find pride in our identity, many gay and lesbian preservationists are profoundly troubled by the way our heritage is represented at historic properties: the glaring omissions, deafening silences, misleading euphemisms, and outright lies we repeatedly encounter in relation to our gay heritage and our gay lives.

For this reason gay preservationists, buoyed by a broader movement for social, political, and cultural equity, are likely to become the principal advocates for improving the protection and interpretation of their heritage. So, too, a number of groups at the periphery of the preservation movement potentially are important allies. A new generation of scholars researching gay and lesbian history provide a foundation for documenting places significant in the past.[5] George Chauncey's prize-winning history of *Gay New York* reaches back to turn-of-the-century urban institutions, such as bars, bathhouses, cafeterias, and residences that were critical to the development of gay consciousness and culture.[6] Esther Newton's study of Cherry Grove, on Fire Island, suggests the importance of resort destinations where gays and lesbians could "be themselves" long before its was socially acceptable to be open about their sexual orientation in the rest of American society.[7] Elizabeth Kennedy and Madeline Davis's study of lesbian bars in Buffalo, New York, *Boots of Leather, Slippers of Gold,* finds that in the period from the 1930s to 1960s these sites were critical to the emergence of the gay and lesbian liberation movement.[8] Accounts that more directly chronicle the emergence of the homophile movement in the 1950s, such as John D'Emilio's *Sexual Politics, Sexual Communities,* suggest the importance of groups such as the Mattachine Society and Daughters of Bilitis.[9] (Founded in Los Angeles in 1951, the Mattachine Society was the first American political organization established for the purpose of defending the rights of homosexuals. The Daughters of Bilitis, founded in San Francisco in 1955, was the first lesbian social and political organization in the United States.)

There has been an outpouring of work on the physical spaces associated with the gay community, from Alan Berube's history of gay bathhouses[10] to the humorously titled collection *Queers in Space,* edited by Gordon Ingram and others and published by Bay Press.[11] Graduate programs in historic preservation are beginning to produce student theses on gay topics.[12] Works focusing on individual urban communities are being published, such as Susan Stryker and Jim Van Buskirk's history of San Francisco, *Gay by the Bay.*[13] The rich detail contained in these and other studies raises the prospect of designating particular properties as gay and lesbian landmarks. So, too, recently published works have begun to interrogate the history of urban renewal and the rise of the preservation movement in light of gay and lesbian history. The History Project's *Improper Bostonians,* for example, showed how at least one public official promoted the destruction of gay bars under the guise of urban renewal, arguing that "we will be better off without these incubators of homosexuality and indecency and a Bohemian way of life."[14]

Gay and lesbian communities have nurtured their own grassroots history projects for more than a decade,[15] in the form of oral history programs, archives, exhibitions, and, more recently, maps and guides to historic sites and buildings in cities such as Boston, New York, Seattle, and Los Angeles.[16] One project in New York City, by the collective Repo-History, produced a series of interpretive signs in the form of pink Masonite triangles on signposts; it was, however, only a temporary project.[17] (I found

Fig. 17.1. New York City, N.Y. The Storefront for Art and Architecture commissioned RepoHistory to develop the project *Queer Spaces* to mark nine sites and buildings significant in gay and lesbian history, including a popular bar known as Bonnie and Clyde's, which operated in Greenwich Village in the 1970s. Photo by Jim Costanzo, courtesy of RepoHistory.

this project moving personally, since it happened to include one of the landmarks of my own adolescent coming-out, a lesbian bar of the early 1970s named Bonnie and Clyde's [fig. 17.1].) While these projects have increased public awareness of gay and lesbian heritage, to date there have been no efforts to secure landmark status for the historic properties identified on these maps or to develop on-site interpretive programs. A partnership between community history projects and local preservation organizations might provide the right mix of skills needed to improve the protection of these resources.

In recent years the preservation movement has taken the first steps toward gaining greater visibility for gay and lesbian heritage. The National Trust's 1996 annual conference featured the first social gathering for gay and lesbian preservationists, followed by the organization's approval of an educational session for the 1997 meeting. Subsequent meetings in Washington, D.C., and Los Angeles have featured field sessions that highlighted the cities' gay and lesbian landmarks and neighborhoods. Dennis Drabelle's 1997 article in *Preservation* magazine, aptly titled "Out and About in the City,"[18] signaled the National Trust's willingness to address this issue in its most public venue (fig. 17.2). A focus on Trevor Hailey's lively San Francisco tour "Cruisin' the Castro" and Jay Gifford's "Victorian Home Walk" introduced Trust members to places of historical significance in the formation of the San Francisco's gay and lesbian community, as well as contemporary landmarks, from a comfortable distance as armchair tourists. Gradually, gays and lesbians within the staff and membership of the Trust have gained space for addressing their concerns.[19] These events have seeded the development of an informal network that is likely to generate future projects aimed at improving the protection and interpretation of so-called lavender landmarks.

Fig. 17.2. San Francisco, Calif. Trevor Hailey's guided walking tour, "Cruisin' the Castro," was the first gay-related subject to appear in the National Trust's *Preservation* magazine. Photo by Emily Louise Scott, courtesy of Trevor Hailey.

Martinac's national guide to gay and lesbian historic places, the maps produced by community-based groups, and increasingly rich scholarship suggest several broad themes and a wide array of property types significant in gay and lesbian history. Within each category public controversy surrounding the protection and interpretation of these sites is likely to crystallize along predictable lines, to which preservationists should be prepared to respond.[20] Places already designated as landmarks are perhaps the most obvious places to begin remedying the omissions and distortions in the presentation of gay and lesbian history. For the most part these take the form of historic houses associated with notable individuals,[21] many of which are open to the public and have ongoing interpretive programs but where little is said about the sexual orientation of the prime subject. M. J. Lowe's article "Outing the National Register" discusses many of these places in greater detail.[22] Examples include:

- Walt Whitman's row house on Mickle Street in Camden, New Jersey, where he lived with his much younger lover, Harry Stafford, who one biographer has called the "central figure of them all."[23] (NR)
- "Clear Comfort," the Staten Island, New York, family seat of pioneering photographer Alice Austen. Austen lived at Clear Comfort for much of her life and shared her life and home there with Gertrude Tate for more than thirty years.[24] (NHL)
- Willa Cather's childhood home in Red Cloud, Nebraska, where she created her alter ego, William J. Cather, whose masculine "dress and manner brought her considerable notoriety and made her the subject of much talk about town," prefiguring her unorthodox adult life, both as a lesbian and as a woman writer. In this setting, one biographer claims, Cather "discovered alternative stories for a woman's life."[25] (NR)
- Gertrude Stein's home on Biddle Street in Baltimore, corresponding to her early days as a medical student at the Johns Hopkins University and her first explorations of her lesbian identity. Although Stein's lifelong partnership with Alice B. Toklas is well acknowledged, her early years at Biddle Street mark her involvement in a love triangle with May Bookstaver and Mabel Haynes which took her "off the academic rails."[26] She wrote about it in the posthumously published *QED,* her first book.[27]
- The Durham Street house in Baltimore's Fell's Point neighborhood, from which a young Eleanora Fagen would make her first sexual ex-

plorations in the area's street culture before changing her name to Billie Holiday and embarking on a stellar musical career. Holiday was known to have had "many affairs with men and women."[28]

- Frances Willard's Evanston, Illinois, home, which also served as headquarters for the Woman's Christian Temperance Union. Willard shared her home there with Anna Gordon for many years. Biographer Ruth Bordin has described them as "almost two sides of a single coin as their years together unfolded and they pursued their common public and private goals."[29] (NHL)

- Potentially the most controversial site is Eleanor Roosevelt's retreat, Val-Kill, in Hyde Park, New York, to which she and her longtime companion, journalist Lorena Hickok, would retire between travels. While many biographers of Roosevelt and Hickok have steadfastly denied the possibility of a lesbian relationship, historian Blanche Wiesen Cook's biography openly explores the possibility of a meaningful love relationship between the two women.[30] (NHS)

Dealing with gay and lesbian history at these types of properties raises a number of important issues: the relevance of so-called private lives to public accomplishments; the propriety of presenting information about homosexuality to public audiences that include children;[31] the ethics of "outing" historical figures who may have wished to remain "closeted";[32] the fluidity of people's sexuality over a lifetime; definitions of sexual identity which are themselves historically contingent; and the danger of reading sexuality into close relationships that were otherwise chaste. Nevertheless, enough is known about the sexual and affectional preferences of many major American figures to justify remedial action that honestly addresses the facts at historic places devoted to their lives and accomplishments.

Lest these properties seem too far removed from the mainstream of preservation, a striking example was included on tours offered in conjunction with the 1997 meeting of the National Trust for Historic Preservation, held in Santa Fe, New Mexico, as well as in the Trust's permanent portfolio of historic properties. Tours of Georgia O'Keeffe's Abiquiu home and studio figured prominently in the 1997 conference program. Those unable to visit had an opportunity to learn about the property from a movie shown in the conference's closing plenary session, which celebrated the Georgia O'Keeffe Foundation's recent gift of the property to the Trust. Yet the information about O'Keeffe's life presented in both settings would have left most site visitors and film viewers deeply surprised about the inclusion of the property in Paula Martinac's guide to gay and lesbian sites, since existing public interpretation reinforces the common view that her most significant relationship "was with her husband, Alfred Stieglitz." As Martinac explains, it was only her most celebrated one, since O'Keeffe "was a bisexual who also enjoyed the company of a number of young women over the years."[33]

Recent scholarship has provided evidence to support Martinac's claims. Jeffrey Hogrefe, in his biography of O'Keeffe, asserts that

> the artist, like many married women in this period, maintained secret homosexual alliances. When asked whether O'Keeffe had any beaus, Phoebe Pack—a close friend for many of her later years—stated that the artist had only women lovers when she knew her in New Mexico and that, as she understood it, her union with Stieglitz had been a "marriage of convenience." Virginia Christianson told me that "All her life, I think, Georgia had been a lesbian." The son of another friend told me that O'Keeffe was a part of a small and select group of women who lived around Santa Fe in the forties and fifties. He said that although many of the women had relationships with men, it was his understanding that they had sexual relations with one another.[34]

O'Keeffe's efforts to hide her lesbian relationships misled some people, although Hogrefe discovered that they were common knowledge in Santa Fe. Those in the know remained silent out of respect for her privacy.

Given O'Keeffe's clear preference for keeping this aspect of her sexual orientation out of public view during her lifetime, the question remains whether it is relevant to the public interpretation of her Abiquiu property. That O'Keeffe's home and studio were renovated and managed by her on-again, off-again lover Maria Chabot suggests the relevance of information about her intimate relationships to an understanding of the landmark. In Martinac's words, "The renovation of the Abiquiu house was overseen by Maria Chabot, a writer who began living with O'Keeffe in 1941 in an intimate friendship—'a tall handsome young woman,' as O'Keeffe described her. Maria planned all the details of the renovation, including the location of the fireplaces, and studied Hopi architecture in order to duplicate its designs." The major biographies of O'Keeffe all acknowledge Chabot's leading role in the renovation. Benita Eisler's study of *O'Keeffe and Stieglitz* is perhaps the most emphatic:

> To her function as majordomo, Chabot now added the roles of architect, designer, and construction superintendent. She commandeered building materials unseen since the construction of Los Alamos—copper wiring, plumbing, electrical fixtures, even hard-to-find nails. She supervised the fabrication of adobe bricks on site, along with the handwork of the women who traditionally smoothed the sand-and-water mixture into facing, covering perpendicular corners with the famed curves of reddish pink. She saw to the traditional interior features of the two main buildings, both painted white. To these, O'Keeffe contributed her preference for minimal furnishings: built-in cushioned benches around the walls, low shelves for books and phonographs, shells and bones, and a country kitchen that could have belonged to a Wisconsin farm.[35]

A fuller and more candid explanation of O'Keeffe's sexual orientation would help the visitor to understand Chabot's instrumental role in the renovation and help to explain her personal stake in the place.

Also listed in Martinac's guide is Philip Johnson's "Glass House" in New Canaan, Connecticut, which the architect designed and built in 1949 and recently willed to the National Trust for Historic Preservation (fig. 17.3). Johnson kept his homosexual orientation a secret for most of his life. As Charles Kaiser wrote, "Johnson was of a class and a generation who were routinely invited to the fanciest dinner parties, but who never brought along a male companion."[36] Later in life, however, Johnson came out of the closet and in recent years has spoken openly about his homosexuality in interviews with members of the press. While some might question the relevance of the architect's sexual orientation to the public interpretation of the Glass House, the fact that it served as Johnson's home makes his personal life more relevant than if it were merely one of his vast number of commissioned works.

Architectural critic Aaron Betsky has offered the novel interpretation that Johnson's sexuality actually is expressed in the "queerness" of the design "of many of his buildings": "Their theatricality, role-playing, licentiousness, twisting of norms and 'passing' as normal—that gives them life. Maybe only a queer could live in a glass house and sleep in a windowless box down the hill on a bed surrounded by domes and floor-to-ceiling cur-

Fig. 17.3. New Canaan, Conn. Architect Philip Johnson has willed the Glass House to the National Trust for Historic Preservation with the intention of opening it up to the public after his death. Time will tell whether the interpretive program skirts or directly addresses Johnson's homosexuality and his more than thirty-year partnership with David Whitney, who curated the Glass House's art collection. Photo by Bill Maris, © Esto.

tains. Only a queer, perhaps, would need to push things to the extreme and then sell them and himself as just the right thing."[37] If this interpretation is not entirely persuasive, some facts help to build the case for interpreting the Glass House in light of Johnson's intimate relationships. The remarkable collection of art within it was collected and curated by Johnson's lover of over thirty years, David Whitney.[38] The intimacy of their relationship was publicly clarified in Martin Filler's 1996 *New York Times* article: "The tall, baby-faced Mr. Whitney was sitting in a sunny corner of the one-bedroom apartment that he and Mr. Johnson, companions now for 36 years, share at the Museum Tower in midtown Manhattan."[39]

Although Johnson's willingness to acknowledge his relationship with Whitney publicly came late in life, his candor in recent years strengthens the case for incorporating this dimension of his life into the interpretation of the Glass House and other Johnson landmarks. In years to come the connection between Johnson's sexual orientation and some of his commissioned works will be difficult to ignore, particularly his design of the two thousand–seat Cathedral of Hope for a gay and lesbian congregation in Dallas, Texas, undertaken at the age of ninety, when he finally was living openly as a gay person. The National Trust has its future work cut out for it, as the owner of two and possibly more nationally significant historic properties associated with gay, lesbian, or bisexual people. These holdings provide the organization with an opportunity to assume leadership by bringing new candor to previously suppressed aspects of history.

Beyond the historic houses associated with notable individuals, there is a pressing need to interpret and preserve places associated with the emergence of homosexual community and identity,[40] many of which meet the fifty-year threshold required to qualify for National Register listing.[41] These properties raise the political stakes even higher, since they are associated with the deeply stigmatized territory of gay men's sexual culture. Landmarks of this period include:

- Gay bars such as the Doubleheader, in Seattle's Pioneer Square, which reputedly is the oldest continually operating gay bar in the country (fig. 17.4).[42]
- Bathhouses such as New York City's famous Everard, Lafayette, St. Marks, and the Mt. Morris.[43] Many are gone or were closed by local authorities in response to the AIDS epidemic; in New York only the Mt. Morris is still in operation.
- YMCAs such as the Army and Navy Y in Newport, Rhode Island; on G Street in Washington, D.C.; and the Harlem branch in New York City.[44]
- Venues in Harlem such as the Hamilton Lodge and the Savoy Ballroom which hosted the colorful costume balls of the Jazz Age and thus were an early focus for the culture of Drag.[45]
- Various forms of public open space which historically served as cruising places for gay men, such as New York's Washington Square Park and Central Park; Seattle's Volunteer Park; and D.C.'s Lafayette Park, across the street from the White House.[46]

- Sections of public beaches and distinctive resort communities, such as Cherry Grove on Fire Island in New York, which began to attract gay people in the 1920s and 1930s and have enjoyed a reputation as a gay haven to the present day.[47] Other resort communities include Provincetown, Massachusetts; Key West, Florida; and Palm Springs, California.
- Homes, churches, and offices that provided havens for the homophile movement, such as the First Universalist Church in Los Angeles and the homes of movement leaders.[48]

In rare cases this sort of site has been added to the list of properties on landmark registers for reasons having nothing to do with its queer connections. Boston's Club Baths, for examine, was housed in a building designed by H. H. Richardson, a fact that secured its place on the city's landmarks register. The failure to recognize this and other buildings' historical (as opposed to architectural) significance means that landmark protection powers rarely extend to interior features that may contribute to the property's integrity of feeling and association with respect to gay heritage. But, because most historic places significant in gay and lesbian history are completely missing from landmark registers, this broad category of properties needs to be surveyed so that individual properties can be assessed for potential listing in the National Register as well as its state and local equivalents.

Harry Hay's home in Los Angeles,[49] which served as the founding place for the Mattachine Society, is a likely prospect for landmark designation based on its significance in gay and lesbian history (fig. 17.5). A pre-application has been filed with the California State Historical Resources Commission that will begin the process of evaluating its eligibility for listing on the California State and National Registers.[50] Fortunately, a foundation has been laid for recognizing the significance of this property and others associated with gay and lesbian history in California. Public comments received on a statewide historic preservation plan led gays and lesbians to be added to the list of state's historically significant communities.[51] This small development in cultural resource management policy probably is a landmark in its own right.

Properties such as these are sure to serve as flashpoints for controversy, since a significant portion of the American public still objects to ho-

Fig. 17.4. Seattle, Wash. The Double Header Tavern, reputedly the oldest continually operating gay bar in the United States, still stands in Seattle's Pioneer Square historic district. Photo by Angela McCarrel, courtesy of the Northwest Lesbian and Gay History Museum Project.

mosexuality on moral and religious grounds. Nevertheless, preservationists and historians have a professional responsibility to tell the truth about the past and to help the public to distinguish between acknowledging historical reality and placing a government stamp of approval on it. If it is even possible to get beyond the political controversy, major issues remain

Fig. 17.5. Los Angeles, Calif. Historic sites and buildings are only beginning to be listed on landmark registers based on their significance in gay and lesbian history. The Stonewall Inn was the first such property to be listed on the National Register of Historic Places. Harry Hay's home, which served as the founding place for the Mattachine Society, is another likely prospect. Photo courtesy of Jeff Samudio.

about the relative significance and physical integrity of the surviving historic properties.

A third category of properties, consisting of sites and buildings connected with the gay and lesbian movement from 1969 onward,[52] raise the issue of preserving the recent past and promise to draw preservationists directly into alliances with the gay community. These include places such as:

- The Stonewall Inn, on New York City's Christopher Street, site of the June 28, 1969, police raid where patrons (mostly drag queens and people of color) fought back in response to police harassment.[53] Listed on the National Register of Historic Places in June 1999, this was the first historic property to be listed on the National Register and designated a National Historic Landmark because of its significance in gay and lesbian history.[54]
- Some gay urban neighborhoods legitimately might be considered historic districts or simply gay-identified districts for the purposes of planning: San Francisco's Castro District, Seattle's Capitol Hill and Pioneer Square, D.C.'s Dupont Circle, Chicago's North Halsted Street, New York's Greenwich Village.
- Individual historic properties finally are being awarded local landmark status, such as Harvey Milk's Castro Street Camera shop, which served as an ad hoc center for gay political organizing in San Francisco.[55]

Finally, there is another type of property which has not yet found its way into maps and guidebooks, namely places connected with the history of homophobia, ranging from mental hospitals[56] and military bases[57] to Anita Bryant's home in Dade County, Florida.[58] Efforts to reclaim interpretive space at sites that have harbored deep hostility to gays and lesbians are guaranteed to provoke fevered political battles. Ultimately, gay and lesbian history may have an even broader reach. Similar to women's history, which offers a reminder that the lives of men and women both merit historical interpretation through the lens of gender, the power of gay and lesbian history ultimately may reside in its ability to reveal the ways in which heterosexuality is socially enforced and culturally constructed, a perspective that draws attention away from gay and lesbian landmarks and, instead, brings a wide range of locations into focus.[59]

If a shared fear is that the preservation movement will be drawn into the culture wars and alienate conservative segments of its membership,[60] perhaps the best hope is that an honest and direct approach to this subject will lead to new alliances and a broader constituency for preservation which is founded on a genuine appreciation of the diverse heritage of the American people. Advocates for improving the preservation and interpretation of gay and lesbian history are likely to find support in several quarters. First, taking on this issue is likely to release new energy from gay

Fig. 17.6. San Francisco, Calif. The historic Fallon Building was threatened with demolition in connection with the construction of a new Lesbian/Gay/Bisexual/Transgender Community Center. Bay area preservationists succeeded in negotiating a revised plan that allows the historic building to coexist with new construction. Photo by Gerald Takano.

people in the preservation movement, who have been eager for affirming policies and initiatives. Second, willing partners are likely to be found in the ranks of the historical profession and grassroots history groups, in which an enormous amount of original work is being done to document gay and lesbian history. Third, gay and lesbian organizations have yet to be approached about the place of preservation in their broader programs, but the need to open a dialogue recently was thrown into high relief when San Francisco's Gay and Lesbian Community Services Center proposed to demolish the historic Fallon Building (fig. 17.6). Ultimately, the building was saved, but the close call with the wrecking ball illuminated the need for focused outreach, not only to preserve gay and lesbian history but also to ensure preservation's place in the ethos and on the agenda of gay organizations. One avenue for getting out the word is a thriving gay media, reflected in dozens of national and innumerable local periodicals that have yet to feature many articles on gay leaders and activists in the preservation movement, historic places of interest to gay travelers, or preservation issues relevant to the gay community.

Finally, support for implementing a gay preservation agenda is likely to be found in some segments of the marketplace,[61] particularly the real estate and travel industries. The existence of well-defined gay neighborhoods in most American cities and realtors who explicitly market their services to the gay community suggests potential alliances. The preservation community has long been aware of the connection between gay people and the revitalization of urban neighborhoods, although for many years this issue was framed exclusively in pejorative terms as "gentrification."[62] The City of Chicago's decision to invest $3.2 million in the renovation of North Halsted Street explicitly recognized the economic and political contributions of a gay neighborhood while raising questions about the form so-called gay-themed street improvements might take.[63]

The emergence of a gay travel market led to the establishment of the International Gay and Lesbian Travel Association over fifteen years ago; it now numbers more than thirteen hundred travel professionals.[64] As the National Trust met in 1997 in Santa Fe, the Fourth International Gay and Lesbian Travel Expo held its meeting at the San Francisco Marriott. Perhaps both organizations might be persuaded to find a common meeting site and agenda in the future. Car rental companies, hotels, and airlines have begun to recognize the economic value of this market, including American Airlines, which counted "$149 million in ticket sales through primarily gay travel agencies or groups" in 1996. Seattle's *Gay Community Yellow Pages* lists more than a dozen travel agencies that cater to the interests of gay and lesbian clients,[65] including American Express Travel, which actively markets its services to the gay and lesbian community; Travel Solutions, which promotes "gay and lesbian tour solutions"; Woodside Travel, which features "Gay Ski Weeks"; and Cathay Express, which offers "gay and lesbian travel packages." Perhaps the best is Royalty Travel, whose motto promises, "Even if you're not a queen, we'll treat you like one."[66]

The rise of this segment of the travel industry suggests that, in their time off, gay people may be seeking a holiday not so much from a heterosexual world as from a homophobic one.[67] This is why the gay travel industry is focused on providing gay-friendly service, carriers, lodging, and tourist destinations. From the perspective of the preservation movement, however, it still has tremendous untapped potential for promoting tourism connected with gay and lesbian heritage. One tour operator featured a gay history canal tour as part of its travel packages for the August 1998 Gay Olympic Games, held in Amsterdam, and for years there has existed a *Pink Plaque Guide to London*.[68] These types of itineraries could be developed for nearly every American city.[69] Mainstream publishers such as *Fodor's* finally have begun to tap pent-up demand for gay travel guides,[70] but it is the responsibility of gay preservationists, their allies, and ultimately the larger preservation movement to ensure that something meaningful remains to visit by preserving the tangible resources associated with gay and lesbian history.

Since this issue is such a new one for the preservation movement, an agenda for improving the protection of gay and lesbian heritage is only now in the formative stages, and debate about strategies and tactics looms in the near future. In the interest of sparking a broader discussion, I offer my own tentative list of priorities in the form of an "Action Agenda":

- There is a need to write gays and lesbians into the history of the preservation movement, both as individuals and as communities vitally involved in urban revitalization and the development of gay-oriented tourist destinations, by documenting their contributions.
- There is a need to reinterpret existing landmarks to provide a more accurate and complete presentation of gay and lesbian history by amending existing landmark nominations[71] and revising the interpretive programs at historic properties.[72]
- There is a need to identify previously undesignated properties significant in gay and lesbian history by undertaking thematic surveys, both nationally and locally, which generate new nominations to landmark registers and, potentially, by conducting campaigns to protect the most significant properties.
- There is a need to develop new tools to increase public education and awareness such as maps, tours, guidebooks, and interpretive signage and to recruit new sources of financial and political support for our projects by forging partnerships with historians, artists, publishers, architects, planners, social and political organizations, and businesses in and marketing to the gay community.
- There is a need to develop new mechanisms of communication, mutual support, and activism on behalf of gay and lesbian heritage by establishing informal communication networks and a formal advocacy organization.

- There is a need to develop strategies for improving the capacity of preservation organizations and agencies to address issues of concern to gays and lesbians by allocating resources, promoting policies, and developing projects that commit preservation institutions to making demonstrable progress.

This agenda for change is not merely wishful thinking. Although advocates for improving the preservation and interpretation of gay and lesbian history are sure to encounter resistance, more acceptance and support may exist than is commonly imagined, even in places far removed from the gay havens of Greenwich Village, Dupont Circle, North Halsted Street, Capitol Hill, and the Castro District. Chris Reed, an art historian at Lake Forest College, makes this point in telling the story of Pendarvis, a Wisconsin State Historical Landmark in the village of Mineral Point (pop. 2,400).

> Although it is nominally a monument to the mid-nineteenth century tin miners of the area, the actual guided tour (local gals in nineteenth century costume) dwells at least as substantially on the two men who purchased, restored, and furnished with antiques the collection of cottages, which they ran as a restaurant. Their cottage (one bedroom) is preserved as it was circa 1965, as is the restaurant (very tiny and no longer functioning), complete with souvenir menus autographed by famous travelers such as JFK. These two structures complete the tour, much of which recounts the details of the men's meeting, their respective interests (cooking and antiquing!), their life in the community. No explicit mention is made of their sexuality, but terms such as "lifelong partnership" and "lifelong friendship" are used—and as I said, there is one bedroom. The whole effect is kind of a shrine to this gay couple, maintained by the State of Wisconsin. In addition to finding this curious, I will confess that I also found it rather touching as an example of the way a small town can ultimately come to accept and even celebrate the presence of a gay couple in its midst.[73]

Perhaps gays and lesbians along with other allies in the preservation movement can help to persuade the ladies leading the Pendarvis tour, as well as the institutions that manage major historic properties such as the homes of Willa Cather, Walt Whitman, Eleanor Roosevelt, Georgia O'Keeffe, and Philip Johnson, that it is acceptable to utter the terrifying words *gay, lesbian, bisexual,* or even the newly reclaimed *queer* in their presentations, if they go on to explain why it is relevant and what it may have meant in a particular time and place.

PART V

Toward an Inclusive Agenda
for Preservation Policy and Practice

CHAPTER 18

Searching for Women in the National Register of Historic Places

Carol D. Shull

The contributions of many American women have been recognized through listings in the National Register of Historic Places, a rich source of information for researchers of women's history in the United States. With more than seventy-four thousand listings by the year 2002,[1] the National Register recognizes and documents historic and cultural units of the National Park System, National Historic Landmarks (NHLs) designated by the secretary of the interior, and places nominated by states, federal agencies, and American Indian tribes. The National Register Information System (NRIS), a computerized index containing some forty-five data elements for each registered historic place, can be queried in a variety of ways to find listings associated with women's contributions to American history, architecture, archeology, engineering, and culture. The NRIS is available on the Internet, and information from both the NRIS and the National Register files may be obtained on request from the National Park Service (NPS), which expands and maintains the National Register. National Register and National Historic Landmark files include descriptions, statements of significance, bibliographies, photographs, and sometimes correspondence and other documents. These records can be invaluable to researchers and add new dimensions to our understanding of many of the conceptual frameworks in women's history dealt with by scholars such as Gerda Lerner and Sara M. Evans.[2] The places associated with individuals, organizations, events, and the daily life of women in America are artifacts of material culture which provide fresh insights about women whose lives may not be well documented in written records.

The National Park Service sought advice from nominating authorities, scholars in a variety of disciplines, and others to determine which data elements to computerize on each National Register listing. The goal was to make the places and the information about them accessible for a wide variety of uses, such as research, preservation planning, public education, and interpretation. After considerable discussion, the National Park Service decided not to include a data field for women's history, primarily because places associated with women were being added to the National Register for their achievements in areas of significance such as architecture, art, education, literature, law, medicine, and science. Gender was not a factor in their selection. In addition, most listings are related to both sexes in one way or another.[3]

The decision not to include a data element for women in the National Register Information System was made in the early 1980s,[4] after Congress had authorized four units of the National Park System honoring women.[5] Later in the decade, scholars focused attention on the need to provide more recognition for historic places associated with women. In 1985 the Organization of American Historians and the National Coordinating Committee for the Promotion of History urged the National Park Service to study additional women's sites for National Historic Landmark designation.[6] Gail Lee Dubrow assessed their representation and found how few properties illustrating the role of women were included in national, state, and local registers.[7] In 1989, after discussions in Congress, the National Park Service was given funds to conduct a study of women's history landmarks.[8]

Through this study and with the passage of time more sites relevant to women's history have been added to the National Register. To aid the researcher who wants to explore topics relating to women, the whole NRIS can be downloaded from the National Register's website for in-depth analysis.[9] Researchers can add their own cross-references. Even though a complete list of places associated with women is not available from the NRIS, the sites in this study and listings added since this study are retrievable for future reference from the NRIS website on the Internet. In addition, the database is searchable using a variety of fields alone and in combination. Properties can be identified by location; resource type; architectural classification; historic and current functions; the criteria for evaluation; significant persons; architect or builder; areas, periods, and dates of significance; cultural affiliation; and so on.[10]

A search of the significant persons field is among the most useful. At the time of the queries for this analysis,[11] the NRIS showed 9,820 listings associated with significant persons, 15 percent of the listings. About 360 (under 4 percent) were women. A researcher can choose names of women, search the NRIS significant persons field by name, and obtain more detailed information from the National Register or NHL file.

Those researching Clara Barton will find four listings, each illustrating her life in a different way: Clara Barton Homestead; St. Mary's Church; Clara Barton National Historic Site, a National Historic Landmark and one of the five units of the National Park System primarily about women; and the Clara Barton Parkway.[12] The Clara Barton Homestead in Oxford, Massachusetts, was her birthplace in 1821 and home for thirty-two years, her family was prominent in local affairs, and she taught school (fig. 18.1). St. Mary's Church in Fairfax Station, Virginia, served as the field hospital for the Union Army after the Second Battle of Bull Run. According to the nomination, Barton arrived at St. Mary's Church on August 31, 1862, and, for three sleepless days and nights, nursed the wounded as violent rains fell and doctors operated in the only dry place available, the church. The files for Clara Barton's house in Glen Echo, Maryland, document her role in establishing the American Red Cross. Originally constructed to house Red Cross disaster supplies and Red Cross workers, the building became her home in 1897 and Red Cross Headquarters until she retired in 1904. The National Historic Landmark records also contain correspondence and photographs that tell the story of the efforts of the Friends of Clara Barton to preserve the house and have it recognized. In commemoration, the section of the George Washington Memorial Parkway in Maryland which leads to her home is named the Clara Barton Parkway.

Searching the significant persons field, researchers will find historic places for famous women such as Jane Addams, Susan B. Anthony, Mary McCleod Bethune, Helen Keller, Annie Oakley, and Eleanor Roosevelt, "female icons."[13] Many are represented by places that illuminate their lives in unique ways. Queries of the data field for significant persons will also reveal numerous women worthy of study whose achievements are not yet well documented in women's history publications.

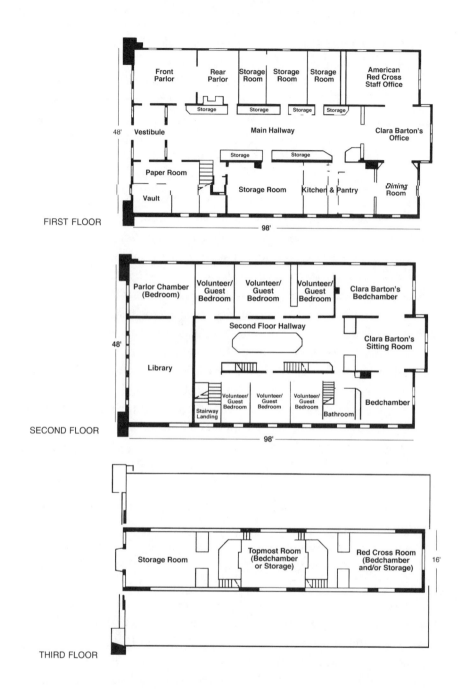

FIRST FLOOR

Front Parlor	Rear Parlor	Storage Room
Storage Room	Storage Room	American Red Cross Staff Office

48'

Vestibule

Main Hallway

Clara Barton's Office

Paper Room

Storage

Storage

Storage Room

Kitchen & Pantry

Dining Room

Vault

98'

SECOND FLOOR

Parlor Chamber (Bedroom)

Volunteer/ Guest Bedroom

Volunteer/ Guest Bedroom

Volunteer/ Guest Bedroom

Clara Barton's Bedchamber

Second Floor Hallway

48'

Clara Barton's Sitting Room

Library

Volunteer/ Guest Bedroom

Volunteer/ Guest Bedroom

Volunteer/ Guest Bedroom

Bedchamber

Stairway Landing

Bathroom

98'

THIRD FLOOR

Storage Room

Topmost Room (Bedchamber or Storage)

Red Cross Room (Bedchamber and/or Storage)

16'

306

A sample gives some indication of the breadth of the National Register.

- The Hulda Klager Lilac Garden in Washington State was the private laboratory and showplace of the nationally recognized horticulturist, a leading authority on the hybridizing of lilacs, who developed over 250 varieties.
- Sarah Clark Case of the Daniel Case/Sarah Case Farmstead was the first licensed woman physician in Hunterdon County and one of the first in New Jersey when granted her medical license in 1816.
- Susan Blow helped create the Des Peres School in St. Louis, the first successful public kindergarten in the United States (fig. 18.2).
- Anna Beir bequeathed her home to the City of Greenville, Ohio, for an art museum. She was the founding spirit behind the Greenville Art Guild; art supervisor in the Greenville schools; and an artist, teacher, and cultural philanthropist.
- The most famous resident of Casa de los Ponce de Leon in Puerto Rico was the nineteenth-century poet and educator, Lola Rodriquez Ponce de Leon.
- Arden served as the California residence of well-known Polish Shakespearean actress Helena Modjeska.
- The Montanez Adobe chapel became the village sanctuary and its owner, Polina Montanez, the spiritual leader of the community in San Juan Capistrano, California (fig. 18.3).

A query of the database for architects and builders identified approximately twenty-five thousand names. The printout suggested that some ninety are women. Several are well known, such as Julia Morgan, the architect of William Randolph Hearst's palatial St. Simeon, with sixteen

---

Fig. 18.1. (opposite) Glen Echo, Md. Floor plans of Clara Barton's home, Clara Barton National Historic Site. In the "Teaching with Historic Places" lesson plan *Clara Barton's House: Home of the American Red Cross*, students are asked to compare the number of rooms used personally by Barton with the area used by the American Red Cross for housing volunteers, for office space, and for storing supplies. As one of the four questions students answer using the floor plan, this activity demonstrates how historic places can provide insights into the lives and work of individuals. Floor plans courtesy of Clara Barton National Historic Site.

listings; and Mary Jane Colter with six, including buildings she designed at the Grand Canyon (fig. 18.4).

The variety of listed buildings designed by Julia Morgan shows the remarkable talent of this pioneer American woman architect. Some of the National Register files for buildings that are her legacy describe the link Morgan had with others of her sex. The nomination for the Mediterranean-style Young Women's Christian Association (YWCA) built in Oakland in 1914 says that it is the first of seventeen YWCAs nationwide designed by Morgan, while the documentation for the YWCA Building in Fresno explains that she was the official architect for the YWCA in the West. The

Fig 18.2. St. Louis, Mo. Des Peres School. Historical photograph taken for the U.S. Centennial celebration, 1876. Inspired by the teaching of Friedrich Froebel, a German educator, Susan Blow became one of the founders of the first successful kindergarten in the United States in this building in 1873. Blow, the well-educated daughter of a wealthy merchant and statesman, was introduced to Froebel's methods when she visited German kindergarten classes on a family trip in 1870. Photo courtesy Missouri Historical Society.

Fig. 18.3. San Juan Capistrano, Calif. The Polonina Montanez Adobe. This place is very significant in the history of the city. From 1886 to 1910 Mission San Juan Capistrano stood empty, a victim of politics, looters, and rain. The tiny chapel in the Montanez Adobe became the village sanctuary, and Polonina Montanez, its owner, became the spiritual leader of the community. This remarkable woman, the daughter of a carpenter at the mission, was also in charge of giving the children of the village religious instruction and served as village nurse and midwife. Photographer unknown, c. 1930.

range of her work for the YWCA is evident in register listings, including the YWCA in Riverside and the magnificent Asilomar, designed in the rustic "Craftsman" mode as the YWCA's national camp and conference grounds in the West. It is located in a spectacular setting on the northern California coast. According to the nomination for the Hostess House, it is the only intact building remaining from the two army training camps established in California during World War I. The War Department requested that the YWCA build Hostess Houses in forty army training camps to establish safe, dignified meeting places for women and children coming to military posts to visit friends, husbands, and relatives in the service. Morgan designed this simple, functional building at Camp Fremont.

Fig. 18.4. Grand Canyon, Ariz. Hopi House at Grand Canyon National Park is one of the few remaining examples of the work of master architect and interior designer Mary Jane Colter. Colter designed Hopi House for the Atchison, Topeka, and Santa Fe Railroad to be used by the Fred Harvey Company to sell Native American arts and crafts to tourists at the South Rim of the Grand Canyon. Colter patterned the building on a Hopi pueblo and included interior murals, fireplaces, and shrines holding Hopi religious artifacts and furnished it with antiques and ceremonial objects she had collected for Fred Harvey. The nomination cites Colter's interest in ethnohistory and scholarly interest in southwestern archaeology when the building was constructed in 1905, right before the passage of the Antiquities Act of 1906, and notes that Colter introduced Indian architecture and culture to travelers at a time when the preservation movement was in its infancy. Photo by Laura Souliere Harrison, National Park Service, 1985.

In 1919 the YWCA gave the building to the City of Palo Alto for one dollar, and with Morgan's approval it was moved there to become the first community center in the United States established and supported by a municipality.

Morgan also designed the Hollywood Studio Club, which was documented by Gail Dubrow and Maren Van Nostrand in a National Historic Landmark nomination for the National Women's Landmark Project. Financed by luminaries of the motion picture field—Mary Pickford, Mrs. Cecil B. DeMille, and Marion Davies, among others—and with contributions from the YWCA, Julia Morgan's 1926 Studio Club was built as a haven for thousands of girls who arrived in Hollywood with the ambition to become stars of the silver screen. Julia Morgan's involvement as architect ensured that all major participants in the project were women, making the Studio Club interesting from the standpoint of women's history in addition to its importance to the history of American filmmaking. The designs of this and other Morgan buildings are worthy of study by social historians for what they tell about the architect and her clients.

Page Putnam Miller gives the best survey to date of what has been done to identify, recognize, and interpret nationally significant historic resources associated with women.[14] These historic resources are either units of the National Park System, such as the Women's Rights National Historical Park and the Maggie L. Walker National Historic Site, or National Historic Landmarks. Some were designated as part of earlier National Historic Landmark theme studies, such as the ones on social and humanitarian movements, American writers, and the African American study, but most resulted from the congressionally mandated theme study on women's history landmarks conducted under a cooperative agreement between the National Park Service, the Organization of American Historians, and the National Coordinating Committee for the Promotion of History.[15] This study and recent NHL theme studies use the more encompassing approaches to American history reflected in the new NPS theme structure and build on current scholarship about women's history.[16]

The NRIS can be searched for NHLs, and the new NPS NHL database is the source of information to find theme studies under which each NHL is designated. Both databases identify areas of significance such as architecture, art, and literature. A review of a few of the landmarks for women demonstrates the range of designated properties.

- The Angelus Temple in Los Angeles served as the base of operations for the colorful preacher and pioneer in the field of radio evangelism Aimee Semple McPherson, who preached there and used it as a center for her social and educational ministry, including providing meals for thousands of hungry people during the Depression.
- The Lukens Historic District in Coatesville, Pennsylvania, is a reminder of Rebecca Lukens (1794–1854) and her family legacy. Lukens, who managed and owned the Brandywine Ironworks (later Lukens Steel Company), one of the iron industry's major firms before the Civil War, was the only woman in the antebellum period to head a heavy industry with interstate and international interests.
- Pewabic Pottery in Detroit was founded by Mary Chase Perry Stratton, an artist of the Arts and Crafts movement. Pewabic Pottery had a national reputation for its iridescent glazes and the production of architectural tile.
- The Triangle Shirtwaist Factory in the Asch Building in New York City is remembered as the site of the disastrous March 25, 1911, fire, which caused the death of 146 of the young women workers whose demands for working fire escapes and open doors had been denied. The nomination says that the events at the Triangle Factory continue to be cited by scholars as a turning point in American labor history which resulted in changes in both factory and fire prevention laws throughout the nation.
- The Philadelphia School of Design for Women, the first school of industrial design for women in the United States, was housed in the building at 1346 North Broad Street from 1880 to 1959.
- The Harriet Taylor Upton House in Warren, Ohio, was the home of Upton, who was nationally important in the woman suffrage movement and as a Republican Party leader and served as national headquarters of the National American Woman Suffrage Association from 1903 to 1909.
- The Madame C. J. Walker Building in Indianapolis functioned as a manufacturing site and national headquarters of the beauty products firm started by Madam C. J. Walker (1867–1919), a black woman who opened the lucrative field of cosmetology to African Americans (fig. 18.5). Her business made her a very wealthy woman.

Fig. 18.5. Indianapolis, Ind. Madame C. J. Walker Building. Madam Walker, the daughter of former slaves, became the first African American woman to become extremely wealthy in business. She developed a highly successful cosmetology company that employed at least three thousand people, mostly women. She expanded from manufacturing to include sales, shops, and schools throughout the United States and in Panama, Cuba, and the West Indies. The Walker Building became the national headquarters and a cultural center with a ballroom and theater. Photo by Eric Gilbertson for the Afro-American Bicentennial Corporation, 1975.

The essays in *Reclaiming the Past: Landmarks of Women's History,* the book edited by Page Putnam Miller which was informed by the National Historic Landmark theme study on women's sites, are organized by some of the primary areas of significance in which women have made outstanding achievements. The book includes essays on architecture, the arts, community, education, politics, religion, and work—all important conceptual frameworks in women's studies. These topics can be searched using the areas of significance in the NRIS, which has identical fields for some (architecture, education, politics, and religion) and is more focused for others (art, performing arts, literature, agriculture, commerce, health and medicine, and law).

An NRIS search of any of the thirty areas of significance will result in a list of all the National Register properties of national, state, and local significance for that area. Those in each category in which the woman is identified in the name of the property will be obvious. For others a query can be run coupling area of significance with another field such as significant person or architect-builder to find women's names. National Register archives also can be hand-searched for sites associated with women.

Research by areas of significance will find the most prominent fields represented by women's sites. For literature, the best represented, 105 places were registered for literary women at the time of our query. Art included places for 38 women artists. Among the most interesting is Grandma Prisbey's Bottle Village in Simi Valley, California, an exceptionally significant and rare folk art environment created by a highly acclaimed, self-taught American folk artist (fig. 18.6). Performing arts had twenty-one listings.

The area of significance and historic function data fields can be used to find sites that provide information for interesting publications about women. One topic is women's colleges. Under the historic function category, college, of the approximately 700 National Register listings, 28 were found to be associated primarily with women. The NRIS can be searched by keyword too. A query for *women* uncovered 58 listings with women in the name. Most were women's clubs, along with some homes, schools, a monument to Confederate women, a hotel, a fountain, a gymnasium, and even a ladies' restroom.

The National Register is being used for research and a variety of publications relating to women's history. Papers presented at the Second National Women in Historic Preservation Conference show the scholarly interest.[17] Historian Mary Jane Lowe used the NRIS and National Register documentation to examine whether National Register files for listings include information on the sexual orientation of a number of famous individuals.[18] Several articles appeared in a 1997 special issue of the National Park Service's *CRM: Cultural Resource Management* publica-

Fig. 18.6. Simi Valley, Calif. Grandma Prisbey's Bottle Village. Courtesy of the Los Angeles Conservancy.

tion, "Placing Women in the Past."[19] Antoinette Lee's study began with a search of the NRIS for YWCAs. Beth M. Boland describes how listed properties and National Register documentation for places such as the homes of Clara Barton and Eleanor Roosevelt became the basis for lesson plans in the National Register's Teaching with Historic Places program. Both authors' studies have been reprinted in an Organization of American Historian's journal devoted to women's history.[20] Carla L. Peterson's essay in *African American Historic Places* surveys listings that illustrate the contributions of black women in American political and social history. Other essays in the book use registered historic places reflecting accomplishments of African American women in various contexts.[21] A National Register of Historic Places travel itinerary describing and linking more than seventy listed places where women made history in Massachusetts and New York is available to the traveling public on the National Register's website. This itinerary, the book, and the Teaching with Historic Places curriculum materials were developed by the National Park Service and outside partners to demonstrate how the National Register can be used for education.

Classroom-ready lesson plans on Clara Barton's house, Eleanor Roosevelt at Val-Kill,[22] the M'Clintock House, the Adeline Hornbek Homestead, and Madam C. J. Walker's business building are among a number of lesson plans focusing on women which are part of the Teaching with Historic Places series.[23] The M'Clintock House lesson uses the Waterloo, New York, residence of the M'Clintock family at Women's Rights National Historical Park to teach young people about the beliefs and backgrounds of the organizers of the first Women's Rights Convention in 1848. Students examine the life of Elizabeth M'Clintock, whose efforts in politics and business illustrate the opportunities and limits on nineteenth-century American women. Students can take a classroom field trip to the Adeline Hornbek Homestead in Florissant Fossil Beds National Monument to study the Homestead Act and how it enabled Adeline Hornbek, a single mother of four, to become a successful homesteader in Colorado. In another lesson achievements of two American entrepreneurs, Madam C. J. Walker and J. C. Penney, are compared and illustrated using their historic places of business. These lesson plans demonstrate how National Register properties can be used to integrate women into the study of broad themes in American history such as equal rights, the settlement of the West, and business.[24] Teaching with Historic Places lesson plans are available in print and on the Internet for use by educators of students in the upper elementary to high school grades.

By organizing National Register files related to women chronologically, Gail Lee Dubrow found that listings until about the mid-1970s tended to recognize women of major significance, such as Juliette Gordon Low, founder of the Girl Scouts, and Harriet Tubman, as well as literary figures such as Louisa May Alcott.[25] Beginning in the mid-1970s, organized initiatives broadened the range of NHLs associated with women such as those done by the American Association for State and Local History and the Afro-American Bicentennial Corporation. The women's theme study has taken the most systematic approach, covering a wider range of subjects, areas of significance, and property types. States have been nominating miscellaneous historic places, usually associated with individuals and a relatively large number of women's clubs. One unusual thematic group of nominations, from the Nebraska State Historic Preservation officer, includes thirty places in Webster County which

Willa Cather used in her writings. Another multiple property submission is for ten buildings designed by California architect Lillian Rice. Several states (Iowa, Michigan, Minnesota, Oregon, Vermont, and Wisconsin) are making a conscious effort to identify women in the names of listings. Georgia is doing a statewide context to evaluate women's history sites. More needs to be done to recognize historic places that chronicle the role of women in American history, including National Historic Landmark designations, thematic surveys, and National Register nominations sponsored by state historic preservation offices, local governments, and Indian tribes. Studies on a variety of topics and properties should integrate the contributions of women as one area of research. Existing listings can be reinterpreted to document the role of women.

Exploring a Common Past: Interpreting Women's History in the National Park Service is a joint effort between the NPS and the Organization of American Historians.[26] Based on current scholarship, it provides information on women's history which will be helpful in identifying new sites and in reinterpreting others in areas such as work, family, life cycle, ideologies about gender, dynamics of difference, public life, and education. Many of these themes can be documented and interpreted at specific historic places that can be used in public education initiatives, as the National Register is doing in the lesson plans relating to women in its Teaching with Historic Places series. Important associations with women at historic places should be reflected in National Register listings, and historians should use these tangible resources to enrich the study and understanding of American history.

Reflections on Federal Policy and Its Impact on Understanding Women's Past at Historic Sites

Page Putnam Miller

Historic sites physically link us to our past, stimulating our imaginations and assisting us in better understanding and appreciating the past. Eudora Welty, one of the most admired American authors, has expressed well the importance and significance of place. In an essay titled "The House of Willa Cather" Welty discusses how inextricably houses are connected to understanding people's lives. She writes: "Set within the land is the dwelling—made by human hands to hold human life." In elaborating on the significance of dwellings, Welty states: "The house is the physical form, the evidence that we have lived, are alive now; it will be evidence someday that we were alive once, evidence against the arguments of time and the tricks of history."[1]

Welty further develops this theme in the essay "Place in Fiction." Place, she argues, is much more than just the framing for the story. We can't understand characters without placing them in identified, concrete, and credible gathering points. It is essential, according to Welty, to see characters "set to scale in his proper world to know his size." She emphasizes this point by asserting, "Place then has the most delicate control over character too: by confining character, it defines it."[2]

What Welty has stated for fiction is all the more true for history. Time and place are two major touchstones for understanding history. Particular places where events occurred and people lived complement the written documents and provide an added vantage point for viewing the past. While honoring the importance of a generalized approach to place, historians have often failed to explore fully the use of buildings, the largest of tangible artifacts, as a research and educational tool.

If we agree both on the importance of understanding women's past and on the critical role that places can play in our understanding of the past, then we must lament that there are so few historic buildings in the United States open to the public with interpretive programs that deal effectively with women's history. Not only are there few sites that focus primarily on women, but there are also few sites that focus on significant historical events and on famous men which also incorporate women's history into the broader story.

If Americans had to rely on existing historic sites for their understanding of women's history, a very limited and distorted picture would emerge. About fifty historic sites, mostly house museums that specialize in the life of a particular woman, have as their primary mission the preservation of structures and the development of interpretive programs about women.[3] One-third of the historic sites open to the public which focus on women are operated by local, state, or federal agencies. The majority, however, have evolved from the efforts of nonprofit organizations and foundations seeking to commemorate their leaders or to preserve the memory of a particular individual. For example, the Woman's Christian Temperance Union and the Girl Scouts of America support historic house museums for their founders. The foundations and associations such as the Rachel Carson Foundation, the Louisa May Alcott Memorial Association, and the Mamie D. Eisenhower Foundation foster the preservation of a historic building associated with the life of a woman they wish to remember and to commemorate.

In the last decade there has been a growing appreciation in the National Park Service (NPS), the lead federal agency for establishing historic preservation policy, of the significance of historic places for understanding women's past. Two NPS initiatives on which I wish to focus are the Women's History Landmark Project and the establishment of a Women's History Education Initiative. Both projects were collaborative ones with the National Park Service working closely with outside specialists in women's history. One focused on sites specifically related to women and the other on integrating women's history into historic sites where women had been present but where their experiences and contribution had been almost totally neglected, with the overwhelming emphasis being, instead, on men's experiences and contributions. The Women's History Landmark Project resulted in the designation of approximately forty additional sites associated with women as National Historic Landmarks. The Women's History Education Initiative led to the publication of a resource booklet titled *Exploring a Common Past: Interpreting Women's History in the National Park Service,* for use by staff at National Parks that are not primarily about women's history but wish to integrate women's history into their interpretations.[4]

The Women's Landmark Project had its roots in the assumption that the first step toward the long-term goal of promoting additional women's history sites open to the public with sound interpretive programs is to identify new sites and to seek increased visibility for their preservation. The National Historic Landmark (NHL) program is one way to identify sites and to gain official recognition. NHLs are designated by the secretary of the interior, possess exceptional value or quality in illustrating and interpreting the heritage of the United States, and are sometimes an avenue for a property becoming a national park.

The origins of the Women's Landmark Project go back to 1985 and to a meeting between Joan Hoff, who was then the executive secretary of the Organization of American Historians (OAH), myself, as director of the National Coordinating Committee for the Promotion of History (NCC), and the deputy director of the NPS. This meeting did not lead immediately to receiving any funds for the project but did result in the signing of a cooperative agreement between the OAH, the NCC, and the NPS to work on designating more sites associated with women as National Historic Landmarks. At that time, of the approximately two thousand National Historic Landmarks, there were only about forty landmarks, or 2 percent, associated specifically with women. Many within the historic preservation and scholarly communities felt that it was important to increase the number of landmarks that focused on women. Yet, without any staff or money assigned to this project, all we managed to do with the cooperative agreement was keep the issue alive.

In 1988 the issue of women and National Historic Landmarks came up at a House congressional hearing. Representative Bruce Vento (D–

Minn.) was at that time chair of the House Subcommittee on National Parks and Public Lands. He was a strong supporter of history and specifically aware of the omissions of women's history, having been well briefed by Heather Huyck, a colleague in the historical profession who was a legislative aide on his staff. Vento's discussion with various witnesses during the hearing resulted in his ensuring that collaboration between scholarly associations and the NPS on the National Historic Landmark Program was part of the committee's report on the NPS budget. The report called for the NPS to establish ongoing and substantial cooperative efforts with major professional and scholarly societies to research and publish National Historic Landmark theme studies.[5] It also laid the groundwork for Congress in 1989 to appropriate modest funding, sixty thousand dollars, for a study on women's history landmarks.

In 1989 the OAH, under the leadership of executive director Arnita Jones; the NCC; and the NPS entered a second phase of a much more substantive cooperative agreement for conducting a Women's History Landmark Project. Funding was extended for this project for two more years. When the project ended, the number of NHLs associated with women had doubled. There were 4 percent, instead of 2 percent, of landmarks associated with women. This was clearly a case of the glass half-empty or the glass half-full. Progress had been made, but there was still a long way to go.

One of the achievements of the Women's History Landmark Project was the 1992 publication of the book *Reclaiming the Past: Landmarks of Women's History.*[6] With its publication the NPS returned to a practice that it had abandoned in the 1970s of including, as a major part of landmark studies, substantive essays to provide the historical context for the theme study. *Reclaiming the Past* provides both the historical context of landmarks associated with women and a discussion of many of the important places and buildings that help to tell the story of American women's struggles and contributions.

The most frustrating part of the Women's History Landmark Project was getting the nomination forms for National Historic Landmark designation through all the various hoops of the NPS process. In the project we worked on about eighty separate properties. Some did not receive the endorsement of the National Park Service staff, some were rejected by

Fig. 19.1. Fort Pierce, Fla. Zora Neale Hurston House. Photo by Jill S. Topalski.

the NPS Advisory Committee, which recommends designation to the secretary of interior, and some were opposed by property owners who did not want their buildings to be designated as landmarks. The NPS rejected about thirty of the properties on which we worked, and owners rejected about ten, leaving us with an addition of forty designated landmarks focusing on women.[7]

One of the success stories of the Women's History Landmark Project was the nomination of the house in Fort Pierce, Florida, where Zora Neale Hurston lived from 1957 until her death in 1960 (fig. 19.1). Hurston, a writer, folklorist, and anthropologist, whom many consider the most noted African American female writer of the mid-twentieth century, never owned a home. She spent her life moving from place to place. This house, which had been discovered by the author Alice Walker, is visited by writers, college students, professors, reporters, and people from all over the world who want to gain a better understanding of Hurston's life. The house is a green concrete-block structure with four rooms, metal windows, and a tar and gravel roof.

There were three strikes against us in our work on the house where Hurston lived. Most of the staff at the NPS and the members of the NPS advisory board had never heard of Hurston, the house was very modest and by some counts most unattractive, and the nomination involved an exception to the National Park Service's fifty-year rule. The first time we made a presentation on this property before the NPS's Advisory Committee's sub-committee on history, only one person on the subcommittee had ever heard of Zora Neale Hurston. But, after several years of persistent effort, we overcame these strikes against us and were successful.

In reflecting on this nomination, it is gratifying to know that it is possible to get a small, ugly cinder block building designated as a National Historic Landmark. But it is well to remember that this accomplishment took considerable persistence. Much groundwork and a great deal of education had to be undertaken to win people over who have little knowledge of women's history. When I appeared before the subcommittee of the NPS which had responsibility for recommending NHL designations to introduce the Hurston house, I saw blank stares indicating their lack of understanding about why this woman was significant. Thus, I started sending the members of the subcommittee background material about her. When this nomination came up a year later, they all knew about Hurston. A production of her work was playing at the Ford Theater in Washington, and the NPS arranged for members of the subcommittee to attend the performance. With time and education it was possible to move the NPS subcommittee with responsibility for recommending NHL nomination from blank stares to celebration of Hurston's life and work.

Next to a lack of knowledge about women's history, the second most difficult hurdle we had to face was the National Park Service's strict application of "integrity." Disagreements frequently occur in the preservation community over whether a building has an adequate degree of "physical intactness," that is, whether it retains enough of its original design and structural materials to have integrity. Judgments about a property's physical integrity often involve subjective factors. The NPS material on evaluating properties for the National Register of Historic Places states that "the evaluation of integrity is sometimes a subjective judgment, but it must always be grounded in an understanding of a property's physical features and how they relate to its significance."[8] A property significant for historical associations should, according to the NPS guide-lines, retain the essential physical features that made up its character or appearance during the period of its association with the important event, historical patterns, or person. If a property is important for illustrating a particular architectural style, the NPS requires that the property retain most of the physical features. The distinction between retaining "the essential physical features" and "most of the physical features" seemed clear in the National Register material. The tendency throughout the Women's History Landmark Project, however, was for the staff of the National Historic Landmark Program to hold properties nominated for historical significance to the same standard as those properties nominated for architectural significance.

One of the properties that had to be dropped from the study because the NPS said that the building lacked integrity was the Lafayette Hotel in Buffalo, New York (fig. 19.2). Louise Blanchard Bethune, the first professional woman architect in the United States designed the Lafayette Hotel, which opened in 1904 and is considered to be her masterpiece. The French Renaissance–style, seven-story hotel with a facade of dark-red brick and white terra cotta trim has 265 rooms and was the first fireproof hotel built in the United States. Throughout the review of the Lafayette Hotel the NPS staff insisted that interior changes to this almost-hundred-year-old building had diminished its integrity and made it an inappropriate candidate to become a landmark site. Since there are very few hundred-year-old buildings that have been frozen in time, the insistence that buildings nominated for historical integrity have the same level of integrity required for buildings of architectural significance eliminated from consideration many buildings that have historical value to understanding women's past.

Another stumbling block was the Park Service's interpretation of "national significance." A property must possess national historical significance to be considered as a landmark. NPS staff frequently rejected properties proposed by the Women's History Landmark Project, arguing that they had only local or regional significance. Those grounded in women's history know that the same standards for national significance which are used in evaluating men's contributions cannot necessarily be applied to women. Women, during much of American history, had to op-

Fig. 19.2. Buffalo, N.Y. Lafayette Hotel. Photo by Joseph Stallone, courtesy of Adriana Barbasch, American Institute of Architects.

erate in a much more confined arena than men, yet women's local and regional activity often had a national impact.

For example, different views between the NPS and the Women's Landmark Project over national significance emerged when we put forward for consideration the Prudence Crandall House in Connecticut, where Crandall had run a girl's school that was the first in the country to admit an African American student (fig. 19.3). The Park Service's first reaction to this nomination was to say that this school had only regional significance. Yet at the time this school was established, in the 1830s, there were no national women's organizations. Women who are denied a national platform can often effect change only on a small scale that in time indirectly influences later national developments. We persisted in making a case for the national significance of the Prudence Crandall House, and we were finally successful. Having to jump through extra hoops was

Fig. 19.3. Canterbury, Conn. Prudence Crandall School. Photo courtesy of The Prudence Crandall Museum, Canterbury, Conn. Administered by the Connecticut Historical Commission.

time-consuming, however, and meant that we couldn't be working on other properties. Furthermore, we sometimes were unsuccessful in making a case for national significance despite support from recent women's history scholarship.

Some properties became stalled in the process because the NPS wished to avoid what it perceived as controversial nominations. The Mary (or Molly, as she was known) Dewson residence in New York City is a prime example (fig. 19.4) The Greenwich Village apartment building where Dewson lived was constructed in 1922. For thirty years Molly Dewson, a social worker and friend of Eleanor Roosevelt, who became a key member of Franklin Roosevelt's political team, lived in this cooperative apartment building with her partner, Polly Porter. In her biography of Dewson, Susan Ware describes the apartment, and Blanche Cook mentions this building in her biography of Eleanor Roosevelt.[9] Most of the twenty-four units in the building were inhabited by other unmarried professional women. Nancy Cook and Marion Dickerman, two women who were also friends of Eleanor Roosevelt, lived across the hall from Dewson.

While many of the women's history scholars who worked on the Women's History Landmark Project thought the Dewson residence was a wonderful site for understanding professional women in the 1920s and 1930s and the culture in which they lived in New York, the NPS was not

Fig. 19.4. New York, N.Y. Molly Dewson Residence. Photo by Andrew Dolkart.

enthusiastic about the site. The first draft of the nomination form for this building came back from the History Division of the NPS with "Lesbian?" written in large letters across the front page. We were unsuccessful in our efforts to gain NPS support for this building, but it is important to note that the exchange took place in 1989 and that the staffer who wrote this comment no longer works for the National Historic Landmark Program (furthermore, that staffer's supervisor and the supervisor's superior have both since retired from the NPS). The official reason given by the NPS for not supporting the nomination was that it was an apartment building and the nomination was based on its association with only one unit of the building. We engaged in a lively challenge of this position but lost.

Concern in the first Bush Administration over possible controversy postponed until 1993 the designation of the Margaret Sanger Clinic as a National Historic Landmark (fig. 19.5). The fear on the part of some administration officials was that Sanger, a pioneer in the birth control movement, would be associated in some way with the abortion movement. Although the Advisory Committee of the National Park Service recommended the designation of the New York City house that had served as the birth control clinic of Margaret Sanger, the nomination languished for several years, unsigned on the desk of the secretary of interior. Only after President Bill Clinton's election did Secretary of Interior Bruce Babbitt sign the forms designating the Sanger Clinic as an NHL.

A number of properties failed to be designated because the owners did not choose to endorse the nomination to NHL status. One of the buildings that fell into this category was the Hollywood Studio Club (NR), a residential facility for women in the Hollywood who worked in the motion picture industry (fig. 19.6). The YWCA, the sponsor of this boarding home, asked architect Julia Morgan to design the club building. Over the years more than ten thousand women associated with the movie industry lived in this building. Several of them became famous—Kim Novak, Dorothy Malone, Donna Reed, Marilyn Monroe, and others. The Hollywood Studio Club primarily provided shelter for single women, who by accepted social standards at that time were not supposed to be living alone, but it also served as an informal extension of the studio casting office, with its most active years in the period 1926–64. The Women's

Fig. 19.5. New York, N.Y. Margaret Sanger Clinic. Photo by Andrew Dolkart.

History Landmark Project claimed in the nomination form that no other single cultural resource in the nation has greater interpretive potential in relation to the history of women in the motion picture industry than the Hollywood Studio Club. The various phases through which the motion picture industry has passed are reflected in the activities and life at the Studio Club.

Fig. 19.6. Hollywood, Calif. Exterior (*top*) and interior (*bottom*) of Hollywood Studio Club. Photo courtesy of Young Women's Christian Association of Los Angeles Collection, Urban Archives Center, University Library, California State University, Northridge.

In reflecting on the nomination process for the Hollywood Studio Club, one of my most vivid memories is a meeting at the NPS office in Washington, D.C., in which specialists in women's history and cultural resources had gathered to evaluate and make recommendations about the draft nomination forms of the Women's History Landmark Project. What I remember so clearly was the way in which those individuals who were scholars of women's history but who knew little about buildings and those who knew about buildings and all about Julia Morgan's career as an architect but who knew little about women's history recognized how much they had to learn from each other. The academic scholars reassured the group that they would be including information about the building in their lectures, and the architectural historians were equally impressed with their newly gained knowledge of the people and events associated with this building.

Throughout the women's landmark project one of the realities with which we had to deal was the fact that there is a tremendous gulf between scholars who focus primarily on words for their research and those who use material culture, with buildings being the largest of tangible artifacts, as research tools. In preparing a single nomination forms for this project, I often had contracts with several people—one to provide the historical significance, another to provide the architectural description, another to take the needed photographs. I hope that there will be more opportunities in the years to come for increased interaction between scholars who focus on the word and those who are specialists in material culture.

Summarizing the experience of the National Park Service's women's landmark initiative, it is important to emphasize that it gave increased visibility to some sites associated with women. The added visibility provided leverage in fund raising to preserve some sites. Also, increased awareness about both the small number of existing sites associated with women and the work to add new sites helped to educate park officials as well as historians and the broader public toward a greater understanding of the importance of having specific programs that focus on incorporating a women's history perspective into historic preservation and interpretation policies. Beyond the value of increasing the number of NHLs associated with women, the Women's History Landmark Project played a key role in setting forth new models for presenting the larger contextual framework for theme studies through publication of a monograph and for developing a partnership between NPS staff and outside scholars which involved an extensive network of specialists in the landmark project. The frustrating aspects of the Women's Landmark Project also served to highlight problems that have continued to face the NHL program in its subsequent work with the labor history theme study. Although some progress has been made in clarifying issues such as the appropriate level of integrity for buildings of historical significance and the meaning of national significance, these remain thorny issues that deserve further deliberation by the NPS at the highest policy levels.

The second NPS initiative related to women which I wish to explore was part of the Women's History Education Initiative and was the development of a resource guide to assist park staff in incorporating women's history into their interpretation of historic sites that are not primarily associated with women. Of the 365 national parks, over half are historic sites. Millions of people every year visit these sites, and they are wonderful classrooms for making history come alive. Since only about half-dozen of the national parks deal specifically with women and since it appears likely that there will be little money available in future budgets for the federal government to purchase new sites, it is increasingly important to be sure that some understanding of women's past is included in all historic parks.

Before considering the specifics of the NPS booklet, *Exploring a Common Past,* it is important to understand the groundwork that was laid over several years which made this publication possible. A whole chain of events contributed to creating the climate for its preparation: a partnership with the OAH dating back to 1985 to undertake collaborate projects with scholarly organizations; revision of the National Park Service's thematic framework in 1993 to incorporate the most recent scholarship; the adoption by the National Park Service Advisory Committee of the report *The Humanities in the National Parks: Adapting to Change;*[10] the 1994 first national conference on women and historic preservation which was held at Bryn Mawr; and a National Park Service working conference held in Lowell National Historical Park in 1995. Additionally, it is doubtful that this initiative would have happened without the internal support within the Park Service of Marie Rust, the Northeast Areas regional director, and Dwight Pitcaithley, chief historian for the NPS.

In describing significant changes and opportunities in the NPS History Program, Pitcaithley emphasizes the importance of the reconceptualization of the NPS thematic framework for history and prehistory and the NPS advisory board's adoption of the report *Humanities and the National Parks,* which recommends the development of partnerships with professional associations and specialists outside the NPS.[11] The new thematic framework adopted in 1994 "brought the NPS's outline for history in line with current scholarship."[12] The new framework, according to Pitcaithley, is built on an understanding of the past which sees human experience as integrated, diverse, and complex. The report specifically recommends the development of partnerships with the scholarly and professional associations that have subsequently been instrumental in enhancing NPS historical research, preservation, and interpretive programs.

While these two developments laid the basic foundation for the NPS accelerating its incorporation of current scholarship and enhancing its working relationship with scholars outside of the NPS, the First National Women in Historic Preservation Conference held at Bryn Mawr in 1994 focused attention on women's history. Although Marie Rust was unable to attend the Bryn Mawr conference, she asked her deputy to convene a breakfast meeting of a few leaders inside and outside the NPS to consider how to increase an understanding of women's history at the national parks. That breakfast meeting then led to a NPS working conference of specialists inside and outside the NPS on how to deal with women's history in the parks.

On May 31, 1995, the National Park Service hosted a small working meeting at Lowell National Historic Park to develop a vision for the role of the National Park Service in the research, identification, interpretation, and commemoration of the contributions and experiences of American women. Marie Rust stressed in her opening remarks a hope that specialists from academe and Park Service staff could form a "learning circle." The NPS organizers of the working meeting established objectives for the thirty people who gathered for two days at Lowell that included the goals of agreeing upon a vision of the role of the NPS in preserving, commemorating, and interpreting the history of American women and developing an action plan for realizing the vision.

Vivien Rose, a historian at the Women's Rights National Historical Park, presented to the Lowell working group a broad overview of how in 1995 the National Park Service was dealing with women's history. She noted that some parks included women only as they were mothers, wives, or daughters of great men, such as Abigail Adams or Mary Todd Lincoln. Other parks included women only if they were heroines whose accomplishments are widely recognized, such as Clara Barton. An increasing number of parks are beginning to include women in what Rose referred to as "sidebars"—such as women nurses at Civil War battlefield sites. She noted, however, that for most parks the full integration of women in the interpretive program is yet to be achieved, despite a realization by many NPS historians that the inclusion of women's history is often indispensable to understanding the American experience.

Rose concluded by asserting that the whole landscape changes where women are included—the whole of history changes as more information is brought to light and there are more letters, more diaries, and more evidence for a more complete history. As new sources on women's history have come to light in the last three decades, there has been rich ferment in the field of women's history scholarship. Many scholars of American history, in fact, are convinced that historians of women's history have been in the forefront of invigorating the study of American history by asking new questions and pursuing new avenues of research. Historical scholarship is rooted in research in new sources and the writing and presentation of an increasingly more comprehensive and accurate view of the past. Dwight Pitcaithley understood well the need to incorporate the large body of new research on women into the interpretation of all historic sites.

As part of the action plan, the Lowell working group identified many possibilities for enhancing the interpretation of women's history at National Park Service sites. One specific recommendation was a collaborative OAH and NPS initiative to develop a resource booklet for National Park staff members who wish to strengthen their work of integrating women's history into their preservation and interpretive programs.

Seven people, four staff from inside the National Park Service and three outside scholars, wrote the resource guide.[13] Because we began with some shared understandings from having participated in the Lowell working group, we were able to prepare the booklet by telephone conferences and e-mail. We kept a steady stream of e-mail exchanges going until we had drafted, refined, and merged various parts to sections of the resource guide to produce a finished booklet, which was published by the History Division of the National Park Service in 1996. Again, the OAH served as the sponsor for this cooperative project.

Exploring a Common Past: Interpreting Women's History in the National Park Service rests on the assumption that it isn't possible merely to "add" women who have been left out of the interpretation of historic sites but that the whole history of a site needs to be rethought because part of the earlier interpretation may have been inaccurate or misleading. Eric Foner, professor of history at Columbia University and a former president of the Organization of American Historians and the American Historical Association, has made the point, echoed frequently by participants in the Lowell working group, that women's history has forced historians not simply to compensate for the previous neglect of half of the population but to rethink some of their basic premises.[14]

The resource booklet *Exploring a Common Past* introduces park staff to key themes in current women's history scholarship, to issues related to the protection of historic sites associated with women, to a means for assessing a park's interpretive program, and to current historical scholarship, providing a bibliography of resources on women's history and the built environment. One of the most important sections of the booklet, in my view, is a set of questions intended to serve as a starting point for evaluating how history is interpreted in a park and exploring ways to provide a more comprehensive and accurate view of what had happened at the park by including women. Park staff are asked to consider, for example: "If visitors ask what were women doing here/were there women here, are interpreters prepared with a knowledgeable answer?" There are almost no National Park Service sites where women were not present, although answering the question often involves research in areas that had previously been considered marginal. Another question—"Does the park recognize that it is not just interpreting one single event but the society that participated in it, the culture that made the event possible or probable?"—gets at issues of the broader context in which specific historical events occur. The question "If the site has been established because of its association with a 'great man,' how are his family and household discussed?" requires a deeper look at the collective effort required to run a household.

This booklet represents a significant step forward in the National Park Service's commitment to making the interpretation of their historic sites more inclusive of women's experiences. The question now is whether the staff at the individual parks will use this resource guide. Early indications are that they are using it. During the Second National Conference on

Women and Historic Preservation in 1997, which was hosted by Arizona State University, National Park Service leaders Marie Rust and Dwight Pitcaithley, on a number of occasions, reaffirmed their commitment to integrating women's history into the parks.

As I reflect on federal policy and its impact on the understanding of women's past at historic sites, I see the National Park Service assuming at the end of the twentieth century a leadership role that it had been unprepared to accept in earlier years. The Women's Landmark Project and the Women's History Education Initiative offer significant beginnings on which to build. This beginning, combined with the broad interest in cultural tourism, can only give a boost to all aspects of historic preservation, including women's history.

CHAPTER 20

Parks Canada
and Women's History

Alan B. McCullough

The growth of women's history during the past thirty years and the related rise in interest in women's heritage has often left major heritage institutions such as the U.S. National Park Service and Parks Canada scrambling to keep up. Not only has the growth of women's history expanded the range of topics considered suitable for commemoration by heritage institutions; it has forced the reevaluation of existing commemorations. In the United States preservation and commemoration is fundamentally a grassroots, decentralized, activity; in Canada a slightly more centralized system has made it possible to begin to refocus the historic sites within the Parks Canada system to recognize the growth of interest in women's history and heritage. In both systems the goal is a more complete, more inclusive, more relevant, system of historic sites. This essay reports on Parks Canada's recent efforts to improve the coverage of women's history within the Canadian system of national historic sites.

In Canada women's history did not emerge as a major field of study until the late 1960s. Early works tended to focus on prominent individuals—great women—active in the public sphere and on organizations that gave women a public voice and presence.[1] Women's labor, both paid and unpaid, also attracted attention.[2] Two influential works, *Many Tender Ties,* by Sylvia Van Kirk, and *Strangers in Blood,* by Jennifer Brown, made the point that women's labor was essential to the fur trade, one of Canada's oldest industries; the works also suggested the importance of family history in studies of women's work.[3] In the 1980s historians began to explore the importance of life cycles and the interaction of the public and private spheres.[4] During the last decade there has been increased interest in extending the concepts and techniques of women's history toward gender history and family history with studies that examine the interplay between home and work for men and women.[5] Women's historians have also extended their studies beyond the majority culture to minority and aboriginal cultures.[6] Although much remains to be done, women's history is now well established in Canada; a recent bibliography of women's history contains 4,761 references.[7]

Women's history as a formal field of academic inquiry is about thirty years old; Canada's national park system dates from 1885, when Canada's first national park, dedicated to preserving natural areas, was established in the Rocky Mountains. Over the next thirty years a growing heritage movement persuaded the Canadian government to help preserve a few historic sites, mostly ones related to the military history of Canada. In 1919 the government appointed the Historic Sites and Monuments Board of Canada (HSMBC) to advise it on heritage issues. The appointment of the board marked the birth of the national historic sites system within Canada's system of national parks; the national parks are dedicated to preserving Canada's natural heritage; the national historic sites commemorate and interpret the country's human heritage.

The HSMBC continues to play a key role in heritage issues. Its membership includes academic historians, historical geographers, archivists, anthropologists, political scientists, and heritage activists representing all of the provinces and territories of Canada. The board meets semiannually to review submissions and to make recommendations to the minister of Canadian heritage on the national historic or architectural significance of various places, individuals, or events. Many of the topics considered by the board are suggested by the public, some originate with other levels of government or other government agencies, and some are generated by the board itself or by Parks Canada.

If the minister of Canadian Heritage accepts the board's recommendation, the site is declared to be of national historic significance and is commemorated or recognized as a national historic site. Since 1919 about 1,600 sites have been declared to be of national historic significance. Commemoration takes several forms. Plaques explaining the significance of the place, event, or person are the most common form of commemoration; they do not involve the acquisition of any property by Parks Canada. At about 130 sites more substantial property has been acquired and the site is administered by Parks Canada. The administered sites include great men's houses, fur trade posts, military sites, historic canals, and industrial sites. Recently, a third type of site, one in which Parks Canada makes financial and technical contributions to a site that it does not own, has become more common; these cost-sharing arrangements at historic sites are likely to be a model for the future.

The existing system of national historic sites is the cumulative product of decisions taken since the HSMBC was created in 1919 and reflects the changing thought in Canadian historiography and heritage over seventy-five years. Until the 1950s commemoration emphasized traditional components of national history: political and military history; and the history of exploration, settlement, and the fur trade. Beginning in the 1950s, there was a perceptible shift toward social, economic, and cultural history as well as an increased interest in preserving buildings of architectural significance. Sometimes the shift in emphasis was subtle and was achieved at the level of interpretation rather than at the level of commemoration. For example, the Fortress of Louisbourg was commemorated for its role in the British and French colonial wars, but it has been interpreted as an eighteenth-century, French colonial garrison / commercial town with social, political, and economic factors receiving almost equal emphasis. In other cases the shift was more overt and led to the commemoration of scientists such as Alexander Graham Bell at his summer home in Cape Breton and industrial complexes such as the Gulf of Georgia Cannery in British Columbia. The interest in fields such as military history has not ended, but it has evolved to recognize previously overlooked aspects of military history; three recent commemorations marked the entry of women into the Canadian army, navy, and air force during World War II.

The shift in commemorative emphasis has included women's history, and over the past decade the proportion of commemorations of women's history has increased. Nevertheless, women remain lamentably under-represented in the system. Of approximately sixteen hundred commemorations made since 1919, only eighty-one are commemorations of women or of institutions that were primarily associated with women. Of the eighty-one commemorations, forty-seven are of individual women, and eighteen are of women's organizations. Thirteen are of places or events associated with women's history. Most of the commemorations are in the arts, religion, health care, and politics, particularly politics associated with the suffrage movement. Thirty-five of the eighty-one commemorations have been made in the last decade (see app. B).

Since 1981 Parks Canada has had a formal, long-range, system-wide plan designed to bring more balance into the commemoration program. The original plan focused on economic and industrial topics but did not include women's history as a priority. When Parks Canada began revising the plan in 1991, however, women's history was identified as a priority along with the history of Aboriginal People and of cultural communities. The decision to include women's history among developmental priorities was largely recognition of the growth of the field and of the need to make the historic sites system more representative of the Canadian population.[8]

For those who had been working in women's history, the decision was overdue. In part the delay can be attributed to one of the constraints on public commemoration. A public commemoration involves an official statement that the site (person, place, or event) is of national historic significance. Not surprisingly, the public often regards commemoration as an official or authoritative version of events and expects to see some reflection of its views in public recognition of historic places and people. Where academic history and public memory are not in agreement, Parks Canada must search for common ground before proceeding to commemoration. The search for a combination of historical accuracy, fairness, and inclusivity is time-consuming and is not always successful.

Even when a decision has been made to include women's history as a priority area for commemoration, the best means of doing so has been far from clear. Parks Canada had little internal expertise in women's history, and hiring freezes made it unlikely that expertise could be hired from outside the program. But the organization had experience in public consultation as a means of seeking advice, of spreading awareness about initiatives, and of building consensus. Building on this experience, the program convened workshops on women's history in 1992 and 1994 to seek advice on how to proceed. The workshops included academic historians, heritage activists representing regional or minority communities, members of the HSMBC, and Parks Canada staff. On the basis of these workshops the HSMBC and Parks Canada have developed some working hypotheses, positions, and understandings that will help guide their commemoration of women's history. These understandings—which relate to point of view, precedents, and policies—and interpretive approaches, are not fixed; they will evolve, and they will be influenced by experience.

Parks Canada's working definition of *women's history* is simply the history of women in Canada and the role of women in Canadian history. What is more important than a definition is a recognition that women's history is more than a field of study; it is an attitude and a way of looking at historical events. We are beginning to speak of applying a gender lens to historical and heritage questions. How this attitude, this lens, is applied to future decisions is a key issue that will affect the success of Parks Canada's plans to commemorate women's history.

It is important to recognize that, over the years, Parks Canada has developed precedents (less charitably, habits) for determining what is and is not historically significant. Often the precedents are a reflection of societal values. Industrialized societies, for example, have generally undervalued unpaid labor. This attitude is reflected in traditional historiography and in the paucity of HSMBC commemorations recognizing the importance of unpaid work. Most women's work has traditionally been unpaid, hence undervalued and not considered of national historic significance. If women's work is to be fully commemorated, it will be necessary to develop new precedents that broaden the understanding of what is significant. Developing new precedents can only be done by doing. What will be essential is remaining open to new topics and considering new approaches to old topics.

In addition to precedents, Parks Canada has formal policies and criteria that guide decisions on what may be commemorated. There was some concern that these policies might hinder the commemoration of women. For example, national historic sites focus on specific places and sites; those that Parks Canada administers usually involve the preservation of important in situ resources such as buildings. It may be that the focus on specific places will work against the commemoration of women participating in social movements involving many individuals at a multitude of sites. Equally, the emphasis on surviving in situ resources might hinder the commemoration of women who were, by and large, not property owners. By focusing on the people who lived and worked at a site in addition to those who owned it, it should be possible to present a more nuanced interpretation of history while highlighting the role of women. The very process of thinking about women's history and identifying new women's history sites is helping to change attitudes and ease the application of old policies to new situations. There is growing confidence that, if there is a general change of attitude, if Parks Canada can apply a gender lens to all topics, then the specific rules and policies should not impede the commemoration of women's history.

Traditionally, major historic sites have been places where pivotal events took place or places that were associated with readily recognizable great men. Battlefields and the homes of leading politicians are prominent in most historic sites systems. Broadly based social changes were less likely to produce identifiable turning points and so, in a traditional commemoration program, were less likely to be commemorated. Parks Canada has begun to work with sites that might not, individually, be of national historic significance but which are representative of important historical developments. For example, a nurses' residence at a teaching hospital or an isolated nursing station could be used as a basis for commemorating the pivotal role of women in health care.[9] The trend to use representative sites will prove useful in commemorating women's history, given that many important developments in women's history were the result of popular movements.

The current Parks Canada systems plan has three priorities: Aboriginal People's history, the history of cultural communities, and the history of women. There are many facets to each of these areas. Within the field of women's history gender is seldom the sole category of analysis; race or ethnicity, class, and region normally must be considered as well. White, middle-class women do not necessarily speak for black women, Asian women, or working-class women or share the same historical experience. These multiple perspectives will have to be considered in all commemorations.

In women's history there are two tendencies: one emphasizing women's oppression or victimization and the other focusing on women's agency or capacity to change their own lives. Traditionally public commemoration has favored a positive or progressive interpretation of history; sites related to the suffrage movement are particularly prone to a progressive interpretation. On the other hand, industrial sites where women worked under harsh conditions might seem susceptible to an interpretation that emphasized oppression. Current writing on a site such as the textile mills of Paris, Ontario, however, emphasizes resistance, coping strategies, and the development of women's cultures in the face of a hostile environment.[10] At most sites it will be necessary to seek a balance between agency and oppression.

Many issues in women's history affect both men and women. For example, the women's suffrage movement is part of the story of the expansion (and occasional contraction) of the franchise. In the context of a program to increase the commemoration of women's history, it may be best to treat the suffrage movement primarily as a women's history issue and highlight the role of women. In other cases, for example the movement of women into the industrial labor force, it might be best to treat the subject as part of a larger issue of the industrialization of labor.

Ideally, if the insights of women's history are incorporated into the Parks Canada culture, they will influence the interpretation of all sites, including those that are perceived to be predominantly male sites. This need not take the form of undue emphasis on the small number of women who were present at a site such as the Bar U Ranch National Historic Site (NHS); instead, it could examine the development and expression of masculine cowboy culture (fig. 20.1).

How these hypotheses and understandings will be applied to expanding the commemoration of women within the Parks Canada system will only become clear with the passage of time. Initially (and this probably means over the next ten years), the goal is to identify and develop several major women's history sites and to expand the proportion of plaques commemorating women. To the outsider these commitments are likely to appear mere token efforts; to an insider they appear to be substantial commitments at a time of declining budgets and staff.

The identification and development of new women's history sites will take several years; preliminary research is focusing on two thematic areas: women and power; and women and health care. The two themes have been chosen both because of their intrinsic importance and because they are comparatively well researched and well known.[11] The theme women

Fig. 20.1. Longview, Alberta. A child of the manager of the Bar U Ranch. Although ranching society projected a masculine image, women and children were a presence on most ranches and played key roles in the production and reproduction of ranching society. Photo courtesy of Glenbow Archives, NA-2467-35.

and power encompasses women's historic relationship to decision-making structures. Women have traditionally been excluded from the formal, public power structures of the Canadian state. Their gradual movement toward political and legal equality is a key development both symbolically and practically and was the focus of some of the earliest women's history studies. Parks Canada has made some commemorations in the area of early female politicians and is in the process of commemorating two key events, the winning of the vote during and after World War I and the Persons Case in 1929.[12] Both events have great symbolic weight and might well be the lynchpins for a wide-ranging interpretation of women's role in electoral politics.

There is a long tradition of women working as health care givers, both formally and informally. To some extent Parks Canada has recognized this tradition through the commemoration of religious orders that operated hospitals. It has also recognized two nurses who directed the nursing service of the Canadian army during World War I and has commemorated two doctors who opened up the medical profession to women in the nineteenth century. A recent commemoration of Women's College Hospital in Toronto opens the possibility of a major commemoration of the theme of women and health care at a site that initiated the provision of health care and medical education for women by women. In general Parks Canada's commemorative initiatives have focused on the role of women as caregivers. In a few cases interpretation at specific sites raises the issue of women as consumers of health care; for example at Bellevue House NHS, for example, where the mistress of the house was a semi-invalid, women's health care is one of the interpretative themes.

The theme of women and work is a broad and important one involving both paid and unpaid labor in and outside the home. At the moment there are no plans to tackle the topic directly, but there is a real possibility of approaching it through the commemoration of different industries in which women were significant components of the labor force. For example, in 1975 the West Coast fishing industry was identified as being of national historic significance, and in 1984 the Gulf of Georgia Cannery was acquired as a site at which to interpret it. Subsequent research revealed that over a third of the cannery workforce was female; at different times Aboriginal Canadians, Japanese Canadians, and Euro-Canadians comprised the majority of the female component of the labor force. The role these women played has been incorporated into the site's themes and forms part of the interpretation of the site. Similarly, women played an important role in Canada's munitions industry in both world wars; their participation in the wartime labor force is generally viewed as an important stage in their entry into the labor force. While women's work in the munitions industry has not been formally commemorated, it is interpreted at Artillery Park NHS in Quebec City (fig. 20.2).

In spite of plans to expand the commemoration of sites related to women's history, it is obvious that for many years to come the system as a whole will continue to be dominated by existing commemorations, most of which were made before women's history became an area of study. Parks Canada has begun a review of the existing system in order to identify any elements that can be made more sympathetic to women's history while respecting the commemorative intent of the site. Initially, Parks

Fig. 20.2. Quebec City, Quebec. A woman worker, Germaine Matte, in the cartridge assembly plant at Quebec City, 1928. Women's work in the Canadian munitions industry is part of the interpretation at Artillery Park National Historic Site. Original source unknown; copy on file, Parks Canada, Quebec.

Canada hopes to expand the interpretation of women's history at a small number of "pilot" sites, which will serve both as a test of the concept and as a source of ideas for other sites.

There is a risk in revisiting and reinterpreting existing sites. It can easily slip into tokenism or into force-fitting women's history into inappropriate sites. But the risk can be minimized by asking the question "What about the women?" and listening carefully to the answer. Detailed and careful research into the history of the site is the key to an appropriate interpretation. At almost all sites women were present, performing essential tasks, even if these tasks were not publicly valued. By interpreting the role of these women, their history will be given value, and the overall balance of the historic sites system will be shifted more rapidly than it could be by commemoration alone.

Parks Canada makes an important distinction between commemoration and interpretation. "Commemoration is the means by which Canada gives official recognition to subjects of national historic significance," while "interpretation seeks to reveal meanings and relationships so that the public will gain an enhanced awareness of what cultural resources signify. Interpretation includes the specialized activities by which the Canadian Parks Service communicates an understanding and appreciation of the historic value of particular places, things, events, and activities to visitors and the public."[13] Commemoration is usually very focused; the focus is maintained through formal statements of commemorative intent which are based on the HSMBC recommendations relating to a site. Interpretation explains and conveys the significance of the site as it is set out in the statement of commemorative intent; to do this interpretation must often go beyond specific individuals and artifacts to provide a context for the site being commemorated. While there is some risk of losing the focus of a site by supplying too much background, there is also an opportunity to provide a multifaceted view, including gender, class, ethnicity, and regional perspectives, of the history of a particular site. If the role of women at national historic sites is to be fully developed, these opportunities must be exploited.

Sites relating to Canada's military history are the largest single category among the sites that Parks Canada administers and interprets directly. Some of the sites are battlefields. Many are obsolete fortifications.

Originally, they were interpreted as male bastions, but we have come to recognize the female presence at many military sites. Military conflict was their raison d'être, but battle was not their normal state, and Parks Canada's interpretation has tended increasingly toward the day-to-day life in a military community. The tradition is quite old and can be traced to early research on the daily life of British soldiers; more recently, the research has extended to the lives of soldier's wives and families.[14]

Before 1870 Canadian fortifications were usually garrisoned by British regiments that, as a matter of course, provided rations and accommodation for a number of wives of soldiers. In addition to their unpaid domestic labor, these women often found paid work as laundresses, seamstresses, housekeepers, and teachers. At Halifax Citadel NHS, where costumed staff have been interpreting the lives of the women attached to the Seventy-eighth Ross Shire Buffs since 1991, the proportion of women is based on the standard allowed by military regulations, six per company (figs. 20.3 and 20.4).[15] Research on another site, Fort Wellington at Prescott, Ontario, has revealed a much higher marriage rate; in 1846 a third of the men were married, and there were over fifty children living at the fort or in the town.[16] "From a twentieth-century point of view, what is the most remarkable feature of this snapshot of military life [at Fort Wellington] is its inconsistency with the stereotypes of military service. The garrison at Fort Wellington was not an isolated male enclave of monastic-like existence, but an alive and vibrant community, literally teeming with the lives and family activities of large numbers of men, women, children and probably animals as well."[17] This "vibrant community" provides an opportunity to interpret nineteenth-century family life in a military environment that is not all musketry drill and mounting guard. It introduces women, and children, into an interpretive environment in which, a decade or two ago, they might well have been overlooked.

After sites related to military history, sites with a link to the fur trade are the most numerous administered sites in the Parks Canada system. Early fur trade historians tended to view the fur trade as a European enterprise, important as an economic activity and as a motivation for the European exploration of Canada. Aboriginal People were not central to the process; at best they were viewed as dependent labor or somewhat troublesome customers. As Aboriginal history developed, Aboriginal

Fig. 20.3. Halifax, Nova Scotia. Many soldiers at Halifax, such as Sergeant Tuite of the Seventy-eighth Ross Shire Buffs, were accompanied by their families. The interpretation of family life in settings that have been traditionally viewed as male offers special opportunities to women's historians. Photo courtesy of Public Archives of Nova Scotia, Notman Collection, 53183, N-0004.

Fig. 20.4. Halifax, Nova Scotia. At Halifax Citadel, National Historic Site interpreters have interpreted the role of soldiers' wives since 1991. Photo courtesy of Parks Canada Collection, 108-57-2-992-0068.

People came to be seen as partners in the process with their own agendas and interests. The unspoken assumption was that Aboriginal men were the principal players in the trade. Since the publication of Sylvia van Kirk and Jennifer Brown's studies on the role of women in fur trade society, however, it has become impossible to interpret the fur trade adequately without reference to Aboriginal women as laborers, wives, traders, diplomats, translators, and cultural mediators.[18]

The growing recognition of the role of Aboriginal women in the fur trade presents a significant opportunity to expand the interpretation of their role at many existing Parks Canada sites in a way that will remain true to the history of the sites. For example, Fort St. James NHS is a nineteenth-century fur trade post in the territory of the Carrier People, in what is now British Columbia. The site was commemorated in 1948 because of its importance in the fur trade; it was acquired by Parks Canada in the early 1970s in order to interpret its role in the trade and to preserve a number of surviving fur trade buildings (fig. 20.5). Although the original commemoration of the site made no mention of either Aboriginal People or of women, research during the 1990s laid the groundwork for expanding the interpretation of the role of Carrier men and women who traded and worked at Fort St. James. Research in fur trade records and secondary literature is helpful, but it usually treats the Carrier People from the perspective of a male outsider. Oral history provides an aboriginal perspective and is particularly useful in defining the women's role at the site. It identifies women as owners of resources, as active traders, and as provisioners as well as wives, mothers, and consumers. Perhaps most important, oral history gives the Carrier women their own voice, and one of the recommendations arising from the research is that "Carrier women should be interpreted as much as possible from their own perspective, with reference to their own historical tradition (oral tradition). As much as possible, the story should be connected with the story-teller, and told in their own voice, so that in the site interpretation programming, whether in the form of personal or taped tours, exhibits, A/V shows, artisan or traditional skill demonstrations, Carrier women themselves will be heard and have a presence. Effectively this means that rather than paraphrasing what a woman said, she should be quoted directly."[19]

The proposed interpretation at Fort St. James also takes a position on the question of whether women's history should be presented as a separate issue or integrated into the general history:

It is noteworthy that to identify "Carrier women's history" as a discrete topic of study is in many respects, artificial. It implies that women somehow lived and moved in a sphere separate from the rest of Carrier history. This categorization grows out of patriarchal traditions where the shapers and preservers of the historical record were overwhelmingly

Fig. 20.5. Fort St. James, British Columbia. Aboriginal women played an important role in the fur trade as traders, translators, processors of furs, and provisioners. These women at Fort St. James, now a national historic site, are making fishing nets. Photo courtesy of Glenbow Archives, NA-1164-3.

male, and tended towards perpetuating a view of the universe that was peculiarly male-centred. This type of historical tradition is not necessarily universal, and Carrier oral tradition is far more likely to portray a picture where men, women and children are inextricably bound in a web of kinship ties, which are naturally the central determinant of social, political and economic life.[20]

Artifacts can also be used to give women a presence or to comment on gender roles. Among the Carrier at Fort St. James in pre-contact days, men hunted big game, women and men trapped, and men and women shared the operation and ownership of fishing sites at which fishing was done using weirs. Women controlled the fisheries where nets were employed; an artifact such as a fishing net provides an opportunity to discuss the gendered use and control of resources among the Carrier People and to highlight the important role that women played in their community.[21]

The homes of leading politicians are another important category of national historic site. Bellevue House in Kingston, Ontario; Maison Cartier in Montreal, Quebec; Laurier House in Ottawa; and the Motherwell Homestead in Saskatchewan were all homes of Canadian politicians. By the nature of their careers the male politicians were often away from their homes; as often as not, the houses were an expression of their wives' tastes and management abilities. They were also the workplace of a largely female domestic staff. If only by default, the interpretation of great men's houses often focuses on women's work in the home, the raising of a family, and the management of a large house.

Bellevue House NHS was designated as being of national historic significance because of its association with Canada's first prime minister, Sir John A. Macdonald, and because of its architectural value. The interpretation of Macdonald's role as a politician is contained, however, in a modern interpretation center; the interpretation of the house by costumed staff emphasizes the operation of a largely female household. Macdonald's wife, Isabella Clarke, was a semi-invalid and managed the house from her bedroom. Interpretation deals with cooking, cleaning, household management, and nineteenth-century medicine as it related to women. It is quite possible that a visitor's lasting impressions of the site are as much of domestic life in a middle-class, mid-nineteenth-century household as they are of Canada's first prime minister.

Sir George-Etienne Cartier NHS provides another example of a politician's house providing a basis for interpreting aspects of women's history. The site, which consists of a double house in Montreal, commemorates the career of Sir George-Etienne Cartier, a colleague of Sir John A. Macdonald. Half of the house is devoted to exhibits on Cartier's political career; the other side is furnished to 1860 and focuses on the Cartier family. At the time Cartier was separated from his wife, Hortense Fabre; the house was normally occupied by Madame Cartier, her two daughters, and servants. Much of the taped narration for the domestic side of the house takes the voices of Cartier's valet and Madame Cartier's maid, adding a class perspective to the interpretation of a well-to-do but troubled family.

The interpretations of family and domestic life at Bellevue House and at Maison Cartier are not directly related to the commemorative intent of the sites, but they provide depth and perspective on what is otherwise a great man in history commemoration. They also raise the profile of women's domestic work and add a class perspective to the interpretation of elites.

It has taken the national historic sites system over seventy-five years to assume the shape it has today; it will take years, probably decades, for it to achieve the changes that women's history, and the histories of aboriginal peoples and of cultural communities, require. The 1991 decision to make women's history a commemoration priority is a recent one, but it is beginning to affect the system. A few individuals and events have been commemorated, and studies offering the promise of major commemorative sites have been put in place. At the level of interpretation things are more advanced if only because the past emphasis on social history has led historians and interpreters into areas that are shared with women's historians. Equally important, reviews of Parks Canada's policies and practices have given some reassurance that increased commemoration of women's history can be achieved with minor changes to existing policies. The increasing willingness to commemorate modest sites that are representative of major phenomena is one change that offers a promise of expanding the range of commemoration. What is crucial is a new openness to the importance of women's history and a willingness to expand the range of subjects that are considered historically important and to look at old subjects from a new perspective.

Proceeding from Here

Heather A. Huyck

Human-created, or at least human-influenced, landscapes, structures, and artifacts give form to the past and help connect us to history. Whether worn wooden spoons, solitary apple trees marking long-abandoned house sites, broken crockery, scarcely worn wedding dresses or quilts frayed and tattered with use, dolls, prairie sunbonnets, or Anasazi turkey feather robes, these rich resources enhance our understanding and help us communicate the past. Tangible history bridges between past and present, created historically but experienced in the present. Historic places both inform us of the past and connect us to it. By evoking a different reality for us, they can powerfully change our understandings, even our identity. Their authenticity provides a way for us to understand our predecessors, to touch objects they touched.

Almost twenty years ago, those of us engaged in public history began grappling with how best to bring women's history and historic preservation together, the one focusing on The Story, the other on The Remains. This volume reflects how far we have come—and how very much farther we must still go. The essays challenge us to do more as we seek to preserve and interpret the "whole story" that includes *everybody* and as we better understand the relationships between women's experiences and extant tangible resources. They promise much richer understandings as we tell that whole story.

Using tangible resources to preserve and interpret women's history both straddles and challenges two often distinct approaches to the past: women's history and historic preservation. Proceeding from here will continue to extract insights from each field, challenge assumptions of both, and, if we are truly successful, contribute as a bridge between them and an infinitely richer understanding of our foremothers (and our forefathers as well).

Preserving and interpreting the tangible resources of women's history pose some interesting challenges. We continue to uncover, sometimes literally, women's presence. We seek ways to share that presence when the tangible remnants are particularly scarce. Sometimes commemoration must substitute for preservation. We work to include everybody in this discovery process, making this truly public history, truly a participatory past.

Much of the last twenty years has appropriately focused on surveying countrywide to see if women's history even existed there. Happily, we found much more than those of us raised on an almost exclusively male history of names and dates and battles dared imagine. We found women in both expected and surprising places. We discovered that we could not assume gender roles, and that gender roles and expectations themselves change. At the same time, we came to see that the female worthies (like male worthies) were the exceptions. Few women lived as they did. Most women were literally embedded in their families and their communities, living mundane lives rather than dramatic ones. They were not individually visible. But they were there. Years ago National Park Service historians debated whether women were present at every park in the National Park System. Alcatraz, the island prison located in San Francisco Bay, seemed the exception, until we learned that the wardens' families lived there and prisoners' families visited there. Another myth gone. Women were historically everywhere—on merchant ships, in Western forts, in mining camps, on battlefields. They had amazing and wonderfully diverse lives, far more complex and interesting than simplistic stereotypes hint. Every site has women's history: it's "simply" a question of how much and how directly. We need to move beyond the few "greats" and the pivotal moments and look at the unpaid, repetitive, and routine work that made both "extravagant" and ordinary lifestyles possible. We must examine all the facets of production and reproduction and look at all the different ways women have configured their lives (including homosocial and homosexual).

Slowly, an intellectual framework has emerged from all these pieces, one that consistently asks where women were and what physical evidence remains from all their lives. Ironically, because historic preservation focuses more on the larger-scale built environment of structures and, sometimes, of cultural landscapes, connecting women's lives with these tangible resources is more difficult than with smaller-scale objects associated with female history frequently collected and displayed in museum settings. This framework both follows previous discoveries and discussions of women's history and challenges them. Most women's history has been based on traditional written archival and manuscript sources, if sometimes creatively reread to tease out women's past. Oral histories and photographs have supplemented these traditional sources. Tangible sources, still relatively untapped, have great potential to contribute much to our understanding.

Where should we go from here? We must enlarge the intellectual framework we are constructing and refine it and redefine it. Doing the careful and comprehensive surveys still needs much work. Such surveys simply locate the tangible remains of female lives. Ensuring that the history of minority women, gay women, and anonymous women's history is fully told becomes equally critical. Omitting such history grotesquely distorts it, as in the cases of Native American women enabling fur traders or eastern wives financing their husbands' California Gold Rush adventures.[1]

The challenges ahead come in three major categories: intellectual, political, and educational. To ensure the preservation and interpretation of women's tangible past, we must succeed with all three. As Susan B. Anthony enjoined us, "Failure is Impossible."[2] Intellectually, we need to ensure that our framework is both truly inclusive and durable, as the Canadian parks have done. We must also continue collecting specific on-the-ground examples such as those of the Los Angeles prostitutes, the Philadelphia servants, and the First Ladies. The states of Pennsylvania and Georgia have shown us the methods, hurdles, and benefits of statewide women's history surveys.

We are still not particularly sophisticated about the interplay of structures built *for* women and the ways women actually lived in them, understood them, and were influenced by them. Careful case studies on how women actually perceived their surroundings and how they actually used them will move us from being simply descriptive to being more analytical. Social workers, real estate agents, and repair people have had better opportunities to see how women actually lived their lives, in contrast to how they were *supposed* to live their lives. Focusing on architecture associated with women's organizations and institutions may help untangle such relationships. Too often, buildings designed by professional architects show prescriptive efforts to shape women's lives rather than describe (much less analyze) women's actual experiences. How much did male architects succeed in shaping women's lives and experiences? How did women reshape those spaces for their own purposes? Here archaeology, generally relying on less-biased resources than written documents, can help us. The Boggsville, Colorado, study found homes that initially seemed to be typically Anglo ones but which had been reconfigured by their residents to reflect their Hispanic and Native American backgrounds.[3] Tracing historical food preparation provides another approach: changing technology and space, from family hearth to separate outbuilding or basement (reflecting climatic and fire safety issues as well as racial and servant/slave relationships) to spaces closer to family living but still peripheral, accommodating "newfangled" technology of stoves, iceboxes, and wringer washers to current fads of "great rooms" with cooking now fully visible and integrated with family and guests. As a universal human activity, usually associated with women, food preparation can link changing gender roles and architectural styles to understand better the interplay between women and physical spaces.

Recognizing how women actually lived also challenges us to understand how different our lives today can be. Historically, very few women could choose to live independently. Most women in the past lived as part of family groups, as daughters, wives, and mothers; sisters, aunts, and grandmothers. Women's lives were marked by these relationships and by life cycle events such as puberty, marriage, pregnancy, and motherhood. We need to acknowledge the women—by far the majority—who had lives barely visible outside their families and respect and share their lives without inappropriately romanticizing their backbreaking labor and repetitious work. We must uncover the evidence of their lives and accomplishments simultaneously, so commonplace and devalued as "women's work," which made preserving their lives' tangible history, or "tangible remains," so little valued. We need to tug on history's apron strings.

Intellectual challenges also come in arguments over whether gender is peripheral or central. This volume strongly argues for gender centrality, but, as the chapter on the National Register of Historic Places makes clear, it has not always been perceived as an essential analytical category. Only many additional case studies showing that tangible resources are essential to understanding the past will give the refusal to recognize gender as a basic human marker its deserved burial.

Political and organizational challenges, so deftly identified by Judith Wellman in her account of the establishment of Women's Rights National Historical Park in Seneca Falls, New York; by Page Putnam Miller on the National Historic Landmark study; and by Edith Mayo on the Smithsonian's First Ladies Exhibit reveal the enormous institutional inertia that has had to be overcome to preserve even the most basic aspects of women's history and present them to the public. As veterans of the field—sometimes scarred from years of arguing the legitimacy of tangible women's history—they show the importance of having support from organized groups, key political figures (congressional members and staff), sympathetic bureaucrats, and the public. Putting together such diverse coalitions dedicated toward a common cause requires skill, determination, and luck. Although such support has grown greatly, it remains inadequate, with the future still uncertain. Educating younger people about the significance of women's history and the special opportunities for understanding that history through historic places remains essential if political and organizational support is to continue. Without such support, places such as the Wesleyan Chapel, site of the first women's rights convention, become Laundromats (as the 1848 site ironically did). Advocates of women's history educate others about the usefulness of tangible resources in understanding women's past and organize to ensure that those resources are preserved.

In so doing, we must argue that, without women's history, national histories are fundamentally flawed. We ourselves have felt the alienation of a history that excludes us, a history not addressed to us, a history defined to eliminate our past, our contributions, our experiences. Women's history—the full inclusion of women's experiences in the nation's past—has the potential to completely rewrite that history for all. Until it does, we are "shortchanging" history and segregating ourselves. National histories cannot be emotionally just or intellectually honest without telling the whole story. That whole story is usually more complicated, always more interesting, and often compelling. We must make the full preservation and interpretation of the whole story compelling for everybody, or we will find ourselves mired in political quicksand. We must appeal to male politicians as well as female ones, or we will not succeed. Allowing our history to be segregated by gender decreases by roughly half the number of potential supporters for telling the whole story.

Educational and interpretive issues also challenge us. We must connect with all the publics who constitute our audiences. Those publics, particularly younger people, often find traditional museum displays boring. Raised on television, videos, and the Internet, they are very visually oriented, with low boredom thresholds. Making women's history exciting, even exhilarating, requires that we avoid static displays and predictable exhibits. At Jamestown, Virginia, site of the first permanent English colony in the North America, an incised brass thimble stuffed with paper marked by a child's scrawl connects us with a little seventeenth-century girl.[4] A woman dressed in period costume interpreting a Jamestown settler in 1638 holds scores of visitors mesmerized as she recounts her life's adventures. Both the thimble and the first-person interpreter show us that this colony was not strictly a military fort or an all-male settlement.

We must also *connect* with audiences. People find genealogy fascinating because by their lineage they are linked to their ancestors. One of the worst mistakes we can make is to define women's history for women only, even if only subtly so. By so doing, we are—inadvertently, I am sure—agreeing with those antediluvian versions of history which believed that the past of males could be understood only by men. We've spent much too much effort arguing for the agency of females to allow ourselves to fall into such a trap. If we believe women affected history, then we must ensure that everybody, females and males, understands their life accomplishments. Linking contemporary experiences with historical ones such as being immigrants or raising children can bridge past and present for visitors.

Recently, Ira Berlin's *Many Thousands Gone* brilliantly synthesized many decades of careful research on African American slavery into a cohesive whole.[5] Women's history has achieved such a synthesis, but tangible women's history has not. In spite of the pathbreaking essays in Page Putnam Miller's *Reclaiming the Past: Landmarks of Women's History*,[6] we still cannot confidently predict where to find women's presence, to see how they affected places, or to know how best to learn from such places. Nor has the study of tangible resources contributed sufficiently to the larger field of women's history. But, as the chapters in this volume reinterpreting Bishop White's or Martin Van Buren's homes clearly indicate, we are beginning to look in the right places for the women who were there all along. When we do, we find greater understanding of how those places really operated and how people actually lived. We are still arguing that it should be done, still framing the questions, still uncovering the resources. Yet all those great men sites were primarily domestic places; their birthplaces had mothers present by definition. Civil War battles were fought in people's front yards, parlors were turned into military headquarters, and bedrooms were made into hospitals. There is an abundance of women's history if we know where to look, if we successfully argue that such history is so critical to understanding the past that it cannot be ignored by anybody.

Asking how people understood their lives on their own terms (rather than ours), greater use of archaeological evidence, and more careful examination of physical landscapes will help us become more precise in our analyses and potent in our conclusions. We know that people approach the material world in quite diverse ways. We can assume that past peoples varied as well, but we lack systematic and comprehensive research about all the different ways of using and understanding the physical aspects of our lives, the human-made environment that includes objects as well as landscapes and architecture.

What is a *place* of women's history? Calling some locales "Places Where Women Made History" implies that women didn't make history elsewhere, much less everywhere. Better to talk about places where previous female inhabitants make women's history focal there. We must keep asking, "What were these women's experiences? What difference did they make? How are their actions reflected in these sites today? How did they perceive their lives? What differences did the women make? What implications do their experiences have for today?"

As preservationists, we must look ahead and consider future genera-tions. We must make women's history indispensable to American history to ensure long-term success. Women are not a special interest: we are the majority of the human race, a race whose history cannot be understood without fully understanding and rightfully incorporating women's experi-ences and contributions into that history.

An agenda for proceeding from here:

• Establish a national collaborative of women's historic sites. With the leadership of Barbara Irvine of Paulsdale (Alice Paul's New Jersey home), an effort is now under way to establish a women's historic sites collabora-tive. Such a collaborative is greatly needed to share resources among the various sites, to garner funding more effectively, and to nurture a com-mon identity and greater visibility. Given the different kinds of women's history–associated sites, various strategies will be needed, primarily de-pending on the prominence of women's lives at particular sites. The col-laborative will initially concentrate on major biographical sites but needs eventually to provide support to all historic sites, so that all sites can fully preserve and interpret women's history. Initially, the collaborative will sup-port sites such as the Susan B. Anthony House in Rochester, New York, or the Maggie Walker House in Richmond, Virginia, which specifically pre-serve and interpret women's history; sites that women directly and obvi-ously affected need greater external visibility and common linkage. Sites such as Lowell Mills or Colonial Williamsburg, where female presence and action is expected but which were not specifically designated for women's history also need greater internal visibility and self-conscious public inter-pretation of women's lives. Eventually, sites such as Golden Spike National Monument, where the transcontinental railroad joined east coast to west, which less obviously document women's history—sites women indirectly affected or which directly affected women—need much more extensive re-search, recognition, and reinterpretation.

• Survey every state for women's historic places. Just as the *Women's History Sources Survey* identified manuscript and archival sources in the late 1970s, we need a thorough state-by-state survey of both existing sites ripe for reinterpretation and new sites that should be recognized.[7] Every state has more women's history to be uncovered. The number of historic sites specifically preserving women's past remains embarrassingly infinitesimal and correspondingly threatened. At the 1984 Southwest Institute for Research on Women conference in Tucson, I called for a National Historic Landmark study to identify potential landmarks for designation.[8] Page Miller and I (as a congressional staffer) worked with others to make that study a congressionally funded reality, which resulted in new National Historic Landmarks and her book, *Reclaiming the Past: Landmarks of Women's History.* Now the challenge is to identify all the appropriate sites in each and every state. Georgia, Pennsylvania, and New Jersey should be commended for their pioneering state surveys.

• Recognize the sites that fully preserve and interpret women's history. Every historic site that does a good job incorporating women's experiences should be recognized and rewarded, by the collaborative or by professional societies or both. They should be given the historical equivalent of Good Housekeeping seals. Sites inadequately telling the whole story should encounter equally strong concern about their poor performance.

• Build intellectual understanding of the relationship between tangible resources and women's history. We need a continued and rigorous discussion on how best to link physical evidence with women's lives at historic sites of all kinds. At the Maria Mitchell house on Nantucket Island in Massachusetts, her desk squeezed into a small nook—essentially a closet with a window—allowed her to study apart from her family's bustle. That space informs us about her, her family's support of her, and their values (of her, of education, of astronomy). The architecture's quirks tell us about the woman.[9] We need a checklist for historic sites to use to "find" the women under their noses and a similar list for historians to use to find the "places" under their feet.

• Emphasize unpaid women's labor. We need to repeat vigorously that this country was built on the unpaid labor of women, of slaves. Without those two essential sources of labor, we wouldn't be here now. Too often, slave cabins, built flimsily, have long disappeared; too often functional areas of historic homes, such as kitchens and laundries, now serve as offices, labs, and libraries, misleading visitors considerably about previous occupants' lives.

• Emphasize and talk about invisible women's lives, those who weren't notable beyond their families. Their experiences were still important, decisions cumulatively momentous (such as the impact of decreasing family size). Too often, historic preservation has emphasized high styles and high society. To tell the whole story, we must go beyond that segment to include everybody.

• Highlight women's indirect as well as their direct presence and effects at historic places. At Theodore Roosevelt National Park we learn that Roosevelt fled to South Dakota's Black Hills reacting to the nearly simultaneous deaths of his wife and mother. But we do not learn that the schemes to raise, slaughter, and ship cattle from near the end of the railroad line would considerably impact women's lives by making quantities of beef available to urban housewives, changing nutritional and culinary possibilities.[10]

Historic places tell us who we are as a people and where we have come from. Omitting any significant portion of our history distorts all of it. Historic places, because they contain so much past evidence and are so powerful in conveying that past to the public, provide great opportunities for sharing women's history by simply asking the right questions about landscapes, structures, and artifacts and by seeing the women's history already there. Incessantly and deliberately, we can—and must—end an inaccurate, misleading, and totally inadequate portrayal of the past at historic places by fully recognizing women's history. That will be our professional contribution to the nation's legacy.

Appendix A

Chester County Historical Society
225 N. High Street
West Chester, PA 19380
(610) 692-4800

Drake Well Historic Site
RD #3, Box 7
Titusville, PA 16354
(814) 827-2797

Folklife Documentation Center for
    Gender Studies
c/o Reeves Memorial Library
Seton Hill College
Greensburg, PA 15601
(724) 838-4270

Hershey Museum
170 W. Hershey Park Drive
Hershey, PA 17033
(717) 534-3439

Historical Society of Western
    Pennsylvania
Senator John Heinz Regional
    History Center
1212 Smallman Street
Pittsburgh, PA 15222
(717) 326-3326

Hopewell Furnace National Historic
    Site
2 Mark Bird Lane
Elverson, PA 19520
(610) 582-8773

Lackawanna County Historical
    Society
232 Monroe Avenue
Scranton, PA 18510
(717) 344-3841

Landis Valley Museum
2451 Kissel Hill Road
Lancaster, PA 17601
(717) 569-0401

Lehigh County Historical Society
Old Courthouse
P.O. Box 1548
Allentown, PA 18105
(610) 435-4664

Library Company of Philadelphia
1314 Locust Street
Philadelphia, PA 19107
(215) 546-3181

Lycoming County Historical Society
858 W. Fourth Street
Williamsport, PA 17701
(717) 326-3326

Old Economy Village
14th and Church Streets
Ambridge, PA 15003
(412) 266-4500

Pennsbury Manor
400 Pennsbury Memorial Road
Morrisville, PA 19067
(215) 946-0400

(Joseph) Priestley House
427 Priestley Avenue
Northumberland, PA 17857
(717) 473-9474

Appendix B

Date of Commemo-ration	Name	Career Area
1927	De Vercheres, M.	Heroine
1937	First Women's Institute	Womens' organization
1939	Albani, Emma	Singer
1947	McKinney, L.	Suffragist, Persons Case
1948	Montgomery, L. M.	Author
1949	Richardson, H. T.	Heritage activist
1952	Blewett, Jean M.	Author
1953	Saunders, M. M.	Author
1954	Hart, Julia C. B.	Author
1954	Dorval, Onésime	Teacher
1957	McClung, Nellie	Suffragist, author
1960	Murphy, E. F.	Suffragist, Persons Case
1962	Hoodless, A. H.	Educator, social activist
1964	Edwards, H. M.	Suffragist, Persons Case
1967	Parlby, M. I.	Suffragist, Persons Case
1973	D'Youville, M.-M.	Founder of a religious order
1974	Grey Nuns' Convent	Architecture, education
1975	Traill, C. P.	Author
1976	De la Roche, Mazo	Author
1978	Edmonton Grads	Sports (basketball)
1981	Duley, M. I.	Author
1981	Ipirvik and Taqulittuq	Inuit guides
1982	Imperial Order Daughters of the Empire	Service club

1983	L'Ancien Hôpital Général des Soeurs grises	Architecture
1983	Crawford, I. V.	Author
1983	Macdonald, M. C.	Nurse (military)
1983	Moodie, Susanna	Author
1984	Miss Davis School	Education
1985	Gaboury, M. A.	Riel family
1985	Macphail, A. C.	Politician
1985	Bourgeoys, M.	Founder of a religious order
1986	Johnson, E. Pauline	Author
1986	Pope, G. F.	Nurse (military)
1987	Carr, Emily	Artist and author
1987	Black, Martha L.	Businesswoman, politician
1987	Rosenfeld, F.	Athlete
1987	Aberdeen, Lady	Social activist
1988	Sisters of Saint Anne	Religious order
1988	Sisters of the Holy Names of Jesus and Mary	Religious order
1988	Sisters of Providence	Religious order
1988	Soeurs de la Charité d'Ottawa	Religious order
1988	Sisters of the Assumption of the Blessed Virgin Mary	Religious order
1988	Soeurs Grises de Montréal	Religious order
1988	Congregation of Notre-Dame	Religious order
1989	Monastère des Ursulines	Architecture
1989	St. Ann's Academy	Education
1991	Lockhart, Grace A.	First female university graduate
1992	Travers, Mary (La Bolduc)	Singer
1993	Abbott, Maude	Medical researcher
1994	Shadd, Mary Anne	Editor, activist
1994	Brant, Molly	Aboriginal leader
1995	Hoodless, A. H. (birthplace)	Social activist
1995	Stowe, Emily	Doctor, activist
1995	Canadian Women's Army Corps	Women in the military
1995	Royal Canadian Air Force, Women's Division	Women in the military
1995	Women's Royal Canadian Naval Service	Women in the military

1995	Trout, Jenny	Doctor
1995	White, Portia	Singer
1995	Women's College Hospital	Medicine
1996	War Brides	War and the family
1996	Newton, Margaret	Agricultural researcher
1996	Ursulines of Three Rivers	Religious order
1997	Persons Case	Women's political rights
1997	Winning the vote	Suffrage
1997	Woman's Christian Temperance Union	Temperance society, suffrage
1997	Hind, E. Cora	Journalist, suffragist
1997	Gérin-Lajoie, M.	Women's legal rights, suffragist
1997	MacMurchy, Helen	Women's health
1997	Archibald, Edith J.	Suffragist
1997	Saint-Jean, Idola	Suffragist, women's legal rights
1997	McNaughton, Violet Clara	Farm activist, health care
1997	Victorian Order of Nurses	Health care
1997	Ann Baillie	Nurses' residence, Kingston
1997	Mailloux Pavilion	Nurses' residence, Montreal
1997	Royal Victoria	Nurses' residence, Montreal
1997	St. Boniface Hospital	Nurses' residence, Winnipeg
1997	Royal Jubilee	Nurses' residence, Victoria
1998	Mance, Jeanne	Nursing leader
1998	Southcott, Mary Meagre	Nursing leader
1998	Newfoundland Outpost Nursing and Industrial Association (NONIA)	Outpost nursing
2000	National Council of Women of Canada	Women's organization

Note: For further information on any of these commemorations, contact: National Historic Sites Directorate, Parks Canada, Department of Canadian Heritage, 25 Eddy Street, Hull, Quebec, Canada, K1A OM5; or parkscanada.pch.gc.ca/parks/main_e.htm.

Notes

CHAPTER 1: RESTORING WOMEN'S HISTORY
THROUGH HISTORIC PRESERVATION

1. Robert B. Konikow, *Discover Historic America* (Chicago: Rand McNally and Co., 1973), 1.

2. "Reclaiming Women's History through Historic Preservation: A National Conference," held at Bryn Mawr College, Bryn Mawr, Pa. (June 17–19, 1994); convened by the Alice Paul Centennial Foundation, Inc., the Preservation Coalition of Greater Philadelphia, and Women's Way. The Second National Conference on Women and Historic Preservation was sponsored by Arizona State University and the National Park Service (March 13–16, 1997). The Third National Conference on Women and Historic Preservation was sponsored by the University of Washington and the National Park Service and was held on the campus of George Washington University at Mount Vernon College, Washington, D.C. (May 19–21, 2000).

3. Charles B. Hosmer Jr., *Presence of the Past: A History of the Preservation Movement before Williamsburg* (New York: G. P. Putnam's Sons, 1965).

4. James M. Lindgren, *Preserving the Old Dominion: Historic Preservation and Virginia Traditionalism* (Charlottesville: University Press of Virginia, 1993), esp. 58–74; and Lindgren, *Preserving Historic New England: Preservation, Progressivism, and the Remaking of Memory* (New York: Oxford University Press, 1995). Also see Lindgren, "A New Departure in Historic Patriotic Work: Personalism, Professionalism, and Conflicting Concepts of Material Culture in the Late Nineteenth and Early Twentieth Centuries," *Public Historian* 18 (spring 1996): 41–60.

5. Jeffrey C. Stewart and Fath Davis Ruffins, "A Faithful Witness: Afro-American Public History in Historical Perspective," in *Presenting the Past: Critical Perspectives on History and the Public*, ed. Susan Porter Benson, Steven Brier, and Roy Rosenzweig (Philadelphia: Temple University Press, 1986); Ruffins, "Mythos, Memory, and History: African American Preservation Efforts, 1820–1990," in *Museums and Communities: The Politics of Public Culture*, ed. Ivan Karp, Christine Mullen Kreamer, and Steven D. Lavine (Washington,

D.C.: Smithsonian Institution Press, 1992), 506–611; and Ruffins, "'Lifting as We Climb': Black Women and the Preservation of African American History and Culture," *Gender and History* 6:3 (November 1994): 376–96.

6. Heather Huyck, "Beyond John Wayne: Using Historic Sites to Interpret Women's History," in *Western Women: Their Land, Their Lives,* ed. Lillian Schlissel, Vicki L. Ruiz, and Janice Monk (Albuquerque: University of New Mexico Press, 1988): 303–29.

7. Patricia West, "'The New Social History' and Historic House Museums: The Lindenwald Example," *Museum Studies Journal* 2:3 (fall 1986): 22–26.

8. See Patricia West, "The Historic House Museum Movement in America: Louisa May Alcott's Orchard House as a Case Study" (Ph.D. diss., Department of History, State University of New York at Binghamton, 1992); and West, *Domesticating History: The Political Origins of America's House Museums* (Washington, D.C.: Smithsonian Institution Press, 1999).

9. National Trust for Historic Preservation, "The View from the Kitchen: Interpreting the Lives of Domestic Workers" (a one-day conference for historic site staff held in Boston, fall 1994). A brief report on this conference by Barbara A. Levy and Susan Schreiber, "The View from the Kitchen," appeared in *History News* 50:2 (March 1995): 16–20. Cassette tapes of the conference and a fourteen-page annotated bibliography are available from the National Trust for Historic Preservation, 1785 Massachusetts Avenue, NW, Washington, D.C. 20036.

10. A brief overview of the historic resources associated with the Young Women's Christian Association has been undertaken by Antoinette Lee, "Supporting Working Women: YWCAs in the National Register," in a special issue on "Placing Women in the Past," ed. Heather Huyck, in *CRM: Cultural Resources Management* 20:3 (1997): 16–17. This article was adapted as "Supporting Working Women: YWCA Buildings in the National Register of Historic Places," in a special issue on "The Stuff of Women's History," ed. Vivien Ellen Rose, in the Organization of American Historian's *Magazine of History* 12:1 (fall 1997): 5–6.

11. Gail Lee Dubrow, "The Interpretation of Women's History at Historic Houses," paper presented at the Winterthur Conference on "The American Home: Material Culture, Domestic Space, and Family Life," Winterthur, Del., October 29–31, 1992.

12. Marion Tinling, *Women Remembered* (Westport, Conn.: Greenwood Press, 1986); and Lynn Sherr and Jurate Kazickas, *Susan B. Anthony Slept Here* (New York: Random House, 1994).

13. Gail Lee Dubrow, "Restoring a Female Presence," in *Architecture: A Place for Women* (Washington, D.C.: Smithsonian Institution Press, 1989), 159–70; and Dubrow, "Preserving Her Heritage: American Landmarks of

Women's History" (Ph.D. diss., Urban Planning Program, University of California Los Angeles, 1991), esp. 18–92.

14. Rights of Women and Anna Davin, *The London Feminist History Walk* (London: Community Press, 1978); Marilyn A. Domer, Jean S. Hunt, Mary Ann Johnson, and Adade M. Wheeler, *Walking with Women through Chicago History: Four Self-Guided Tours* (Chicago: Salsedo Press, 1981); Karen Mason and Carol Lacy, *Women's History Tour of the Twin Cities* (Minneapolis: Nodin Press, 1982); Mary Gehman and Nancy Ries, *Women and New Orleans: A History* (New Orleans: Margaret Media, Inc., 1985); Jennifer Clarke, *In Our Grandmothers' Footsteps: A Walking Tour of London* (New York: Atheneum, 1986); *Boston Women's Heritage Trail: Four Centuries of Boston Women: A Guide to Five Walks: Downtown, North End, Beacon Hill, South Cove/Chinatown, Back Bay* (Gloucester, Mass.: Curious Traveller Press, 1991), revised and reprinted as *The Boston Women's Heritage Trail: Four Centuries of Boston Women: A Guide to Five Walks* (Gloucester, Mass.: Curious Traveller Press, 1999); Katherine Sturtevant, *Our Sisters' London: Feminist Walking Tours* (Chicago: Chicago Review Press, 1991); Catherine Cullen, *Paris: The Virago Woman's Travel Guide* (Berkeley: Ulysses Press, 1993); Ros Belford, *Rome: The Virago Woman's Travel Guide* (Berkeley: Ulysses Press, 1993); and Gayle Brandow Samuels with Lucienne Beard and Valencia Libby, *Women in the City of Brotherly Love and Beyond: Tours and Detours in Delaware Valley Women's History* (Philadelphia: By the author, 1994).

15. Suzanne Spencer-Wood, "A Survey of Domestic Reform Movement Sites in Boston and Cambridge, MA, 1865–1905," *Historical Archaeology* 21:2 (1987): 7–37.

16. Gail Lee Dubrow, "Claiming Public Space for Women's History in Boston: A Proposal for Preservation, Public Art, and Public Historical Interpretation," *Frontiers: A Journal of Women's Studies* 13:1 (winter 1992): 111–48. An extended discussion of the Boston sites is included in this essay; and Dubrow, "Preserving Her Heritage," 306–631.

17. *Boston Women's Heritage Trail: Four Centuries of Boston Women: A Guide to Five Walks.*

18. *Reclaiming the Past: Landmarks of Women's History,* ed. Page Putnam Miller (Bloomington: Indiana University Press, 1992), esp. 1–26.

19. *Cultural Resource Management in Wisconsin,* ed. Barbara Wyatt (Madison: Wisconsin State Historic Preservation Office, June 1986), 1–4; cited in Page Putnam Miller, "Landmarks of Women's History," in Miller, *Reclaiming the Past,* 10.

20. This study provides an opportunity to identify previously overlooked local resources while addressing issues relevant to the broader preservation

community, such as: what makes a place significant in women's history, what types of properties are linked to the history of women, how do places associated with women's history meet and challenge established standards of eligibility for listing on the National Register of Historic Places, and what strategies will promote the preservation and public interpretation of cultural resources significant in the history of women? The context document is an outgrowth of the Historic Preservation Division's (HPD) broader Women's History Initiative, launched in 1995 by Beth Gibson and Leslie Sharp. The first major project was a March 1996 regional conference on women's history and historic preservation, "Telling Her Story: Expanding the Past of Georgia's Women through Historic Places." In May 1998 the HPD advertised its "Request for Proposals for the Development of a Women's History Context for Women-Related Historic Resources in Georgia." The team of Darlene Roth, Beth Gibson, Bamby Ray and Associates, and Gail Lee Dubrow was awarded the contract. See Leslie N. Sharp, "The Role of Women in Preservation: A Georgia Perspective," in a special issue on "Placing Women in the Past," ed. Heather Huyck, *CRM: Cultural Resources Management* 20:3 (1997): 18–19; and her chapter in this collection.

21. "Whitman to Sign Women's Heritage Trail Bill at Paulsdale, Birthplace of Suffragist Alice Paul: Bill Funds Research to Identify Women's History Sites," press release, Alice Paul Centennial Foundation, September 7, 1999.

22. Personal communication from Shanna Stevenson to Gail Lee Dubrow, electronic mail (October 14, 1998).

23. David W. Dunlap, "Stonewall, Gay Bar That Made History, Is Made a Landmark," *New York Times,* June 26, 1999, late edition (East Coast), 1.

24. Other sites that merit reinterpretation are Francis Willard's Evanston, Illinois, home, which also served as headquarters for the Woman's Christian Temperance Union, and potentially the most controversial site, Eleanor Roosevelt's retreat, Val-Kill.

There is a pressing need to interpret and preserve, beyond the homes of notable individuals, places associated with the emergence of homosexual community and identity in the twentieth century, many of which meet the fifty-year threshold for listing on the National Register. The National Trust for Historic Preservation finally has begun to address this issue by sponsoring a session on preserving gay and lesbian history at its national conferences and by publishing an article on the subject in each of its flagship publications, *Preservation* and *Forum.* Some of the most interesting projects, however, have been done outside of preservation's mainstream, such as RepoHistory's *Queer Spaces* Project, which erected pink Masonite triangles, with descriptive text, on signposts near nine places significant in gay and lesbian history in New York

City, and community-based projects that have developed guides to gay and lesbian historic sites in Boston, New York, Seattle, and Los Angeles, among other cities. The directness and vitality of this maverick work indirectly illuminates the polite censorship and uncomfortable silences that prevail at sites managed by the preservation establishment.

CHAPTER 2: WOMEN IN THE NINETEENTH-CENTURY PRESERVATION MOVEMENT

Portions of this chapter previously appeared in a different form in Barbara J. Howe, "Women in Historic Preservation: The Legacy of Ann Pamela Cunningham," *Public Historian* 12:1 (1990): 31–61, © by the Regents of the University of California; and Barbara J. Howe, "Women and Architecture," in *Reclaiming the Past: Landmarks of Women's History*, ed. Page Putnam Miller (Bloomington: Indiana University Press, 1992), 27–62, and are used with the permission of the Regents of the University of California and Indiana University Press. The author also thanks Sarah L. Burks, Eve Carr, Judith Anne Mitchell, Francesca Morgan, and Susan E. Schnare for permission to cite their papers presented at the Second National Women in Historic Preservation Conference, Tempe, Ariz., 1997.

1. See, for example, Barbara Berg, *The Remembered Gate: Origins of American Feminism, 1800–1860* (New York: Oxford University Press, 1978).

2. See, for example, Francesca Morgan, "One Fine and Harmonious Whole: Nation, Public History, and the Daughters of the American Revolution, 1890–1930," paper presented at the Second National Women in Historic Preservation Conference, Tempe, Ariz., March 1997.

3. See, for example, Fath Davis Ruffins, "Lifting as We Climb: Black Women and the Preservation of African American History and Culture," *Gender and History* 4 (November 1994): 376–96; Fath Davis Ruffins, "Mythos, Memory, and History: African American Preservation Efforts, 1820–1990," in *Museums and Communities: The Politics of Public Culture*, ed. Ivan Karp, Christine Mullen Kreamer, and Steven D. Lavine (Washington, D.C.: Smithsonian Institution Press, 1992), 506–611; James Oliver Horton and Spencer R. Crew, "Afro-Americans and Museums: Towards a Policy of Inclusion," in *History Museums in the United States: A Critical Assessment*, ed. by Warren Leon and Roy Rosenzweig (Urbana: University of Illinois Press, 1989), 215–36; and Eve Carr, "The Preservation of African American History and Culture: An Overview" (MS, Department of History, Arizona State University, 10 December 1997).

4. Gail Lee Dubrow, "Restoring a Female Presence: New Goals in Historic Preservation" in *Architecture: A Place for Women*, ed. Ellen Perry Berkeley

and Matilda McQuaid (Washington D.C.: Smithsonian Institution Press, 1989), 159–60; and Paul S. Boyer, "Sarah Josepha Buell Hale," in *Notable American Women, 1607–1950: A Biographical Dictionary* (*NAW*), ed. Edward T. James et al. (Cambridge, Mass.: Belknap Press of Harvard University Press, 1971), 2:111.

5. Lamia Doumato, "Louisa Tuthill's Unique Achievement: First History of Architecture in the U.S.," in Berkeley and McQuaid, *Architecture: A Place for Women*, 5–13.

6. Horton and Crew, "Afro-Americans and Museums," 217; and James Oliver Horton and Lois E. Horton, *Black Bostonians: Family Life and Community Struggle in the Antebellum North* (New York: Holmes and Meier, 1979), 57, 118, 124.

7. "Sale of Mount Vernon—Sailing of the Pacific Surveying Expedition," *Wheeling (Va.) Intelligencer,* June 16, 1853, 3:3.

8. "Mount Vernon," *Wheeling Intelligencer,* August 15, 1853, 2:2.

9. Charles B. Hosmer Jr., *Presence of the Past: A History of the Preservation Movement in the United States before Williamsburg* (New York: G. P. Putnam's Sons, 1965), 45.

10. Untitled, *Wheeling Intelligencer,* March 14, 1854, 2:1; and Wallace Evan Davies, "Ann Pamela Cunningham," in *NAW*, 1:416.

11. "Mount Vernon," *Wheeling Intelligencer,* December 13, 1853, 2:1.

12. "Mount Vernon," *Wheeling Intelligencer,* January 27, 1854, 2:3.

13. "Purchase of Mount Vernon," *Wheeling Intelligencer,* July 26, 1854, 2:1.

14. Davies, "Ann Pamela Cunningham," 416–17.

15. Judith Anne Mitchell, "Ann Pamela Cunningham: 'A Southern Matron's Legacy'" (Master's thesis, Middle Tennessee State University, 1993), chap. 3.

16. Hosmer, *Presence of the Past,* 43, 49–50, 44.

17. Untitled, *Wheeling Intelligencer,* December 24, 1859, 2:3.

18. Untitled, *Wheeling Intelligencer,* January 19, 1859, 2:1.

19. Mitchell, "Ann Pamela Cunningham," chap. 3.

20. Untitled, *Wheeling Intelligencer,* January 19, 1859, 2:1.

21. "Young Girls Mount Vernon Fair," *Martinsburg Advertiser and Gazette,* May 4, 1859, 2:6.

22. Untitled, *Wheeling Intelligencer,* December 24, 1859, 2:3.

23. Susan E. Schnare, "Women's Organizations and Landscape Preservation," paper presented at the Second National Women in Historic Preservation Conference, Tempe, Ariz., March 1997, 1.

24. Davies, "Ann Pamela Cunningham," 416–17.

25. Edward C. Smith, "The Keeper of the Keys," *Civil War* 21 (1984): 16–18; and Karen Byrne, "The Remarkable Legacy of Selina Gray" (MS, Arling-

ton House, Arlington, Va., provided courtesy of Frank Feragasso, National Capital Parks East).

26. Smith, "Keeper of the Keys," 16–18; and Byrne, "Remarkable Legacy of Selena Gray."

27. Davies, "Ann Pamela Cunningham," 416–17.

28. Hosmer, *Presence of the Past*, 55.

29. Hosmer, *Presence of the Past*, 56–57, 62; and James Lindgren, *Preserving the Old Dominion: Historic Preservation and Virginia Traditionalism* (Charlottesville: University Press of Virginia, 1993), 60.

30. William J. Murtagh, *Keeping Time: The History and Theory of Preservation in America* (Pittstown, N.J.: Main Street Press, 1988), 30.

31. Hosmer, *Presence of the Past*, 57–60, 70, 105.

32. See, for example, Morgan, "'One Fine and Harmonious Whole.'"

33. Lindgren, *Preserving the Old Dominion*, 61, 66, 59.

34. Lindgren, *Preserving the Old Dominion*, 58, 59.

35. Lindgren, *Preserving the Old Dominion*, 61, 62.

36. Lindgren, *Preserving the Old Dominion*, 66, 63.

37. Lindgren, *Preserving the Old Dominion*, 68, 73.

38. Lindgren, *Preserving the Old Dominion*, 67–68.

39. Lindgren, *Preserving the Old Dominion*, 68–69.

40. John M. Coski, "A Century of Collecting: The History of the Museum of the Confederacy," *Museum of the Confederacy Journal* 74 (1996): 3.

41. Lindgren, *Preserving the Old Dominion*, 63.

42. Lindgren, *Preserving the Old Dominion*, 64.

43. Coski, "Century of Collecting," 2–6.

44. Juliette Baker Boyer, comp. and ed., *West Virginia State History of the Daughters of the American Revolution* (n.p., n.d. [1928]), 5; and Martha Strayer, *The D.A.R.: An Informal History* (Washington, D.C.: Public Affairs Press, 1958), 3.

45. Hosmer, *Presence of the Past*, 88–91; and "Annual Report of the National Society of the Daughters of the American Revolution" (NSDAR), submitted to the U.S. Congress by the Secretary of the Smithsonian Institution (March 2, 1901), 235–36.

46. "Annual Report of the NSDAR," 1901, 57–59.

47. Morgan, "One Fine and Harmonious Whole," 9.

48. "Annual Report of the NSDAR," 1901, 238; and National Park Service, *The National Parks: Index 1987* (Washington, D.C.: U.S. Department of the Interior), 65.

49. "Annual Report of the NSDAR," 1901, 239–40.

50. "Annual Report of the NSDAR," 1901, 117, pl. 24 (following 118), 114.

51. "Annual Report of the NSDAR," 1901, 110, 145.

52. In 1901 the men's group became the American Scenic and Historic Preservation Society. For more information, see Hosmer, *Presence of the Past,* 96; *Twelfth Annual Report of the American Scenic and Historic Preservation Society to the Legislature of the State of New York* (Albany, N.Y.: J. B. Lyon Co., State Printers, 1907), 14-16, 92; and Sarah L. Burks, "The Women's Auxiliary to the American Scenic and Historic Preservation Society," paper presented at the Second National Women in Historic Preservation Conference, Tempe, Ariz., March 1997, 1–3.

53. *Twelfth Annual Report, 1907,* 69, 91–92; and Burks, "Women's Auxiliary," 4–12.

54. Marion Tinling, *Women Remembered: A Guide to Landmarks of Women's History in the United States* (Westport, Conn.: Greenwood Press, 1986), 276.

55. Gilbert Wenger, "The Story of Mesa Verde," www.mesaverde.org/smvf/p78.html.

56. Gilbert Wenger, "The Story of Mesa Verde," www.mesaverde.org/smvf/p85.html.

57. Leah Dilworth, *Imaging Indians in the Southwest: Persistent Visions of a Primitive Past* (Washington, D.C.: Smithsonian Institution Press, 1996), 13, 15.

58. Robert F. Berkhofer Jr., *The White Man's Indian: Images of the American Indian from Columbus to the Present* (New York: Alfred A. Knopf 1978), 54.

59. Dilworth, *Imaging Indians,* 15.

60. Dilworth, *Imaging Indians,* 16.

61. Dilworth, *Imaging Indians,* 17.

62. Dilworth, *Imaging Indians,* 47.

63. Dilworth, *Imaging Indians,* 16-17.

64. Gilbert Wenger, "The Story of Mesa Verde," www.mesaverde.org/smvf/p85.html.

65. Tinling, *Women Remembered,* 642–43; *National Parks: Index 1987,* 29; Mrs. J. C. Croly, *The History of the Woman's Club Movement in America* (New York: Henry G. Allen and Co., 1898), 266; and William C. Everhart, *The National Park Service* (New York: Praeger Publishers, 1972), 12.

66. Ruffins, "'Lifting as We Climb,'" 376–77; and Cathy Ingram, museum curator at the Frederick Douglass National Historic Site, e-mail communication to author, December 17, 1997; and Ruffins, "Mythos, Memory, and History," 516–17.

67. Paul A. Shackel, "The John Brown Fort: African-Americans' Civil War Monument," *CRM: Cultural Resources Management* 20:2 (1997): 23–24.

CHAPTER 3: SPECIAL PLACES SAVED

1. Dorothy and Carl J. Schneider, *American Women and the Progressive Era, 1900–1920* (New York: Anchor Books/Doubleday, 1993), 98.

2. For more information on the history of the Mount Vernon Ladies' Association (MVLA), see Barbara J. Howe's chapter "The Role of Women in the Nineteenth-Century Preservation Movement."

3. Mount Vernon Ladies' Association of the Union (MVLAU), minutes of the Mount Vernon Ladies' Association of the Union, 1901, 1915.

4. MVLAU, minutes, 1901, 1915.

5. MVLAU, "Annual Report" (Mount Vernon, Va., 1932, 1935, 1936, 1938, 1987, 1990).

6. MVLAU, minutes, 1889, 1891, 1915.

7. MVLAU, "Annual Report," 1993.

8. Polly Welts Kaufman, *National Parks and the Woman's Voice* (Albuquerque: University of New Mexico Press, 1996), 28.

9. Charles B. Hosmer Jr., *Preservation Comes of Age,* 2 vols. (Charlottesville: University Press of Virginia, 1981), 898.

10. Dorothy Hunt Williams, *Historic Virginia Gardens* (1975; rpt., University Press of Virginia, 1985), xii.

11. Garden Club of Virginia, *The Restored Historic Gardens of Virginia,* pamphlet.

12. Garden Club of Virginia, "Restored Historic Gardens of Virginia."

13. Williams, *Historic Virginia Gardens,* xii–xiii.

14. Garden Club of Virginia, "Restored Historic Gardens of Virginia."

15. Garden Club of Virginia, "Restored Historic Gardens of Virginia"; Williams, *Historic Virginia Gardens,* xii–xiii.

16. Hosmer, *Preservation Comes of Age,* 307–9.

17. See Louise Shelton, *Beautiful Gardens in America* (New York: Charles Scribner's Sons, 1915); and Alice Morse Earle, *Old Time Gardens* (New York: Macmillan, 1901).

18. See Alice G. B. Lockwood, comp., *Gardens of Colony and State,* 2 vols. (New York: Charles Scribner's Sons, 1931 and 1934).

19. Mac Griswold and Eleanor Weller, *The Golden Age of American Gardens* (New York: Harry N. Abrams, in association with the Garden Club of America, 1992), 17.

20. See Edith Tunis Sale, ed., *Historic Gardens of Virginia* (Richmond: William Byrd Press, 1930). The James River Garden Club, originally a member of the Garden Club of America, became one of the founding members of the Garden Club of Virginia. When the book was first published, it was affiliated with the GCA.

21. See T. A. Daly, comp, *The Wissahickon* (Philadelphia: Garden Club of Philadelphia, 1922); Louise Bush-Brown, and James Bush-Brown, *Portraits of Philadelphia Gardens* (Philadelphia: Dorrance and Co., 1929); Mrs. William R. Massie and Mrs. Andre H. Christian, *Descriptive Guide Book of Virginia's Old Gardens* (Richmond: J. W. Fergusson and Sons, 1929); Florence Marye, *Garden History of Georgia, 1723–1933* (Atlanta: Peachtree Garden Club, 1933); and Winifred Starr Dobyns, *California Gardens* (New York: Macmillan, 1931).

22. Hosmer, *Preservation Comes of Age*, 1, 289.

23. Guide to African American Preservation Foundation, Inc., *African American Heritage Preservation Foundation, Inc., Website,* November 28, 1997, Internet, July 24, 1998.

24. See, for example, Ethan Carr, *Wilderness by Design: Landscape Architecture and the National Park Service* (Lincoln: University of Nebraska Press, 1998).

25. Schneider, *American Women and the Progressive Era*, 98.

26. Kaufmann, *National Parks and the Woman's Voice*, 32–35.

27. Pat Tolle, "Stepping in to Save the Everglades," *Courier* 32 (April 1987): 7.

28. New Jersey State Federation of Women's Clubs, *A Century of Challenge* (New Brunswick, N.J.: New Jersey State Federation of Women's Clubs, 1994), 431.

29. New Jersey State Federation of Women's Clubs, *Century of Challenge,* 433.

30. Kaufmann, *National Parks and the Woman's Voice*, 40.

31. Lewis L. Gould, *Lady Bird Johnson and the Environment* (Kansas City: University Press of Kansas, 1988), 3.

32. Elizabeth B. Lawton, "What Progress in Roadside Control?" *American Planning and Civic Annual* (1937): 315.

33. Gould, *Lady Bird Johnson and the Environment*, 4.

34. Susan Q. Stranahan, "State Looses New Species of Litterbug on a Persistent Nuisance: The Slob," *Philadelphia Inquirer*, March 28, 1997, B2.

35. Gould, *Lady Bird Johnson and the Environment*, 4.

36. Lewis F. Fisher, *Saving San Antonio: The Precarious Preservation of a Heritage.* (Lubbock: Texas Tech University Press, 1996), x.

37. Fisher, *Saving San Antonio*, 92.

38. Fisher, *Saving San Antonio*, 181–207, 262–76, 161.

39. Fisher, *Saving San Antonio*, 262–76.

40. Fisher, *Saving San Antonio*, 161.

41. See, for example, John C. Teaford, *The Rough Road to Renaissance* (Baltimore: Johns Hopkins University Press, 1990).

42. Walter C. Kidney, *A Past Still Alive* (Pittsburgh: Pittsburgh History and Landmark Foundation, 1989), 122.

43. See Louise Bush-Brown, *Garden Blocks for Urban America* (New York: Charles Scribner's Sons, 1969).

CHAPTER 4: FOUR AFRICAN AMERICAN WOMEN
ON THE NATIONAL LANDSCAPE

I want to acknowledge the support of my colleague and friend Jeffrey C. Stewart for his numerous conversations about this chapter. I also wish to thank my husband, Paul Ruffins, and children, Joy and Robert, for sharing their Sag Harbor time with it in the summer of 1998.

1. Over time people of African descent within the United States have changed how they wished to be named. In the eighteenth century *sons and daughters of Africa* was a common appellation. During the 1830s *Colored American* and *People of Color* had come into colloquial use, although *Afro-American* was often used in newspapers, books, and other published sources. In the 1890s a younger generation adopted the capitalized word *Negro* as an assertion of pride, while in the 1960s the term *Black* took on that connotation. By the late 1980s *African American* began to be used in published sources, although colloquially the simpler term *Black* still remains important. Because these name changes reflect significant shifts in cultural discourse, in this chapter I have used the ethnic self-designations that were used in their relevant historical periods, with capitalization as rendered in African American publications of the time. I also do this to help contextualize any original sources quoted.

2. From the ParkNet–National Park Service website, www.cr.nps.gov/crweb1/nr/travel/pwwmh/ny13.htm.

3. Many of the United States' history museums and historic houses are on the eastern seaboard (North and South) with a smaller number in the Midwest. Before 1990 most African American historical museums and sites were in New England and the Mid-Atlantic region, with a smaller number in midwestern cities and California. In the 1990s, however, a number of civil rights museums and sites have sprung up in many cities across the South.

4. Philadelphia was probably the most significant community of free Afro-Americans in the late eighteenth century. Most but not all of its members were free by 1800. Over the years Philadelphia has been the home of a multigenerational concern for documenting local Black history. Today there is a vibrant branch of the Afro-American Historical and Genealogical Society, an Afro-American Museum of History and Culture, the American Women's Heritage Society, and a very active chapter of the Association for the Study of Afro-

American Life and History (ASALH). In addition, the Philadelphia area is the home of Charles Blockson, the preeminent late-twentieth-century Black bibliophile and memorabilia collector. His collection is now owned by Temple University, and he is the primary curator.

5. I am indebted for much of my information about the Tubman House to Pauline Johnson (telephone interview, July 17, 1998). She has lived in Auburn her whole life and is the great-great-grandniece of Harriet Tubman. Although she is presently semi-retired, Mrs. Johnson has long given and continues to give tours to the public of the Tubman estate. I also spoke with Reverend Paul G. Carter, who is the resident manager of the estate for the A.M.E. Zion Church, which owns the whole property (telephone interview, July 17, 1998). I also met with Reverend Carter on November 12, 1998. He graciously delivered two photographs that I needed for this chapter to my home in Washington, D.C.

6. Information on Tubman's life is paraphrased from the following sources: Jesse Carney Smith, ed., *Epic Lives: One Hundred Black Women Who Made a Difference* (Detroit: Visible Ink Press, 1993), 529–37 (profile by Nancy A. Davidson); and Philip Sterling, *Four Took Freedom: The Lives of Harriet Tubman, Frederick Douglass, Robert Smalls, and Blanche K. Bruce* (Garden City, N.Y.: Doubleday, 1967), 2–34. See also Sarah Bradford, *Harriet Tubman: The Moses of Her People,* first published in 1868. I used the edition with an introduction by Butler A. Jones (Gloucester, Mass.: Peter Smith, 1981). See also National Park Service website, www.cr.nps.gov/crweb/nr/travel/pwwmh/ny13 .htm.

7. For more information on the A.M.E. Zion Church, see David Henry Bradley, *A History of the A.M.E. Zion Church,* pt. 1: *1796–1872* (Nashville: Parthenon Press, 1956); Edward Smith, *Climbing Jacob's Ladder: The Rise of the Black Church in Eastern American Cities, 1740–1877* (Washington, D.C.: Smithsonian Press, 1988); and Gayraud S. Wilmore, *Black Religion and Black Radicalism: An Interpretation of the Religious History of African Americans* (Maryknoll, N.Y.: Orbis Books, 1998).

8. Of course, there are innumerable school buildings, organizations, and other forms of memorial to Douglass and to a lesser extent Truth and Tubman. I have examined the preservation of the Douglass home in detail in two previous articles: see Fath Davis Ruffins, "'Lifting as We Climb': Black Women and the Preservation of African American History and Culture," *Gender and History* 6:3 (November 1994): 376–96; and "Mythos, Memory, and History: African American Preservation Efforts, 1820–1990," *in Museums and Communities: The Politics of Public Culture,* ed. Ivan Karp, Christine Mullen Kreamer, and Steven D. Lavine (Washington, D.C.: Smithsonian Institution Press, 1992), 506-611.

9. The primary collections on Truth include: Berenice Bryant Lowe's "Sojourner Truth" Collection in the Bentley Historical Library at the University of Michigan at Ann Arbor; the Willard Library of the Battle Creek Historical Society; and the Westchester County Archives in New York. See Nell Irwin Painter, *Sojourner Truth: A Life, A Symbol* (New York: W. W. Norton, 1996). See also *The Narrative of Sojourner Truth,* intro. Jeffrey C. Stewart, Schomburg Library of Black Women Authors (New York: Oxford University Press, 1991).

10. Douglass, Truth, and Tubman are all celebrated in many ways in neighborhoods throughout the nation: by the naming of public and private buildings such as school or libraries; by the naming of commemorative festivals, private clubs, and organizations, and by the naming of children or by adults taking new symbolic names. Indeed, during the era of American segregation (c.1880–1965) Afro-Americans were able to tell where the "safe" parts of a new town might be by the naming of certain streets, neighborhoods, or buildings. I first explored this concept in greater detail while curating an exhibition at the National Afro-American Museum and Center in Wilberforce, Ohio. The exhibition, *From Victory to Freedom: Afro-American Life in the Fifties, 1945–1955,* opened in 1988 and can still be visited.

11. According to my interview with Pauline Johnson, Tubman left the Brick House to her daughters, who were impoverished. They had to sell the house to pay for her funeral expenses. The next owners upon leaving, however, offered to sell the house back to A.M.E. Zion Church in the 1930s. With the help of the National Council of Negro Women, the house was reunited with the rest of the property. It appears that the contents of the house were dispersed among Tubman's heirs. Today the Brick House has only two objects directly related to the time Tubman lived there. The Home for the Aged has a small number of original objects, but they include the bed and other furnishings from Tubman's time living in the home in the years right before her death.

12. The Nineteenth Amendment to the U.S. Constitution in 1920 gave women the vote in state and federal elections.

13. Information on Bethune's life is paraphrased from the following sources: Jesse Carney Smith, ed., *Epic Lives: One Hundred Black Women Who Made a Difference* (Detroit: Visible Ink Press, 1993), 39–47 (profile by Elaine M. Smith); and Cindi Brownfield, "A Walk through Time: Historic Sites on B-CC Tour," *News-Journal* (Daytona Beach, Fla.), February 9, 1998, sec. C, cover story. This article was faxed to me by Jean Fives of the Public Information Office of Bethune Cookman College. It also draws on information from the National Park Service (NPS) website, www.cr.nps.gov/mame/bethune/welcome/mission.htm, and other links from this site. Susan McElrath, curator

of the Council House, gave me numerous free handouts as well as copies of key articles I have cited in this chapter and answered questions about the operations of the NPS during my August 19, 1998, visit. Ms. Fives and Ms. McElrath were essential in helping me to complete this section of the chapter.

14. Apparently, President Roosevelt's customary greeting to her was "I'm always glad to see you, Mrs. Bethune, for you always come asking help for others, never for yourself." Upon Franklin Roosevelt's death, Eleanor Roosevelt gave Bethune a silver-tipped mahogany cane that had belonged to him. When asked how she felt about it, Bethune replied: "I swagger it sublimely. It gives me strength and nothing to fear." This brief story provides a sense of the nature of Bethune's relationship to the two Roosevelts as well as a glimpse of her fascinating personality. I received this information in a fax from Jean Fives of the Public Affairs Office of Bethune-Cookman College on August 19, 1998. Fives also sent me a needed photograph for this chapter in early November 1998.

15. A copy of her will can be downloaded from the National Park Service website, www.cr.nps.gov/mamc/bethune/meet/will.htm.

16. Booker T. Washington's (1856–1915) autobiography, first published in 1901, is titled *Up from Slavery*. Washington was born enslaved at the end of the slave era and became one of the most important Colored persons in the United States by the turn of the twentieth century, especially in the years after the death of Frederick Douglass (1895). Washington attended college at Hampton Institute during the 1870s (founded in Virginia in 1865) and went on to found Tuskegee Institute in Alabama in 1881. Today both are thriving universities with endowments, active alumni, and a resurgence of tremendous interest among young African Americans in attending them.

17. For more on Dorothy Porter and Sue Bailey Thurman, see Ruffins, "Mythos, Memory, and History." Esme Bhan, a former archivist at Moorland-Spingarn at Howard University, is working on a full-scale biography of Dorothy Porter. The work of Sue Bailey Thurman (now deceased) has been formally celebrated by the Boston Afro-American Museum, but she is worthy of a full-scale biography. Mrs. Thurman, the wife of noted theologian Howard Thurman, was involved in the founding and support of Afro-American cultural institutions in Boston, Washington, and San Francisco from the 1930s through the 1960s. For more information on the National Council of Negro Women's (NCNW) cultural work, see Bettye Collier-Thomas, "Towards Black Feminism: The Creation of the Bethune Museum-Archives," in *Women's Collections: Libraries, Archives and Consciousness*, ed. Suzanne Hildenbrand (New York: Haworth Press, 1986), 43–66. Dr. Collier-Thomas was the head of the Bethune Archives for many years and was instrumental in the building of a memorial to Bethune in a park on Capitol Hill in Washington, D.C. Prior to

the acquisition of the Council House by the National Park Service, Collier-Thomas became a professor of history at Temple University. See also Linda J. Henry, "Promoting Historical Consciousness: The Early Archives Committee of the National Council of Negro Women," *Signs: Journal of Women in Culture and Society* 7:11 (1981): 251–59.

18. The NCNW recently moved into lavish new headquarters in a former Riggs Bank at 301 Pennsylvania Avenue, facing the National Gallery of Art East Building. NCNW has sponsored the annual Black Family Reunion on the Mall in Washington, D.C., Los Angeles, and other major cities for eight years. On September 17, 1998, the longtime president of NCNW, Dorothy Height, was feted at her official retirement party by First Lady Hilary Clinton, Oprah Winfrey, Camille and William Cosby, Jesse Jackson, Gladys Knight, and other celebrities. This event was widely reported in newspapers nationwide, including the *Washington Post* (September 18, 1998). This coverage points to the NCNW's continuing importance as an organization.

19. Villa Lewaro and the present owners, Harold and Helena Doley, are the subject of an article by Beverly Lowry, "A Mansion for MmeWalker," *Preservation* 50:3 (May-June 1998): 62–69.

20. A'Lelia Perry Bundles is the author of a biography for young people, *Madam C. J. Walker, Entrepreneur* (New York: Chelsea House Publishers, 1991). Her website is www.madamcjwalker.com/. Authoritative biographical information comes from these two sources as well as through the NPS website, www.cr.nps.gov/crweb1/nr/travel/pwwmh/ny22.htm. I wish to thank A'Lelia Bundles for numerous conversations over the years about Madam Walker and her legacy.

21. Bundles, *Walker,* 35.

22. The world of direct sales is finally beginning to attract the attention of young historians. There are a couple of dissertations in progress about the California Perfume Company, which later became Avon, an early leader in direct marketing and self-employment for women. This research may provide a point of comparison with the similar work on Madame Walker analyzed in Bundles, *Walker.* See Kathy Lee Peiss, *Hope in a Jar: The Making of America's Beauty Culture* (New York: Metropolitan Books, 1998); see also Robert Weems, *Desegregating the Dollar: African American Consumerism in the Twentieth Century* (New York: New York University Press, 1998).

23. Bundles, *Walker,* 69.

24. Bundles, *Walker,* 91.

25. Tandy was New York State's first certified Afro-American architect. He attended Tuskegee Institute as an undergraduate and earned a master's de-

gree from the Cornell University School of Architecture. Tandy is another person deserving of a full-scale biography.

26. The Madame Walker Theater Center can be found at the website www.mmewalkertheatre.org/Home.html. You can also link from the Bundles website, cited in note 20. The theater uses the later spelling of Madam's name with an *e* added: *Madame.*

27. Information about Maggie Lena Walker comes from two sources: the Maggie Lena Walker Historic Site NPS website, www.cr.nps.gov/malw/details .htm; and "The Banker," by Gene Smith in the "Pathfinders" column of the magazine, created in 1998, *American Legacy: Celebrating African-American History and Culture* 4:3 (fall 1998): 12,14.

28. The NPS website, www.cr.nps.gov/malw/details.htm, 1.

29. The role of these "firsts" is so important for understanding the post–World War II years that, when I curated an exhibition on Afro-American life in the 1950s, I named one entire section of the show " Negro Firsts." That exhibition is entitled *From Victory to Freedom: Afro-American Life in the Fifties, 1945–1965.* It opened in 1988 at the National Afro-American Museum in Wilberforce, Ohio, and remains up today.

30. See Ruffins, "'Lifting as We Climb.'"

31. For more on the contemporary Black middle class, see Charles T. Banner-Haley, *The Fruits of Integration: Black Middle Class Ideology and Culture* (Jackson: University of Mississippi Press, 1994); Sharon M. Collins, *Black Corporate Executives: The Making and Breaking of a Black Middle Class* (Philadelphia: Temple University Press, 1997); Ellis Cose, *The Rage of a Privileged Class* (New York: HarperCollins, 1993); Joe Feagin, *Living with Racism: The Black Middle Class Experience* (Boston: Beacon Press, 1994); and Bart Landry, *The New Black Middle Class* (Berkeley: University of California Press, 1987).

CHAPTER 5. UNCOVERING AND INTERPRETING
WOMEN'S HISTORY AT HISTORIC HOUSE MUSEUMS

1. For further discussion of the cultural politics of the house museum, see Patricia West, *Domesticating History: The Political Origins of America's House Museums* (Washington, D.C.: Smithsonian Institution Press, 1999).

2. Perspectives on the problems and possibilities in the American historic house museum include John Herbst, "Historic Houses," in *History Museums in the United States,* ed. Warren Leon and Roy Rosenzweig (Urbana: University of Illinois Press, 1989), 98–114; Michael Wallace, "Visiting the Past," in *Presenting the Past: Essays on History and the Public,* ed. Susan Porter Benson, Stephen Brier, and Roy Rosenzweig (Philadelphia: Temple University Press, 1986), 137–61; Peter O'Connell, "Putting the Historic House into the

Course of History," *Journal of Family History* 6 (spring 1981): 28–40; Mary Lynn Stevens, "Wistful Thinking: There Is More at Historic House Museums than Nostalgia," *History News* 36 (December 1981): 10–13. On women's history in museums, see Barbara Melosh and Christina Simmons, "Exhibiting Women's History," in *Presenting the Past: Essays on History and the Public,* ed. Susan Porter Benson, Stephen Brier, and Roy Rosenzweig (Philadelphia: Temple University Press, 1986), 203–21; and the essays in the November 1994 special issue of *Gender and History* on public history.

3. William T. Alderson and Shirley Paine Low, *Interpretation of Historic Sites,* 2d ed. (1976; rpt., Nashville: American Association for State and Local History, 1985), 16–17.

4. On the roots of this phenomenon, see Richard Bushman, *The Refinement of America: Persons, Houses, Cities* (New York: Alfred A. Knopf, 1992), esp. 262–63. On its full flowering and later reversal, see Clifford Edward Clark Jr., *The American Family Home, 1800–1960* (Chapel Hill: University of North Carolina Press, 1986), 131–92.

5. Historians have argued that the ideology of feminine domesticity arose in part as a means by which middle-class women could distinguish themselves from the new class of working women. See Linda Kerber's discussion of the historiography of nineteenth-century domesticity in "Separate Spheres, Female Worlds, Woman's Place: The Rhetoric of Women's History," *Journal of American History* 75 (June 1988): 9–39.

6. For a concise history of American material culture studies, see Thomas Schlereth, "Material Culture Studies in America, 1876–1976," in *Material Culture Studies in America,* ed. Thomas Schlereth (Nashville, Tenn.: American Association for State and Local History, 1982), 1–78.

7. For further detail, see Patricia West, "Irish Immigrant Workers in Antebellum New York: The Experience of Domestic Servants at Van Buren's Lindenwald," *Hudson Valley Regional Review* 9 (September 1992): 112–26; and "'The New Social History' in Historic House Museums: The Lindenwald Example," *Museum Studies Journal* 2 (fall 1986): 22–26.

8. The roots of this dimension of nineteenth-century American political ideology are described by Bernard Bailyn, *The Ideological Origins of the American Revolution* (Cambridge, Mass.: Harvard University Press, 1967); and Gordon Wood, *The Creation of the American Republic* (Chapel Hill: University of North Carolina Press, 1969); among others. The phrase *haven in a heartless world* is from Christopher Lasch, *Haven in a Heartless World: The Family Besieged* (New York: Basic Books, 1977).

9. Faye E. Dudden, *Serving Women: Household Service in Nineteenth-Century America* (Middletown, Conn.: Wesleyan University Press, 1983). In

making this case, Dudden implicitly challenged the tendency of historians of nineteenth-century women to construct arguments based on the rhetoric of "separate spheres." Nancy Cott, for example, used Thompson's concept of "time discipline" to argue that industrialization caused male work life to differ markedly from that of women, creating separate, gendered cultures because women's work continued along traditional lines. Dudden's predecessors in the study of domestic service had by and large concurred, arguing that the "servant problem" was caused by an anachronistic "master-servant" relationship ill suited to the modernizing world. Nancy Cott, *The Bonds of Womanhood: "Woman's Sphere" in New England, 1780–1830* (New Haven, Conn.: Yale University Press, 1977); Daniel E. Sutherland, *Americans and Their Servants: Domestic Service in the United States from 1800 to 1920* (Baton Rouge: Louisiana State University Press, 1981); David Katzman, *Seven Days a Week* (New York: Oxford University Press, 1978).

10. Hence the double-edged meaning of Dudden's title, *Serving Women.*

11. See Sean Wilentz, *Chants Democratic* (New York: Oxford University Press, 1984); Paul Johnson, *A Shopkeepers' Millennium* (New York: Hill and Wang, 1978); Paula Baker, "The Domestication of Politics: Women and American Political Society, 1780–1920," *American Historical Review* 89 (June 1984): 620–47.

12. Classics include Wilentz, *Chants Democratic;* Daniel Walker Howe, *The Political Culture of the American Whigs* (Chicago: University of Chicago Press, 1979); Edward Pessen, *Jacksonian America: Society, Personality, and Politics* (Hornewood, Ill.: Dorsey Press, 1978); Glyndon Van Deusen, *The Jacksonian Era* (New York: Harper and Row, 1963); Arthur M. Schlesinger Jr., *The Age of Jackson* (Boston: Little, Brown, 1953). On the election identified as spawning the "modern" presidential campaign, see William Nisbet Chambers, "The Election of 1840," in *History of American Presidential Elections,* ed. Arthur Schlesinger Jr. (New York: McGraw-Hill, 1971), 1:651, 647–49.

13. For definitive studies of Van Buren's life and career, see John Niven, *Martin Van Buren: The Romantic Age of American Politics* (New York: Oxford University Press, 1983); and Donald Cole, *Martin Van Buren and the American Political System* (Princeton, N.J.: Princeton University Press, 1984). See also James C. Curtis, *The Fox at Bay: Martin Van Buren and the Presidency* (Lexington: University Press of Kentucky, 1957); Robert Remini, *Martin Van Buren and the Making of the Democratic Party* (New York: Columbia University Press, 1968); Richard P. McCormick, "Van Buren and the Uses of Politics," in *Six Presidents from the Empire State,* ed. Harry J. Sievers (Tarrytown, N.Y.: Sleepy Hollow Restorations, 1974), 30–32.

14. Kerby Miller, *Emigrants and Exiles: Ireland and the Irish Exodus to America* (New York: Oxford University Press, 1985); Hasia R. Diner, *Erin's Daughters in America: Irish Immigrant Women in the Nineteenth Century* (Baltimore: Johns Hopkins University Press, 1983).

15. Curtis, *Fox at Bay,* 63, 191–94; Robert Gray Gunderson, *The Log Cabin Campaign* (Lexington: University Press of Kentucky, 1957); Remini, *Martin Van Buren,* 125; Chambers, "Election of 1840," 647; McCormick, "Van Buren and the Uses of Politics," 30–32; James C. Curtis, "In the Shadow of Old Hickory: The Political Travail of Martin Van Buren," *Journal of the Early Republic* 1 (fall 1981): 249–67.

16. Martin Van Buren to James Wadsworth, National Park Service, Martin Van Buren National Historic Site, Kinderhook, N.Y., June 8, 1844.

17. "Interpretive Prospectus," Martin Van Buren National Historic Site, Kinderhook, N.Y., 1985.

18. "Interpretive Prospectus," Martin Van Buren National Historic Site.

CHAPTER 6: DOMESTIC WORK PORTRAYED

The authors wish to thank the Friends of Independence National Historical Park for their generous financial assistance in preparing the expanded versions of this chapter: Karie Diethorn, "Domestic Servants in Philadelphia, 1780–1830" (MS, National Park Service, Independence National Historical Park, August 1986); and John Bacon, "Cellars, Garrets, and Related Spaces in Philadelphia Houses, 1750–1850" (MS, National Park Service, Independence National Historical Park, August 1991).

1. Traditional interpretation at historic sites is well represented by William T. Alderson's seminal monograph *The Interpretations of Historic Sites* (Nashville, Tenn.: American Association for State and Local History, 1976). More recently, the discussion of whose stories are told at historic sites has become more heated; see Gerald George, *Visiting History: Arguments over Museum and Historic Sites* (Washington, D.C.: American Association of Museums, 1990); and Michael Sorkin, ed., *Variations on a Theme Park* (New York: Noonday Press, 1992). Patricia West's *Domesticating Clio: The Political Origins of America's House Museums* (Washington, D.C.: Smithsonian Institution Press, 1999) chronicles the growing interpretive interest in alternative pasts and how these histories can be introduced to mainstream visitors.

2. Recently, new interpretive approaches to women's history as presented at historic sites has fostered interdisciplinary programming at a range of museums in Pennsylvania. Funded by the Pennsylvania Humanities Council, "Raising Our Sites" explored women's roles at nine sites across the common-

NOTES TO PAGES 97–106

wealth. The process at several of these sites is documented in Virginia K. Bartlett, *Women's Lives in Western Pennsylvania, 1790–1850* (Pittsburgh: University of Pittsburgh Press, 1994).

3. See Bird Wilson, *Memoir of the Life of the Right Reverend William White, D.D.* (Philadelphia: James Kay, Jun. and Bro., 1839); and "Historic Building Report on the Bishop White House" (MS, Independence National Historical Park, April 1958).

4. Studies of domestic work have increased during the last decade. Notable among them are Faye E. Dudden, *Household Service in Nineteenth-Century America* (Hanover, N.H.: Wesleyan University Press, 1983); Barbara T. Ryan, "'Uneasy Relations': Servants' Place in the Nineteenth-Century American Home" (Ph.D. diss., Department of History, University of North Carolina, Chapel Hill, 1994); and Debra M. O'Neal, "Mistresses and Maids: The Transformation of Women's Domestic Labor and Household Relations in Late Eighteenth-Century Philadelphia" (Ph.D. diss., University of California, Riverside, 1994).

5. See Statutes at Large of Pennsylvania from 1682 to 1809 (Harrisburg, Pa.: Clarence and Busch, 1896–1911), 4:62, for the mandatory indenture of free blacks until age twenty-one.

6. See Gary B. Nash, *Forging Freedom: The Formation of Philadelphia's Black Community, 1720–1840* (Cambridge, Mass.: Harvard University Press, 1988), for a detailed discussion of the city's late-eighteenth- and early-nineteenth-century free African community.

7. Eliza Leslie, *The House Book: or, a Manual of Domestic Economy* (Philadelphia, 1840), 121 and 247.

8. Elizabeth Drinker diary, August 3, 1803, Historical Society of Pennsylvania Manuscript Department.

9. Drinker diary, April 22, 1784.

10. Benjamin Franklin (as "Anthony Afterwit"), *Pennsylvania Gazette*, July 10, 1732; quoted in Elisabeth Garrett, *At Home: The American Family, 1750–1870* (New York: Abrams, 1990), 249.

11. See Robert Roberts, *The House Servant's Directory* (Boston: Munroe and Francis, 1827), 155; and Drinker diary, October 10, 1803, and January 27, 1804.

12. On servant dining, see Margaret Hill Morris to Robert Morris, Philadelphia, October 12, 1793; quoted in *Letters of Richard Hill and his Children: or, the history of a family as told by themselves. Collected & analyzed by John Jay Smith* (N.p.: privately printed, 1854), 379. On servant sleeping quarters, see Drinker diary, October 6, 1803; George Washington to Tobias Lear, Balti-

more, September 5, 1790, in *Writings of George Washington*, ed. John C. Fitzpatrick (Washington, D.C.: U.S. Government Printing Office, 1939), 31:110.

13. See Dell Upton, "Vernacular Domestic Architecture in Eighteenth-Century Virginia," *Winterthur Portfolio* 17 (summer-fall 1982): 104–6; Anthony N. B. Garvan, ed., *The Mutual Assurance Company Papers*, vol. 1: *The Architectural Surveys, 1784–1794* (Philadelphia: Mutual Assurance Co., 1976), xv; George B. Tatum, *Philadelphia Georgian: The City House of Samuel Powel and Some of Its Eighteenth-Century Neighbors* (Middleton, Conn.: Wesleyan University Press, 1976), 60.

14. Alexander Smith advertised his services as a bell hanger, lately from London, to Philadelphians in the September 19, 1778, issue of the *Royal Gazette*. The Boston Academy of Arts and Sciences related the stories of two Philadelphia homes in which bell systems conducted lightning into the houses and caused fires in 1781; see "Historic Structures Report, Part II on the Dilworth-Todd-Moylan House" (MS, Independence National Historical Park, July 1960), chap. 3, sec. 1, 7–9.

15. Mrs. Eliza Farrar, *The Young Lady's Friend* (Boston: American Stationers' Co., 1837), 238.

16. See "Contributionship Survey," bk. 1 (1768–94), 140; bk. 2 (1768–94 cont.), 43; bk. 3 (1794–1809), 86; bk. 5 (1824–37), 395; Mutual Assurance Surveys, policy 3568.

17. From 196 Philadelphia inventories dated 1790 to 1795 and 24 Philadelphia inventories dated 1775 to 1836 (all are transcribed in the files of Independence National Historical Park), 43 separate estates with rooms labeled "Garret" or "Kitchen Chamber/Room over Kitchen" by their evaluators were chosen for this study. Thirty-six of these inventories had a garret chamber. Seven inventories had a kitchen chamber. Fifteen inventories had both kitchen and garret chambers. A total of 68 rooms were examined. A few of these rooms were clearly servants' quarters, since they contained "servant bed(s)" or were labeled as servants' rooms.

18. See Drinker diary, May 23, 1795, and March 25, 1805.

19. See Ronald D. Clifton, "Forms and Patterns: Room Specialization in Maryland, Massachusetts, and Pennsylvania Family Dwellings, 1725–1834" (Ph.D. diss., American Civilization Program, University of Pennsylvania, 1971), 13–15, 31.

20. See Farrar, *Young Lady's Friend*, 53: "The best dinner-set is often kept in the closet of a spare chamber; so piles of plates and arms full of dishes are seen walking down stairs on company days, and walking up again the day after."

CHAPTER 7: PUTTING WOMEN IN THEIR PLACE

1. See Ellen Cochran Hicks, ed., *Women's Changing Roles in Museums* (Washington, D.C.: Smithsonian Institution, Office of Museum Programs, 1986); and Jane R. Glaser and Artemis Zenetou, eds., *Gender Perspectives: Essays on Women in Museums* (Washington, D.C.: Smithsonian Institution Press, 1994).

2. For information about "Raising Our Sites," write to the Pennsylvania Humanities Council, 320 Walnut Street, Philadelphia, PA 19106.

3. *Exploring a Common Past: Interpreting Women's History in the National Park Service* (Washington, D.C.: National Park Service, 1996).

4. *PresHERvationist* (Moorestown, N.J.) 1:3 (September 1996). This newsletter is published three times a year by the Alice Paul Centennial Foundation, which preserves the birthplace of Alice Paul, militant woman suffrage leader, as a historic landmark. Write to *PresHERvationist,* Alice Paul Centennial Foundation, Inc., P.O. Box 472, Moorestown, NJ 08057.

5. For articles on the presentation of women's history exhibitions in museums and historic sites, see Barbara Melosh and Christina Simmons, "Exhibiting Women's History," in *Presenting the Past: Essays on History and the Public,* ed. Susan Porter Benson, Stephen Brier, and Roy Rosenzweig (Philadelphia: Temple University Press, 1986), 203–21; Barbara Melosh, "Speaking of Women: Museums' Representations of Women's History," in *History Museums in the United States: A Critical Assessment,* ed. Warren Leon and Roy Rosenzweig (Urbana: University of Illinois Press, 1989), 183–214; Barbara J. Howe and Emory L. Kemps, eds., *Public History: An Introduction* (Malabar, Fla.: Robert E. Krieger Publishing, 1986); Edith Mayo, "Women's History and Public History: The Museum Connection," *Public Historian* 5:2 (spring 1983): 63–73; Heather A. Huyck, "Beyond John Wayne: Using Historic Sites to Interpret Western Women's History," in *Western Women: Their Land, Their Lives,* ed. Lillian Schlissel, Vicki Ruiz, and Janice Monk (Albuquerque: University of New Mexico Press, 1988); and Heather A. Huyck, ed., "Placing Women in the Past," *CRM: Cultural Resources Management* 20:3.

6. Leon and Rosenzweig, *History Museums.*

7. Edith Mayo, ed., *American Material Culture: The Shape of Things around Us* (Bowling Green, Ohio: Bowling Green State University Popular Press, 1984); Thomas J. Schlereth, ed., *Material Culture Studies in America* (Nashville, Tenn.: American Association for State and Local History, 1982); Robert Blair St. George, ed., *Material Life in America, 1600–1860* (Westford, Mass.: Murray Printing Co., 1988); and Ann S. Martin and J. Ritchie Garrison, eds., *American Material Culture: The Shape of the Field* (Winterthur, Del.:

Henry Francis du Pont Winterthur Museum, 1997), are but a few of the many texts available.

8. Important scholarly articles about the construction of historical memory are: Michael Frisch, "The Memory of History," and Michael Wallace, "Reflections on the History of Historic Preservation," both in Benson, Brier, and Rosenzweig, *Presenting the Past,* 5–17 and 165–99. See also Michael Wallace, "The Future of History Museums," *History News* 44 (July–August 1989): 5–8, 30–33.

9. See Carol Berkin, "'Dangerous Courtesies' Assault Women's History," *Chronicle of Higher Education,* December 11, 1991, A44, for a variety of ways to incorporate women into historical texts "but keep them out of interpretation."

10. See Edith Mayo, "New Angles of Vision" in *Gender Perspectives:Essays on Women in Museums,* ed. Jane R. Glaser and Artemis A. Zenetou (Washington, D.C.: Smithsonian Institution Press, 1994), 57–62.

11. Barbara Clark Smith, "A Case Study of Applied Feminist Theories," in *Gender Perspectives: Essays on Women in Museums,* ed. Jane R. Glaser and Artemis A. Zenetou (Washington, D.C.: Smithsonian Institution Press, 1994), 137–46.

12. Smith, "Case Study," 140.

13. Smith, "Case Study," 141.

14. Smith, "Case Study," 145.

CHAPTER 8: ROOMS OF THEIR OWN

The author gratefully acknowledges the support of the McGill Centre for Research and Teaching on Women and the insightful assistance of David Theodore. Many others also contributed to the effort, especially Suzelle Baudouin, Linda Cohen, Peter Gossage, Rhona Kenneally, Karen Kingsley, Marie-Alice L'Heureux, Tania Martin, Rob Michel, Debbie Miller, Dianne Newell, Françoise Roux, Conor Sampson, and Gordon Whiteside. Graduates of the RVH Training School for Nurses and the staff of the Royal Victoria Hospital generously shared their material and memories, particularly Lorine Besel, Pat Blanshay, Helen Belschner, Brenda Cornell, Lynda deForest, and Martin Entin. A longer version of this article first appeared in *Material History Review* 40 (fall 1994): 29–41.

1. The Maxwells were the winners of a limited competition held in 1905. See House Committee, RVH, Minute Book 2, 1903–15. The most comprehensive study of the Maxwells' career is *The Architecture of Edward and W. S. Maxwell* (Montreal: Montreal Museum of Fine Arts, 1991). Hutchison and Wood designed numerous extensions and alterations to the hospital from 1905

to 1912. The drawings for the Lawson and Little extension to the Hersey Pavilion are in the Canadian Centre for Architecture. See D. Sclater Lewis, *Royal Victoria Hospital, 1887–1947* (Montreal: McGill University Press, 1969), 250.

2. Dianne Dodd, "Nurses' Residences: Commemoration of Canadian Nursing," Historic Sites and Monuments Board of Canada, Agenda Paper, n.d.

3. The architecture of nursing has been little explored by historians; the most thorough study is Karen Kingsley, "The Architecture of Nursing," in *Images of Nurses: Perspectives from History, Art, and Literature,* ed. Anne Hudson Jones (Philadelphia: University of Pennsylvania Press, 1988), 63–94. On the RVH Training School in particular, see *The Alumnae Association Incorporated of the Royal Victoria Hospital Training School for Nurses, 1896–1972,* prepared by Kathryn Catterill in 1972; Lynda deForest, Proud Heritage: A History of the Royal Victoria Hospital Training School for Nurses, 1894–1972 (Montreal: Alumnae Association, 1994); and Marjorie Dobie Munroe, *The Training School for Nurses, Royal Victoria Hospital, 1894–1943* (Montreal: Gazette Printing, 1943). The school closed in 1972, although the association is still active today. A longer history of nursing education at the Montreal General Hospital, an English-speaking hospital that was founded in 1819, is offered in Hugh Macdermot, *History of the School of Nursing of the Montreal General Hospital* (Montreal: Alumnae Association, 1940). Alternatively, the histories of francophone nursing education offered at Montreal hospitals are found in Johanne Daigle, "Devenir infirmière: le système d'apprentissage et la formation professionnelle à l'Hôtel-Dieu de Montréal, 1920–1970" (Ph.D. diss., Department of History, Université du Québec à Montréal, 1990); and *L'Ecole d'infirmières de l'Hôpital Notre-Dame, Montreal, 1898–1968* (Montreal: Association des infirmières diplômées de l'Hôpital Notre-Dame, 1968). On the history of nursing in Canada, see John Murray Gibbon and Mary S. Mathewson, *Three Centuries of Canadian Nursing* (Toronto: Macmillan, 1947); and Kathryn McPherson, *Bedside Matters: The Transformation of Canadian Nursing, 1900–1990* (Toronto: Oxford University Press, 1996).

4. Excerpted from the RVH's act of incorporation, Charter of the Royal Victoria Hospital, Statutes of Canada, 50–51, Victoria (1887), chap. 125; reproduced in Lewis, *Royal Victoria Hospital,* 311–15. The main responsibilities of a new probationer at the hospital in 1894 are listed in Gibbon and Mathewson, *Three Centuries,* 159.

5. A five-story wing of the administration building was added to the original Snell complex in 1898–99, designed by Andrew Taylor. This included a nurses' dining room and extra bedrooms. This dining room, illustrated in Lewis (fig. 10), was accessible from the hospital's main staircase. It became the doctors' dining room after construction of the Maxwells' residence for nurses and stood

until the construction of the new surgical wing after World War II. The plans in the Maxwells' possession which show a dining room in the western end of the administration building do not reflect what was built. See Lewis, *Royal Victoria Hospital*, 128. The Royal Infirmary at Edinburgh, the model for the RVH, had a separate dining room for nurses, as designed by David Bryce.

6. "On the Mountain's Breast," *Gazette* (Montreal), November 12, 1891, 2, cols. 1–2.

7. These drawings were produced by Snell's office; copies are now in the National Archives of Canada. An axonometric drawing of the complex, also drawn by Snell, names portions of block 7, 8, and 9 for nurses; it is likely from scattered references that the fourth floor of the administration block was largely occupied by the nurses (block 8).

8. D. Sclater Lewis says they slept on the fourth floor; see Lewis, *Royal Victoria Hospital*, 26; according to "The Royal Victoria Hospital," *Montreal Medical Journal* 22:7 (January 1894): 536: "The second and third stories contain the apartments of the Lady Superintendent, her assistant and the nursing staff. J. Robson, "The Royal Victoria Hospital, Montreal," in *Hospitals, Dispensaries, and Nursing*, ed. J. S. Billings and Henry M. Hurd (Baltimore: Johns Hopkins Press, 1894), 416, offers a description: "The upper floors contain a large number of bedrooms for the nurses, together with their common sitting and dining rooms, library, linen and bath rooms, lavatories, etc."

9. On the pavilion plan, see Jeremy Taylor, *The Architect and the Pavilion Hospital: Dialogue and Design Creativity in England, 1850–1914* (London: Leicester University Press, 1997).

10. On the Royal Infirmary at Edinburgh, see *Builder* 28:1454, December 17, 1870, 1006–7, 1009. The "Scottishness" of the RVH was noted by many visitors at the time. A journalist in one Montreal newspaper, for example, said that "the whole structure has the appearance of one of the embattled fortalices for which old Scotland was once so famous." See "On the Mountain's Breast," 2, cols. 1–2.

11. Lewis, *Royal Victoria Hospital*, 135.

12. The instructional aspects of mid-twentieth-century nurses' residences are mentioned in Fred L. Townley, "The Planning of Nurses' Homes," *RAIC Journal* (August 1944): 169–70. Examples are illustrated in "Burton Hall Women's College Hospital Residence and School of Nursing," *RAIC Journal* (April 1956): 124; "Student Nurses' Residence, Royal Victoria Hospital, Barrie, Ontario," *RAIC Journal* (October 1952): 293; "Royal Alexandra Nurses Residence and School of Nursing," *RAIC Journal* (January 1962): 48. The nurses' home constructed at the Montreal General Hospital in 1926 also contained "a complete teaching unit of laboratories and class rooms, all on one floor." See Macdermot, *History of the School*, 65.

13. The hospital-based training of nurses in Canada was gradually replaced by college and university programs, beginning in 1920 at the University of British Columbia (Judy Coburn, "'I See and Am Silent': A Short History of Nursing in Ontario," *Women at Work, Ontario 1850–1930* [Toronto: Women's Press, 1974], 153; and Lee Stewart, *It's Up to You: Women at UBC in the Early Years* [Vancouver: University of British Columbia Press, 1990], 31–42). Stewart has noted that the establishment of this pioneering program satisfied a need on the part of hospital administrators to create a hierarchy within nursing, rather than reflecting a sincere interest on the part of the university to welcome women. For more information on the history of nursing in Quebec, see Yolande Cohen and Michèle Dagenais, "Le métier d'infirmière: savoirs féminins et reconnaissance professionnelle," *Revue d'Histoire de l'Amerique Française* 41:2 (fall 1987): 155–77; and Johanne Daigle, Nicole Rousseau, and Francine Saillant, "Des traces sur la neige. La contribution des infirmières au développement des régions isolées du Québec au XXe siècle," *Recherches Féministes* 6:1 (1993): 93–103.

14. Snell's hospital appeared symmetrical, but the west and east wings actually differed significantly due to the steep slope of the site. Note that the bridge linking the third level (D) of the central administration section led to the second floor of the west wing, while it led to the fourth floor in the east wing.

15. 1933 *Yearbook,* 19.

16. Nineteenth-century medical advice literature written for women, for example, is full of suggestions that menstruation, conception, and even childbirth would be eased by rural or natural surroundings. See Pye Henry Chavasse, *Advice to a Wife,* 12th ed. (London: Churchill, 1887), 17, 19–22.

17. On ideologies of women and nature informing the process of suburbanization, see Gwendolyn Wright, *Moralism and the Model Home: Domestic Architecture and Cultural Conflict in Chicago, 1873–1913* (Chicago: University of Chicago Press, 1980); and Annmarie Adams, "The Eichler Home: Intention and Experience in Postwar Suburbia," in *Gender, Class, and Shelter: Perspectives in Vernacular Architecture V,* ed. Elizabeth Collins Cromley and Carter L. Hudgins (Knoxville: University of Tennessee Press, 1995), 164–78.

18. The RVH has never actually owned property east of University Street; it has always belonged to the Royal Institute for the Advancement of Learning (McGill University).

19. These prestigious structures included the first pathology building and medical theater (1894), the new pathology building by Nobbs and Hyde (1924), and the Montreal Neurological Institute by Ross and Macdonald (1933–34).

20. Eileen C. Flanagan, "An Address Given at the 75th Reunion Royal Victoria Hospital Nurses' Alumnae," May 9, 1972, 7.

21. Kingsley has remarked that many nurses' residences had doors of exceptional architectural merit, which lent the institution "identity and stature" and also marked the transition between work and home. Many of the doors in her study were the main entries to the building from the exterior, which she notes were more often used by guests, ironically, than by the nurses. This door at the RVH, however, was an interior door from the hospital. RVH nurses were often photographed at the entry to the Lawson and Little extension.

22. Gibbon and Mathewson, *Three Centuries,* 376.

23. Edward F. Stevens, *The American Hospital of the Twentieth Century,* 3d ed. (New York: Dodge, 1928), 403; Stevens designed both the Ross Memorial Pavilion and the Royal Victoria Montreal Maternity Hospital at the RVH. See Annmarie Adams, "Modernism and Medicine: The Hospitals of Stevens and Lee, 1916-1932," *Journal of the Society of Architectural Historians* 58:1 (March 1999): 42–61. Thomas Harris, on the other hand, writing twenty-five years earlier, remarked that most nursing homes adjoined general hospitals. See Thomas Harris, "Notes on a Short Visit to Some of the Hospitals and Medical Educational Institutions in the United States and Canada," *Montreal Medical Journal* 32:2 (February 1903): 114.

24. Stevens, *American Hospital,* 403.

25. Photographs of these social spaces intended as enticements to the profession appear throughout the promotional literature. See *So You Want to Be a Nurse?* (pamphlet, RVH, 1955).

26. E. A. E. MacLennan, "The New Residence," 1933 *Yearbook,* 18–19.

27. Martha Vicinus, *Independent Women: Work and Community for Single Women, 1850–1920* (Chicago: University of Chicago Press, 1985), 129; the book includes a chapter on reformed nursing (85–120).

28. Comments on the uniform are taken from a letter from Miss Janet Marlane to a friend, reprinted in the 1925 *Yearbook;* Coburn, "I See and Am Silent," 135–40.

29. Stevens, *American Hospital,* 406.

30. The Weir survey of 1932 emphasized the role of the dietetic lab in nursing education so that nurses could become "ambassadors to the people of the new preventive medicine" (Gibbon and Mathewson, *Three Centuries,* 376).

31. 1933 *Yearbook,* 19. Extensive documentation is drawn from Stevens, *American Hospital,* 403–39. Stevens illustrated the plans of fifteen nurses' residences, many of which include educational spaces, in his chapter on the building type. Some large hospitals even had separate educational facilities for nurses at this time (437–39), especially the model plan of an educational build-

ing for nurses as suggested by the New York State Board of Nurse Examiners (435). The Royal Victoria Montreal Maternity Hospital, designed by Stevens and Lee, included housing for its nurses on its sixth floor, with a demonstration room, living room, and library (193).

32. Mrs. Daley applied to Sir Donald A. Smith for admission to the school. The House Committee Minute Book documents that "as it appeared that Mrs. Daley was married and at present living with her husband it was decided that it would not be advisable to accept her application." See House Committee RVH, Minute Book, 1893–1903 (June 12, 1895), 98.

33. Flanagan, " Address Given," 7.

34. 1933 *Yearbook,* 19.

35. This innovative designed was featured in a photograph of a double room in the 1933 *Yearbook,* 19.

36. Telephone interview with Lynda deForest, March 31, 1994.

37. Flanagan, "Address Given," 2; Flanagan was elected president of the Alumnae Association in 1939. The changes carried out during her term are outlined in the Alumnae Association booklet.

38. Hersey's obituary by Elsie Allder appeared in *Canadian Nurse* 101 (February 1949): 3. Some of her accomplishments are cited in Gibbon and Mathewson, *Three Centuries,* 172–73.

39. Lewis, *Royal Victoria Hospital,* 135; the possibility exists, of course, that the lady superintendent resided in the first nurses' home despite the suggestions of the medical board.

40. Coburn, "I See and Am Silent," 155.

CHAPTER 9: ON THE INSIDE

1. For recent library preservation efforts, see *Architecture Minnesota* 15 (September–October 1989); *American Libraries* 21 (April 1990); and *Indiana Preservationist* (September–October 1993).

2. Summarized in Richard Wagner, "Rehabilitation Standards," in *Landmark Yellow Pages,* ed. Pamela Dwight (New York: John Wiley, 1993), 129.

3. Richard Wagner, "Adaptive Use," in *Landmark Yellow Pages,* ed. Pamela Dwight (New York: John Wiley, 1993), 26.

4. For more on women as users of nondomestic space, see Abigail A. Van Slyck, "The Lady in the Library Loafer: Gender and Public Space in Victorian America"; and Carolyn Brucken, "In the Public Eye: Women and the American Luxury Hotel," both in a special issue of the *Winterthur Portfolio* 31 (winter 1996) on "Gendered Spaces and Aesthetics"; see also Cynthia A. Brandimarte, "'To Make the Whole World Homelike': Gender, Space, and America's Tea Room Movement," *Winterthur Portfolio* 30:1 (spring 1995): 1–19; Ann-

marie Adams, "Rooms of Their Own: The Nurses' Residences at Montreal's Royal Victoria Hospital," *Material History Review* 40 (fall 1994): 29–41; Mary P. Ryan, *Women in Public: Between Banners and Ballots, 1825–1880* (Baltimore: Johns Hopkins University Press, 1990); Katherine C. Grier, "Imagining the Parlor, 1830–1880," in *Perspectives in American Furniture*, ed. Gerald W. R. Ward (New York: W. W. Norton, for the Henry Francis du Pont Winterthur Museum, 1988), 205–39; Helen Lefkowitz Horowitz, "Hull-House as Women's Space," *Chicago History* 12 (winter 1983): 40–55.

5. "The New Librarians," *Library Journal* 15 (November 1890): 338.

6. For the remasculinization of American culture more generally at the turn of the century, see Jackson Lears, *No Place of Grace: Antimodernism and the Transformation of American Culture, 1880–1920* (New York: Pantheon Books, 1981).

7. For recent scholarly assessment of this demographic change, see Dee Garrison, *Apostles of Culture: The Public Librarian and American Society, 1876-1920* (New York: Free Press, 1979), 173–241. For contemporary commentaries, see Melvil Dewey, *Librarianship as a Profession for College-Bred Women: An Address Delivered before the Association of Collegiate Alumnae* (Boston: Library Bureau, 1886); M. S. R. James, "Women Librarians," *Library Journal* 18 (May 1893): 146-48; Celia A. Hayward, "Woman as Cataloguer," *Public Libraries* 3 (April 1898): 121–23.

8. The link between sex discrimination and an uncertain professional status has been made explicitly for other fields in these same years. For architecture, see Elizabeth Grossman and Lisa Reitzes, "Caught in the Crossfire: Women and Architectural Education, 1880–1910," in *Architecture: A Place for Women*, ed. Ellen Perry Berkeley (Washington, D.C.: Smithsonian Institution Press, 1989), 27–40.

9. Salome Cutler Fairchild, "Women in American Libraries," *Library Journal* 29 (December 1904): 161.

10. John Cotton Dana, "Women in Library Work," *Independent* 71 (August 3, 1911): 245–46.

11. For more on the Carnegie program, see Abigail A. Van Slyck, *Free to All: Carnegie Libraries and American Culture, 1890–1920* (Chicago: University of Chicago Press, 1995); and George Bobinski, *Carnegie Libraries: Their History and Impact on American Public Library Development* (Chicago: American Library Association, 1969).

12. Mary Denson Pretlow, "The Opening of a Public Library," *Charities and the Commons* 15 (March 17, 1906): 889.

13. This analysis of professional space builds on Bledstein's discussion of largely nonspatial rituals of professional culture (Burton J. Bledstein, *The Cul-*

ture of Professionalism: The Middle Class and the Development of Higher Education in America [New York: W. W. Norton, 1976], 94–96).

14. Or, as Ellen Lupton notes, the woman worker and her machine in the modern office environment function "as a technological conduit for male thought" (*Mechanical Brides: Women and Machines From Home to Office* [New York: Cooper-Hewitt National Museum of Design, Smithsonian Institution, and Princeton Architectural Press, 1993], 42).

15. Lillian Gunter, diary entry, January 12, 1923, Lillian Gunter Papers, Archives Division, Texas State Library. For more on Gunter's career, see "Lillian Gunter [obituary]," *Handbook of Texas Libraries,* no. 4 (Houston: Texas Library Association, 1935), 143; Alice J. Rhoades, "Early Women Librarians in Texas," *Texas Libraries* 47 (summer 1986): 48; Lillian Gunter biography, typescript in Lillian Gunter Papers, Cooke County Heritage Society.

16. For an example of how children's librarians at the turn of the century linked theories of child psychology to the arrangement of their work space in the children's reading room, see Clara W. Hunt, "Maintaining Order in the Children's Room," *Library Journal* 28 (April 1903): 164–67. For parallel survival strategies developed by women in medicine, scientific research, and social work, see Penina Migdal Glazer and Miriam Slater, *Unequal Colleagues: The Entrance of Women into the Professions, 1890–1940* (New Brunswick, N.J.: Rutgers University Press, 1987), 217–19.

17. Nicholson Baker, "Discards," *New Yorker* 70, April 4, 1994, 78.

18. Judy Anderson, Gail Lee Dubrow, and John Koval, *The Library Book* (Seattle: Seattle Art Commission, 1991), 23–25, 69–70.

19. George S. Bobinski, "Carnegies," *American Libraries* 21 (April 1990): 301. As of June 1997, this campaign has stalled. One prominent open-air museum is enthusiastic about including a Carnegie library in its collection, if the museum does not have to pay for the purchase or relocation of the building. Bobinski has approached several foundations about funding these costs, but financial assistance has not been forthcoming.

CHAPTER 10: WOMEN IN THE SOUTHERN
WEST VIRGINIA COALFIELDS

1. Women were not allowed to work in the mines until 1973 because it was considered bad luck, but there were exceptions. During World War II, for example, women worked as "bone pickers," sorting out "bone" and other impurities from the coal at a large "shaker table" that stood over a moving conveyor belt of coal at the tipple (Crandall A. Shiflett, *Coal Towns-Life, Work and Culture in Company Towns of Southern Appalachia* [Knoxville: University of Ten-

nessee Press, 1991], 81; and "Women Enter Coal Industry during World War II," *Bluefield Daily Telegraph,* March 13, 1983).

2. Janet Greene, "Strategies for Survival: Women's Work in the Southern West Virginia Coal Camps," *West Virginia History* 49 (1990): 38.

3. Cindy Dobson, Stacy Sone, and Kim Valente, *Coal Heritage Survey: Southern West Virginia Reconnaissance Study of Sites Related to the History of Coal Mining,* Phase 1 Final Report and Inventory (Charleston: West Virginia Division of Culture and History, 1991).

4. There are a variety of good secondary sources that discuss coal mining, its built environment, and its labor history: Ronald Eller, *Miners, Millhands, and Mountaineers* (Knoxville: University of Tennessee Press, 1982); David Corbin, *Life, Work and Rebellion in the Coal Fields* (Urbana: University of Illinois Press, 1981); and Phil Conley, *History of the West Virginia Coal Industry* (Charleston, W.Va.: Charleston Printing Co., 1960). Two other sources are Mack Gillenwater, *Cultural and Historical Geography of Mining Settlements in the Pocahontas Coal Fields of Southern West Virginia, 1880–1930* (Knoxville: University of Tennessee Press, 1972); and Ken Sullivan, *Coal Men and Coal Towns: Development of the Smokeless Coalfields of Southern West Virginia, 1873–1923* (New York: Garland, 1989).

5. David A. Edwards and John S. Salmon, "Pocahontas Historic District," National Historic Landmark Nomination Form (Richmond: Virginia Department of Historic Resources, 1992), sec. 7.

6. Edwards and Salmon, "Pocahontas Historic District," sec. 8, 52.

7. Edwards and Salmon, "Pocahontas Historic District," sec. 8, 53.

8. Lathrop writes that "we were awakened by a terrific noise which sounded like an explosion. This was followed by three others in rapid succession, and before we could determine in our half dazed condition just what it was, one of the office men called . . . from outside, just below our window: 'oh, Mr. Lathrop, there's been an awful explosion in the mine, one hundred and fifty men and boys, and there's not a living soul in there now'" (Edwards and Salmon, "Pocahontas Historic District," sec. 8, 56).

9. "The Lathrop Memoirs," *The Pocahontas Coalfield: Early Recollections and Happenings* (Marceline, Md.: Walsworth Publishing Co., 1984), 21–45.

10. Beth A. Hager, Bramwell National Register Historic District Nomination (Charleston: West Virginia Division of Culture and History, 1992), sec. 8, 3. See also Beth A. Hager, "Bramwell, West Virginia: The Development of a Coal Operator's Town, 1884–1933" (Master's thesis, University of Delaware, 1984), 93–96.

11. Hager, "Bramwell, West Virginia," 50–51.

12. Hager, "Bramwell, West Virginia," 93–95.

13. Hager, "Bramwell, West Virginia," 98.

14. Special Resource Study, vol. 2: Resource Inventory/Descriptions, Bramwell, West Va. (Denver, Colo.: National Park Service, Denver Service Center, 1992), 153.

15. Beth A. Hager, "Millionaire's Town," *Goldenseal* 8:4 (winter 1982): 43–54.

16. Michael Gioulis, Bramwell Additions Historic District (Boundary Increase), West Virginia Division of Culture and History, Charleston, W.Va., listed August 3, 1995.

17. Gioulis, Bramwell Additions Historic District (Boundary Increase), sec. 8, 9.

18. Stuart McGehee, "Gary: A First-Class Operation," *Goldenseal* 14:3 (fall 1988): 28–32.

19. McGehee, "Gary" 28–32. See also Dobson, Sone and Valente, "Coal Heritage Survey Report," McDowell County overview, n.p.

20. Drawings of the elevations and floor plans for house types are available for review at the Eastern Regional Coal Archives, Craft Memorial Library, Bluefield, West Virginia.

21. Hornick Photographic Collection, Eastern Regional Coal Archives (ERCA), Craft Memorial Library, Bluefield, W.Va.

22. Dobson, Sone, and Valente, "Coal Heritage Survey Report," West Virginia State Historic Inventory Forms, MD744–771 and MD705–743. These forms represent remaining building stock of Elbert and Filbert, two towns from the planned Gary Works.

23. Dobson, Sone, and Valente, survey report, MD805.

24. Hornick Photographic Collection, ERCA.

25. J. Greene, "Strategies for Survival," 40–43.

26. Veena Gupta, Oral History Research Project, ERCA, Bluefield, W.Va. (summer 1992).

27. Hornick Collection, ERCA, Bluefield, W.Va.

28. Gupta, interview with Frances Huffman, 1992.

29. Gupta, interview with Frances Huffman, 1992.

30. Virginia Ladd, *Sodom and Gomorrah of Today; or the History of Keystone, West Virginia* (pamphlet, West Virginia State Archives, Charleston, 1912).

31. Ladd, *Sodom and Gomorrah of Today.*

32. Priscilla Long, *Mother Jones, Woman Organizer* (Boston: South End Press, 1976), 14.

33. Page Putnam Miller, "Mother Jones' Prison," National Historic Landmark Nomination, National Coordinating Committee for the Promotion of History, 1990, sec. 8, 7.

34. Miller, "Mother Jones' Prison," sec. 8, 3.

35. "Woman Saves Artifacts from Mother Jones' Former Jail," *Charleston Gazette,* May 10, 1996, 4D.

36. Gioulis, Bramwell Additions Historic District, sec. 8, 10.

37. Gioulis, Bramwell Additions Historic District, sec. 8, 13.

38. H.R. 4236, *Congressional Record,* October 1, 1996.

CHAPTER 11: "A NIGHT WITH VENUS, A MOON WITH MERCURY"

1. The two principal investigators for the project were Julia G. Costello, of Foothill Resources, Ltd., Mokelumne Hill, Calif.; and Adrian Praetzellis, of California State University, Sonoma; project manager was Susan Goldberg, of Applied Earthworks, Hemet, Calif.

2. The Metropolitan Water District is a regional water agency that imports water from northern California and the Colorado River and delivers it on a wholesale basis to the coastal plain of southern California. Through its twenty-seven-member public agencies, the district provides almost 60 percent of the water used by nearly sixteen million people living in portions of Los Angeles, Orange, Riverside, San Bernardino, San Diego, and Ventura Counties.

3. The research was in compliance with legal mandates set forth in the California Environmental Quality Act. The formal report on the project is in two volumes: *Historical Archaeology at the Headquarters Facility Project Site,* vol. 1: *Data Report* (1998); and vol. 2: *Interpretive Report* (1999). They are to be published by the Metropolitan Water District of Southern California.

4. Joan M. Gero and Margaret W. Conkey, eds., *Engendering Archaeology: Women and Prehistory* (Cambridge: Basil Blackwell, 1991); and Donna J. Seifert, ed., special issue on *Gender in Historical Archaeology, Historical Archaeology* 25:4, Ronald L. Michael, journal ed. (Society for Historical Archaeology, 1991).

5. Kathleen Deagan, "Mestizaje in Colonial St. Augustine" *Ethnohistory* 20:1 (1973): 55–65; Diana diZerega Wall, *The Archaeology of Gender: Separating the Spheres in Urban America* (New York: Plenum Press, 1994); Elizabeth M. Scott, ed., *Those of Little Note: Gender, Race, and Class in Historical Archaeology* (Tucson: University of Arizona Press, 1994); Janet D. Spector, *What This Awl Means: Feminist Archaeology at a Wahpeton Dakota Village* (St. Paul: Minnesota Historical Society Press, 1993).

6. Most of the historical information in this chapter is derived from the summary history of the project area written by historian Judith Marvin which appears in the *Data Report* volume. She obtained rich descriptive information from accounts in the *Los Angeles Daily Star,* while the Great Register, census

reports, city directories, and lease agreements detailed occupants of specific buildings. Problematically, police records did not exist, assessments were rare, and title searches unusually difficult. Of enormous help was *Tarnished Angels: Paradisiacal Turpitude in Los Angeles Revealed,* by W. W. Robinson (Los Angeles: Ward Ritchie Press, 1964), which includes a reproduction of the "Souvenir Sporting Guide" (flier, Los Angeles, 1897).

7. *Los Angeles Times,* March 20, 1887.

8. Jaqueline Baker Barnhart, *The Fair but Frail: Prostitution in San Francisco, 1849–1900* (Reno: University of Nevada Press, 1986), 26–27, 31, 37; Ruth Rosen, *The Lost Sisterhood: Prostitution in America, 1900–1918* (Baltimore: John Hopkins University Press, 1982), 76, 90–97; Howard B. Woolston, *Prostitution in the United States* (1921; rpt., Montclair, N.J.: Patterson Smith, 1969), 104, 132–36 (relies mainly on investigative reports from 1910 to 1916).

9. Barnhart *Fair but Frail,* x, 25–31, 32; Rosen, *Lost Sisterhood,* 78–79, 92, 94; Woolston, *Prostitution in the United States,* 136–37.

10. The leases in 1893 to Blanche Laborde (later Rappet) for the Horseshoe Saloon and the old Keller winery building by Frank and George Shafer and the lease to Sarah Kornfeld for the three cribs at 734, 734 1/2, and 736 Alameda Street (for three years, at seventy-five dollars per month) by George Shafer are recorded in the Books of Lease at the City of Los Angeles (bk. 22, 122–33).

11. *Los Angeles Daily Times,* December 13, 1903.

12. *Los Angeles Daily Times,* February 2, 1904.

13. *Los Angeles Daily Times,* December 14, 1907.

14. Al Rose, *Storyville, New Orleans* (Birmingham: University of Alabama Press, 1974), 75–76, 80.

15. Rose, *Storyville,* 163, 164.

16. John S. Haller and Robin M. Haller, *The Physician and Sexuality in Victorian America* (Urbana: University of Illinois Press, 1974), 257–58.

17. *Physician and Sexuality in Victorian America,* 115.

18. *Physician and Sexuality in Victorian America,* 262.

19. *Physician and Sexuality in Victorian America,* 266.

20. Kay Devner, *Patent Medicine Picture* (Tucson, Ariz.: Russell White, 1968).

21. *Physician and Sexuality in Victorian America,* 302.

22. Details on the ingredients and effects of Shiloh's Consumption Cure and Jamaica Ginger were supplied by bottle analyst Jane Russell, of Sutter Creek, Calif.

23. Advertisement in the *Philadelphia Record-Union,* April 20, 1897.

24. Advertisement in *Good Housekeeping,* May 30, 1885.

25. Richard E. Fike, *The Bottle Book: A Comprehensive Guide to Historic, Embossed Medicine Bottles* (Salt Lake City, Utah: Peregrine Smith Books, 1987), 93.

26. May (Maimie) Pinzer, *The Maimie Papers,* ed. Ruth Rosen (Old Westbury, N.Y.: Radcliffe College, The Feminist Press at CUNY, 1977), 52.

CHAPTER 12: THE POWER OF PLACE PROJECT

1. John Brinckerhoff Jackson, *Discovering the Vernacular Landscape* (New Haven, Conn.: Yale University Press, 1984), xii.

2. These questions are fully explored in Dolores Hayden, *The Power of Place: Urban Landscapes as Public History* (Cambridge, Mass.: MIT Press, 1995). An earlier version of this essay appeared in the *Journal of Urban History* (August 1994).

3. A pioneering work with a multiethnic approach is Carey McWilliams, *Southern California: An Island on the Land* (Salt Lake City, Utah: Peregrine Smith Books, 1983). This is a classic from the 1940s. Other recent overall treatments include Robert Fogelson, *The Fragmented Metropolis: Los Angeles, 1850–1930* (Cambridge, Mass.: Harvard University Press, 1967); Scott Bottles, *Los Angeles and the Automobile: The Making of the Modern City* (Berkeley: University of California Press, 1987); and Mike Davis, *City of Quartz: Excavating the Future in Los Angeles* (New York: Verso, 1990). Examples of ethnic studies include Rudolfo Acuna, *A Community under Siege: A Chronicle of Chicanos East of the Los Angeles River, 1945–1975* (Los Angeles: UCLA Chicano Studies Center, 1980); Richard Griswold del Castillo, *The Los Angeles Barrio, 1850–1890: A Social History* (Berkeley: University of California Press, 1979); Ricardo Romo, *East Los Angeles: History of a Barrio* (Austin: University of Texas Press, 1983); Lonnie G. Bunch III, *Black Angelenos* (Los Angeles: California African-American Museum, 1989); and Noritaka Yagasaki, "Ethnic Cooperativism and Immigrant Agriculture: A Study of Japanese Floriculture and Truck Farming in California" (Ph.D. diss., Department of Geography, University of California, Berkeley, 1982).

4. The brief walking tour is given in Dolores Hayden, Gail Lee Dubrow, and Carolyn Flynn, *Los Angeles: The Power of Place* (Los Angeles: The Power of Place, 1985).

5. State of California, Department of Parks and Recreation, *Five Views: An Ethnic Sites Survey for California* (Sacramento: Department of Parks and Recreation, 1988).

6. Dolores Hayden, "Biddy Mason's Los Angeles, 1856–1891," *California History* 68 (fall 1989): 86-99, carries the full documentation.

7. Laurel Ulrich, *A Midwife's Tale: The Life of Martha Ballard, Based on Her Diary, 1785–1812* (New York: Alfred A. Knopf, 1991).

8. Susan E. King, *HOME/stead* (Los Angeles: Paradise Press, 1987).

9. Hayden, "Biddy Mason"; Dolores Hayden, *The Power of Place: Urban Landscapes as Public History* (Cambridge, Mass.: MIT Press, 1995).

10. Mario Garcia, *Mexican Americans* (New Haven, Conn.: Yale University Press).

11. Celia Alvarez Munoz, *If Walls Could Speak / Si Las Paredes Hablaran* (Arlington, Tex.: Enlightenment Press, 1991).

CHAPTER 13: BEST PRACTICES FOR
SAVING WOMEN'S HERITAGE SITES

1. Two of these case studies were presented as papers for the "Reclaiming Women's History through Historic Preservation" conference, June 17–19, 1994: "Relocation and Rehabilitation of Charlotte Perkins Gilman House," by Marguerite Duncan-Abrams and Elizabeth Neaves; and "Women Saving Women's History: The Alice Paul Stokes Home," by Barbara Irvine. I want to thank the many preservationists associated with these case studies for their assistance in developing this chapter, especially Duncan-Abrams, Neaves, Irvine, and Joan Maynard of the Weeksville Society. I am also very grateful to my brother, Jonathan Goodman, and my husband, Fred Richards, for editorial assistance, and my father, Paul Goodman, for his encouragement.

2. Although the preservation of Weeksville involves both women and men, the case study offers important insights regarding common preservation challenges faced by cultural heritage sites.

3. Dolores Hayden, *The Grand Domestic Revolution: A History of Feminist Design for American Homes, Neighborhoods, and Cities* (Cambridge, Mass.: MIT Press, 1981), 183. Committed to improving domestic architecture and women's economic roles in the home, Gilman argues for central kitchens, dining rooms, and day care centers to free women from isolating household tasks.

4. Charlotte Perkins Gilman, *The Living of Charlotte Perkins Gilman* (1935; rpt., Salem, N.H.: Ayer Co., 1987), 107.

5. Polly Wynn Allen, *Building Domestic Liberty: Charlotte Perkins Gilman's Architectural Feminism* (Amherst: University of Massachusetts Press, 1988), 177.

6. Gilman, *Living of Charlotte Perkins Gilman*, 334.

7. The Pasadena Cultural Heritage Commission could only delay the demolition of a cultural landmark; they could not prevent it.

8. Susan Mossman, telephone interview with Jennifer Goodman, April 24, 1998.

9. Joan Huff, "Women and Politics," in *Reclaiming the Past: Landmarks of*

Women's History, ed. Page Putnam Miller (Bloomington: Indiana University Press, 1992), 161–63.

10. National Register nomination, Alice Paul Home, prepared by Gail Greenberg, Alice Paul Centennial Foundation, 1988.

11. Barbara Irvine, "Women Saving Women's History: The Alice Paul Stokes Home" paper presented at "Reclaiming Women's History through Historic Preservation," Bryn Mawr, Pa., June 1994, 1.

12. Barbara Irvine, telephone interview by Jennifer Goodman, February 18, 1998.

13. Joan Maynard, telephone interview by Jennifer Goodman, April 24, 1998.

14. Maynard, telephone interview, April 24, 1998.

15. Many publications offer suggestions regarding environmental and preservation advocacy: "Rescuing Historic Resources: How to Respond to a Preservation Emergency," *National Trust for Historic Preservation Information Series,* no. 51 (1991); Peggy Cohen, "Saving the Neighborhood," *National Trust for Historic Preservation Information Series,* no. 65 (1992); and Maritza Pick, *How to Save Your Neighborhood, City, or Town* (San Francisco: Sierra Club Books, 1993).

16. For survey information, see "Basic Preservation Procedures," *National Trust for Historic Preservation Information Series,* no. 48 (1991); *National Register Bulletin no. 24: Guidelines for Local Surveys,* by Patricia L. Parker, rev. ed. (Washington, D.C.: USGPO, 1985).

17. See Sondra C. Shaw and Martha A. Taylor, *Reinventing Fundraising: Realizing the Potential of Women's Philanthropy* (San Francisco: Jossey-Bass, 1995), 6, 11, 12–16, 41–42, and 98.

18. Lucienne Beard, telephone interview by Jennifer Goodman, June 24, 1998.

CHAPTER 14: "IT'S A WIDE COMMUNITY INDEED"

This chapter is dedicated to the women and men of the Elizabeth Cady Stanton Foundation and the National Park Service and to those individuals and organizations across the country whose support helped bring Women's Rights National Historical Park into existence. This chapter is also dedicated to the creators and keepers of the records, including the *Seneca Falls Reveille* (esp. Howard Van Kirk, editor, and Pam Quiggle, photographer), the *Auburn Citizen* (esp. to Martin Toombs, reporter), and the *Rochester Democrat and Chronicle* (esp. Carol Ritter, reporter), who covered the original stories so well. Very special thanks to Mary Curry, whose work as archivist to the Eliza-

NOTES TO PAGES 230-237

beth Cady Stanton Foundation generated files of clippings, newsletters, and minutes, without which I could not have written this chapter. Thanks also to Vivien Rose for suggesting this topic and for being such a persistent and successful midwife to so many women's history projects.

All sources except published books and articles are from the Elizabeth Cady Stanton Foundation (ECSF) Papers, located in Special Collections, Penfield Library, State University of New York at Oswego. Special thanks to Elisabeth Dunbar, Nancy Osborne, and Edward Vermue, whose archival work made this collection available to the public, and to Terry Bales for her research assistance.

1. For a survey of women in the United States as preservationists, see Gail Lee Dubrow, "Restoring a Female Presence: New Goals in Historic Preservation," in *Architecture: A Place for Women,* ed. Ellen Perry Berkely (Washington, D.C.: Smithsonian Institution Press, 1989), 159–70; and Barbara J. Howe, "Women and Architecture," in *Reclaiming the Past: Landmarks of Women's History,* ed. Page Putnam Miller (Bloomington: Indiana University Press, 1992), 27–62. For general considerations relating to the interpretation of women at historic sites, see Heather A. Hyuck, "Beyond John Wayne: Using Historic Sites to Interpret Women's History," in *Western Women: Their Land, Their Lives,* ed. Lillian Schlissel, Vicki L. Ruiz, and Janice Monk (Albuquerque: University of New Mexico Press, 1988), 303–30.

2. David Lowenthal, *Possessed by the Past: The Heritage Crusade and the Spoils of History* (New York: Free Press, 1996).

3. Mrs. George W. Campbell to Mrs. S. E. Johnson Hudson, September 1897, quoted in Charles B. Hosmer Jr., *Presence of the Past: A History of the Preservation Movement in the United States before Williamsburg* (New York: G. P. Putnam's Son, 1965), 45.

4. Elizabeth Cady Stanton to Mary Morris Hamilton, "The Purchase of Mount Vernon," *National Anti-Slavery Standard,* September 4, 1858.

5. Hosmer, *Presence of the Past,* 57; Murtagh, *Keeping Time* (New York: Sterling Publishing Co., 1990), 30.

6. *The Spirit of Houston: The First National Women's Conference* (Washington, D.C: National Commission on the Observance of International Women's Year, 1978), 177, 193–203.

7. Lucille Povero, *ECSF Newsletter,* December 14, 1978.

8. Judy Hart, quoted in Philip Burnham, *How the Other Half Lived: A People's Guide to American Historic Sites* (Boston: Faber and Faber, 1995), 149.

9. Honorary trustees included Lois Banner and Elisabeth Griffith, both biographers of Stanton; philosopher and anthropologist Ashley Montagu; Betty

Bone-Schiess, the first woman to be ordained in the Episcopal Church; artist Judy Chicago; author Adrienne Rich; Karen DeCrow, lawyer and former national president of the National Organization for Women; Nancy Dubner, historic preservationist; Frances Farenthold, president of Wells College; Congresswoman Shirley Chisholm; Lynda Johnson Robb, then chair of the President's Advisory Committee for Women; author and organizer Betty Friedan; actor Alan Alda; Sey Chessler, editor of *Redbook;* Gloria Steinem, editor of *Ms.;* Rhoda B. Jenkins, Stanton's great-granddaughter; and Ralph Peters and his ex-wife, Marjorie Smith (Minutes, ECSF, September 19, 1979; letters from each of these in ECSF Papers, February 11 to November 20, 1979; *ECSF Newsletter* 1:1 [January 1980]; and 1:2 [March 1980]).

10. *ECSF Newsletter* 1:1 (January 1980), ECSF Papers; Pat Holland and Ann Gordon, eds., *Papers of Elizabeth Cady Stanton and Susan B. Anthony* (Wilmington, Del.: Scholarly Resources, 1989); Lois Banner, *Elizabeth Cady Stanton: A Radical for Woman's Rights* (Boston: Little, Brown, 1980); Elisabeth Griffith, *In Her Own Right: The Life of Elizabeth Cady Stanton* (New York: Oxford University Press, 1984); Margaret Hope Bacon, *Valiant Friend: The Life of Lucretia Mott* (New York: Walker and Co., 1980); Judith Wellman, "The Seneca Falls Women's Rights Convention: A Study of Social Networks," *Journal of Women's History* 3:1 (spring 1991).

11. *ECSF Newsletter* 7:7 (January 1980).

12. Minutes, ECSF, December 19, 1979; and February 20, 1980.

13. *ECSF Newsletter* 1:3 (July 1980).

14. *ECSF Newsletter* 1:2 (March 1980); 1:3 (July 1980); and 1:4 (October 1980).

15. Quoted in *ECSF Newsletter* 2:1 (January–February 1981).

16. Quoted in *ECSF Newsletter* 2:1 (January–February 1981); *Seneca Falls Reveille,* July 14, 1982, 2.

17. *ECSF Newsletter* 2:1 (January–February 1981).

18. *ECSF Newsletter* 2:2 (May–June 1981).

19. *ECSF Newsletter* 2:2 (May–June 1981); "Certification," Corinne Guntzel, treasurer, ECSF, May 14, 1979, enclosed in (Judy Hart), park coordinator to chief, Land Acquisition, North Atlantic Region (NAR), December 23, 1981.

20. August P. Sinicropi to members of the Seneca Falls Historic District Commission and the Urban Cultural Park Advisory Council, April 16, 1981; (Judy Hart), park coordinator to chief, Land Acquisition, NAR, December 23, 1981.

21. "Seneca Falls Consortium Formed to Promote Women's History," *New York State Network* 3:2 (fall 1981): 7; *ECSF Newsletter* 2:3 (September–October

1981); and 3:1 (winter 1982); program, "Upstate: Dialogues on the Cultural Background," Regional Conference of Historical Agencies (RCHA), July [1981].

22. *ECSF Newsletter* 2:3 (September–October 1981).

23. *ECSF Newsletter* 2:3 (September–October 1981); Carol Ritter, "Owner of the Stanton house won't sell," clipping from *Rochester Democrat and Chronicle,* n.d.

24. Ralph Peters and Marjorie Smith to Steven H. Lewis, deputy regional director, National Park Service, September 28, 1981; Chessler to Ralph Peters, October 1, 1981.

25. Paul Cotter, acting chief, Land Acquisition Division, NAR, "Trip Report," January 27 1981; Steven H. Lewis, acting regional director, National Park Service, to Ralph Peters and Marjorie Smith, October 30, 1981; Emil J. Bove to Ralph Peters, November 10, 1981.

26. Bove to Cables, October 26, 1981; Cables to Bove, December 22, 1981; purchase offer enclosed in letter from Bove to Cables, December 18, 1981; (Judy Hart), park coordinator to chief, Land Acquisition, NAR, December 23, 1981.

27. *ECSF Newsletter* 3:1 (winter 1982).

28. *ECSF Newsletter* 3:2 (summer 1982).

29. *Seneca Falls Reveille,* "Souvenir Section: Convention Days '82," July 14, 1982; *ECSF Newsletter* 3:3 (fall 1982). The play was written by Betsy Shultis and directed by Ann Kieffer.

30. The list of historians who participated read like a "who's who" in women's history, beginning with an opening address by Gerda Lerner and continuing with presentations by such people as Carol Berkin, Joan Jacobs Brumberg, William Chafe, Ellen DuBois, Sara Evans, Elizabeth Fox Genovese, Nancy Hewitt, Joan Hoff, Julie Roy Jeffrey, Kathryn Kish Sklar, Suzanne Lebsock, Edith Mayo, Mary Beth Norton, Nancy Grey Osterud, Dwight Pitcaithley, Anita Rapone, Carroll Smith, and Judith Wellman (program, "Daughters of Clio and Daughters of Eve: Seneca Falls, N.Y.—The Second Seneca Falls Women's History Conference," *Women and Community,* July 15–17, 1982).

31. "Editorial," *Seneca Falls Reveille,* July 14, 1982.

CHAPTER 15: "RAISING OUR SITES"

1. Barbara Melosh, "Speaking of Women: Museums' Representations of Women's History," in *History Museums in the United States: A Critical Assessment,* ed. Warren Leon and Roy Rosenzweig (Urbana: University of Illinois Press, 1989).

CHAPTER 16: FINDING HER PLACE

1. LeeAnn Whites, "Rebecca Latimer Felton and the Wife's Farm: The Class and Racial Politics of Gender Reform," *Georgia Historical Quarterly* 76 (summer 1992): 359. One of many versions of the Tybee Island, Ga., speech, Rebecca Latimer Felton, newspaper clipping, n.d., scrapbook, Rebecca Latimer Felton Papers, Special Collections, University of Georgia Libraries. Felton was influential in farmer politics in Georgia and was dedicated to improving the lives of women.

2. The following information on the Georgia Women's History Initiative draws upon the work of Catherine Lewis and Beth Gibson as well as my own work. In 1999 Leslie Sharp was invited to testify before the President's Commission on the Celebration of Women in American History. The commission's recommendations highlighted the Georgia Women's History Initiative as a model project.

3. National Register of Historic Places statistics for Georgia were obtained from the National Park Service's National Register of Historic Places Database and by interviewing Georgia's National Register staff. The statistics for the Georgia Historical Marker Program were obtained by looking at the text of each marker in Carroll P. Scruggs, *Georgia Historical Markers* (1973; rpt., npp., 1984), and by interviewing Billy Townsend, historian and former head of the marker program within the Parks and Historic Sites Division of the Georgia Department of Natural Resources. As of February 1997, the Georgia Historical Marker was no longer part of the Georgia Department of Natural Resources. In 1998 the Georgia Historical Society reactivated a revised Georgia Historical Marker Program.

4. The word *significance* in this chapter is defined as the National Park Service defines it, as the "importance of a property to the history, architecture, archaeology, engineering, or culture of a community, state, or nation" (*National Register Bulletin 15: How to Apply the National Register Criteria for Evaluation*, U.S. Department of Interior, National Park Service [Washington, D.C.: U.S. Government Printing Office, 1991]).

5. Carol D. Shull, "Women's History in the National Register and the National Historic Landmarks Survey," *CRM: Cultural Resources Management* 20:3 (1997): 12.

6. Carroll Van West, "Assessing Significance and Integrity in the National Register Process: Questions of Race, Class, and Gender," paper presented at the conference "Preservation of What, for Whom: A Critical Look at Historical Significance," Goucher College, Baltimore, Md., March 20–22, 1997.

7. Gerda Lerner, *The Majority Finds Its Past: Placing Women in History* (New York: Oxford University Press, 1979), 145–60.

8. Page Putnam Miller, ed., *Reclaiming the Past: Landmarks of Women's History* (Indianapolis: Indiana University Press, 1992), 13.

9. Darlene R. Roth-White, "Atlanta Is a Female Noun: Evidence of City-Building among Women," paper prepared for the meeting of the American Historical Association, December 1975. Roth has continued to write on collective female efforts and organizations which have shaped the built environment with her most recent work, *Matronage: Patterns in Women's Organizations, Atlanta, Georgia, 1890–1940* (New York: Carlson Publishing, 1994).

10. Gretchen E. Maclachlan, "Atlanta's Women Workers and Industrial Districts and Sites," paper presented at the conference "Telling Her Story: Expanding the Past of Georgia's Women through Historic Places," Decatur, Ga., March 1996.

11. The final report from the conference is on file at the Historic Preservation Division of the Georgia Department of Natural Resources, Atlanta, Ga.

12. The consulting team is made up of Darlene Roth, Ray and Associates (Bamby Ray, Lynn Speno, and Ced Dolder), Gail Lee Dubrow, Sarah Boykin, and Beth Gibson.

13. Carole Merritt, *Historic Black Resources: A Handbook for the Identification, Documentation, and Evaluation of Historic African-American Properties in Georgia* (Atlanta: Historic Preservation Section, Department of Natural Resources, 1984).

14. Section 106 is a federal planning process that takes into consideration historic resources in undertaking federally funded and licensed projects. The process involves participation from state agencies and the public.

15. Miller, *Reclaiming the Past,* 23.

16. Heather A. Huyck, "Placing Women in the Past," *CRM: Cultural Resources Management* 20:3 (1997): 6.

CHAPTER 17: BLAZING TRAILS WITH PINK TRIANGLES
AND RAINBOW FLAGS

This chapter draws on a brief discussion of preserving gay and lesbian history contained in Gail Dubrow, "Feminist and Multicultural Perspectives on Preservation Planning," in *Making the Invisible Visible: A Multicultural Planning History,* ed. Leonie Sandercock (Berkeley: University of California Press, 1988), 55–77. An earlier version of this work was published in *Historic Preservation Forum* 12:3 (spring 1998): 31–44. References to properties owned by the National Trust were censored in that version. The author wishes to express gratitude for Coll-Peter Thrush's able research assistance.

1. See Antoinette Lee's writings on the subject of preserving cultural diversity, including: "Discovering Old Cultures in the New World: The Role of Ethnicity," in *The American Mosaic*, ed. Robert E. Stipe and Antoinette Lee (Washington, D.C.: US/ICOMOS, 1987); "Cultural Diversity and Historic Preservation," *CRM: Cultural Resources Management* 15:7 (1992); "Multicultural Building Blocks," in *Past Meets Future: Saving America's Historic Environments*, ed. Antoinette Lee (Washington, D.C.: Preservation Press, 1992); and, with Elizabeth Lyon, "Cultural and Ethnic Diversity in Historic Preservation," *National Trust for Historic Preservation Information Series*, no. 65 (1992). Also see Dolores Hayden, *The Power of Place: Urban Landscapes as Public History* (Cambridge, Mass.: MIT Press, 1995).

2. Two recent publications on the culture wars are recommended reading for those preservationists who intend to take on the controversial issue of addressing gay and lesbian history in public venues: Martin Harwit, *An Exhibit Denied* (New York: Copernicus, 1996); and *History Wars: The* Enola Gay *and Other Battles for the American Past,* ed. Edward T. Linenthal and Tom Engelhardt (New York: Metropolitan Books, 1996).

3. For Gary Larson's collected cartoons, see *The Far Side* and *The Far Side Gallery* (Kansas City, Mo.: Andrews and McMeel, 1982–).

4. Paula Martinac, *The Queerest Places: A National Guide to Gay and Lesbian Historic Sites* (New York: Henry Holt, 1997), xi.

5. Recent works on the history of gays and lesbians in the United States include Lillian Faderman, *Odd Girls and Twilight Lovers: A History of Lesbian Life in Twentieth-Century America* (New York: Columbia University Press, 1991); Eric Marcus, *Making History: The Struggle for Gay and Lesbian Equal Rights, 1945–1990: An Oral History* (New York: HarperCollins, 1992); James T. Sears, *Lonely Hunters: An Oral History of Lesbian and Gay Southern Life, 1948–1968* (Boulder, Colo.: Westview Press, 1997); Charles Kaiser, *The Gay Metropolis, 1940–1996* (Boston: Houghton Mifflin, 1997); and Neil Miller, *Out of the Past: Gay and Lesbian History from 1869 to the Present* (New York: Vintage, 1995); among others.

6. George Chauncey, *Gay New York: Gender, Urban Culture, and the Making of the Gay Male World, 1890–1940* (New York: Basic Books, 1994). This history will be brought up to date in his forthcoming work, *The Making of a Modern Gay World, 1935–1975* (New York: Basic Books).

7. Esther Newton, *Cherry Grove, Fire Island: Sixty Years in America's First Gay and Lesbian Town* (Boston: Beacon Press, 1993).

8. Elizabeth Lapovsky Kennedy and Madeline D. Davis, *Boots of Leather, Slippers of Gold: The History of a Lesbian Community* (New York: Routledge, 1993).

9. John D'Emilio, *Sexual Politics, Sexual Communities: The Making of a Homosexual Minority in the United States, 1940–1970* (Chicago: University of Chicago Press, 1983).

10. Alan Berube, "The History of Gay Bathhouses," in *Policing Public Sex: Queer Politics and the Future of AIDS Activism,* ed. Dangerous Bedfellows (Boston: South End Press, 1996).

11. Examples of work focusing on the architectural and spatial dimensions of gay lives include Manuel Castells, *The City and the Grassroots* (Berkeley: University of California Press, 1983); *Queers in Space: Communities, Public Places, Sites of Resistance,* ed. Gordon Brent Ingram, Anne-Marie Bouthillette, and Yolanda Retter (Seattle: Bay Press, 1997); *The Margins of the City: Gay Men's Urban Lives,* ed. Stephen Whittle (Aldershot, Hants, U.K.: Arena; Brookfield, Vt.: Ashgate, 1994); *Mapping Desire: Geographies of Sexualities,* ed. David Bell and Gill Valentine (London: Routledge, 1995); Manuel Castells and Karen Murphy, "Cultural Identity and Urban Structure: The Spatial Organization of San Francisco's Gay Community," in *Urban Policy under Capitalism,* ed. Norman I. and Susan S. Fainstein (Beverly Hills, Calif.: Sage Publications, 1982), 237–59; Elizabeth A. Grosz, *Space, Time, and Perversion: Essays on the Politics of Bodies* (New York: Routledge, 1995); Aaron Betsky, *Queer Space: Architecture and Same-Sex Desire* (New York: William Morrow and Co., 1997); and Moira Rachel Kenney, "Remember, Stonewall Was a Riot: Understanding Gay and Lesbian Experience in the City," in *Making the Invisible Visible,* 120–32.

12. See Ken M. Lustbader, *Landscape of Liberation: Preserving Gay and Lesbian History in Greenwich Village* (Master's thesis, Historic Preservation Program, Columbia University, 1993). Master's theses and doctoral dissertations in planning also address these issues; see Moira Rachel Kenney, "Strategic Invisibility: Gay and Lesbian Place-Claiming in Los Angeles, 1970–1994" (Ph.D. diss., Urban Planning Program, University of California Los Angeles, 1994); Eric Reyes, "Queer Spaces: The Spaces of Lesbians and Gay Men of Color in Los Angeles" (Master's thesis, Graduate School of Architecture and Urban Planning, University of California, Los Angeles, 1993); and a work in progress on preserving Seattle's gay and lesbian heritage by Angela McCarrel (Master's thesis, Department of Urban Design and Planning, University of Washington, forthcoming).

13. Susan Stryker and Jim Van Buskirk, *Gay by the Bay: A History of Queer Culture in the San Francisco Bay Area* (San Francisco: Chronicle Books, 1996).

14. The History Project, *Improper Bostonians: Lesbian and Gay History from the Puritans to Playland* (Boston: Beacon Press, 1998), 190.

15. Lisa Duggan, "History's Gay Ghetto: The Contradictions of Growth in Lesbian and Gay History," in *Presenting the Past: Essays on History and the Public,* ed. Susan Porter Benson, Stephen Brier, and Roy Rosenzweig (Philadelphia: Temple University Press, 1986). Garry Wotherspoon raises the issue of interpreting gay and lesbian history in public places in "From Private Vice to Public History: Homosexuality in Australia," *Public History Review* 1 (1992): 148–59.

16. New York: *A Guide to Lesbian and Gay Historical Landmarks* (New York: Organization of Lesbian and Gay Architects and Designers, 1994 [P.O. Box 927, Old Chelsea Station, New York, NY 10113]); Seattle: *Changing Space: A Historical Map of Lesbian and Gay Seattle* (Seattle: Northwest Lesbian and Gay History Museum Project, June 1996); *Gay and Lesbian L.A. History Map* (Los Angeles: Center for Preservation Education and Planning, 2000); Boston: Gay and Lesbian Architects and Designers; and Boston Area Gay and Lesbian History Project (1995). The most recent compilation is *Creating a Place for Ourselves: Lesbian, Gay, and Bisexual Community Histories,* ed. Brett Beemyn (New York: Routledge, 1997). Also see Simon LeVay and Elisabeth Nonas, *City of Friends: A Portrait of the Gay and Lesbian Community in America* (Cambridge, Mass.: MIT Press, 1995); and Kevin Murphy, "Walking the Queer City," *Radical History Review* 62 (spring 1995): 195–201.

17. Pink Masonite triangles served as temporary historical markers at nine sites that the artists' collective RepoHistory designated as significant in New York City's gay and lesbian history. "Queer Spaces: Places of Struggle, Places of Strength" was commissioned by the Storefront for Art and Architecture, June 18–July 30, 1994.

18. Dennis Drabelle, "Out and About in the City," *Preservation* 49:1 (January–February 1997): 74, 76–78.

19. Two regional meetings were convened by the Western Regional Office of the National Trust for Historic Preservation. The first, "Learning within the Castro," was held in San Francisco on March 15, 1997. A follow-up meeting was held in Seattle on August 10, 1997. These meetings forged connections among gay and lesbian preservationists and galvanized plans for the educational session, "Hidden History: Identifying and Interpreting Gay and Lesbian Places," at the October 18, 1997, meeting of the National Trust for Historic Preservation in Santa Fe, N.M.

20. For an overview of the Christian right's antigay rhetoric, see D. Herman, "(Il)legitimate Minorities: The American Christian Right's Anti-Gay Discourse," *Law and Society* 23:3 (September 1996): 346–63.

21. For a list of important gay figures in history, see Paul Elliott Russell, *The Gay One-Hundred: A Ranking of the Most Influential Gay Men and Lesbians,*

Past and Present (New York: Carol Publishing Group, Citadel Press Book, 1995). The study of gay and lesbian writers is relevant because so many historic houses are associated with major literary figures. For an overview of the subject, see *Professions of Desire: Lesbian and Gay Studies in Literature,* ed. George E. Haggerty and Bonnie Zimmerman (New York: Modern Language Association of America, 1995); *The Gay and Lesbian Literary Heritage: A Readers Companion to the Writers and Their Works, from Antiquity to the Present,* ed. Claude J. Summers (New York: Henry Holt, 1995); and Eve Sedgewick, *Tendencies* (Durham, N.C.: Duke University Press, 1993).

22. Mary Jane Lowe, "Outing the National Register," first was presented in a session on "Lavender Landmarks" at the Second National Conference on Women and Historic Preservation, sponsored by Arizona State University and the National Park Service.

23. A discussion of the homoerotics of Whitman's poetry and his sexual orientation is pervasive in recent literary criticism and biography. For example, see Gary Schmidgall, *Walt Whitman: A Gay Life* (New York: NAL/Dutton, 1997); *Breaking Bounds: Whitman and American Cultural Studies,* ed. Betsy Erkkila and Jay Grossman (New York: Oxford University Press, 1996); David Reynolds, *Walt Whitman: A Cultural Biography* (New York: Alfred A. Knopf, 1995); Byrne R. S. Fone, *Masculine Landscapes: Walt Whitman and the Homoerotic Text* (Carbondale: Southern Illinois University Press, 1992).

24. Martinac, *Queerest Places,* 124–25. On Austen, see Ann Novotny, *Alice's World: The Life and Photography of an American Original: Alice Austen, 1866–1952* (Old Greenwich, Conn.: Chatham Press, 1976); and Oliver Jensen, "The High Summer of Alice Austen: Rediscovering the Pioneer Photographer and Her House on Staten Island," *House and Garden* 159:8 (August 1987): 94–99.

25. For biographies that explicitly address Cather's sexual identity, see Hermione Lee, *Willa Cather: Double Lives* (New York: Pantheon, 1989); Sharon O'Brien, *Willa Cather* (New York: Chelsea House, 1995); and Sharon O'Brian, *Willa Cather: The Emerging Voice, 1873–1912* (New York: Oxford University Press, 1987).

26. Diana Souhami, *Gertrude and Alice* (New York: Pandora Press, 1991), 52–55, esp. 54.

27. Also see Linda Wagner-Martin, *"Favored Strangers": Gertrude Stein and Her Family* (New Brunswick, N.J.: Rutgers University Press, 1995), esp. 28–55.

28. Martinac, *Queerest Places,* 65–67. On Billie Holiday, see Donald Clark, *Wishing on the Moon: The Life and Times of Billie Holiday* (New York: Viking, 1994); and Stuart Nicholson, *Billie Holiday* (Boston: Northeastern University Press, 1995).

29. See Frances Willard's own comments about companionship in her autobiography, *Glimpses of Fifty Years* (Chicago: Woman's Christian Temperance Union, 1889); and recent biographies such as Ruth Bordin, *Frances Willard: A Biography* (Chapel Hill: University of North Carolina, 1986).

30. The first scholarly work to address Eleanor Roosevelt's relationship with Lorena Hickok fully was Blanche Wiesen Cook, *Eleanor Roosevelt* (New York: Viking, 1992). Cook's view was bolstered by the recent publication of correspondence, *Empty without You: The Intimate Letters of Eleanor Roosevelt and Lorena Hickok,* ed. Rodger Streitmatter (New York: Simon and Schuster, 1998). Nevertheless, this view remains controversial.

31. For an excellent discussion of the presentation of gay topics and the experience of gay students in the schools, see Debra Chasnoff and Helen Cohen's film *It's Elementary* (San Francisco: Women's Educational Media, 1996); and Jeff Dupre's film *Out of the Past* (New York: Zeitgeist Distributors, 1998).

32. Here I am thinking of the many individuals who managed same-sex relationships during their lives with an extraordinary degree of candor and discretion, then destroyed their personal papers or directed their families to do so upon their death to avoid exposure. But it also brings to mind flamboyantly gay figures who adamantly remained closeted, such as Liberace. On the broader subject of "outing," see Larry P. Gross, *Contested Closets: The Politics and Ethics of Outing* (Minneapolis: University of Minnesota Press, 1993).

33. Martinac, *Queerest Places,* 296–97.

34. Jeffrey Hogrefe, *O'Keeffe: The Life of an American Legend* (New York: Bantam Books, 1992), 26–27.

35. Benita Eisler, *O'Keeffe and Stieglitz: An American Romance* (New York: Doubleday, 1991), 482.

36. Kaiser, *Gay Metropolis,* 213.

37. For his interpretation of Johnson's oeuvre, see Aaron Betsky, "Owner of the Avant-Garde: A Review of Philip Johnson: Life and Work," *Blueprint* (February 1995): 46–47; and Betsky, *Queer Space,* esp. 114–17.

38. Martin Filler, "The Architect of a Master Builder's Store of Art," *New York Times,* June 2, 1996, sec. 2, 37, 40.

39. Filler, "Architect," 37, 40.

40. Many historical works on the pre-Stonewall period already have been noted. Others include *Growing Up before Stonewall: Life Stories of Some Gay Men,* ed. Peter Nardi, David Sanders, and Judd Marmor (London: Routledge, 1994); *Wolf Girls at Vassar: Lesbian and Gay Experiences, 1930–1990,* comp. and ed. Anne McKay (New York: St. Martin's Press, 1993); Andrea Weiss and Greta Schiller, *Before Stonewall: The Making of a Gay and Lesbian Commu-*

nity (Tallahassee, Fla.: Naiad Press, 1988); *Last Call at Maud's* (video recording about a San Francisco lesbian bar), by the Maud Project (New York: Water Bearer Films, 1993); *Forbidden Love: The Unashamed Stories of Lesbian Lives* (video recording of a National Film Board of Canada Studio D Production about Canadian lesbians' experience in the bars of the 1950s and 1960s) (New York: Women Make Movies, 1992); Katie Gilmartin, "'We Weren't Bar People': Middle-Class Lesbian Identities and Cultural Spaces," *GLQ* 3:1 (1996): 1–51; and Thomas Noel, "Gay Bars and the Emergence of the Denver Homosexual Community," *Social Science Journal* 15 (April 1978): 59–74.

41. *National Register Bulletin 16A,* "How to Complete a National Register Form," neatly summarizes the qualifications for listing properties on the National Register.

42. Don Paulson has documented one aspect of Seattle's gay history and associated bar scene in *An Evening at the Garden of Allah* (New York: Columbia University Press, 1996).

43. Martinac, *Queerest Places,* 104. For a detailed history of gay bathhouses in New York City, including the surviving Mt. Morris Baths, see Chauncey, *Gay New York,* 207–25, esp. 218. Also see Randy Shilts, "Big Business: Gay Bars and Bathhouses," *Advocate,* June 2, 1976, 37–38; and "The Dressed Up Look of the Club Baths, New York," *Advocate,* June 2, 1976, 39.

44. Martinac, *Queerest Places,* 41–42, 60–61, 94–95, 226, and 309. The role of YMCAs in orienting newcomers to the gay urban scene is described in great detail in Chauncey, *Gay New York,* 151–77.

45. Martinac, *Queerest Places,* 93–94. For greater detail, see Chauncey, *Gay New York,* 227–67 and 271–99. Other works that deal with camp sensibility include Andrew Ross, "Uses of Camp," in *No Respect: Intellectuals and Popular Culture,* ed. Andrew Ross (New York: Routledge, 1989), 135–70; *Camp Grounds: Style and Homosexuality,* ed. David Bergman (Amherst: University of Massachusetts Press, 1993); and *The Politics and Poetics of Camp,* ed. Moe Meyer (London: Routledge, 1994).

46. Martinac, *Queerest Places,* 53–54. Also see Chauncey, *Gay New York,* 179–205. For a pioneering study of the public sites of gay male sexual encounters, see Laud Humphreys, *Tearoom Trade: Impersonal Sex in Public Places* (Chicago: Aldine, 1975).

47. Newton, *Cherry Grove, Fire Island.*

48. Perhaps the best history of male and female homophile organizations is contained in D'Emilio, *Sexual Politics, Sexual Communities.* On the founding of the Daughters of Bilitis, also see Del Martin and Phyllis Lyon, *Lesbian/Woman* (San Francisco: Glide Publications, 1972; also available in a twentieth-anniversary edition from Volcano, Calif.: Volcano Press, 1991). For oral histo-

ries that provide different views of the founding of the Mattachine Society and Daughters of Bilitis, see Marcus, *Making History.*

49. On Hay's historical significance, see D'Emilio, *Sexual Politics, Sexual Communities,* esp. 58–70. Also see Stuart Timmons, *The Trouble with Harry Hay: Founder of the Modern Gay Movement* (Boston: Alyson, 1990); Harry Hay, *Radically Gay: Gay Liberation in the Words of Its Founder,* ed. Will Roscoe (Boston: Beacon Press, 1996); and an interview with Hay in Jonathan Katz, *Gay American History: Lesbians and Gay Men in the U.S.A.: A Documentary History* (New York: Crowell, 1976), 406–20.

50. Jeff Samudio and Howard Smith to Gail Lee Dubrow, personal correspondence, October 3, 1997.

51. Office of Historic Preservation, Department of Parks and Recreation, Resources Agency, *Forging a Future with a Past: A Comprehensive Statewide Historic Preservation Plan for California,* report, December 1997. Thanks to Jeff Samudio for pointing this out.

52. On the historical significance of the Stonewall riot, see Martin B. Duberman, *Stonewall* (New York: Dutton, 1993). On Stonewall's aftermath, see Leigh W. Rutledge, *The Gay Decades: From Stonewall to the Present—The People and Events That Shaped Gay Lives* (New York: Plume, 1992).

53. Martinac, *Queerest Places,* 120.

54. For a report of the pathbreaking landmark designation of Stonewall Inn, see David W. Dunlap, "Stonewall, Gay Bar That Made History, Is Made a Landmark," *New York Times,* June 26, 1999, late ed. (East Coast), 1. Christopher Thomson also provided an insider's account of the NRHP and NHL designation process in an oral presentation at the Third National Conference on Women and Historic Preservation, Washington, D.C., May 20, 2000.

55. Harvey Milk's contributions to the rise of gay political power in San Francisco have been chronicled by Randy Shilts, *The Mayor of Castro Street: The Life and Times of Harvey Milk* (New York: St. Martin's Press, 1982); and an Academy Award–winning film released on video, *The Times of Harvey Milk* (Beverly Hills, Calif.: Pacific Arts Video, 1986).

56. The pathbreaking film *Word Is Out* contains a moving account of the institutionalization of homosexuals in the 1950s and 1960s, before the American Psychological Association's 1973 decision to remove homosexuality from its list of mental disorders. See the book based on that film, Nancy and Casey Adair, *Word Is Out: Stories of Some of Our Lives* (San Francisco: New Glide Publications, 1978).

57. The history of gays in the military is well documented in Alan Berube, *Coming Out under Fire: The History of Gay Men and Women in World War Two* (New York: Free Press, 1990); and in a related film of the same name by

Arthur E. Dong, Salome Jens, and Alan Berube (Zeitgeist Films; a Deepfocus Production, 1995). On the oppression of homosexuals in the 1950s, see Alan Berube and John D'Emilio, "The Military and Lesbians during the McCarthy Years," in *The Lesbian Issue: Essays from SIGNS* (Chicago: University of Chicago Press, 1985), 279–95; Nicholas von Hoffman, *Citizen Cohn: The Life and Times of Roy Cohn* (New York: Doubleday, 1988); and Faderman, *Odd Girls and Twilight Lovers*, 118–87.

58. For her early volley in the emerging culture wars, see Anita Bryant, *The Anita Bryant Story: The Survival of Our Nation's Families and the Threat of Militant Homosexuality* (Old Tappan, N.J.: Revell, 1977).

59. Jonathan Katz, The *Invention of Heterosexuality* (New York: Dutton, 1995).

60. Lest we stereotype gays as liberals, a number of publications offer a helpful reminder that gay people can be found at every point in the political spectrum. For example, see Marvin Liebman, *Coming Out Conservative* (San Francisco: Chronicle Books, 1992); and Steve Gunderson and Rob Morris, with Bruce Bawer, *House and Home* (New York: Dutton, 1996).

61. The consumer behavior of gays and lesbians has been the subject of several works, including *Gays, Lesbians, and Consumer Behavior: Theory, Practice, and Research Issues in Marketing,* ed. Daniel L. Wardlow (New York: Harrington Park Press, 1996); and Grant Lukenbill, *Untold Millions: Positioning Your Business for the Gay and Lesbian Consumer Revolution* (New York: HarperCollins, 1995). For a more critical study, see *Homo Economics: Capitalism, Community, and Lesbian and Gay Life,* ed. Amy Gluckman and Betsy Reed (New York: Routledge, 1997). On the broader influences of gay culture in straight America, see David Van Leer, *Queening of America: Gay Culture in Straight Society* (New York: Routledge, 1995).

62. On the dynamics of gay involvement in the gentrification of a New Orleans neighborhood, see Lawrence Knopp, "Some Theoretical Implications of Gay Involvement in an Urban Land Market," *Political Geography Quarterly* 9:4 (1990): 337–52. Contrary to expectations, Knopp finds that "those most active in advancing gay community development were gay speculators and developers, while those most resistant to promoting a gay political and social agenda were gay neighborhood activists." Also see Knopp, "Gentrification and Gay Neighborhood Formation in New Orleans," in Gluckman and Reed, *Homo Economics*, 45–64; Mitchell L. Moss, "Reinventing the Central City as a Place to Live and Work," *Housing Policy Debate* 8:2 (1997): 471–90, which focuses "on the role that nontraditional households [such as gays and lesbians] can play in urban redevelopment"; Mickey Lauria and Lawrence Knopp, "Toward an Analysis of the Role of Gay Communities in the Urban Renaissance,"

Urban Geography 6 (1985): 651–69; Felix Javerne Boyle, "Gay Ghettos and Gentrification: Separate Issues, Misunderstood Processes—Toward an Understanding of the Gay and Lesbian Role in Gentrification" (Master's thesis, Urban Planning, Columbia University, 1985); Lauri Johnston, "Christopher Street: From Farm to Gay Center," *New York Times*, July 26, 1971, 27; and Karen DeWitt, "Gay Presence Leads Revival of Declining Neighborhoods," *New York Times,* September 6, 1994, A14. Fewer works address the presence of gays in the suburbs; see, however, Frederick Lynch, "Non-Ghetto Gays: A Sociological Study of Suburban Homosexuals," *Journal of Homosexuality* 13:4 (summer 1987): 13–42.

63. Alexandra Zavis, "City to Renovate Chicago's Gay Halsted Street," *Associated Press*, August 29, 1997. Christopher Reed reported on this development at the "Future of the Queer Past: A Transnational History Conference," convened by the Center for Gender Studies, University of Chicago, September 14–17, 2000.

64. Briavel Holcomb and Michael Luongo, "Gay Tourism in the United States," *Annals of Tourism Research* 23:3 (July 1996): 711–13; and Christopher Reynolds (*Los Angeles Times*), "Gay Travelers Draw Ever More Mainstream Interest," *Seattle Times*, Travel section, May 27, 1997, D5.

65. *Seattle's Gay and Lesbian Community Yellow Pages,* 1997–98 ed. (Phoenix, Ariz.: Community Yellow Pages, 1997–98), 130–33.

66. American Express and Royalty Travel were listed in the *Greater Seattle Business Directory* (Seattle: Emerald City Arts, 1996-97), 237–42.

67. For a discussion of the discomforts of traveling as a gay couple in a homophobic world, see Lindsay Van Gelder, *Are You Two Together?* (New York: Random House, 1991).

68. See Michael Elliman and Frederick Roll, *The Pink Plaque Guide to London* (London: Gay Men's Press, 1995).

69. See Daniel Hurewitz, *Stepping Out: Nine Walks through New York City's Gay and Lesbian History* (New York: Henry Holt, 1997).

70. Gay and lesbian travel guides have been published under the imprint of Fodor, Detour, Out and About, Severe Queer Review, and others. For example, see *Fodor's Gay Guide to the U.S.A.* (New York: Fodor's Travel Publications, 1998).

71. *National Register Bulletin 16A*, "How to Complete National Register Forms," explains the process for amending National Register forms.

72. A recent series of projects aimed at improving the interpretation of women's history at historic properties provides useful models for new initiatives in the area of gay and lesbian history. On this subject, see Gail Lee Dubrow, Sara Evans, Page Putnam Miller, Danyelle Nelson, Dwight Pitcaith-

ley, and Sandy Weber, *Exploring a Common Past: Interpreting Women's History in the National Parks*, National Park Service, Resource Guide Series, no. 1. (Washington, D.C.: Organization of American Historians and National Park Service, 1996); and R*eclaiming the Past: Landmarks of Women's History*, ed. Page Putnam Miller (Bloomington: Indiana University Press, 1992); as well as the other chapters in this collection.

73. Chris Reed to Gail Lee Dubrow, personal correspondence, October 3, 1997.

CHAPTER 18: SEARCHING FOR WOMEN
IN THE NATIONAL REGISTER OF HISTORIC PLACES

Special thanks to Mary McCutchan (former National Conference of State Historic Preservation Officers staffer working for the National Register) and John Byrne of the National Register staff, for gathering facts and figures from the National Register Information System and National Register files, and to Nathan Poe, then a National Council for Preservation Education intern, for additional assistance. Thanks also to state historic preservation office staff for information about women and the National Register, including Jim Draeger (Wis.), Beth Foster (Iowa), Elsa Gilbertson (Vt.), Rolene Schliesman (N.D.), Kathryn Eckert and Laura R. Ashlee (Mich.), Susan Roth (Minn.), and Elisabeth B. Potter (Oreg.); to National Park Service staffers Beth Boland, Harry Butowsky, Marilyn Harper, Paul Lusignan, and Dwight Pitcaithley; and to then National Conference of State Historic Preservation Officers staffers Sarah Dillard and Susan Kline, who recommended places to include or provided comments.

1. Information on the number and kinds of listings in the National Register of Historic Places comes from querying the National Register Information System (NRIS), the computerized index of historic districts, sites, buildings, structures, and objects listed in the National Register. This database is maintained by the U.S. Department of the Interior, National Park Service, at www .cr.nps.gov/nr.

2. Gerda Lerner, *The Majority Finds Its Past* (Oxford: Oxford University Press, 1979); Sara M. Evans, *Born for Liberty: A History of Women in America* (New York: Free Press, 1989).

3. As a member of the National Park Service's National Register, I reviewed the recommendations and participated in the discussions about what data elements should be included in the National Register Information System. These observations are from my memory.

4. Diane Miller, "23 Years of Automating the National Register," in *CRM: Cultural Resources Management* 14:4 (1991). Efforts to computerize the Na-

tional Register began as early as 1968, but data entry for the NRIS did not begin until the mid-1980s. Miller's article provides a good summary of efforts to computerize the National Register. See also my article "Computerizing the National Register of Historic Places" in *CRM: Cultural Resources Management* 21:4 (1998).

5. Clara Barton National Historic Site in 1974, Eleanor Roosevelt National Historic Site in 1977, Maggie L. Walker's home in 1978, and Women's Rights National Historical Park in 1980. Since then, three more units with a focus on women have been added to the National Park System: Mary McLeod Bethune Council House National Historic Site; Rosie the Riveter/World War II Home Front National Historic Park, and First Ladies National Historic Site. As of 2002, 7 of the 385 units of the National Park System have been designated for primary associations with women.

6. Page Putnam Miller, ed., *Reclaiming the Past: Landmarks of Women's History* (Bloomington: Indiana University Press, 1992), 15.

7. Gail Lee Dubrow, "Preserving Her Heritage: American Landmarks of Women's History," paper delivered at the annual meeting of the National Council on Public History, Washington, D.C., April 25, 1987 (and Ph.D. diss., Graduate School of Architecture and Urban Planning, University of California, Los Angeles, 1991).

8. Miller, ed., *Reclaiming the Past*, 15–16. Miller's introduction, "Landmarks of Women's History," includes an account of the growing interest in recognizing historic places highlighting the achievements of American women.

9. The Internet address for the National Park Service, National Register of Historic Places website is www.cr.nps.gov/nr.

10. Explanations and definitions of the categories of information found on National Register of Historic Places registration forms, many of which are included in the National Register Information System, can be found in *How to Complete the National Register Registration Form, National Register Bulletin* (Washington, D.C.: National Park Service, 1997).

11. The queries of the National Register Information System for this analysis were made in the last half of 1996.

12. All of the information on registered historic properties in this study comes from the National Register of Historic Places and National Historic Landmark registration files that are maintained by the National Park Service in Washington, D.C.

13. See Holly Brubac et al., "Heroine Worship," in *New York Times Magazine*, 24 November 1996.

14. Miller, *Reclaiming the Past*, 12–23.

15. It is interesting to note that in 1975, on the eve of America's bicenten-

nial, the National Register of Historic Places launched a study of listed properties associated with minority groups. The National Register files were searched by hand to identify and produce card files recording listings associated with a variety of groups, including women. While the results of the findings on women were not published, the card file was used as one reference source to identify sites to be considered for NHL designation in the women's history theme study (interview with Beth Boland, the National Register staff historian who participated in the study).

16. *Revision of the National Park Service's Thematic Framework*, National Park Service, 1996.

17. The Second National Women in Historic Preservation Conference, sponsored by the Women's Studies Program and the Graduate Program in Public History at Arizona State University and by the National Park Service, March 13–15, 1997.

18. Mary Jane Lowe, "Outing the National Register: Sites Related to Lesbians, Gay Men, and Bisexuals," paper delivered at the Second National Women in Historic Preservation Conference, Mesa, Ariz., March 14, 1997.

19. Heather A. Huyck, ed., "Placing Women in the Past," *CRM: Cultural Resources Management* 20:3 (1997); Antoinette J. Lee, "Supporting Working Women: YWCAs in the National Register," 16–17; and Beth M. Boland, Keeping Women in their Historic Places—Bringing Women's Stories into the Classroom," 35–38.

20. "The Stuff of Women's History," Organization of American Historian's *Magazine of History* 12:1 (fall 1997).

21. Beth L. Savage, ed., *African American Historic Places* (Washington, D.C.: Preservation Press, National Trust for Historic Preservation, 1994).

22. Joan S. Pryor, *Clara Barton's House: Home of the American Red Cross;* and Todd Stoeberl, *First Lady of the World: Eleanor Roosevelt at Val-Kill,* National Trust for Historic Preservation, 1995; and www.cv.nps.gov/nv/twhp.

23. For information on Teaching with Historic Places lesson plans, see the National Register's website, www.cr.nps.gov/nr/twhp; or contact the National Park Service, National Register of Historic Places.

24. Felicia Moss, *The M'Clintock House: A Home to the Women's Right Movement;* Laine Weber, *Adeline Hornbek and the Homestead Act: A Colorado Success Story;* Rita G. Koman, *Two American Entrepreneurs: Madame C. J. Walker and J. C. Penney.*

25. Personal communication with Gail Lee Dubrow, associate professor of Urban Design and Planning and director, Preservation Planning and Design Program, University of Washington.

26. *Exploring a Common Past: Interpreting Women's History in the Na-*

tional Park Service (Washington, D.C.: National Park Service and Organization of American Historians, 1997).

CHAPTER 19: REFLECTIONS ON FEDERAL POLICY AND ITS IMPACT ON UNDERSTANDING WOMEN'S PAST AT HISTORIC SITES

1. Eudora Welty, *The Eye of the Story: Selected Essays and Reviews* (New York: Vintage International, 1990), 56.

2. Welty, *Eye of the Story,* 122.

3. From consulting staff and directories of the major national historical and museum associations, I was unable to locate any survey or list of public historic sites associated primarily with women. The following analysis is based on information and an informal working list that I developed in the course of working on the Women's History Landmark Project in 1992.

4. National Park Service, "Exploring a Common Past: Interpreting Women's History in the National Park Service" (Washington, D.C.: National Park Service, 1996).

5. House Committee on Interior and Insular Affairs, *Report to the Committee on the Budget,* 100th Cong., 2nd sess., 1988, H. Rept., 100-4, 73.

6. Page Putnam Miller, ed., *Reclaiming the Past: Landmarks of Women's History* (Bloomington: Indiana University Press, 1992).

7. The NCC served as the coordinating organization for the Women's History Landmark Project. As the director of the NCC, I devoted one day a week to the project, and Jill Mesirow, the research assistant for the project, provided day-to-day coordination. Most of the work of the project was handled by contracts with dozens of historians and preservationists from around the country assisting in the writing of essays and the preparation of National Historic Landmark nomination forms.

8. National Park Service, "National Register of Historic Places' Bulletin 15, How to Apply the National Register Criteria for Evaluations" (Washington, D.C.: U.S. Department of the Interior, NPS, Interagency Resource Division, 1991), 44.

9. Susan Ware, *Partner and I: Molly Dewson, Feminism, and New Deal Politics* (New Haven, Conn.: Yale University Press, 1987), 134; Blanche Wiesen Cook, *Eleanor Roosevelt,* vol. 1: *1884–1933* (New York: Viking Press, 1992), 296.

10. "Humanities and the National Parks: Adapting to Change—A Report by the Humanities Review Committee of the National Park System Advisory Board" (Washington, D.C.: National Park Service, 1994).

11. Dwight T. Pitcaithley, "The Future of the NPS History Program," *CRM: Cultural Resources Management* 20:7 (1997): 5.

12. National Park Service, "History of the National Park Service: Themes and Concepts," adopted by the NPS in 1994, first printing 1996 (Washington, D.C.: National Park Service, 1996).

13. The seven individuals involved in writing this resource guide were Page Putnam Miller, director of the National Coordinating Committee for the Promotion of History and coordinator for the project; Gail Lee Dubrow, associate professor of Urban Design and Planning at the University of Washington; Sara Evans, professor of history at the University of Minnesota; Danyelle A. Nelson, historian at the City Point Unit of the Petersburg National Battlefield; Dwight T. Pitcaithley, chief historian of the National Park Service; Sandy Weber, interpretive specialist of the National Park Service; and Heather A. Huyck, director, Strategic Planning Office of the National Park Service.

14. Eric Foner, "Introduction," in Linda Gordon, *U.S. Women's History* (Washington, D.C.: American Historical Association, 1990), viii.

CHAPTER 20: PARKS CANADA AND WOMEN'S HISTORY

The opinions expressed in this chapter are the author's and are not an official expression of Parks Canada policy.

1. For example, Mary Qualye Innis, ed., *The Clear Spirit: Twenty Canadian Women and Their Times* (Toronto: University of Toronto Press, 1966); Veronica Strong-Boag, *The Parliament of Women: The National Council of Women of Canada, 1893–1929* (Ottawa: National Museum of Man, 1976).

2. One of the earliest collections was Janice Acton et al., *Women at Work: Ontario, 1850–1930* (Toronto: Canadian Women's Educational Press, 1974).

3. Sylvia Van Kirk, *Many Tender Ties: Women in Fur-Trade Society, 1670–1870* (Winnipeg: Watson and Dwyer, 1979); and Jennifer Brown, *Strangers in Blood: Fur Trade Company Families in Indian Country* (Vancouver: University of British Columbia Press, 1980).

4. Margaret Conrad, Toni Laidlaw, and Donna Smyth, eds., *No Place like Home: Diaries, and Letters of Nova Scotia Women, 1771–1938* (Halifax, N.S.: Formac Publishing Co. Ltd., 1988); Angus and Arlene Tigar McLaren, *The Bedroom and the State: The Changing Practices and Politics of Contraception and Abortion in Canada, 1880–1980* (Toronto: McClelland and Stewart, 1986).

5. Joy Parr, *The Gender of Breadwinners: Women, Men and Change in Two Industrial Towns, 1880–1950* (Toronto: University of Toronto Press, 1990); Bettina Bradbury, *Working Families: Age, Gender, and Daily Survival in Industrializing Montreal* (Toronto: McClelland and Stewart, 1993).

6. Julie Cruickshank in collaboration with Angela Sidney, Kitty Smith, and Annie Ned, *Life Lived like a Story: Life Stories of Three Yukon Elders* (Van-

couver: University of British Columbia Press, 1991); Peggy Bristow et al., *"We're Rooted Here and They Can't Pull Us Up": Essays in African Canadian Women's History* (Toronto: University of Toronto Press, 1994).

7. Diana Pedersen, *Changing Women, Changing History: A Bibliography of the History of Women in Canada* (Ottawa: Carleton University Press, 1996).

8. Personal communication, Christina Cameron, director-general, National Historic Sites, January 6, 1998.

9. For more on the tangible remains of women and nursing in Canada, see Annmarie Adams's chapter in this volume.

10. Parr, *Gender of Breadwinners*. The Penman knitting mills at Paris were identified as being of national historic significance in 1989.

11. One of the earliest Canadian works on women's history is Catherine Cleverdon's study *The Woman Suffrage Movement in Canada* (Toronto: University of Toronto Press, 1950). The struggle for, and the exercise of, political rights (only one aspect of "Power"), is the subject of 205 entries in Diana Pedersen's *Changing Women, Changing History*. The bibliography contains 301 entries under the heading "Health/Medicine."

12. The Persons Case is a landmark legal decision of 1929 by which Canadian women were found to be persons for the purposes of the British North America Act and hence eligible for appointment to the Canadian Senate. It has subsequently come to be viewed by many Canadians as a legal declaration that women were persons in all respects.

13. Canadian Heritage, Parks Canada, *Guiding Principles and Operation Policies* (Ottawa: Minister of Supply and Services Canada, 1994), 71, 112.

14. Carol Whitfield, "Tommy Atkins: The British Soldier in Canada, 1759–1870," *History and Archeology* (Parks Canada, Ottawa) 56 (1981); Katherine M. J. McKenna, "Family Life in a Military Garrison: History of the Routines and Activities of the Royal Canadian Rifle Regiment at Fort Wellington, Prescott, 1843–1856" (MS, Parks Canada, 1995).

15. Personal communication, Barbara Schmeisser, project historian, Halifax Defence Complex, October 23, 1996.

16. McKenna, "Family Life in a Military Garrison," 178.

17. McKenna, "Family Life in a Military Garrison," 181.

18. Van Kirk, *"Many Tender Ties"*; Brown, *Strangers in Blood*.

19. Frieda Esau Klippenstein, "Resources on Carrier Women's History" (MS, Parks Canada, Fort St. James National Historic Site, March 1966), 34.

20. Klippenstein, "Resources on Carrier Women's History," 3–4.

21. Joanne Fiske, "Fishing Is Women's Business: Changing Economic Roles of Carrier Women and Men," in Bruce Cox, ed., *Native People, Native Lands* (Ottawa: Carleton University Press, 1988), 186–97.

AFTERWORD: PROCEEDING FROM HERE

The views expressed here are solely the author's.

1. Heather A. Huyck, "Placing Women in the Past," *CRM: Cultural Resources Management* 20:3 (1997): 4–6.

2. Susan B. Anthony, quoted in Ida Husted Harper, *Life and Work of Susan B. Anthony* (Salem, N.H.: Ayer Co., 1983), 1409.

3. Bonnie J. Clark, "The Women of Boggsville: Life along the Santa Fe Trail," technical document for Site Interpretation and Investigation and Documentation for the Women of Boggsville brochure (Denver: National Park Service, 1997).

4. Colonial National Historical Park, Jamestown collection, Jamestown, Va.

5. Ira Berlin, *Many Thousands Gone: The First Two Centuries of Slavery in North America* (Cambridge, Mass.: Belknap Press of Harvard University Press, 1998).

6. Page Putnam Miller, ed., *Reclaiming the Past: Landmarks of Women's History.* (Bloomington: Indiana University Press, 1992).

7. Andrea Hinding, Ames Sheldon [Bower], and Clarke Chambers, eds., *Women's History Sources: A Guide to Archives and Manuscript Collections in the United States* (New York: R. R. Bowker, in association with the University of Minnesota, 1979).

8. See Heather A. Huyck, "Beyond John Wayne: Using Historic Sites to Interpret Women's History," in *Western Women, Their Land, Their Lives,* ed. Lillian Schlissel, Vicki L. Ruiz, and Janice Monk (Albuquerque: University of New Mexico Press, 1988), 318.

9. Personal visit to Maria Mitchell home, Nantucket, Mass., 2000.

10. Personal visit to Theodore Roosevelt National Park, Medora, N.D., 1999.

Contributors

Annmarie Adams is an associate professor at the School of Architecture, McGill University. She is the author of *Architecture in the Family Way: Houses, Doctors, and Women, 1870–1900* and coauthor (with Peta Tancred) of *Designing Women: Gender and the Architectural Profession.*

John Bacon received his Master of Arts in Early American Culture from the Winterthur Program, University of Delaware (1990). Formerly a museum intern, Independence National Historical Park, and collections manager, Philadelphia Maritime Museum, he now works as an attorney in New York City.

Julia G. Costello, Ph.D., co-owner of a cultural resource management firm for over twenty years, is a recognized authority on historic period archaeological sites. She has published widely on her work on the Spanish and Mexican periods, the California Gold Rush and mining, and on sites occupied by Chinese, Japanese, and Italian immigrants. Dr. Costello has conducted projects in the Middle East and represented the United States on the Archaeology Committee of the International Council on Monuments and Sites. She has served as President of the Society for Historical Archaeology and of the Society for California Archaeology, and on the Ethics Committee of the Society for American Archaeology.

Karie Diethorn received her Master of Arts in American History and Museum Studies from the University of Delaware (1984). She was formerly a museum intern, Independence National Historical Park; curator of Collections, Old Economy Village, Pennsylvania Historical and Museum Commission (Ambridge, Pa.); curator, Henry Wadsworth Longfellow National Historic Site (Cambridge, Mass.); and associate curator, Independence National Historical Park. She became chief curator at Independence National Historical Park in 1993.

Gail Lee Dubrow is professor of Architecture, Landscape Architecture, Urban Design and Planning and director of the Preservation Planning and Design Program at the University of Washington, where she also serves as associate dean for academic affairs in the College of Architecture and Urban Planning. She received a bachelor's degree in Architecture from the University of Oregon and a doctoral degree in Urban Planning from the University of California, Los Angeles. Her research and practice are devoted to integrating the history of women, ethnic communities of color, and gay and lesbian people into the practice of preservation planning. Support for this work has been provided by the Seattle Arts Commission, the National Park Service, the National Endowment for the Humanities, the American Institute of Architects/American Architectural Foundation, and the American Association of University Women. She is the author, with Donna Graves, of *Sento at Sixth and Main: Preserving Landmarks of Japanese American Heritage.*

Shaun Eyring is the Cultural Resources Group manager in the National Park Service's Philadelphia Support Office. She received a master's degree in Landscape Architecture and a Certificate in Historic Preservation from the University of Virginia in Charlottesville in 1987. In 1992, after working in the private sector in Charlottesville and Philadelphia, she joined the National Park Service to develop and implement a region-wide historic landscape preservation program. Currently, she manages an interdisciplinary team that provides cultural resources technical expertise to national parks and partners in the northeast region.

Jennifer B. Goodman served a leadership role in producing the first "Reclaiming Women's History through Historic Preservation" conference, held in Bryn Mawr, Pennsylvania, in 1994, which brought together scholars, practitioners, and other interested parties to explore the documentation, interpretation, and preservation of women's heritage sites. As the executive director of the New Hampshire Preservation Alliance, and in previous management positions in Philadelphia- and Boston-based preservation advocacy organizations, she has led many community-based preservation planning and public awareness initiatives for cultural heritage sites including African American sites, long-standing businesses, and civic landmarks. Goodman has also published, and presented at national and regional conferences, on varied topics including conservation districts, preservation development charettes, barn preservation, and effective public policy strategies for preservation and conservation initiatives.

Dolores Hayden is professor of architecture, urbanism, and American studies at Yale University and the author of several books on the politics of design, including *The Grand Domestic Revolution: A History of Feminist Designs for American Homes, Neighborhoods, and Cities* and *The Power of Place: Urban Landscapes as Public History.* She is currently completing a history of American suburbs and their landscapes from 1820 to the present.

Barbara J. Howe received her M.A. in history from the University of Wisconsin–Milwaukee in 1971 and her Ph.D. degree in history from Temple University in 1976. She was a regional preservation officer for the Ohio Historic Preservation Office from 1976 to 1980. She directed the West Virginia University (WVU) public history program from 1980 to 2000, served as chair of the Department of History from 1995 to 1998, was interim director of the WVU Center for Women's Studies from 1998 to 2000, and became director of the Center for Women's Studies in 2000. Howe has published articles on West Virginia women's history and contributed an essay on "Women and Architecture" to Page Putnam Miller's *Reclaiming the Past: Landmarks of Women's History.*

Heather A. Huyck has been a public historian for the past thirty years. Formerly the Jamestown 400th Project Director, in 2002 she became Regional Chief Historian for the National Park Service's Northeast Region and Visiting Lecturer at William and Mary College. She was head of Strategic Planning for the National Park Service and spent eight years working as a congressional staff member for the U.S. House of Representatives Subcommittee on National Parks and Public Lands. She has visited over 279 units of the National Park System.

Edith Mayo is curator emeritus in political history at the Smithsonian's National Museum of American History, where she worked for over thirty years as a curator and historian. Ms. Mayo currently teaches a course in material culture in the American Studies Department at the George Washington University and is curating an exhibit on successful women business entrepreneurs, *Enterprising Women,* for the Radcliffe Institute for Research of Harvard University.

Alan B. McCullough, who served as a historian with Parks Canada prior to 1998, was responsible for the research aspects of Parks Canada's initiative to expand the commemoration of women's history. He is now a historical consultant.

431

Page Putnam Miller, Ph.D., holds an appointment as distinguished visiting lecturer in the History Department of the University of South Carolina. In 2000 she stepped down after twenty years as director of the National Coordinating Committee for the Promotion of History, a national advocacy office for the historical and archival professions. She has written extensively on legislative issues and has testified frequently before congressional committees on federal information policy, access to federal records of historic value, preservation and interpretation of cultural resources, and support of the National Archives and the National Endowment for the Humanities. She served from 1990 to 1993 as the Washington coordinator of the women's history landmark project, a cooperative project of the National Park Service, the Organization of American Historians, and the National Coordinating Committee for the Promotion of History.

Kim Moon is the former assistant director of the Pennsylvania Humanities Council and was project director for the pilot of "Raising Our Sites: Women's History in Pennsylvania." She holds a B.A. from the University of Richmond in English and women's studies and an M.A. in English from Villanova University, where she focused her work on the literary lives of African American women in the post-Reconstruction era. She currently serves as Director of Foundation Relations of Partners for Sacred Places, a national, nonsectarian, nonprofit organization based in Philadelphia which is dedicated to helping citizens embrace and care for older and historic religious properties that are centers of cultural and community life and irreplaceable works of architecture.

Susan M. Pierce is the deputy state historic preservation officer for the Division of Culture and History, Charleston, W.Va. As a graduate of Columbia University's master's degree program in historic preservation, she has worked for the division since 1987. Other areas of research have included Cold War–era bomb shelters and agricultural settlement pattens in West Virginia. Prior research has included New York regional history, most notably the architectural history of Raynham Hall, Oyster Bay, N.Y.

Fath Davis Ruffins has been a historian at the National Museum of American History (NMAH), Smithsonian Institution, since 1981. Since 1988 she has been the head of the Collection of Advertising History in the Archives Center. She co-curated two exhibitions at NMAH which opened in 1988: *1848: New Border, New Nation* and *A Collector's Vision of Puerto Rico*. She has published widely on the "history of Black history," has served as an officer of two national

African American cultural organizations, and is working on a book on history museums at the millennium.

Leslie N. Sharp is currently pursuing a Ph.D. in the History of Technology at the Georgia Institute of Technology. From 1993 to 1999 she worked at the Historic Preservation Division of the Georgia Department of Natural Resources, where she coordinated the National Register of Historic Places and the Georgia Women's History Initiative as well as chairing the Georgia Centennial Farm Committee. A native of Georgia, Ms. Sharp received her B.A. in history from the University of Georgia and her M.A. in history with an emphasis in historic preservation from Middle Tennessee State University.

Carol D. Shull is keeper of the National Register of Historic Places and chief of the National Historic Landmarks Survey, National Park Service, U.S. Department of the Interior. She has more than twenty-five years of experience and has written and lectured extensively in the historic preservation field.

Abigail A.Van Slyck is the Dayton Associate Professor of Architectural History at Connecticut College, where she directs the Architectural Studies Program. She is the author of *Free to All: Carnegie Libraries and American Culture, 1890–1920* and is at work on a social and architectural history of children's summer camps.

Judith Wellman is Director and Historian for Historical New York, a research and consulting firm. She is Professor Emerita at the State University of New York at Oswego and was the first historian at Women's Rights National Historical Park.

Patricia West is the author of *Domesticating History: The Political Origins of America's Historic House Museums* (Washington, D.C.: Smithsonian Institution Press, 1999). She teaches in the Public History Graduate Program at the University at Albany and is curator of the Martin Van Buren National Historic Site.

Index

Abbott, Harold, 39
abolitionism, 60, 61
aboriginal cultures, 338, 340, 342, 345, 348, 350–352, 354. *See also* Native Americans
Abzug, Bella, 225
Acuna, Rodolfo, 201
Adams, Abigail, 31, 333
Adams, Annmarie, 131–144
Adams, John, 232
Adams, Louisa Catherine, 124
Addams, Jane, 305
Adeline Hornbek Homestead, 316
advocacy, legislative: federal, 47–48, 64, 238–239, 241; state, 48–50, 52, 276
AfraAmerican Journal, 70
Africa, 73
African American Heritage Preservation Foundation, 46
African American Historic Places (Peterson), 315
African Americans, 5, 30, 36, 58–80, 99, 121, 125, 127, 226, 256, 257, 261, 262, 270, 311, 360; preservation and commemoration of heritage sites and people, 18, 19, 35, 46, 59, 63, 77–80, 117, 175, 203–208, 213, 214, 221–223, 271, 277–278, 312, 315, 322, 325; preservation efforts of, 4, 18, 19, 59, 63–66, 70–71, 75, 221–223, 271; urban landscapes, 54, 55, 200, 201, 206, 212, 221–223
African-American Historic Places and Culture: A Preservation Resources Guide for Georgia, 278

African Methodist Episcopal (A.M.E.) Zion Church, 60, 62, 63, 64
Afro-American Bicentennial Corporation, 316
Alabama, 75; Birmingham, 78
Alcatraz National Park, 356
Alcott, Louisa May, 316
Alda, Alan, 237, 239, 240, 245
Alderson, William T., 84
Alice Paul Centennial Foundation, 218, 225, 227, 228
Allen Memorial, 138
Alliance for Historic Landscape Preservation, 56
American Airlines, 297
American Association for State and Local History (AASLH), 84, 255, 316
American Association of University Women, 228, 234
American Civic Association, 51
American Express Travel, 297
American Historical Association, 271, 335
American Library Association, 148
American Red Cross, 305
Anderson, Judy, 159
Andes, Cindy, 260
Angelou, Maya, 233
Angelus Temple, 312
Anthony, Susan B., 2, 9, 17, 61, 121, 238, 305, 357
anthropology, 33, 179
archaeology, 8, 9, 10, 34, 39, 42, 177–196, 238, 361

architectural and site integrity, 131, 223, 323–324; examples of, 215–218, 220–221, 222–223. *See also* interiors

architectural features, and cultural significance, 100–109, 131–144, 210, 214, 224, 292, 357–358, 363

Arizona: Tucson, 363

Arizona State University, 3, 112, 336

Arnold Arboretum, 39

Artillery Park National Historic Site (Canada), 345

Asian Americans, 201, 213. *See also* Chinese and Chinese Americans; Japanese Americans; Japanese Canadians

Asilomar, 309

Association for the Preservation of Virginia Antiquities (APVA), 17, 24, 25, 27, 28, 46

Association for the Study of Negro Life and History (ASNLH), 75

Atchison, Topeka and Sante Fe Railroad, 34

Athens YWCA, 267

Attucks, Crispus, 19

Austen, Alice, 286

Azurest, 59

Babbitt, Bruce, 328

Bacon, John, 7, 96–110

Bacon, Margaret Hope, 238

Baker, Nicholson, 158

Balcony House, 33

Ballerino, Bartolo, 183

Banner, Lois, 238

Barney, John, 237

Barton, Clara, 305, 315, 316, 333

Bar U Ranch National Historic Site (Canada), 343

Beard, Lucienne, 220, 228

Beard, Mary Ritter, 2

Beautiful Gardens in America (Shelton), 44

Beckley Exhibition Mine, 176

Beir, Anna, 307

Bell, Alexander Graham, 339

Bellevue House National Historic Site (Canada), 345, 353

Benson, Susan Porter, 113

Berg, Shary, 236

Berlin, Ira, 360

Bertram, James, 150–153

Berube, Alan, 283

Bethune, Louise Blanchard, 324

Bethune, Mary McLeod, 5, 58, 63, 66–71, 76, 77, 78, 79, 80, 305

Bethune-Cookman College, 59, 66, 69, 71, 78

Betsky, Aaron, 289

Betsy Ross House, 28

Beulah Rucker School/House, 271

Biddy Mason: Time and Place (de Bretteville), 207

Biddy Mason's House of the Open Hand (Saar), 206

Bill of Rights, 248

Bingham, Jonathan, 238

Black Women's Research Archives, 71

Block Candy Company, 273

Blow, Susan, 307

Bobinski, George, 159

Boggs, Mrs., 99

Boland, Beth M., 315

Bookstaver, May, 286

Boots of Leather, Slippers of Gold (Kennedy and Davis), 283

Bordin, Ruth, 287

Bove, Emil, 242

Breedlove, Sarah, 72

Brett, William Howard, 150

de Bretteville, Sheila Levrant, 203, 207, 208, 211

Brier, Stephen, 113

de Bright, Josefina Fierro, 210, 211

British National Trust, 31

Brown, James Bush, 46

Brown, Jennifer, 337, 350

Brown, John, 18

Brown, Marina, 234

Bruton Parish Church, 27

Bryan, Isobel Lamont Stewart, 28

Bryan, Joseph, 28

Bryans, Jennie, 272
Bryant, Anita, 295
Bryce, David, 135
Bryn Mawr College, 3, 112, 332, 333
Buckley, Chris, 183
Bumpers, Dale, 239
Bunch, Lonnie, 201
Bundles, A'Lelia P., 72, 73, 75
Bureau of American Ethnology, 33
Burton, Phillip, 238, 239
Bush, President George H. W., 328
Bush-Brown, Louise, 46, 54
Business and Professional Women, 228, 234

Cabell, James Alston, 25
Cables, Herbert, Jr., 240, 242, 243
California, 46, 208, 292, 309, 317; Arden, 307; Fresno, 308; Hollywood, 328; Los Angeles, 12, 177–196, 199–212, 283, 285, 292, 312, 357; Oakland, 308; Palm Springs, 292; Palo Alto, 310–311; Pasadena, 215, 225; Riverside, 309; San Bernadino, 204; San Francisco, 180, 183, 283, 285, 295, 296, 297, 299, 356; San Juan Capistrano, 307; Simi Valley, 314
California Afro-American Museum, 203
California Gardens (Dobyns), 46
California History, 208
California Roadside Council, 51
California State Historical Resources Commission, 292
Camarillo, Albert, 201, 210
Canada, 62, 131 144, 337 354, 357; British Columbia, 351; Cape Breton, 339; Kingston, Ont., 353; Montreal, 8, 131–144, 353; Ottawa, 353; Paris, Ont., 343; Prescott, Ont., 348; Quebec City, 345; Saskatchewan, 353; St. Catharines, 60; Toronto, 345
Cannery Women, Cannery Lives (Ruiz), 210
Carnegie, Andrew, 150
Carter, President Jimmy, 233, 238, 239
Carter, Judy, 233

Carter, Rosalynn, 234
Cartier, Sir George-Etienne, 353
Caruso, Enrico, 75
Case, Sarah Clark, 307
Caswell Coal and Coke Company, 168
Catharine Memorial Society, 27
Cathay Express, 297
Cathedral of Hope, 291
Cather, Willa (aka William J. Cather), 13, 286, 299, 317
Caucasian women, 270, 271
Center for Right Living, 10
Chabot, Maria, 288, 289
Channing, Grace, 215
Charitable and Parochial Establishments (Snell), 133
Charleston Mercury, 19
Chauncey, George, 282
Chessler, Sey, 237, 239, 242
Chester County Historical Society, 255, 260
children, involving in advocacy and education, 224, 225, 359
Chinese and Chinese Americans, 179, 185, 195, 201
Chisolm, Shirley, 225
Christianson, Virginia, 288
Civil War, 22, 24, 27, 28, 271, 276, 282, 305, 312, 314, 334, 361
Clara Barton Homestead, 305
Clara Barton National Historic Site, 305
Clara Barton Parkway, 305
Clark-Atlanta University, 273
Clarke, Isabella, 353
Clinton, President Bill, 328
Clinton, Hillary Rodham, 58, 66
Coal Heritage Area, 169, 176
Coal Heritage Survey, 169, 175
coal mines, 161–176
Coburn, Judi, 144
Coleman, Cynthia Beverley Tucker, 24, 27
collaborations and coalitions, 203, 212, 226–227, 229, 251–253, 359, 362
Collins, Jeffrey, 260
Colonial America, 30
Colonial Williamsburg, 2, 41, 362

Colorado, 41, 316; Boggsville, 358; Denver, 33, 34, 73; Durango, 33; Mesa Verde, 33, 41
Colorado Cliff Dwellings Association, 34
Colored Women's Clubs, 121
Colter, Mary Jane, 308
Columbia University, 335
Commission on Interracial Cooperation, 67
Community Development Block Grants, 277
Confederate Memorial Literary Society (CMLS), 17, 28
El Congreso, 210
Congress Hall, 30, 97
Congressional Women's Caucus, 238
Conkey, Margaret, 180
Connecticut, 325; New Canaan, 289; Norwalk, 31
Consolidated Bank and Trust Company, 76
Constitution, 248
context. See historic context studies
Continental Congress, 7
Cook, Blanche Wiesen, 287, 326
Cook, Nancy, 326
Cookman Institute for Boys, 66
Cooper, John, 168
Cooper, Mrs., 175
Costello, Julia G., 8–9, 177–196
Crater Lake National Park, 239
Crescent Avenue Apartments, 269
CRM: Cultural Resource Management (NPS), 314
Cuba, 21
Cunningham, Ann Pamela, 17, 19, 20, 21, 23, 28, 230, 232, 233, 246
Cunningham, Floride, 28
Curry, Mary, 234
Custis, George Washington Parke, 22
Custis, Mary Anna Randolph, 22

Daily Star, 184
Dana, John Cotton, 149
Daniel Case / Sarah Case Farmstead, 307
Daughters of Bilitus, 283

Daughters of the American Revolution (DAR), 4, 17, 18, 24, 25, 28, 30, 31, 32, 46, 271
Davies, Marion, 311
Davis, Madeline, 283
Dawes General Allotment Act (1887), 33
Daytona Educational and Industrial Institute for Colored Girls, 66
Deagan, Kathleen, 180
Declaration of Independence, 231, 232, 243
Declaration of Sentiments (1848), 58, 230, 231, 233, 243
Degler, Carl, 243
del Castillo, Richard Griswold, 201
D'Emilio, John, 283
DeMille, Mrs. Cecil B., 311
Depression Era, 167, 312
Descriptive Guide Book of Virginia's Old Gardens (GCV), 46
Des Peres School, 307
Dewey, Melvil, 153
Dewson, Mary "Molly," 326, 327
De Zavala, Adina, 32
Dickenson, Russell, 242
Dickerman, Marion, 326
Dickinson, Emily, 2
Diethorn, Karie, 7, 96–110
Dilworth, Leah, 33
Discover Historic America (Konikow), 1
Dobyns, Winifred Starr, 46
Doe, Jane, 181
Doley, Harold, 72
domesticity: as limiting perspective for women's history, 7, 85; as motivation for preservation, 17; and patriotism, 24, 27, 28
domestic service, as museum theme, 6–7, 86–95, 98–110, 256–257, 261
Douglass, Frederick, 18, 35, 60, 62, 63, 70
Douglass, Helen Pitts, 18, 35
Dozier, Henrietta, 277
Drabelle, Dennis, 285
Drake, Laura, 252
Drake Well, 252, 259, 260

Draper, Elizabeth, 76
Drinker, Elizabeth, 104
Driscoll, Clara, 32
Dubner, Nancy, 237, 238
Dubrow, Gail Lee, 1–14, 159, 201, 281–299, 304, 311, 316
Dudden, Faye, 87, 88
Dupree-Begos, Jane, 257

Earle, Alice Morse, 44
Echo Cliff House, 33
Edwards, Emily, 53
Eisenhower College, 241, 244
Eisler, Benita, 289
Elizabeth Cady Stanton Foundation (ECSF), 234, 236–240, 242, 243, 245, 246
Ellamae Ellis League's House, 276
Elliman, Michael, 298
Engendering Archaeology: Women in Prehistory (Gero and Conkey), 180
England, 133; London, 114, 193, 194
Equal Rights Amendment, 231, 238, 244, 247
ethnography, and preservation, 33, 34
Euro-Canadians, 345
Europe, 188, 195, 215
Evans, Sara M., 303
Everett, Edward, 19, 21
Everglades National Park, 48
Exploring a Common Past: Interpreting Women's History in the National Park Service (NPS and OAH), 317, 320, 332, 334, 335
Eyring, Shaun, 5, 37–57

Fabre, Hortense, 353
Fagen, Eleanora (Billie Holiday), 286–287
Federal-Aid Highway Act (1956), 54
Federal Council on Negro Affairs, 69
Federal Emergency Management Agency (FEMA), 169
Federal Era, 97–110
Federal Highways Administration, 52
Felton, Rebecca Latimer, 263
Fields, Kate, 18, 35

Filler, Martin, 290
First African Methodist Episcopal Church (FAME), 203, 206
First Street National Register Historic District, 211
Fitzhugh, Krucker, & Deckbar, 210
Five Views (State of California), 201
Flanagan, Eileen, 143
Florida, 71, 295; Daytona Beach, 59, 69; Fort Pierce, 10, 322; Key West, 292; Paradise Key, 48; St. Augustine, 180
Florida Federation of Women's Clubs, 48
Florissant Fossil Beds National Monument, 316
Flynn, Carolyn, 201
Fodor's, 298
Fogelson, Robert, 201
Folger Foundation, 66
folklore, as preservation tool, 224
Foner, Eric, 335
Ford, Betty, 234
Ford Theater, 323
Fortress of Louisbourg (Canada), 339
Fort St. James National Historic Site (Canada), 351, 352
Fort Wellington (Canada), 348
Fox, Hilda, 51
France, Paris, 190, 193
Franklin, Benjamin, 97, 105
Fraunces Tavern, 31–32
Frederick Douglass Memorial and Historical Association, 35
Freeland, Robert, 243
Freeman (newspaper), 71
Freeman, John, 168
French, Georgie, 181
Friends of Clara Barton, 305
Fugitive Slave Law (1850), 60
Fulton Bag and Cotton Mill, 273
fund raising, 21, 22, 23, 53–54, 228, 236, 238, 239–240, 242–243

Galt, Annie, 25
Galt, Mary Jeffery, 24
Gamble, James, 66

Garcia, Mario, 201
Garcia, Rupert, 210
Garden Club of America (GCA), 5, 38, 44–46, 50, 52
Garden Club of Natchez, Mississippi, 44
Garden Club of Philadelphia, 46
Garden Club of Virginia (GCV), 38, 41–44
Garden History of Georgia (PTGC), 46
gardens, 5, 39, 41–46, 54–56, 171
Gardens of Colony and State (Lockwood), 44
Gay by the Bay (Stryker and Van Buskirk), 283
Gay Community Yellow Pages, 297
Gay New York (Chauncey), 282
gays and lesbians, 12, 13, 229, 281–299, 328, 357
Gender in Historical Archaeology (Seifert), 180
General Federation of Women's Clubs (GFWC), 10, 17, 32, 34, 47–50, 56
George Washington Memorial Parkway, 305
Georgia, 11, 50, 263–280, 317, 357, 363; Athens, 279; Atlanta, 46, 78, 269, 276; Columbus, 269; Gainesville, 271; Indian Springs, 272; Macon, 276; Savannah, 269; Tybee Island, 263
Georgia Department of Natural Resources, 263
Georgia Historical Marker, 276
Georgia Office of Historic Preservation, 277
Georgia O'Keeffe Foundation, 287
Georgia Women's History Initiative, 264, 265, 267, 269, 275, 276, 279
Gero, Joan, 180
Gertrude "Ma" Rainey House, 269
Gibson, Beth, 263
Gifford, Jay, 285
Gillette, Charles, 43
Gilman, Charlotte Perkins, 12, 214–218, 224
Girl Scouts of America, 319
The Golden Age of American Gardens (Griswold and Weller), 46
Golden Spike National Monument, 362

Goldman, Emma, 12
Gold Rush, 357
Gone with the Wind (Margaret Mitchell), 269
Goodman, Jennifer B., 11–12, 214–229
Goodwill, Phoebe Douty, 166, 167, 176
Gordon, Ann, 238
Gordon, Anna, 287
Grandma Mason's Place: A Midwife's Homestead (de Bretteville), 207
Grandma Prisbey's Bottle Village, 314
Graves, Donna, 203, 207, 210
Gray, Selina, 18, 22
Grebinger, Paul, 238
Greek Slave (sculpture; Hiram Powers), 114
Green, Pamela, 222
Green, Rena Maverick, 53
Greenbush Manor House, 30
Greene, Janet, 161–162
Greenville Art Guild, 307
Griffin, Elisabeth, 238
Griswold, Mac, 44, 46
Griswold, Ralph, 43
Guatemala, 210
guides and tours, 1–3, 9–10, 176, 201–202, 203, 279, 282, 283, 285, 286, 287, 296–298, 315
Gulf of Georgia Cannery (Canada), 339, 345
Guntner, Lillian, 157
Guntzel, Corinne, 234, 236, 238

Hager, Beth, 166, 167
Hailey, Trevor, 285
Hale, Sarah Josepha, 18, 19
Halifax Citadel National Historic Site (Canada), 348
Harding, Florence, 124, 125
Harding, Warren, 124
Harper's, 125
Harriet Taylor Upton House, 312
Harriet Tubman Brick House, 58, 59, 60, 65, 66
Harriet Tubman Home for the Aged, 59, 60, 64
Harrison, Caroline Scott, 31

Hart, Judy, 236, 240, 242, 243
Harvard University, 39
Hata, Don, 201
Hata, Nadine, 201
Hawaii, 21
Hay, Harry, 292
Hayden, Dolores, 12, 199–213, 208
Hayes, Lucy Webb, 124
Haynes, Joseph, 221
Haynes, Mabel, 286
Hearst, Phoebe, 23
Hearst, William Randolph, 23, 307
Heinzeman, C. F., 191
Heritage Conservation and Recreation
    Service, 238
The Hermitage, 23, 41
Hersey, Mabel, 143
Hershey Museum, 261
Hewitt, Katherine, 167
Hickok, Lorena, 287
Higginson, Thomas Wentworth, 64
Highway Beautification Act (1965), 52
Hispanics and Latinos, 55, 127, 200, 201,
    208, 210, 212, 213, 229, 307, 358
Historic Aberdeen Gardens, 46
Historical Society of Western
    Pennsylvania, 255
Historic and Architectural Resources
    Associated with Women's Clubs and
    Organizations in the State of Georgia,
    276
*Historic Black Resources: A Handbook
    for the Identification, Documentation,
    Evaluation of Historic African
    American Properties in Georgia*
    (Merritt), 277, 278
historic context studies, 228, 275, 276,
    277, 331; effectiveness, 277–278. *See
    also* National Register of Historic
    Places
historic districts, 78, 228, 240, 295
Historic Gardens of Virginia (JRGC),
    46
historic houses and museums, 5, 6,
    17–36, 58–80, 83–95, 96–110,
    214–229, 248–262. *See also* interpre-
    tation

Historic Sites and Monuments Board of
    Canada (HSMBC), 131, 338, 339,
    340, 341, 347
historic structures, relocation of, and in-
    terpretation, 215–218
*History Museums in the United States: A
    Critical Assessment* (Rosenzweig and
    Leon), 113
*History of Architecture from the Earliest
    Times; its Present Condition in
    Europe and the United States; With a
    Biography of Eminent Architects and
    a Glossary of Architectural Terms by
    Mrs. L. C. Tuthill, with Numerous
    Illustrations* (Tuthill), 18–19
Hoes, Mrs. Rose Gouveneur, 123, 124
Hoff, Joan, 241, 320
Hogrefe, Jeffrey, 288
Holiday, Billie, 286–287
Holland, Pat, 238
Hollywood Memorial Association
    (HMA), 27, 28
Hollywood Studio Club, 311, 328–330
Holstein, Mrs. William H., 23
HOME/stead (King), 207
Hopewell Furnace National Historic
    Park, 260
Hopkins, Alden, 43
Hornbek, Adeline, 316
Hosmer, Charles, Jr., 4, 38, 233
Hospital Construction and Management
    (Snell), 133
Hostess House, 309
House Book (Leslie), 102
House Subcommittee on National Parks
    and Public Lands, 321
Howard University, 70
Howe, Barbara J., 4, 17–36, 113
Huffman, Frances, 172
Hulda Klager Lilac Garden, 307
Hull House, 120, 123
*The Humanities in the National Parks:
    Adapting to Change* (NPS), 332
Hurley, Jim, 221
Hurston, Zora Neale, 10, 77, 322, 323
Hutchinson & Woods, 131
Huyck, Heather A., 6, 14, 321, 355–364

If Walls Could Speak (C. Munoz), 211
Ignacio, Chief, 33
Illinois, 50; Chicago, 34, 35, 79, 120, 208, 295, 297, 299; Evanston, 287
Improper Bostonians: Lesbian and Gay History from the Puritans to Playland (The History Project), 283
Independence Hall, 30, 97
Independence National Historical Park, 97
Independent Order of St. Luke, 75, 76
Indiana: Indianapolis, 31, 59, 71, 74, 75, 312
Ingram, Gordon, 283
Inman, Emily MacDougald, 276
InSites (newsletter), 255
integrity. *See* architectural and site integrity
interiors, and preserving integrity, 145–147, 158–160, 217, 292
International Gay and Lesbian Travel Association, 297
International Ladies' Garment Workers Union (ILGWU), 210
interpretation, at historic houses and museums, 97, 107–110, 119, 210, 248–262, 347–354; challenges, 83–89, 99–101, 126–128, 249–250; examples, 90–95, 107–110, 117–118, 120–125
interpretation, of history and architecture, 131–144, 145–160, 161–176, 177–196, 210, 281–299, 334–335, 347–354, 356, 362
Interpretation of Historic Sites (Alderson and Lowe), 84
Iowa, 317
Irish, 87, 88, 89, 95
Irvine, Barbara, 219, 220, 225, 362
Ishii, Sonya, 211
Italy, 75

J. H. Zeilin and Company, 188
Jackson, Col. Andrew, 23, 41
Jackson, John Brinckerhoff, 199
Jacksonian Era, 88–89
James, Mrs. Cassie Myers, 123, 124

James River Garden Club, 46
Japanese Americans, 201, 203, 211, 212
Japanese Canadians, 345
Javits, Jacob, 238, 239
Jefferson, Thomas, 97, 232
Jenkins, Rhoda Barney, 237
Jenkins-Sahline, Colline, 237
Jennings, Mae Mann, 48
John (coachman at Bishop White House), 99
John Brown Fort Company, 35
Johns Hopkins University, 286
Johnson, Joseph, 21
Johnson, Lady Bird, 52, 234
Johnson, Lyndon B., 52
Johnson, Philip, 289–291, 299
Jones, Arnita, 321
Jones, Elizabeth Owen, 175
Jones, Mary Harris "Mother," 173, 175, 176
Joseph Priestley House, 257, 261
Juliette Gordon Low House, 269
Jumel Mansion, 32
Junior League, 228

Kaiser, Charles, 289
Kansas, 23; Kansas City, 78; Pittsburg, 145
Kazickas, Jurate, 9, 269
Keemle, Mary Katherine, 35
Keller, Helen, 305
Keller, Matthew, 180, 183
Kemp, Emory, 113
Kennedy, Elizabeth, 283
Kennedy, John F., 299
King, Susan E., 203, 207
Klager, Hulda, 307
Koval, John, 159
Krupsak, Mary Ann, 234
Ku Klux Klan, 66
Kunz, Mary Ellyn, 257, 260
Kuttner, Hans, 234

Ladd, Virginia, 172
Ladies Advisory Group, 66
Ladies Hermitage Association, 23, 41

Ladies Memorial Association, 271
Lake Forest College, 299
Lancaster County Historical Society, 261
Landis Valley Museum, 252
landmark designation: in Canada, 131,
    347, 351, 354; local, 227; obstacles,
    12, 321–322, 323–331; women's lack
    of representation, 3, 23, 201, 265,
    304, 339–340. *See also* National
    Historic Landmark; National Register
    of Historic Places
landscape preservation, 5, 8, 27–28,
    33–35, 38, 39–57, 161–176, 220–221,
    276; gardens, 5, 39, 41–46, 54–56,
    171. *See also* urban preservation
Lanier, May, 41
Lansdale, Mrs. Philip, 50
Lathrop, Harriet, 163–166, 176
Latinos. *See* Hispanics and Latinos
Lauren, Ralph, 58
Laurier House National Historic Site
    (Canada), 353
Lawson & Little, 131, 141, 142, 143
Lawton, Elizabeth, 50, 51
League, Ellamae Ellis, 276, 277
League of Women Voters, 228
Lee, Antoinette, 315
Lee, Gary, 238
Lee, Mary Anna Randolph (Custis), 22
Lee, Robert E., 22, 41
Lehigh University, 256
Lelia College, 74
Leon, Warren, 113
Lerner, Gerda, 243, 269, 271, 303
lesbians and gays, 12, 13, 229, 281–299,
    328, 357
Leslie, Eliza, 102
Leslie's Illustrated Newspapers, 125
Levin, Brenda, 210, 211
Lewis, Steve, 242
Liberia, 75
libraries, 8, 33, 145–160
The Library Book (Anderson, Dubrow,
    and Koval), 159
Lincoln, Abraham, 61
Lincoln, Mary Todd, 333

Lindenwald, 89, 90, 93, 94, 95
Lindgren, James, 4, 25
Lithuanians, 55
Lockwood, Alice G. B., 44
Lofty, Mary, 257
Longfellow, Alice, 23
Longfellow, Henry Wadsworth, 23
Los Angeles Community Redevelop-
    ment Agency (CRA), 203, 211
Louisa May Alcott Memorial Association,
    319
Low, Juliette Gordon, 269, 316
Lowe, Mary Jane, 286, 314
Lowe, Shirley Paine, 84
Lowell National Historical Park, 8, 332,
    333, 334, 335
Lowenthal, David, 232
Lower East Side Tenement House
    Museum, 8
Lukens, Rebecca, 312
Lukens Historic District, 312

Macdonald, Sir John A., 353
Maclachlan, Gretchen, 273
Madam C. J. Walker Hair Culturists
    Union of America, 74
Madame C. J. Walker Building, 312
Madame Walker Theater Center, 59, 71,
    75
Maggie Lena Walker National Historic
    Site, 77, 311
Maggie Walker House, 362
Malone, Dorothy, 328
Mamie D. Eisenhower Foundation, 319
Many Tender Ties (Van Kirk), 337
Many Thousands Gone (Berlin), 360
Margaret Sanger Clinic, 328
markers, historic, 31, 58, 59, 62, 63, 175
Martinac, Paula, 282, 286, 288, 289
Martin Van Buren National Historic
    Site, 6, 86, 89
Maryland, 41; Baltimore, 54, 76, 286;
    Cambridge, 60; Glen Echo, 305
Maryland Federation of Garden Clubs,
    44
Mason, Biddy, 12, 203–212

Massachusetts, 315; Boston, 10, 18, 19,
31, 54, 56, 70, 283, 292; Brockton, 31;
Cambridge, 10; Jamaica Plains, 10;
Lowell, 112, 333, 362; Nantucket
Island, 363; New Bedford, 62;
Oxford, 305; Pittsfield, 1;
Provincetown, 292
Mattachine Society, 283, 292
Maxwell, Edward, 131–132, 135, 136,
138, 139, 141, 142, 143
Maxwell, William Sutherland, 131–132,
135, 136, 138, 139, 141, 142, 143
Maynard, Joan, 221, 222, 223
Mayo, Edith, 7, 111–128, 359
McClintock, Elizabeth, 231, 316
McClintock, Mary Ann, 61, 231, 316
McClurg, Virginia Donaghe, 33, 34
McCullough, Alan B., 13, 337–354
McDowell, Brig. Gen. Irwin, 22
McGill University, 133
McKim, Mead & White, 199
McPherson, Aimee Semple, 312
McWilliams, Carey, 201
McWilliams, Lelia, 73
McWilliams, Moses, 73
McWilliams, Sarah (Breedlove), 73
media, use of, 227, 238
Meigs, Q.M. Gen. Montgomery, 22
Melosh, Barbara, 260
Melville, Herman, 85
Merritt, Carole, 277
Mesa Verde National Park, 34
Methodist Episcopal Church, 62
Metropolitan Water District of Southern
California, 178
Mexico, 210
Michigan, 317; Detroit, 54, 312
A Midwife's Tale (Ulrich), 206
military history, 338, 339, 347–348, 361
Milk, Harvey, 295
Mill Creek Coal and Coke Company, 168
Millennium Project, 58, 60, 66
Miller, Page Putnam, 10, 11, 12, 13, 270,
279, 311, 313, 318–336, 359, 361, 363
Minnesota, 321
Mississippi, 204, 208; Natchez, 44;
Vicksburg, 73

Missouri: St. Louis, 73, 74, 75, 307
Mitchell, Elizabeth, 76
Mitchell, Maggie Lena, 76
Mitchell, Margaret, 269
Mitchell, Maria, 10, 363
Mitchell, William, 76
Modjeska, Helena, 307
Monroe, President James, 123
Monroe, Marilyn, 328
Montanez, Polina, 307
Montanez Adobe Chapel, 307
Monticello, 43
Moon, Kim, 11, 248–262
Moore, Millicent Brady, 233
Moorland-Spingarn Research Center, 70
Moreno, Luisa, 210
Morgan, J. P., 168
Morgan, Julia, 307–309, 311, 328, 331
Morgan Farm, 278
Mormons, 204, 206
Mossman, Susan, 216
Mother Jones Prison, 173, 175
Motherwell Homestead National
Historic Site (Canada), 353
Mott, Lucretia, 17, 238
Mount Vernon, 18–23, 36, 38–41, 230,
233, 246
Mount Vernon College, 3
Mount Vernon Ladies' Association of the
Union (MVLA), 4, 17, 19–23, 25,
38–41, 232, 233, 246
Moynihan, Daniel Patrick, 238, 239, 241
Ms., 238
Munoz, Celia Alvarez, 210
Munoz, Garcia, 210
Munroe, Mary Barr, 48
Murase, Mike, 201
Murphy, Alexander, 35
Murtagh, William J., 23, 233
Museum of Afro-American History, 70
Museum of American History, 117
Museum of the City of New York, 119

Nagasawa, Nobuho, 211
National Air and Space Museum, 116
National American Woman Suffrage
Association, 312

National Association for African American Heritage Preservation, 229

National Association for the Advancement of Colored People (NAACP), 75, 79

National Association of Colored Women (NACW), 67–68

National Coalition for Roadside Beauty, 50

National Coordinating Committee for the Promotion of History (NCC), 304, 311, 320, 321

National Council of Negro Women (NCNW), 65, 69, 70, 71, 78

National Endowment for the Arts, 281

National Endowment for the Humanities (NEH), 112, 241, 250, 251, 261, 281

National Federation of Afro-American Women, 63

National Historic Landmark (NHL), 13, 60, 72, 173, 228, 266, 295, 303, 304, 305, 311, 313, 316, 359, 363; criteria for funding, 227; nominating sites, 10, 12, 277, 317, 320–331. *See also* landmark designation

National Historic Preservation Act, Section 106, and historic context studies, 277

National Historic Sites, 63, 72

National Housing Act (1949), 54

National League of Colored Women, 35

National Museum of American History (NMAH), 58, 114, 118, 119, 120

National Negro Business League, 72

National Organization for Women, 228, 234, 236

National Park Service (NPS), 3, 13, 22, 47, 58, 61, 62, 63, 72, 97, 108, 112, 162, 173, 230, 234, 236, 238, 240, 241, 242, 243, 246, 253, 266, 267, 281, 303, 304, 305, 311, 315, 317, 319–328, 330–336, 337, 356

National Park Service Special Resource Study, 175

National Park System, 12, 303, 311

National Register Bulletin, 266

National Register Historic District, 212

National Register Information Service, 13

National Register Information System (NRIS), 266, 303, 304, 305, 311, 314, 315

National Register of Historic Places, 3, 13, 56, 58, 169, 173, 264, 265, 269, 271, 295, 303, 305, 314, 315; criteria for grant funding, 227, 277; definitions of women's historic site, 266–267, 272, 273, 275, 276, 279, 280, 303–317, 359; eligibility, 174, 175, 267, 277, 291, 292, 323–324; nominating sites, 11, 12, 166, 168, 273, 276, 278, 279; teaching aid, 315–316. *See also* landmark designation

National Roadside Council, 47, 50–52, 56

National Society of the Colonial Dames, 25, 46

National Trust for Historic Preservation, 6, 7, 213, 281, 284, 285, 287, 288, 289, 291, 297

National Women's Hall of Fame, 230, 234, 240

National Women's History Project, 255

National Women's Landmark Project. *See* Women's History Landmark Project

National Youth Administration, 69

Native Americans, 1, 4, 24, 30, 33–35, 36, 53–54, 127, 180, 200, 261, 281, 288, 303, 317, 357, 358. *See also* aboriginal cultures

Nature, 51

Neaves, Elizabeth, 217

Nebraska: Red Cloud, 13, 286

Nebraska State Historic Preservation, 316

neighborhood conservation, 54–56, 221–223, 230, 283

Netherlands: Amsterdam, 298

New England Hospital for Women and Children, 10

New England Women's Fund, 228

New Jersey, 11, 227, 307, 362, 363; Camden, 13, 286; Mt. Laurel, 218; Newark, 149; Palisades, 48–50, 74

New Jersey Federation of Women's Clubs, 48–50
New Jersey Register of Natural Areas, 50
New Mexico, 288; Los Alamos, 289; Santa Fe, 287, 288, 297
Newnan Cotton Mills, 268
Newton, Esther, 282
New York, 20, 61, 62, 79, 88, 193, 234, 236, 240, 315; Albany, 30; Auburn, 59, 60, 61, 62, 63; Buffalo, 156, 159, 324; Fire Island, 282, 292; Hyde Park, 287; Irvington-on-Hudson, 59, 71, 74; Kinderhook, 6, 86, 88, 89; New York City, 8, 12, 31, 54, 56, 62, 63, 72, 74, 75, 153, 155, 158, 180, 199, 221, 283, 290, 291, 295, 299, 312, 326, 328; Rochester, 60, 63, 230, 362; Sag Harbor, 59; Seneca Falls, 12, 58, 60, 200, 230–247, 359; Solvay, 153; Staten Island, 286; Syracuse, 230; Waterloo, 230, 316
New York City Landmarks Commission, 225, 227
New York Council for the Humanities, 234, 241
New York Express, 20
New York Graphic, 33
New York State Council on the Arts, 234, 241
New York State Council on the Humanities, 238
New York State Office of Parks and Recreation, 238
New York State Studies Group, 234, 241
New York Times, 227, 290
Nightingale, Florence, 133, 141
Nobb, Percy, 137
nonprofit preservation, 11, 199–213, 214–229, 319
Norfolk and Western Rail Road, 168
North Carolina, 50, 208; Chapel Hill, 112
Notes on the Erection of Library Bildings [sic] (Bertram), 150, 152, 153
Novak, Kim, 328

Oakley, Annie, 305

O'Connor, Flannery, 268
Ohio, 40, 124; Cincinnati, 54, 158; Cleveland, 150; Greenville, 307; Warren, 312
O'Keeffe, Georgia, 287–289, 299
O'Keeffe and Stieglitz (Eisler), 289
Old Sturbridge Village, 1, 2
Old Time Gardens (Earle), 44
Order of St. Luke, 79
Oregon, 50, 317
Organization of American Historians (OAH), 13, 112, 241, 243, 304, 311, 315, 317, 320, 321, 332, 334, 335
Outdoor Advertising Association of America, 50

Pack, Phoebe, 288
Palmer, Minnie, 181
Parks Canada, 13, 337–354
Pasadena Heritage, 215, 216, 217, 225, 227, 228
Pathological Institute, 137
Paul, Alice, 12, 214, 218–221, 224, 225, 228, 362
Peach Tree Garden Club (PTGC), 46
Peirce, Melusina Fay, 31, 32
Pemberton, Abigail, 257
Penn, William, 55, 256, 257
Penney, J. C., 316
Pennsbury Manor, 256, 257, 260, 261
Pennsylvania, 60, 112, 164, 166, 248, 249, 253, 257, 357, 363; Coatesville, 312; Gettysburg, 1, 2; Lancaster, 229; Levittown, 8; Philadelphia, 7, 28, 30, 54, 55, 59, 74, 97, 99, 101, 102, 104, 109, 188, 208, 229, 243, 256, 312, 357; Pittsburgh, 54, 56, 74, 75, 145, 255; Shamokin, 166; Valley Forge, 23, 30, 31
Pennsylvania Abolition Society, 99
Pennsylvania Federation of Museums and Historic Organizations, 250
Pennsylvania Heritage Affairs Commission, 250
Pennsylvania Historical and Museum Commission (PHMC), 229, 250, 253, 261

Pennsylvania Horticultural Society, 56
Pennsylvania Humanities, 255
Pennsylvania Humanities Council
 (PHC), 11, 112, 248–251, 252, 255,
 261, 262
Pennsylvania Roadside Council, 51, 52
Pennsylvania School of Horticulture, 54
Pennsylvania Society of the Colonial
 Dames, 30
Pesotto, Rose, 210, 211
Peters, Ralph, 236, 238, 241–242, 243
Peterson, Carla L., 315
Pewabic Pottery, 312
Philadelphia Neighborhood Gardens
 Association (PNGA), 54–55
Philadelphia School of Design for
 Women, 312
philanthropy. *See* fund raising
Pickford, Mary, 311
Pierce, Susan M., 8, 161–176
Pink Plaque Guide to London (Elliman
 and Roll), 298
Pinzer, Maimie, 196
Piscataway National Park, 40
Piscataway National Park Expansion Act
 (1994), 41
Pitcaithley, Dwight, 332, 333, 334,
 336
Pittsburgh History and Landmark
 Foundation, 54
plaques. *See* markers
Poe, Edgar Allan, 32
Ponce de Leon, Lola Rodriguez, 307
Poro Company, 73
Porter, Dorothy, 70
Porter, Polly, 326
Portraits of Philadelphia Gardens
 (Brown and Brown), 46
Povero, Lucille, 234, 236, 238–239, 240
*The Power of Place: Urban Landscapes
 as Public History* (Hayden), 208
Power of Place Project, 199–213
Powers, Hiram, 114
Praetzellis, Adrian, 178
Pratt Neighborhood College, 221
Presbyterians, 66
Presence of the Past (Hosmer), 4, 38

*Presenting the Past: Essays on History
 and the Public* (Benson, Brier, and
 Rosenzweig), 113
Preservation, 282, 285
Preservation Pennsylvania, 229
Preserving Historic New England
 (Lindgren), 4
Preserving the Old Dominion
 (Lindgren), 4
Priestley, Elizabeth Ryland, 257
Priestley, Joseph, 257
Procter and Gamble, 66
Progressive movement, 78, 183, 271
prostitution, 172, 177–196
Prudence Crandall House, 325
public art, as preservation tool, 203, 212;
 examples of, 206–208, 210–211
Public Historian, 113
Public History: An Introduction (Howe
 and Kemp), 113
Puerto Rico: Casa de los Ponce de Leon,
 307

QED (Stein), 286
Quakers, 60, 218
The Queerest Places (Martinac), 282
Queers in Space (Ingram et al.), 283
Quinn, Susan, 233

Rachel Carson Foundation, 319
Rainey, Gertrude "Ma," 77, 269
Raitzsky, Constantine, 120
Rand McNally, 1
Randolph, A. M., 25
Rappet, Blanche, 183
Rappet, Jean, 183, 184
Reagan, President Ronald, 231, 239, 241,
 242
*Reclaiming the Past: Landmarks of
 Women's History* (Miller), 10, 228,
 270, 313, 321, 361, 363
Red Bone Community Club, 267
Reed, Chris, 299
Reed, Donna, 328
Regional Conference of Historical
 Agencies, 234, 236, 241
reinterpretation. *See* interpretation

Repo-History, 283
Republicans, 312
Revolutionary War, 24, 25, 27, 28, 30, 31, 32, 35, 246
Reynolds, Helen, 51
Rhode Island: Newport, 291; Providence, 194
Rice, Lillian, 317
Richards, Ellen Swallow, 10
Richardson, H. H., 292
Rivers, Gypsy, 181
Robb, Lynda Johnson, 239
Robert E. Lee Memorial Foundation, 41
Robinson, A'Lelia Walker, 74, 75
Robinson, Sallie B., 172
Rockmart Woman's Club, 267
Roddy, Miss, 172
Roll, Frederick, 298
Romo, Ricardo, 201
Roosevelt, Eleanor, 69, 287, 299, 305, 315, 316, 326, 327
Roosevelt, Franklin, 69, 326
Rose, Vivien, 333, 334
Rosenzweig, Roy, 113
Ross Memorial Pavilion, 138
Roth, Darlene, 271, 276
Royalty Travel, 297
Royal Victoria Hospital (RVH), 131–144
Rucker, Beulah, 271
Ruffin, Josephine St. Pierre, 121
Ruffins, Fath Davis, 5, 58–80
Ruiz, Vicki, 201, 210
Russia, 210
Russian Jews, 210
Russian Molokans, 210
Rust, Josephine, 41
Rust, Marie, 332, 333, 336

Saar, Betye, 203, 206
Sam (slave at Pennsbury Manor), 257
Sampson, Deborah, 30
San Antonio Conservation Society, 47, 52–54, 56
Sanchez, George, 210
Sanger, Margaret, 12, 328
Sarbanes, Paul, 41
Sargent, Charles Sprague, 39

Scenic America, 52
Scenic Byways, 52
Scholer, Ethel, 181
Scotch-Irish immigrants, 261
Scotland, 133; Edinburgh, 135
Scott, Elizabeth, 180
Seifert, Donna, 180
Senator John Heinz Pittsburgh Regional History Center, 255
Seneca Falls Consortium, 240, 244
Seneca Falls Historical Society, 230, 234, 240
Seneca Falls Historic District Committee, 240
Seneca Falls Reveille, 246
Seneca Falls Urban Cultural Park, 240
Seneca Falls Women's Rights National Historical Park, 213, 359
Seward, William H., 61, 64
Sexual Politics, Sexual Communities (D'Emilio), 283
Shafer, Frank, 183, 195
Shafer, George, 183, 195
Sharp, Leslie N., 11, 263–280
Shelton, Louise, 44
Sheppard, Beverly, 256, 260
Sherman, Mary Belle King, 47
Sherr, Lynn, 9, 269
Shull, Carol D., 13, 266, 303–317
Shurcliff, Arthur, 43
Sir George-Etienne Cartier National Historic Site (Canada), 353
Smith, Barbara Clark, 119, 120, 122, 127
Smith, Marjorie, 236, 242
Smithsonian Institution, 33, 44, 58, 111, 112, 114, 123, 124, 252, 281, 359
Smithsonian Museum of African Art, 63
Snell, Henry Saxon, 133, 135
Society for the Preservation of Weeksville and Bedford-Stuyvesant, 221–227
Society of Masons, 21
Soderlund, Jean, 256
Sodom and Gomorrah of Today or the History of Keystone (Ladd), 172
Sons of the American Revolution, 18, 28
South Carolina, 28, 71; Mayesville, 66, 71

South Dakota: Black Hills, 364
Southeastern Association of Colored
  Women (SACW), 67
Southwest Library Association, 157
Southwest Pennsylvania Heritage
  Preservation Commission, 250
Southwest Virginia Improvement
  Company, 163
Spector, Janet D., 180
Spelman College, 271
Spencer, Anne, 175
Spencer-Wood, Suzanne, 10
St. Luke Herald, 76
St. Luke Penny Savings Bank, 76
St. Mary's Church, 305
St. Simeon, 307
de Stael, Madame, 188
Stafford, Harry, 286
Stanton, Elizabeth Cady, 17, 61, 230,
  232–234, 237, 238, 239, 246, 247
Stanton Family Cemetery, 46
State University of New York, 159
Stein, Gertrude, 286
Stevens, Edward, 139, 141
Stevenson, Shanna, 11
Stieglitz, Alfred, 288
Stowe, Harriet Beecher, 2
Strangers in Blood (Brown), 337
Stratton, Mary Chase Perry, 312
Strong, Mrs. S. deL. Van Rensselaer, 30
Stryker, Susan, 283
Sue (slave at Pennsbury Manor), 257
Survey of Nursing Education in Canada
  (Weir), 139
surveys and inventories, as planning
  tools, 50–51, 162–163, 227–228, 298,
  357, 362–363. *See also* historic con-
  text studies
Susan B. Anthony House, 362
Susan B. Anthony Slept Here (Sherr and
  Kazickas), 9, 269
Swan House, 276
Sztaray, Susan, 211

Tachau, Mary Kay, 243
Tandy, Vertner, 72, 75
Tate, Gertrude, 286

Tennessee, 23; Nashville, 41
Teper, Doug, 276
Terrell, Mary Church, 35
Terry, Maude, 59
Texas: Dallas, 291; Gainesville, 157;
  Houston, 233; San Antonio, 47,
  52–54
Theodore Roosevelt National Park, 364
Thomas, Marlo, 225
*Those of Little Note: Gender, Race, and
  Class in Historical Archaeology*
  (Scott), 180
Three Tiered House, 33
Thurman, Sue Bailey, 70
Tinling, Marion, 9, 269
Toklas, Alice B., 286
tourism, 34, 176, 272, 297–298
tours and guides, 1–3, 9–10, 44, 176,
  201, 203, 279, 282, 283, 285, 286,
  287, 296–298, 315
Town Young People's Committee, 234
Tracey, Sarah C., 22
Travel Solutions, 297
Triangle Shirtwaist Factory, 312
Trio Laundry, 273
Truth, Sojourner, 60, 62
Tubman, Harriet, 5, 58, 59–66, 70, 72,
  78, 79, 80, 316
Tubman, John, 60
Tuskegee Institute, 73, 75
Tuthill, Louisa, 18–19

U.S. Coal and Coke Company, 168, 169,
  172
U.S. Postal Service, 72, 225
U.S. Steel, 169
Ulrich, Laurel, 206
United Cannery, Agricultural, Packing,
  and Allied Workers Association
  (UCAPAWA), 210
United Daughters of the Confederacy
  (UDC), 18, 25
United Negro College Fund, 71
University of California, Los Angeles
  (UCLA), 200, 201, 203, 211
University of Massachusetts, 238
University of Pennsylvania, 257

University of Southern California (USC), 210, 211
University of Virginia, 41, 43
Upjohn, Richard, 89
Upstate New York Women's History Organization, 234, 241
Upton, Harriet Taylor, 312
urban preservation, 53–56, 57, 97–109, 120, 199–213. *See also* African Americans
Utah: Salt Lake City, 204

Valley Forge Association, 23
Valley Forge Centennial Association, 46
Valley Forge National Park Association, 30–31
Van Buren, President Martin, 88–95, 361
Van Buren, Smith Thompson, 89
Van Buskirk, Jim, 283
Van Kirk, Howard, 246
Van Kirk, Sylvia, 337, 350
Van Lew, Elizabeth, 76
Van Nostrand, Maren, 311
Van Rensselaer, Kilaen, 30
Van Slyck, Abigail A., 8, 145–160
Van West, Carroll, 267
Vassar College, 241
Vento, Bruce, 320, 321
Vermont, 317
Vicinus, Martha, 140
Victorian Era, 84–85, 87–95, 168, 182, 190
Viets, Cassius, 33
Villa Lewaro, 59, 71, 72, 75
Virginia, 25, 46; Bishop, 172; Fairfax Station, 305; Fredericksburg, 25, 27, 41; Jamestown, 25, 27, 360; Martinsburg, 21; Mount Vernon, 1, 5, 18–23, 36, 38–41, 230; Pocahontas, 163–165, 167; Richmond, 25, 27, 28, 59, 60, 71, 72, 76, 79, 362; Williamsburg, 24, 27
Virginia Historical Society, 24
Von Wagener, Isabella (Sojourner Truth), 60, 62

Wakefield Memorial Association, 41
Walker, Alice, 77, 322
Walker, Armstead, Jr., 76

Walker, Charles Joseph, 73
Walker, Hattie, 181
Walker, Madam C. J. (Sarah Breedlove), 5, 58, 71–75, 77, 78, 79, 80, 312, 316
Walker, Maggie Lena (Mitchell), 5, 58, 59, 63, 71, 72, 75–77, 78, 79, 80
Wall, Diana diZerega, 180
Ware, Susan, 326
Washington, 50, 307; Olympia, 11; Seattle, 158, 159, 236, 242, 283, 291, 295, 297, 299
Washington, Booker T., 73
Washington, D.C., 3, 10, 22, 35, 50, 54, 58, 59, 62, 63, 66, 68, 71, 123, 285, 291, 295, 299, 323
Washington, George, 9, 22, 38, 39–41, 97, 232, 233, 246
Washington, John A., 21
Washington, Margaret Murray, 73
Washington, Martha, 22
Watt, James, 231, 239–240, 241
Weeks, James, 221
Weir, George, 139
Weller, Eleanor, 44, 46
Wellman, Judith, 12, 230–247, 243, 359
Welty, Eudora, 318
Wesleyan College, 276
West, Patricia, 6, 83–95
West Virginia, 8, 161, 162, 168, 176; Beckley, 176; Bramwell, 163, 165–169, 175; Charleston, 173; Gary, 169, 172; Harpers Ferry, 18, 35; Maybeury, 172; Pratt, 173, 175
West Virginia State Historic Preservation Office, 162
West Virginia University, 176
West Virginia Women's Commission, 176
What This Awl Means (Spector), 180
Wheeling (Va.) Intelligencer, 19
Whigs, 88, 89
White, Thomas H., 66
White, Bishop William, 7, 97–101, 361
White Sewing Machine Company, 66
Whitman, Walt, 13, 286, 299
Whitney, David, 290
Wilburn, Lelia Ross, 267, 277

Willard, Frances, 9, 287
William Penn Foundation, 261
Williams, Morley, 39, 43
Wilson, President Woodrow, 218
Wisconsin, 11, 289, 317; Mineral Point, 299
Wisconsin State Historical Landmark, 299
Wolf, Stephanie Grauman, 257
Woman's Christian Temperance Union, 124, 287, 319
Women in Philanthropy, 228
Women-Related Historic and Architectural Resources Associated with the Civil War in Georgia, 276
Women Remembered (Tinling), 9, 269
Women's College Hospital (Canada), 345
Women's History Education Initiative, 13, 319, 320, 332, 336
Women's History Initiative, 264
Women's History Landmark Project, 13, 311, 319, 320, 321, 322, 324, 325, 327, 329, 330, 331, 336
Women's Pavilion Hospital, 138

women's rights and suffrage, 33, 60, 61, 62, 77, 122, 125, 218, 219, 231, 232, 233, 236, 243, 246–247, 344
Women's Rights Historic District, 234
Women's Rights National Historical Park (WRNHP), 12, 230–247, 311, 316, 333, 359
Woodside Travel, 297
Woodson, Carter G., 75
World War I, 116, 150, 167, 309, 344, 345
World War II, 77, 118, 339, 345

Yagasaki, Noritaka, 201
Yellowstone Park, 242
The Yellow Wallpaper (Gilman), 215
YMCA, 291
YWCA, 8, 74, 249, 267, 308, 309, 310, 315, 328

Zion Church, 62
Zolli, Barbara, 259